THE SUGAR INDUSTRY
AND THE ABOLITION OF THE SLAVE TRADE,
1775–1810

Florida A&M University, Tallahassee
Florida Atlantic University, Boca Raton
Florida Gulf Coast University, Ft. Myers
Florida International University, Miami
Florida State University, Tallahassee
University of Central Florida, Orlando
University of Florida, Gainesville
University of North Florida, Jacksonville
University of South Florida, Tampa
University of West Florida, Pensacola

The Sugar Industry
and the Abolition of the Slave Trade,
1775–1810

Selwyn H. H. Carrington

Foreword by Colin Palmer

University Press of Florida

GAINESVILLE   TALLAHASSEE   TAMPA   BOCA RATON

PENSACOLA   ORLANDO   MIAMI   JACKSONVILLE   FT. MYERS

First cloth printing, 2002
First paperback printing, 2003

Library of Congress Cataloging-in-Publication Data
Carrington, Selwyn H. H., 1937–
The sugar industry and the abolition of the slave trade. 1775–1810 /
Selwyn H. H. Carrington.
p. cm.
Includes bibliographical references and index.
ISBN 0-8130-2557-5 (cloth: alk. paper)
ISBN 0-8130-2742-x (pbk.)
1. Sugar trade—West Indies, British—History. 2. Slavery—West Indies, British
—History. 3. Slaves—Emancipation—West Indies, British—History.
4. West Indies, British—Economic conditions. I. Title.
HD9114.W42 C37 2002
972.9'03—dc21   2002018073

The University Press of Florida is the scholarly publishing agency for the State
University System of Florida, comprising Florida A&M University, Florida Atlantic
University, Florida Gulf Coast University, Florida International University, Florida
State University, University of Central Florida, University of Florida, University
of North Florida, University of South Florida, and University of West Florida.

University Press of Florida
15 Northwest 15th Street
Gainesville, FL 32611–2079
http://www.upf.com

To Glyn

Contents

Figures

Tables

Weight and Measure Equivalents

Gallons are imperial, but as they were supplied by the planters, they may also reflect American measurement.

Measure	Equivalent	
bag	cotton	208–300 lbs.
	ginger	100 lbs.
	pimento	200 lbs.
	sugar	cwt (112 lbs.) or hhd (12–18 cwt)
bale	cotton	150 lbs.
barrico	14 gals.	
	8 barricoes	1 puncheon
barrel (bbl)	beef	95 lbs.
	flour	204 lbs.
	herring	95 lbs.
	oil	31½ gals.
	pork	95 lbs.
	rum	36 gals.
	tongue	95 lbs.
box	candles	56–65 lbs.
	soap	240 lbs.
bundle (bdl)	onions	100 lbs.
bushel (bu)	8 gals.	
	flour	56 lbs.
cargo	cocoa	81 lbs.

Measure	Equivalent	
cask	varying sizes (smaller than a hhd)	
	coffee	112–336 lbs.
	ginger	300 lbs.
	gunpowder	1 cwt.
	indigo	250 lbs.
	pimento	300 lbs.
	sugar	see bag, sugar
fanega	55.7 litres	
	grain	1.58 bu. (Am.)
	cocoa	110 lbs.
firkin	¼ bbl.	
	butter	56–66 lbs.
	rice	54 lbs.
foot (ft.)	lumber	1 solid ft.
gallon (gal.)	231 cu. in.	
hogshead (hhd)	12–18 cwt	
	molasses	100 gals.
	rum	56 gals.
	salt	20 bu.
	sugar	9 bags or 12 cwt
	wine	63 gals.
hundredweight (cwt)	long (Br.)	112 lbs.
	short (Am.)	100 lbs.
keg	14–15 gals.	
	tallow	50 lbs.
pipe, wine	126 gal.	
pound (lb.)	16 ounces (oz.)	
pot	sugar	ca. 5 lbs.
	11 pots	½ cwt (56 lbs.)
	352 pots	1 hhd (16 cwt)
puncheon (pun)	varying capacity (about 80 gals.)	
	rum	240 gals.
	salt	15 bu.
quintal (quin.)	1 cwt/220.46 lbs.	

Measure	Equivalent	
quart (qt.)	dry	67.20 cu. in.
	liquid	57.75 cu. in.
soron		
	pimento	102–250 lbs.
	cocoa	210 lbs.
tierce (t/ce)	46 gals. liquid	
ton		
	long (Br.)	20 cwt/2240 lbs.
	short (Am.)	2000 lbs.
	wood=48 solid ft.	

Sources: S.H.H. Carrington, "Statistics for the Study of Caribbean Economic History," manuscript; Long Papers, BL, Add. MSS 12,413, fols. 23, 24d; contain all measurements.

Note: These measures and values vary according to item and according to the source or origin of the goods. If not all are used in the book, many will have been encountered by the student of British Caribbean history, often without explanation, in other works.

Currency Equivalents

British (Sterling) Coins/Notes

Denomination	Symbol	Value
farthing	f	smallest coin
penny (*pl.* pence)	d	4 farthings (4f)
shilling	s	12 pence (12d)
pound	£	20 shillings (20s)
guinea	gn	21 shillings (£1 1s)

Equivalents in West Indies

Island	Value of £1 Sterling in Island Currency
Barbados	from £1 8s to £1 12s
Dominica	£2
Jamaica	£1 8s
Leeward Is.	£1 12s
Windward Is.	£2

Source: Long Papers, BL, Add. MSS 12,413, fols. 23, 24d.

Foreword

The debate over the state of the economy of the British Caribbean islands in the decades preceding the abolition of the slave trade in 1807 and thereafter remains unabated and vigorous.

Selwyn H. H. Carrington has entered this important debate with impressive credentials and his well-known penchant for clinically dissecting the arguments and conclusions of less careful and gifted scholars. His book is a product of more than two decades of laborious research. It builds upon his earlier studies on the American War of Independence and its impact on the Caribbean economies, most notably his monograph *The West Indies during the American Revolution.*

Writing in 1928, Lowell J. Ragatz in his *The Fall of the Planter Class in the British West Indies, 1763–1833* identified a complex set of factors that were already in evidence in the 1760s and that led inexorably to the decline of the fortunes of the sugar industry and the plantocracy. Ragatz's decline thesis did not establish a direct connection between the abolition of the slave trade, the emancipation of the slaves, and naked economic imperatives, but the informed reader could make such linkages. A veritable revolution in the historiography of the Caribbean was in the making, since Ragatz provided some potent ammunition to challenge the prevailing view that the emancipation of the slaves was essentially an exercise in British humanitarianism.

Sixteen years after the appearance of Ragatz's provocative work, the young West Indian scholar Eric Williams published his classic work *Capitalism and Slavery.* Building upon the arguments of a number of earlier scholars, Williams presented the intellectually pugnacious thesis that there was an unexplored relationship between emancipation and the decline of the British West Indian sugar economies. *Capitalism and Slavery* showed that the seeds of decline could be traced to a number of internal factors such as the diminishing fertility of the soil in the older colonies and the persistence of anachronistic agricultural techniques. These and other local conditions were exacerbated by the disruption in trade caused by the American War of Independence. Among other consequences, Williams's book permanently altered the terms of the debate over the centrality of the slave trade and slavery in the Caribbean to the construction and growth of the British industrial economy. While most scholars in the developing world embraced the attractive and persuasive Williams thesis, imperial historians were generally more critical of it. Williams had punctured British claims to altruism in the abolition of the slave trade and slavery, and some scholars dismissed his arguments outright, accusing the scholar of an unacceptable economic determinism in his conclusions. Some critics, at the time the book was published and later too, based their assertions less on credible evidence than on a transparent determination to rescue a tarnished reputation concerning the primary impetus for abolition and emancipation.

Carrington's *The Sugar Industry and the Abolition of the Slave Trade* is nothing less than a major reconsideration of the "decline thesis" in Caribbean history. Taking issue with the conclusions of several contemporary scholars, Carrington provides a trenchant and provocative analysis of the nature of the British West Indian economies during the last third of the eighteenth century and the first decade of the nineteenth. He has mined the archives in England and the Caribbean to provide a detailed and comprehensive analysis of the economies of the islands and the impact on them of the American war.

Carrington shows that the war adversely affected the West Indian economies, not only by producing food shortages but also by closing American markets during the hostilities. He charts a picture of sustained decline in the island economies after the war. His chapter on the indebtedness of the sugar planters is particularly important. Carrington examines the ways in which the West Indians responded to the economic crises, particularly those involved in the sugar industry. He concludes that the decline of the West Indian economies had a direct bearing on the abolition of the British slave trade in 1807.

Selwyn Carrington's book is a model of exhaustive research, measured in its analysis and brilliant in its conclusions. It is likely to be the most important work on the economic history of the Caribbean and the relationship of the state of the island economies to abolition and emancipation since Eric Williams published *Capitalism and Slavery* in 1944. Carrington has amassed a wealth of data to support his conclusions and he has presented these judiciously, insightfully, and persuasively. Scholars are going to discuss them for a very long time. I predict that this book will be honored as a classic study in the tradition of Lowell Ragatz and Eric Williams. It deserves to be read, reread, and debated. It is a significant accomplishment.

Colin Palmer
Dodge Professor of History
Princeton University

Preface

Over the last thirty years I have worked assiduously in the period of West Indian history that has become associated with the decline of the British West Indies and the abolition of the slave trade. My interest in the area was initiated by my decision to undertake a doctoral thesis at the University of London and my ambition to return to lecture at the University of the West Indies at St. Augustine. To achieve these goals, I had to find a thesis topic that accommodated my knowledge of American history and my desire to return to the Caribbean. With this in mind, I chose the period of the American Revolution. My research connected me with those historians who opposed the traditional view that the slave trade was abolished because of a Christian fervor that had inspired the humanitarians in England. This group saw the decision to end the trade as arising out of the decline of the British West Indian economy, the rise of the free trade movement, and the increasing availability of cheaper sugar on the international market.

My contribution to the historiography is my research on, and interpretation of, the impact of the American Revolution and of postwar British policy on the continued profitability of sugar production in the British West Indies. My earlier book *The British West Indies during the American Revolution* and several other articles demonstrate clearly that the West Indian sugar industry was dependent on the American markets for the supply of both provisions and lumber. The significance of this theme is evident in Andrew O'Shaughnessy's *An Empire Divided*. Land and labour were made available for concentration on the production of sugar and other tropical commodities. The American trade did not drain off any significant amount of specie because supplies from the American continent were paid for in rum and molasses, with a small quantity of bills of exchange.

In an effort to correct the misconceptions caused by Seymour Drescher's study *Econocide: British Slavery in the Era of Abolition,* I have undertaken this detailed project titled *The Sugar Industry and the Abolition of the British Slave Trade, 1775–1810.* It will analyse the British West Indian economy at the end of the eighteenth century to determine the state of its development during one of the most crucial periods of West Indian slavery and the slave trade. The humanitarian explanation for abolition was not universally accepted among contemporary British historians, as witness William Darity Jr., who has written extensively on profitability and decline. On the former, he contends that the slave trade achieved profits as high as those claimed by Williams. Similarly, he supports the claims of decline and not humanitarianism as the basis for abolition. Here he cites the Victorian economic historians to show that, even if the islands were profitable at the end of the eighteenth century, the plantation system could not advance the interests of industrial capitalism. Furthermore, the West Indian interests could not counter the governing elite's transition from mercantilism to Adam Smith's doctrine of laissez-faire capitalism.

The primary goal of the study is to test the Ragatz-Williams hypothesis that the British sugar islands declined at the end of the eighteenth century as a result of events that affected the sugar industry, thus weakening the islands' economies. Eric Williams contends that this decline led to the abolition first of the slave trade, then of slavery, and finally of the sugar duties in 1846. Since many historians accept the second assumption—that decline led to abolition of slavery—there is no necessity to carry the research beyond the British slave trade period. Even Drescher acknowledges the decline of the sugar industry after 1820.

My study supports the decline theory of the British West Indies in the post-1775 period. It unearths and analyses numerous problems affecting the economies of the sugar islands from 1775 to 1810. It also considers the profitability of plantation agriculture in the West Indies during much of the eighteenth century. The islands were not at their highest point of production when the debate over the abolition of the slave trade began in the 1780s. These were trying years during which sugar production was static at best; recovery was minimal, production costs high. Of greater importance, however, the future for investments in the sugar industry in the West Indies was uncertain because of the rising free trade doctrine, coupled with the fast-growing industrial economy in Britain and the development of sugar production in new areas within the British

Empire and those countries with which Britain was establishing preferential trade relations.

Research for this project has been undertaken in repositories and libraries in Britain, Canada, the United States, Trinidad and Tobago, and Jamaica. Such diverse labour has enabled me to view a wealth of documentation including plantation papers, Colonial Office records, contemporary historical writings, secondary works, and statistical information highlighting the performance of the West Indian economy.

This work would not have been possible without the help and assistance of my family and friends. Several of the latter have unselfishly allowed me to stay at their residences or have entertained me on my visits to England for research purposes. For this, I thank Dave and Stephanie Shill, Daphnie and Eric Smith, and Beverly and David Clark; in Canada, Sybil and Eugene Lamkin and Franklin and Sheryl Lewis and family; and Susan and Tony Sookram. I thank my former supervisor, now supporter, Glyn Williams (to whom this work is dedicated), for his continued belief in my work and his faith in my ability to get the job done. I thank my parents, the Reverend William H. T. Carrington and Beata L. Carrington, for their support. My children, Marcia Ann Yvette and Leah Natalia Susan, were without my company for the summers from 1989 to 1993. I give thanks to them for their understanding. I further thank my brothers and sister for housing me while I did research. And I thank my wife, Lesly Ann Carrington, not only for tolerating my long absences from home during the periods when I was not teaching but also for reading the chapters and making invaluable suggestions.

My colleagues have from time to time supported my endeavours. Dr. Kathleen Phillips Lewis has never refused my request to read a draft and has directed me to relevant material. Dr. Fitzroy A. Baptiste, Professor K. O. Laurence, and Professor Bridget Brereton receive my gratitude for their criticisms and suggestions for revision. Professor Barry Higman must also be thanked for commenting on several of the chapters. Professor Winston Richards of Pennsylvania State University provided advice on the preparation of the statistics. Professors Richard B. Sheridan, Emeritus, University of Kansas, Colin Palmer, Princeton University, and Stanley Engerman, University of Rochester, provided critical comments. Special thanks to Colin for his strong faith in the work and for writing the foreword. Thanks to his secretary, Sebony Burris, for typing and forwarding the piece with such efficiency. I also received invaluable help from Graham Taylor and Wayne Shepherd, formerly of the Computer Centre, University of the West Indies, St. Augustine Campus. I wish to thank the Rev. Mr. Dave St. Aubyn Gosse, ABD, for painstakingly assisting me in revising the copyedited version of the book.

I acknowledge the assistance of the staff of the following institutions for their help and guidance: in London, the Public Records Office, the Historical Manuscript Commission, the London Metropolitan Archives, the Lambeth Palace Library, the Institute of Historical Research, and the Library, University of London; in Oxford, the Bodleian and Rhodes House Libraries; in Bristol, the Archives, the Reference Library, and the University Library; the Somerset Record Office; the Surrey Record Office; the East Riding of Yorkshire Record Office, Beverley; the National Library and Registry of Archives, Edinburgh, Scotland; the National Library of Wales; the Library of Congress, Washington; the University of Manitoba Library and the Legislative Library, Winnipeg; and the University of the West Indies libraries at St. Augustine, Mona, and Cave Hill. I am greatly indebted to those institutions for affording me access to their manuscript holdings and other collections.

Grants from the Research and Publication Committee of St. Augustine Campus, University of the West Indies, and from the Central Research Fund, University of London, as well as a Professor Dame Lillian Penson Travel Grant, 1989, and a Professor Dame Lillian Penson Research Award, 1992, were instrumental in enabling me to travel to Britain.

At Howard University, thanks to Provost A. Toy Caldwell-Colbert, Mr. Rohinton Tengra, Dr. Orlando Taylor, dean of the Graduate School, and Dr. Emory J. Tolbert, chair of the History Department, for their unwavering support.

While many individuals shared in providing me with the facilities for undertaking the research and with the comfort of their homes, the ideas and concepts and analysis of the material are mine only, as is full responsibility for any mistakes and oversights. Of course, the interpretation is influenced not by any person but by the historical material alone.

Introduction

Methodology and Historical Assessment of the Literature

Beginning with the establishment of the plantation system in the British West Indies in the decade preceding the middle of the seventeenth century and for almost 125 years afterwards, the islands became increasingly dependent on American food and lumber. The size of the islands limited the quantity of prime land for concurrent sugar and provision cultivation. Even the use of labour was confined to the production of export commodities. Sugar production would not have thrived without the American continental colonies. In fact, dependency emerged because of the planters' need for both product and input markets. The American colonies became equally dependent on West Indian demand, which, throughout the first half of the eighteenth century, was large enough to consume most, if not all, of the lumber and foodstuffs produced for export in the thirteen continental colonies. After the mid-eighteenth century, however, American production and consumption were steadily exceeding West Indian demand and supply. There were other suppliers of tropical commodity products, so competition arose. Nevertheless, the British West Indies remained the single most important market for American goods. In return, the mainland colonies took all British West Indian rum and secondary crops, including coffee, cocoa, ginger, cotton, and a small quantity of molasses and sugar. This mutual trade was preeminent in colonial commercial relations, fostering cultural and social ties, and leading to the expansion and consolidation of the plantation system throughout the West Indies.

Caribbean trade with the American colonies and British West Indian dependence on American supplies of food and lumber are two of the well-documented themes in British colonial history. Herbert C. Bell's "The West India Trade before the American Revolution" is one of the earliest historical analyses of commercial relations between the two sets of colonies. The most comprehensive study on the subject thus far is Richard Pares's *Yankees and Creoles: The Trade Between North America and the West Indies Before the American Revolution.* Another work that traces the contribution of the American colonies to the growth and expansion of the sugar economy in the British West Indies and its contribution to the accumulation of wealth in Britain is Richard B. Sheridan's *Sugar and Slavery: An Economic History of the British West Indies, 1623–1775.*

The threatened outbreak of war between Britain and the American colonies disturbed West Indian planters and colonial officials alike. Contemporary commentators forecast a disastrous outcome for the sugar islands. However, the impact of the American Revolution on the political economy of the islands and the survival problems of the sugar planters was not considered until recent times.[1] These received some attention from Lowell J. Ragatz's *The Fall of the Planter Class in the British Caribbean, 1763–1833,* which demonstrates that events during the period of the War of American Independence contributed to the decline of the British West Indies. A further article from Sheridan amplifies on the problem of slave subsistence in the colonies, which was due in large part to the termination of American commerce. Sheridan discusses the numerous periods of shortage of food and lumber and the resultant reduction in tropical products exported to Britain, and he shows quite conclusively that shortages of foodstuffs contributed significantly to increased death rates among the black population mainly from malnutrition.

For the Caribbean, the War of American Independence was unique among major eighteenth-century wars. It was the first time that traditional supply markets were barred to the planters. Previous wars had little or no significant impact on American supplies reaching the islands. But the passage of the Prohibitory Act in December 1775 threatened the plantation system, the very foundations of the West Indian economy. This act stopped the free movement of goods between the islands and the rebellious colonies. Ships belonging to, or found trading with, the continental colonies were to be seized and "libelled" in any court of Vice-Admiralty in the British Empire. The measure did incorporate several provisos aimed at exempting certain classes of American ships—for example, a limited trade was allowed between the West Indies and those colonies that were not in revolt, as well as those areas under the control of British military forces—and these provisos enabled some merchants to engage in a profitable illegal trade. Nevertheless, the quantity of supplies reaching the West Indies by this means was much smaller than in previous years.

The disruption of commerce between America and the sugar colonies, when compounded by soil exhaustion and adverse weather conditions, had a deleterious effect on the islands' economies. Eric Williams cites the disruption of the American trade as marking the beginning of the uninterrupted decline of the West Indies, stressing that "it was current saying at the time that the British ministry had lost not only thirteen colonies but eight islands as well."[2] This edition of *Capitalism and Slavery* is dedicated to "Professor Lowell Joseph Ragatz whose monumental labors in this field may be amplified and developed but can never be superseded." Of course, Williams was giving due credit to the modern initiator of the decline thesis. Ragatz's *The Fall of the Planter Class in the British Caribbean, 1763–1833,* remains the seminal work in the overall interpretation of decline. Williams's major contribution was to link decline with abolition. It is my view, however, that while credit must be given to Williams and Ragatz for their insightful assessment of the West Indian economy at the end of the eighteenth century, the originator of the thesis was Hall Pringle in *The Fall of the Sugar Planters of Jamaica.* Pringle contended that West Indian decline, "if not regular and continuous, recurred repeatedly and at short intervals. Indeed, as early as 1689 we begin to hear of the 'Groans of the Plantations'" in which the sugar planters complained of their "present decline." In the years of the abolition of the slave trade, Pringle continues, reports showed that Jamaica was deeply in trouble and the distress of the sugar planters, already desperate, was increasing with alarming rapidity.[3]

This thesis found support among historians such as David H. Makinson, Sheridan, Barbara Solow, and William Darity Jr.[4] In Roger B. Anstey's *The Atlantic Slave Trade and British Abolition, 1760–1810,* there is a measure of consensus about the downturn in the economies of the sugar islands, yet Anstey refutes the Williams contention that it led directly to abolition. David Brion Davis has made the point about decline most succinctly in "Reflections on Abolitionism and Ideological Hegemony." Here he emphasises that the "opposition to slavery cannot be divorced from the vast economic changes that were intensifying social conflicts and heightening class consciousness," and that these changes were reflected in the West Indian economy, which even before the American

Revolution had weakened significantly; the sugar colonies by the end of the eighteenth century were overvalued only because "sugar was a symbol of national power." Of the state of the West Indian economy, Davis wrote: "The West Indies decline thus appeared all the more dramatic. Sugar and slaves were not a source of opulence, one discovered, but of debt, wasted soil, decayed properties and social depravity.... In the popular view there was thus a total dissociation between the old empire of plantation slavery and the new imperial search for raw materials and world markets. The emergence of the second empire involved a repudiation of the first. The second might depend on millions of involuntary labourers, but it was, by definition, a 'free world.'"[5]

New literature has surfaced in an effort to overturn the previously accepted view of the decline of the West Indian economy. This opposition to the decline-and-abolition thesis has its most powerful supporter in Seymour Drescher, whose monograph *Econocide* is one of the most polemical books since Adam Smith's *Wealth of Nations*. Drescher could have made greater use of the material available in the repositories in Britain. He accepts decline but dates its beginnings to the abolition of the slave trade. This old view was refuted in 1869 by Pringle, who emphasised that the abolition of the slave trade and slavery was "not needed to ruin the Jamaica sugar-planters and that the system was doomed to destruction from inherent causes." Of the "journalists and other writers" whom he termed "apologists of slavery," he wrote that they sought "to lead their readers inferentially to the belief that the abolition of [the slave trade and] slavery has been equally fatal to the interests of owners of sugar plantations in the other British colonies. These are persons careless of the dishonour thus sought to be brought on this country, who are bold enough to assert, that though England was first to suppress negro slavery, the nation has now discovered its mistake."[6]

Like the nineteenth-century commentators, Drescher equates the abolition of the slave trade with British altruism in her economic policy. He argues that the abolition occurred at the highest point of West Indian production, when the sugar colonies were growing in both absolute and relative value, which at the end of the eighteenth century had reached levels above those of any putative "golden age" before the American Revolution. This interpretation has been endorsed by David Brion Davis, who wrote earlier that "slave labour itself was inefficient, unprofitable and an impediment to economic growth," without any further research into the question.[7] David Eltis is also supportive, but unconvincing, mainly because his evidence is drawn from Drescher, whose thesis is that the long-term prospects of the slave trade and slavery were bright "when the British Parliament severed the umbilical link with Africa." Eltis argues that Britain stood to make significant profits from the slave trade at the time when it was abolished. It is quite ironic that, when it suits Eltis, he reconstructs his material to show that the slave trade was not very profitable to British entrepreneurs.[8]

Some critics have turned their attention to an analysis of Drescher's work and have found it wanting. Walter Minchinton has determined that Drescher's claims of an advancing West Indian economy were possible only because of flaws in his research technique. When his assumptions are put under the microscope, they are far less forceful than his supporters would have them. Drescher used only a part of the information available to him, in order to arrive at the conclusions he desired. For Minchinton, the evidence does not support Drescher's hypothesis; on the contrary, the available statistics are more likely to support the Ragatz/Williams doctrine of West Indian decline.[9]

I published one of the first full critiques of Drescher's arguments in my 1984 article "'Econocide'—Myth or Reality?" Here I showed that Drescher's book served only to confuse the issues. Unlike the case during previous eighteenth-century wars, decline was already evident during the War of American Independence. Furthermore, what appeared to be growth during the French Revolution and the Napoleonic Wars was not even a full return to pre-1776 conditions of profitability. Similarly, the destruction of St. Domingue did cause the value of West Indian goods to appreciate initially, but British policy and increased costs of production led to diminishing profits, as is clearly shown by J. R. Ward.[10] In the article I also undertook a crop-by-crop analysis of the performance of the West Indian economy. It was clear from this examination that the islands were in decline generally.

Even the number of slaves retained on the islands fell as the profits of the planters dwindled. David Richardson has found a direct but lagged relationship between changes in Jamaican planters' gross receipts from sugar sales in England between 1748 and 1775 and the number of slaves retained in the colonies. According to Richardson's findings, there were two peaks in slave imports into the British West Indies: one in the 1720s–1730s and the other in the period 1763–1775, shortly before the American Revolution, when "British vessels carried more slaves from Africa than in any previous or subsequent period of thirteen years."[11]

The Sugar Industry and the Abolition of the Slave Trade seeks to clarify in a conclusive manner the state of the British West Indian economy from 1775 to 1810. For this, the disruption of trade between the United States and the sugar colonies must be considered, since it had adverse effects on the islands' economies, compounding the already negative situation caused by soil exhaustion and poor weather conditions. I have therefore addressed, examined, and analysed the numerous conceivable issues that had an impact on the economy of the British West Indies for the period 1775–1810. In so doing, I have asked the following questions: (1) What was the state of the economies of the sugar colonies in the period immediately preceding the American Revolution? (2) What impact did the War of Independence have on the islands? (3) What was the overall result of Anglo-American trade relations on the economies of the sugar islands in the immediate postwar period and during the French Wars?

After the Treaty of Paris in 1763, the British West Indian planters settled down to cultivate their estates and to reap the benefits Britain had gained from a successful war. The Ceded Islands—Grenada, Tobago, St. Vincent, and Dominica—were being settled and developed as sugar colonies; sugar production was increasing as the interior of Jamaica was now cultivated. With the acquisition of the Ceded Islands and the expansion of agriculture in Jamaica, cocoa and coffee were significant additions to the list of articles exported from the British sugar islands. Coffee plantations became an important feature of the Jamaica landscape. A larger number of captive Africans were retained annually, and everywhere throughout the English-speaking Caribbean there were signs of increased economic activity. Planters were thus ever ready to take any risk involved in the plantation economy. To be sure, there were disquieting signs. In some colonies, planters were experiencing prolonged periods of poor crops from severe dry weather. Yet there were no signals of the immediate disintegration of the British Caribbean sugar economy. Chapter 1, "Sugar Production and British Caribbean Dependence on External Markets, 1769–1776," is the first of four chapters that are concerned mainly with the external aspects of the British Caribbean economy. It establishes and analyses the state of the West Indian economy in the pre–American Revolution period and shows its reliance on external markets.

Chapter 2 looks at the West Indian economy's rapid deterioration after the outbreak of hostilities in the American colonies. It identifies and assesses many of the major problems evident within a plantation economy. It analyses the effect of food shortages during the American War on slave subsistence and sugar production, and it examines the planters' search for alternative supply markets. Apart from concentrating on the problems affecting production, it establishes the beginnings of the decline in imports of new captive Africans and also in the number retained. Furthermore, it highlights how these shortfalls affected the growth of the black population and as a consequence the level of productivity in the sugar industry. "The American War and the British Caribbean Economy" focuses on all these issues to 1783.

In the third chapter, "British Policy, Canadian Preference, and the West Indian Economy, 1783–1810," I establish that conditions existing during the war years continued during the postwar period precisely because the British government adopted an insensitive and restrictive policy in its attempt to regulate British West Indian trade. This chapter demonstrates that the British plantation system was tested severely by the continued restriction on trade with the United States. It shows that attempts by the metropolitan government to force the islands to develop trading links with Canada to the exclusion of their historical trading partners simply intensified conditions of decline that existed from 1776 to 1783. Canadian performance throughout the period is compared with that of West Indian trade with the United States and other commercial partners.

We have seen that, as a result of British policy, the United States market was tapped and serviced by other sugar-producing areas. Canada was too limited in population and experience to meet the needs of the British West Indies. Ireland had little interest in taking West Indian products, as evidenced by her import figures. The majority of Irish imports of tropical products were through ports in Britain. The British market could not expand to accommodate the increased West Indian production of tropical products, including sugar, and its failure to do so helped to exacerbate decline. Furthermore, Parliament adopted measures to destabilize the sugar industry and to reduce the handsome prices that planters were receiving for their sugar and rum following the destruction of the St. Domingue economy and the loss of its supply. Cheap sugar, important to consumers, was a political weapon. The sugar industry was thrown into a state of trauma. Market conditions and the industry's responsiveness are analysed in chapter 4, "The Sugar Market after 1775." In this chapter, I also show that Britain reduced the drawback and bounty to prevent the export of sugar to Europe, and Parliament passed legislation importing sugar from India, which led to overstocking of the British market.

The next three chapters investigate how the planters turned to their own local resources to help in rationalizing the sugar industry. They are therefore chiefly concerned with internal issues. British policy led to spiralling costs through high prices for provisions, lumber, captive Africans, and supplies from Britain. In addition, duties on West Indian products increased, while transportation costs advanced significantly. On the other side of the ledger, the returns to West Indian planters, though higher in gross earnings, declined in terms of net returns. All in all, West Indian planters found themselves sinking further into debt. Yet they could not abandon their estates because of the nature of sugar investment and debt commitment. Chapter 5, "Debt, Decline, and the Sugar Industry, 1775–1810," assesses the evolution and growth of indebtedness of the West Indian plantations as a result of the American Revolution and British policy. Its main focus is to show that at the end of the eighteenth century indebtedness increased and extended the decline of the sugar colonies.

Of course, the economic security of the sugar islands was inextricably linked to the commerce of American colonies. The dependence of the islands on the American market has been indelibly established. The termination of unlimited trade forced the sugar planters and their attorneys to deal with the critical problem of procuring food supplies for their slaves while maintaining and even increasing production levels of sugar, rum, and coffee in order to meet rising costs. Chapter 6, "New Management Techniques and Planter Reforms," while dealing with the management of these problems, highlights planters' attempts at amelioration on individual plantations. It also assesses the efforts of many West Indian legislatures to adopt policies of amelioration to safeguard plantation labour. One solution offered in illustration was to purchase female slaves for the sake of breeding—a policy geared to achieve long-term effects. In the short term, planters attempted more humane actions such as allowing limited marriages and introducing religion in order to create an atmosphere of family life and so maintain slavery by natural increase.

The War of American Independence had unleashed a series of crises in the British West Indies and brought immense hardships, which led to near economic ruin. None was more devastating than the impact of this war and the succeeding ones on the labour force and its ability to perform all the duties required on a West Indian plantation. In order to counter the shortfall, the planters and their managers turned to hired labour to meet their needs as well as to ease the plight of their slaves. Chapter 7, "Hired Slave Labour," assesses labour on the plantations and the effect of decline on labour practices.

The last group of four chapters continues the analysis of the West Indian economy between 1789 and 1810 to determine the performance of the sugar industry in a rapidly changing environment. Chapter 8, "British Caribbean

Slavery and Abolition," deals in greater detail with the institution of slavery itself. It analyses the changes made to the institution and the measures adopted to enable it to confront the threat to its existence. The rationale for slavery's continuation, at a time when its viability was questioned by free trade ideology, depended on the planters' ability to demonstrate that as a labour force it was cheaper than free labour. Unfortunately for them, such an argument was limited by the state of the markets that consumed British West Indian products.

The next chapter, "The Sugar Industry and Eighteenth-Century Revolutions," deals almost totally with the performance of this mainstay of the West Indian economy during this critical period, beginning with the Colonial Office's investigations into the slave trade and slavery in the British West Indies, and ending with a brief analysis of conditions three years after the slave trade was abolished. The chapter highlights how the industry fared during the French Wars, looks at its problems with markets and profitability, and concludes that, in spite of adjustments, it was certainly in decline. The sugar industry had always had problems during wartime, though Britain maintained its lifeline by protecting colonial trade during eighteenth-century wars. But certainly the irony was that British interests had expanded by the wars and the British West Indies were now the least attractive investment area. British industrial capitalists saw a long-term future in the imperial colonies to the east. The old sugar colonies had served their purpose. Their sun had set. It was rising in the East with full glow with sugar production in Mauritius and India.

In spite of the problems that faced the West Indian planters, they were committed to the continued production of sugar. Not all abandoned their estates for the safety of the coffeehouses in London. Many remained to struggle on during these critical years. Chapter 10, "War, Trade and Planter Survival, 1793–1810," examines the efforts of the planter class to surmount the problems of war and the devastating hardships brought about by British policy including the abolition of the slave trade. The plantations survived, and this chapter reveals how that was achieved. Further adjustments would become necessary with the abolition of the slave trade. This area of research will have to be accomplished by other scholars.

This work, having employed several new sources of information to examine the decline hypothesis, concludes with "Profitability and Decline: Issues and Concepts—An Epilogue." This epilogue summarises the discussion and uses a variety of documentation showing that the British West Indies were in decline and that the decline was an important factor in the decision of the British government to end the slave trade in captive Africans—though this did not end British involvement in the trade of other countries, which Parliament outlawed only in the 1840s.

My study has set out to identify, analyse, and understand the thorny issue of the decline of the British West Indian economy in the period 1775–1810. It has accomplished this through the assessment of a wide range of official documents, plantation papers, contemporary published letters, and historical works. The study has been fertilized by modern scholarship through historical investigations.

Most valuable to this work has been the availability of the papers of so many plantations. The survival of these papers is reminiscent of the survival of the plantations themselves through the long line of hardships and setbacks that their owners faced. Complementing these invaluable sources are the hundreds of volumes of Colonial Office Papers with their extensive statistical data. The plantation papers also contain a wealth of statistical offerings which, although limited to a few estates throughout the islands, inform us on such matters as the prices of enslaved persons, of sugar, of rum. They enable the researcher to make comparisons with the official documents. There are in the Colonial Office Papers very extensive collections of statistics on numerous areas of commercial and shipping activities—trade figures on captive Africans, prices for enslaved workers, exports of sugar and rum to Britain and the United States, prices of American goods, and many more.

These statistics are extremely useful in helping us to fathom the economic conditions that shaped the ideas and policy of both the British government and the West Indian planters. I have therefore complemented the straightforward historical analysis with detailed statistical analysis in order to consolidate our quantitative knowledge of the late eighteenth century and better understand why certain decisions were made. In achieving this, models are used if applicable, but the work depends more heavily on tabular and graphical presentations of data sets to allow the reader to evaluate the conclusions. There is also regression and correlation testing, and frequency distribution charts for periods of four years or five, whichever allows for greater and more effective analysis of the period, unhindered by wars or natural disasters.

The use of these statistics has enhanced the study and has helped to clarify the work's conclusions. Many data may suffer from irregularities—mainly to do with the recording and copying of figures and the conversion of measurements from one system to another—without negating their value to the work.

The principal aim surrounding the collection of import and export statistics was to determine the balance of trade between England and other countries. From this standpoint, the statistics may have limited value. As an indicator of what happened, however, they are particularly valuable, at least as records of the quantities of goods, if not of money. Even in the matter of quantity, they cannot account for all the goods that entered a country, since only goods passing through the customs were listed and valued. In the British West Indies there were numerous inlets and bays that had no customhouses. Furthermore, large quantities of smuggled goods are not included in the statistics. Similarly, ship-owners understated the tonnage of their vessels in order to save on charges. There may have also been a measure of complicity between traders and customs officers in the colonies, causing smaller quantities of items to be registered than were actually traded. When Thomas Irving became inspector-general, he routinely added one-third to shipping tonnages in order to arrive at a more accurate total, as he believed that freight (that is, transport costs) was an important component in determining the balance of trade.

It is almost impossible, and probably bootless to attempt to make adjustments. In the case of shipping, the quantity remained constant. For other goods too, the chief achievement would be an inflation of the figures. In the particular case of Barbados, the trade with England may at times have been considered larger than it was, because the island was normally the landfall for outward ships from the United Kingdom, and it became a transshipment base for the newly settled Windward Islands.

The values assigned to imports and exports are of immense significance to researchers who wish to calculate the value of a particular activity, as in the case of the trade in captive Africans. The islands had their own currencies, and the rate of exchange is not always known on a regular basis. One has to assume that it was fairly stable for the eighteenth century. Furthermore, the statistics do not always identify the currency in which the prices of enslaved workers were quoted, especially in the plantation papers. The researcher has to assume that, when not specifically given in sterling, the attorneys' quotations are in the local currency, whereas quotations in official documents are normally given in sterling. Still, it is possible to use the figures by converting to one currency. After the independence of the United States, the prices of its exports were sometimes quoted in dollars. This poses greater difficulty, because the ratio of sterling or even local currency to dollars is seldom found in the documents.

In a period marked by so many wars, the shipping statistics may be inaccurate because ships were prone to sail under several colours, including those of the enemy. In these cases, it may be enough for the researcher to establish the problem without attempting to adjust the figures, as with tonnage. I have high-lighted these problems, not to negate the value of the statistics, but in the hope that their use will be understood better. In conjunction with the manuscript material covering the period under study, the statistics reinforce emphatically the claims of decline and the continued loss of profitability by the planters and their attorneys. With this added evidence at the disposal of the researcher, it is now possible to analyse the statistical material, despite the problems outlined, with a measure of precision and stability.

$\backsim$ 1 $\backsim$

Sugar Production and British Caribbean Dependence on External Markets, 1769–1776

The economic development and growth of the British Caribbean islands depended on their unrestricted commercial intercourse with the continental American colonies. Before 1776 the sugar islands and the thirteen continental colonies carried on a mutual trade and intercourse fostered by, and developed under, the protection of British mercantilist policies, since the trade between Britain and her colonies operated within a closed system that functioned well until it was terminated by the War of American Independence. Although strict commercial laws governed trade within the empire, the British West Indian planters profited because they were able to sell their products at guaranteed markets while receiving cheap, steady, and reliable supplies of provisions, lumber, captive Africans, and manufactured goods.

In the eighteenth-century British commercial system, the Caribbean colonies played a very important role, which an examination of the commerce of the islands for the period 1769–75 clarifies. These were indeed the last truly prosperous years for the West Indian planters; while there were fluctuations in the quantity of staples exported to England and America, overall there was a significant increase in the total of British Caribbean products shipped.

This resulted mainly from the acquisition and development of the Ceded Islands, with the extension of sugar and coffee plantations in Jamaica, and with the establishment of sugar estates in the new colonies. Cocoa and coffee plantations had already existed in many of the new British colonies. However, with the British occupation of Grenada and Tobago, sugar plantations were quickly established and the sugar industry gained prominence. From the trade statistics, significant quantities of cocoa and coffee were still produced in Grenada. It would appear that cocoa remained one of the chief exports of St. Vincent. None was sent from Tobago until 1779, when 37 hundredweight were exported to England. Tobago's development in the period 1771–75 was phenomenal and is demonstrated in table 1.1.

The importance of the coffee and cocoa plantations is shown in table 1.2. Cocoa exports from Grenada to England increased fivefold in seven years, from approximately 1,000 hundredweight in 1764 to more than 5,000 in 1771. However, between the latter year and 1775 there was a decline in the quantity of British plantation cocoa sent to England from Grenada. And during the American Revolution, cocoa exports fell to a low of only 2,219 hundredweight in 1779—the year in which the French captured the island. Similarly, the quantity of British-grown cocoa imported into England from St. Vincent increased unevenly from approximately 270 hundredweight in 1765 to 2,201 in 1769, then fell drastically to 530 in 1777.[1]

Of the older islands, Jamaica was the only colony in which the planters had attempted to diversify their agricultural system, although sugar production remained their chief interest. Diversification was the result of the availability of thousands of acres of land unsuitable for sugarcane but suited to the cultivation of other crops. In 1773 Jamaica had 110 cotton works occupying 48,000 acres, 500 breeding pens totalling 500,000 acres, 600 provision plots, and 150 coffee plantations occupying in excess of 6,000 acres.[2] A small quantity of cocoa was cultivated, and exports to England increased unevenly from 241 hundredweight in 1770 to 939 in 1775. The largest quantities exported from Jamaica to England were 1,900 and 1,267 hundredweight in 1772 and 1773 respectively.

With the acquisition of the Ceded Islands and the expansion of coffee plantations in Jamaica, the quantity of coffee sent to England from the West Indies increased significantly after 1763. From 1769 to 1775, coffee exports from Grenada almost doubled, from 12,443 hundredweight to 24,423. St. Vincent coffee exports increased even more: in 1769 a total of 4,818 hundredweight were sent to England; this rose to 10,568 in 1775. British plantation-grown coffee imported into England from Dominica was exceeded only by that from Grenada and rose from 10,480 hundredweight in 1770 to 21,134 in 1774 and to 25,165 in 1776. Only very small quantities of coffee were exported from Barbados and the Leeward Islands to England.

Coffee production became increasingly important in Jamaican agriculture

Table 1.1. Development of Tobago

	Unit	1771	1772	1773	1774	1775
White men		284	416	431	367	391
Slaves		5,028	7,342	7,192	7,635	8,643
Acres cleared		7,402	9,601	12,451	15,000	17,514
Mules/oxen		651	1,315	1,477	1,712	1,823
Sugar	cwt	12,545	36,296	39,494	64,220	75,528
Rum	gal	40,800	62,240	90,000	206,520	389,040
Cotton	lb	—	—	—	96,500	285,031
Coffee	cwt	—	—	—	—	650
Indigo	lb	—	—	—	3,600	4,620

Sources: W. Young, *Growth of Tobago* (1807); Stowe MSS 922; see also Drescher, *Econocide*.

Table 1.2. Coffee and cocoa exports to Britain, 1769–80

	Dominica	St. Vincent		Jamaica	Grenada	
Year	Coffee	Coffee	Cocoa	Coffee	Coffee	Cocoa
1769	14,163	4,818	2,201	—	12,443	2,343
1770	10,480	2,995	936	1,711	15,927	3,054
1771	16,449	7,685	921	2,123	13,749	5,048
1772	20,321	10,503	1,381	5,900	24,740	3,424
1773	15,709	7,348	2,082	3,770	17,396	3,074
1774	21,134	8,111	1,784	4,831	23,299	2,811
1775	15,792	10,568	1,192	4,029	24,423	2,667
1776	25,165	6,827	2,037	3,396	16,403	2,386
1777	16,121	7,120	530	3,987	21,027	2,413
1778	14,306	3,531	724	651	20,124	2,384
1779	—	5,320	751	6,260	12,158	2,219
1780	—	—	—	7,176	—	—

Sources: PRO, CH 3/69–80; Minutes of the West India Merchants, vol. 1, fols. 9, 18, 28, 47, 51, 76, 115, 147, 174; vol. 2, fols. 20, 58d, 112d.

Note: Quantities of coffee and cocoa are given in hundredweight.

in the decade after 1765. Not only were the planters concerned with the increased production of that commodity for the British and European markets, they were encouraged by the legislature to produce the best types of beans, equal in quality to "mocha coffee."[3] To achieve this, assistance was provided to the coffee planters. Beginning in 1773, the legislature instituted cash incentives to planters who produced quality coffee beans. In 1774 the awards were increased, from £100 to £150 for the best sample and from £50 to £100 for the second, and a third prize of £50 was added. For the information of others, each planter submitting samples was required to list the type of soil for cultivation, particulars pertaining to growth, times when beans were picked, and the method used to cure them. This information was published and the best coffee samples were sent to England to be evaluated.[4] Other incentives were added later. It must be noted that there was a general increase in exports during the early part of the 1770s. The planters in Jamaica had increased coffee cultivation, and the establishment of plantation societies in the Ceded Islands sent increased exports to England.

After settlement of the Ceded Islands, cotton exports to England (shown in table 1.3) were boosted. Grenada and the Grenadines became the chief exporters, and the quantity of cotton sent from there increased to 368,032 pounds. Jamaica, which had led in cotton exports to England prior to 1763, not only lost its place but saw its exports decline between 1770 and 1775. However, there was no cause for alarm: in 1776 the island exported more than 775,000 pounds of cotton to England. The most significant gains occurred in Tobago after 1770. Before 1772 no cotton was exported from there to England; in 1780 more than 1,450,000 pounds were sent. Cotton exports from Barbados, as from Jamaica, lost ground to other producers during the years 1769–75. But between 1775 and 1780 cotton sent to England averaged nearly 350,000 pounds, a substantial increase over the 1769 figure of 112,000. More important, the cotton industry was assuming greater significance in the Barbados economy, as sugar declined. Favourable reports of increased production inspired the Assembly to adopt unanimously a private bill to encourage "Pearce Archer in his new projection of a Windmill for Ginning and cleaning the seeds out of Cotton."[5] George Pinckard reported seeing these mills on his visit to Barbados in 1798; they were driven by wind power, and some were operated by hand.[6] It is not clear how far this technological development was adopted in cotton production, but it shows that some planters were aware of a need for mechanization to reduce costs and boost production.

Despite a general desire among West Indian planters to diversify their agricultural system, the British West Indian economy remained one based mainly on the production of sugar and rum. Given the demand for sugar in the American, British, and European markets, the planters were forced not only to continue but to increase production. Also, as I have indicated, two other factors led

Table 1.3. Cotton exports to Britain, 1769–80

Year	Barbados	Grenada	St. Vincent	Tobago
1769	112,083	969,093	46,602	—
1770	114,055	966,496	63,964	—
1771	65,877	629,228	67,895	—
1772	129,892	1,069,261	84,627	33,000
1773	161,139	1,028,802	199,670	2,000
1774	165,988	1,175,913	342,228	96,500
1775	230,291	729,949	271,472	285,031
1776	201,850	561,949	374,229	381,355
1777	491,849	1,225,201	219,329	408,974
1778	253,915	1,296,723	577,911	1,459,614
1779	434,785	1,176,026	26,500	728,506
1780	461,933	—	—	1,452,002

Source: PRO, CH 3/69–80.

Note: Quantities of cotton are given in pounds.

to increased quantities of sugar reaching the ports of England between 1769 and 1775: the establishment of sugar estates in the Ceded Islands, and increased investments in sugarcane cultivation in Jamaica after 1763. In 1769 Jamaica's exports to Britain of 43,091 hogsheads of sugar were 8 percent above the 1767 figures, and in 1773 her exports of 54,302 hogsheads had advanced in excess of 26 percent over those of 1769.[7] Extensive cultivation of sugarcane was the most significant feature of British settlement of the Ceded Islands. For example, Grenada increased her sugar exports to England from 64,458 hundredweight in 1765 to 198,159 in 1773; by 1775 exports had risen more than 190 percent. Imports of sugar into England from St. Vincent increased from 700 hundredweight in 1766 to 62,599 in 1774. The Tobago planters also concentrated on the production of sugar. Before 1769 none was exported, but in 1770, 1,686 hundredweight were imported into England, and in 1775 the island's exports reached 50,385. Dominica showed a similar rate of growth in sugar exports to England, up from 1,560 hundredweight in 1769 to 53,464 in 1774. Table 1.4 shows sugar exports from the Ceded Islands and Jamaica for the period 1769–82.

Exceptions to this general growth in sugar exports from the British colonies were to be found in Barbados and for periods in the Leeward Islands. Soil exhaustion has usually been listed as the main reason for the decline, though lesser factors such as land distribution and increased cultivation of root veg-

Table 1.4. Sugar and rum exports from Jamaica and Ceded Islands to Britain, 1769–82

Year	Dominica		Grenada		Jamaica		St. Vincent		Tobago	
	Sugar (cwt)	Rum (gal)	Sugar (cwt)	Rum (gal)	Sugar (hhd)	Rum (casks)	Sugar (cwt)	Rum (gal)	Sugar (cwt)	Rum (gal)
1769	1,560	6,604	126,228	94,030	—	—	21,174	5,878	—	—
1770	13,940	793	196,131	158,066	39,760	8,743	38,395	34,694	1,686	60
1771	10,258	25,489	157,762	161,189	39,136	10,737	44,359	48,047	4,450	29
1772	10,371	18,706	194,452	90,143	45,889	12,483	53,551	20,350	13,625	619
1773	26,705	10,867	198,159	63,664	54,302	12,596	58,691	26,071	14,153	171
1774	53,464	11,707	179,375	72,318	51,218	10,493	62,599	16,342	30,985	550
1775	40,682	50,800	189,939	143,138	50,340	11,564	51,643	79,603	50,385	2,845
1776	49,837	74,955	147,722	292,953	40,799	14,257	45,975	88,089	47,146	66,656
1777	35,462	26,444	115,740	98,078	33,856	10,034	50,381	39,330	17,754	16,782
1778	38,855	44,729	122,254	148,351	40,509	12,320	43,080	58,883	26,922	35,351
1779	—	—	103,292	67,223	42,876	14,250	40,877	16,763	15,591	4,998
1780	—	—	—	—	49,158	12,014	—	—	22,149	5,850
1781	—	—	—	—	38,509	8,189	—	—	—	—
1782	—	—	—	—	30,282	7,820	—	—	—	—

Sources: Same as table 1.2.

etables for food were contributory. Yet despite the reduced production in Barbados, sugar remained a very lucrative industry. Commenting on the ability of the Barbados planters to manage their estates profitably, Edward Long, planter and historian, remained convinced that they had enough experience to remedy the infertility of their lands. In 1774 he wrote: "We can hardly therefore form any conception of the industry practiced by the Barbadians from 1689 to the present time, in manuring their land, and retaining it in a degree of fertility sufficiently to continue the planting of Sugarcanes for so many years, and to make the business at all profitable."[8]

The decline of sugar exports from Barbados was in many ways unique in the West Indies. In the Leeward Islands, sugar production in Antigua had recovered from the slump of the early 1770s, and in 1774 and 1775 the island sent to England a total of 233,441 and 241,595 hundredweight of sugar respectively. Also, although there were fluctuations in the sugar exports from Montserrat and Nevis between 1770 and 1775, the quantity sent to England by each island remained constant during this period. St. Kitts exported significantly large quantities of sugar to England between 1770 and 1775. The worst year was 1773, when only 106,367 hundredweight were exported. The Custom House accounts put the annual sugar imports into England from St. Kitts at 120,164 hundredweight in 1770, at 210,134 in 1772, at 204,743 in 1774, and at 197,437 in 1775. Taken as a whole, sugar exports from the Leeward Islands to England increased during the five years prior to the outbreak of the war. In 1773 Governor Sir Ralph Payne wrote to the Earl of Dartmouth, colonial secretary, that all the planters were expecting bumper crops. In 1774 his prediction was proven right, and he wrote that the very large crops had "surpassed the Expectations of the Planters." Similar ones were expected in 1775.[9] Table 1.5 gives the quantities of sugar and rum imported into England from Barbados and the Leeward Islands. The uneven nature of the figures seems to be the result of seasonal variations caused by adverse weather conditions.

The only manufactured article exported from the British sugar islands was rum, but a relatively small quantity of that distilled in Barbados, the Ceded Islands, and the Leeward Islands was sent to Britain. The greater portion was exchanged for American products. A detailed look at the statistics shows that the quantity exported from Antigua to England stood at 21,840 gallons in 1770 and at 32,400 gallons in 1775. Rum exports to England from Montserrat and Nevis also declined between 1770 and 1775, while those from Barbados fell

Table 1.5. Sugar and rum exports from Barbados and Leeward Islands to London, 1769–75

Year	St. Kitts Sugar	Rum	Nevis Sugar	Rum	Antigua Sugar	Rum	Montserrat Sugar	Rum	Barbados Sugar	Rum
1769	12,584	69	2,149	12	11,567	17	4,032	22	9,449	23
1770	17,183	49	3,738	60	17,445	91	4,049	11	8,353	91
1771	13,884	62	3,336	37	7,391	38	3,000	95	4,903	77
1772	15,681	47	3,992	34	8,692	55	4,513	3	7,339	71
1773	6,908	33	2,060	6	6,387	16	2,806	17	5,259	40
1774	15,839	60	5,284	17	21,125	112	3,981	4	6,929	79
1775	13,520	76	3,705	13	14,190	135	3,307	9	3,594	135

Source: Compiled from the West India Committee Records, Minutes of the Society of West Indian Merchants, vol. 1.

Note: Quantities of sugar are given in casks, of rum in puncheons.

Table 1.6. Selected British West Indian exports to Britain, 1771–76

Year	Sugar (cwt)	Rum (gal)	Coffee (cwt)	Cocoa (cwt)	Pimento (lb)
1771	1,492,092	2,728,565	40,026	6,882	1,793,154
1772	1,786,045	2,284,163	62,206	6,802	1,450,575
1773	1,762,386	2,282,544	44,745	7,813	2,282,071
1774	2,015,911	1,703,222	57,694	5,227	2,530,939
1775	2,002,224	2,305,808	54,937	5,334	2,522,356
1776	1,656,934	3,341,025	51,833	6,536	1,589,145

Sources: "Account of the Imports and Exports between . . . England and the British West Indies . . . for Christmas 1773 to 1783," PRO, T 38/269, fols. 1–11 (hereafter cited as "Imports and Exports"); Edwards, *History,* 1:509–10; Ragatz, *Statistics,* 22.

moderately from 30,720 gallons in 1770 to 26,640 gallons in 1775. Exports from the Ceded Islands to Britain were likewise small in relation to the quantity of rum produced. Between 1770 and 1775 all the sugar colonies, with the exception of Jamaica, depended on American markets to take the bulk of their excess rum. An assessment of the total statistical data indicates quite conclusively that the overall picture of exports of tropical products to England between 1770 and 1776 was one of growth, as is illustrated in table 1.6.

For the seven years prior to the commencement of the American War, 1769–

75, the total value of imports from Britain to the sugar colonies amounted to £9,768,303, for an annual average of £1,395,472.[10] However, the importance of the West Indian colonies to the British imperial commercial system, unlike those of North America, lay not in their imports from Britain but in their exports.[11] The produce of the islands when exported to England was an "appropriated fund" used to pay for British supplies consumed in the islands, and was independent of the foreign commerce carried on by the merchants.[12] The total value of exports to Britain from the West India colonies in the seven years before the American War amounted to £21,006,618, or more than £3 million a year.[13]

Similarly, between 1769 and 1775 there was a steady increase in British West Indian imports from Britain. The rate of growth of the economy of the British islands had always fluctuated from the beginning of the eighteenth century. Some years showed continuing economic prosperity, others a downturn, but the latter was always temporary. Looking at the state of the trade between Britain and the West Indies in the four decades from 1740 to 1780, one finds that the average annual value of exports to Britain for the 1740s amounted to about £1,200,000; for the 1750s this increased to £1,779,000, and in the 1760s the average annual value of West Indian exports to Britain increased by almost a million pounds to some £2,730,000. Because of the American War, the 1770s showed a smaller increase than the previous ten years, yet the annual average rose to £2,943,000. The exports from England to the British West Indies showed a similar pattern of growth. The average annual value of the exports from England increased from £725,664 in the 1740s to £1,133,233 in the 1760s.[14] The data for the years from 1769 to 1782 are given in table 1.7. There is fairly steady growth until 1776 and then an overall drop.

An examination of the statistics for the individual islands for 1770–75 (table 1.8) shows that the trade of most of the islands was progressing satisfactorily. But such figures give only a partial picture of the balance of trade position of the West Indian colonies. The islands' exports to England, and not their imports, were always rated at the real value. The freight and other charges upon the goods exported to the West Indies were not included in the total value of British goods imported into the islands. By contrast, the official value of imports from the sugar islands into Britain included the cost of freight and other charges. The islands were apparently given this credit in assessing their exports. Since the freight and handling charges belonged to the British merchants, the apparent balance of trade in the islands' favour was not as large as the Custom House books would indicate. Yet the planters were not impoverished and many were

Table 1.7. Shipping figures, Britain–West Indies trade, 1769–82

Year	To the West Indies			From the West Indies		
	Ships	Tonnage	Cargo value (£)	Ships	Tonnage	Cargo value (£)
1769	474	80,986	1,346,247	564	89,466	3,002,679
1770	398	69,153	1,313,676	610	89,683	3,418,823
1771	430	77,335	1,209,822	502	77,584	2,972,203
1772	433	78,942	1,433,028	579	90,187	1,465,404
1773	464	86,257	1,338,703	608	84,206	2,848,613
1774	472	87,694	1,420,524	498	82,327	3,622,948
1775	498	93,717	1,706,301	592	103,045	3,675,948
1776	490	85,753	1,602,713	594	97,972	3,329,920
1777	420	76,861	1,247,771	464	76,900	2,794,457
1778	504	90,834	1,151,594	568	92,298	3,057,424
1779	522	97,135	1,127,465	553	86,196	2,811,909
1780	535	101,798	1,675,313	475	88,726	2,450,078
1781	353	64,851	1,031,028	474	88,562	1,860,546
1782	452	80,726	1,289,552	471	89,123	2,217,928

Sources: "An Account of the Number of Ships, with Their Tonnage, Which Cleared Outwards from Great Britain to the British West India Islands, in Each Year, from 1765, Together with the Total Value of Exports from Great Britain to the West Indies . . . to the nearest (£)," *Parliamentary Papers* (HMSO), vol. 84, app. pt. 4, nos. 687.

Table 1.8. Selected trade balances with England and Scotland, 1770–75

Year	Island	Exports (£)	Imports (£)	Balance	Trading partner
1770	Antigua	349,102	112,533	+236,569	England
1770	Antigua	65,660	8,141	+57,519	Scotland
1772	St. Kitts	302,952	118,914	+184,038	England
1772	St. Kitts	14,635	10,054	+4,581	Scotland
1774	Dominica	244,729	46,952	+197,777	England
1775	Grenada	486,035	137,946	+348,089	England
1775	Grenada	22,565	5,235	+17,330	Scotland
1775	Jamaica	1,653,735	786,728	+867,007	England
1775	Barbados	112,971	138,384	-25,413	England
1775	Barbados	57	6,600	-6,543	Scotland

Source: Compiled from Whitworth, *State of the Trade*, PRO, BT 6/185.

Note: The figures have been rounded to the nearest £.

satisfied with the functioning of the system. This is supported by a quotation from Edward Long that gives the view of the typical eighteenth-century English mercantilist who worked and operated West Indian plantations. Long carefully argued that "every shilling of West India produce is English property. . . . In regard to our colonies, both the Import and Export are our own. The whole revolves and Circulates in . . . [England] and is, so far as it regards our profit, in the nature of home trade as much as if all our Dominions in America were fixed to Cornwall."[15]

The West Indian planters had numerous other obligations in Britain, apart from the freight and port charges, to fulfil. These included commissions to factors and agents, interest on debts, annuities, and allowances for their children sent to be educated there. These consumed a large portion of their profits, and many of the West Indian planters were always indebted to the British merchants. With their accounts constantly overdrawn, their exports from the colonies in one year were consigned to the merchants to pay for goods sent out the preceding year.[16] Even the planters of the Ceded Islands were affected in this way. The result was a loss of specie from the islands. The show of progress and wealth among many of the planters was therefore deceptive. In 1775 Lord Macartney, governor of Grenada, highlighted the problems facing the colonists, in a letter to Lord George Germain, Secretary of State. He cited the financing of estates as the chief reason for the economic state of the islands. Many commission houses had financed the purchase of these estates "on the condition that all the produce would be consigned to them. By this means the profit of commission and interest together amounted to nearly 20 percent, whilst the planter lay under every disadvantage for being entirely dependent on his London Creditor and obliged to remit the produce to him only, losing the choice of his correspondent and the chance of the Market. Thus although . . . [Grenada] itself was rich, the individual was poor."[17]

Compounding the indebtedness of the planters to local and British merchants, the effects of the bankruptcies of 1772 were still being felt in the West Indies as late as 1776. After 1763, as we have seen, large sums of money were invested in the establishment of sugar and coffee plantations in Jamaica and the Ceded Islands. The failure of the banks in Britain and Europe in 1772 caused universal panic. It had greatly distressed the planters in the British colonies, and had given rise to distrust and loss of confidence. In Dominica and Grenada, many planters and land speculators were financially ruined.[18]

An assessment of the sugar colonies' trade with Britain must also consider that with Ireland. From there, the West Indies imported chiefly beef, pork, butter, and herring. In 1773 Jamaica took from Ireland 19,923 barrels of beef, 4,308 barrels of pork, 15,876 firkins of butter, and 21,300 barrels of herring. The total value of Irish imports into Jamaica in that year was put at £113,901 10s sterling. The high price of Irish beef was the chief factor—which gave its American counterpart, though inferior in quality, preference in the West Indian markets.[19] In 1774 Irish exports to the British Caribbean colonies were valued at approximately £260,000, and Irish imports from the islands at only £147,384.[20] (The main West Indian products imported into Ireland were rum, cotton, and sugar. Rum was taken directly, but sugar had to be landed first in England.) This trade deficit forced the West Indian planters to send large amounts of bills of exchange to Ireland.

During most of the eighteenth century, a great number and variety of businesses in Britain and Ireland depended upon the importation of West Indian products, as well as on West Indian markets, for their daily existence. Many artisans and tradesmen were employed in building, repairing, victualling, and equipping the ships engaged in the West Indian trade, and thousands more earned their living by loading and unloading these ships. West Indian commerce thus established several important linkages. "The Benefits derived from our West India islands," wrote Edward Long,

are not merely [that] which we gain from them per annum on the Gross Balance of Trade. Call this sum 4 millions, we are to consider at the same time, that this 4 million is coming in and moving on in circulation; the constant regular demands from the colonies, requires as constant, and regular a preparation for answering them, and therefore it is neither absurd nor fallacious to say that double the sum is in effect acting with unremitted operation [in the] Employment of our fellow subjects both at home and abroad, & our ships & marines at Sea.... There is no artificer, manufacturer or mechanic in ... Britain whose fabrics are not comprehended in the West India demand. Thousands there are in this Kingdom whom it keeps in constant Employment, others Incidentally; & if when the Gain of these people comes to be diffused for the Support of the numerous families, & the multitudes of Inferior workmen labourers and other Dependents the whole which are entirely or partially subsisted will be found to exceed computation.[21]

Another writer, Sir John Dalrymple, voiced a similar opinion. He estimated "that the sugar colonies added to the wealth of ... [Britain] annually, £3,852,962 or £12 5s 1d per head for their inhabitants, employed 5,600 ... seamen, or one to every 55 of their people, and increased the population of the kingdom by a variety of means."[22]

The development, growth, and economic progress of the British Caribbean islands depended on their unrestricted commercial intercourse with the continental American colonies. Since the British colonial plantation system was based on a monocultural slave society dependent on an external supply of provisions and lumber, the American colonies became the suppliers of every class of foodstuffs and lumber consumed in the British islands. West Indian trade with the mainland colonies worked well, and despite a series of wars affecting the Caribbean during the eighteenth century, the weaknesses inherent in this artificial monocultural slave economy never became apparent until the years of the American War and after. From the establishment of the plantation system in the Caribbean, the sugar islands relied almost solely on the continental colonies for their sustained growth. The economies of the two groups of colonies became closely interwoven, their interdependence as indispensable to the growth and prosperity of the British islands as to the agricultural, industrial, and commercial development of the mainland colonies. As long as each group of colonies progressed in conjunction with the needs of the other, the economic development of the British West Indies was secure.

Although an illegal trade had grown up between the non-British West Indies and the American colonies in the eighteenth century, the greater part of the continental trade was still with the British islands, which provided a steady and reliable market to the northern agriculturists for their provisions, to the New England fishermen for their inferior grades of fish, to the lumbermen of the middle and southern colonies, and to the American farmers for their coarse salted beef and pork as well as their livestock. In addition, the New England shipping industry with its numerous artisans was kept in steady employment, building and repairing ships for the West Indian trade.

Each continental colony had a stake in the continued growth and prosperity of the British sugar colonies. After the middle of the eighteenth century, the North Americans supplied the islands with slaves, through their commerce with Africa. They also provided board, joists, planks, shingles, and complete house frames for the buildings; staves, heading, and hoops for casks for sugar and rum; fish, flour, biscuit, rice, beef, pork, livestock, tobacco, lamp oil, candles, soap, and pitch for household consumption; horses, cattle, and oxen for plantation uses; and a small quantity of manufactured goods, mainly hats, shoes, iron implements, and furniture.

By 1774 the export of manufactured articles from the continental colonies had become an important feature of West Indian–American trade, and a source of worry to colonial officers who saw the Americans as competing with manufacturing interests in Britain. In 1773 Lieutenant-Governor Stuart of Dominica informed the Earl of Dartmouth that "the North American have lately enlarg'd a trade with these islands in the articles of shoes, and all kinds of Household furniture which . . . is contrary to the Rights and Interest of Great Britain. *The Pretence* is that there are no Acts of Parliament But against the Article of Hatts, And is likewise an Excuse for the Revenue Officer permitting them."[23]

The framers of British commercial policy had probably preferred to overlook this problem. The Earl of Dartmouth, in commenting on the state of the trade, acknowledged that the increased importation of slaves and manufactured goods from America deserved very serious consideration: "Such a Trade . . . is highly prejudicial to the interest of great Britain and repugnant to every purpose of Government in planting those colonies, but as there are no laws in being which prohibit the importation from North America of the articles you mention, I cannot give you any instruction thereto until it shall have become the object of consideration in Parliament."[24]

The exports from the mainland colonies came from every area of the continent. An examination of the agricultural, industrial, and commercial development of the individual continental colonies shows conclusively that the economy of each colony was but a part of the whole imperial commerce, at the centre of which was the West Indian trade. Fishing was an important industry of the Massachusetts Bay Colony. Some eight or nine hundred sloops and schooners were employed in the cod, whale, and mackerel fisheries. To carry on this industry, about 22,500 hogsheads of molasses were distilled annually. A part of the rum was consumed in the colony, but a significant portion was shipped to Newfoundland, Nova Scotia, and Quebec for the fishing there, to the southern colonies to pay for provisions, and to the Guinea coast for slaves for the West Indian trade.[25] Rhode Island also manufactured significant quantities of rum. Approximately forty distilleries processed a total of 12,000 hogsheads of molasses annually. Most of the rum was sent to Africa for slaves. Domestic trade was mainly with the southern colonies, to which the merchants annually sent rum and a portion of the molasses imported, in exchange for bread, flour, grain, beef, and pork for its West Indian trade. On the other hand, most of the 12,000 hogsheads of molasses imported into Connecticut were consumed in that colony. Only a small portion was distilled and shipped to Guinea, Newfoundland, and Nova Scotia in exchange for slaves and other articles of trade. Connecticut exported to the West Indies horses, cattle, sheep, beef, pork, maize, bread, flour, lumber, masts, and hoops.[26]

In New Hampshire, which had only one distillery, most of the rum consumed was imported from the British West Indies. New York imported about 14,000 hogsheads of molasses, of which two-thirds was distilled and shipped to Newfoundland, Africa, and the southern colonies. Because the rum produced was insufficient for domestic consumption, New York imported a significant quantity from the British West Indies, as well as from the coastwise trade. In return it exported to the sugar colonies bread, flour, beef, pork, hams, and a small quantity of boards, staves, and shingles. New Jersey, on the other hand, had very little direct trade with the West Indies; most of its produce went to Philadelphia and New York for reexportation, and it received most of its imports of West Indian commodities via those ports. Philadelphia imported a considerable quantity of rum from the British islands—about 735,000 gallons annually. In turn, it exported to them bread, flour, beef, pork, grain, and lumber.[27]

The five southern colonies, Maryland, Virginia, North and South Carolina, and Georgia, imported most of their rum and molasses from the British West Indies and the northern colonies. They exported chiefly tobacco, grain, pork, beef, flour, and lumber—boards, shingles, and planks. Added to these articles, North Carolina exported tar, turpentine, peas, and maize. South Carolina and Georgia also sent beans, rice, wax, tallow, and leather.[28]

Although each American colony contributed to the needs of the sugar colonies, certain continental colonies controlled a majority of the exports to the islands. The New England colonies supplied most of the lumber, shingles, staves, and hoops, and as a result of their trade with Newfoundland, Nova Scotia, and Canada (then essentially meaning Quebec), these colonies also supplied almost five-eighths of all the fish consumed in the islands. Of the total of 21,271,995 feet of lumber imported into the British West Indies from North America in 1771, the New England colonies supplied more than two-thirds. They sent half the shingles, about one-third of the staves, and nearly all the hoops. Of the total amount of bread and flour exported to the West Indies, Pennsylvania sent slightly less than two-thirds. The rest came from Virginia, New York, and Maryland. Of the 75,000 barrels of beef consumed in the islands annually, the American colonies supplied about 14,000 barrels. Of the 15,129 barrels and 9,651 tierces of rice imported into the British islands in 1771, 13,308 barrels and 7,967 tierces were sent from South Carolina, while the majority of horses, oxen, and other livestock reaching the islands went from the New England colonies.[29] Significant quantities of all classes of American products reached the British West Indies. This commerce gives a clear indication of the food and lumber requirements of the sugar colonies, and their sources of origin.

The annual value of North American products exported to the British West Indies was averaged at £745,000 for the three years immediately preceding the American Revolution, and included the cost of freight, which was approximately £245,000.[30] In 1770 the continental colonies exported £844,178 worth of products to the British and foreign West Indies, of which the majority went to the British islands.[31] Jamaica alone took from one-third to one-half of some articles. For example, of the 14,500 barrels of beef sent to the sugar colonies annually, Jamaica imported some 7,903 barrels.

On average, Jamaica imported 29,674 barrels of flour, 6,557 barrels and 3,450 kegs of bread, 6,479 tierces of rice, above 15 million staves, shingles, and headings, 6,197,322 feet of boards, and large quantities of other articles annually. In 1774 the value of American products to Jamaica was put at £177,746. According to the estimates of a Jamaica planter, the value of North American exports to Jamaica in 1775 was approximately £210,000.[32] Detailed statistics of the chief articles imported into Jamaica for the years 1768–74 show conclusively the extent of Jamaican reliance on American supplies (see table 1.9). The fluctuation of the quantities of some articles also indicates the changing nature of Jamaican demand. The figures show no significant increase in imports of most articles. Those for Canadian trade with that island indicate the insignificant position of those colonies in the West Indian trade in this period.

This brings us to consider the trade between the British West Indies as a whole and Nova Scotia, Newfoundland, and Canada. It is not surprising that, as with Jamaica, the pre-Revolutionary trade that developed between these northernmost colonies and the sugar islands was of little importance. Lumber exports from the new North American colonies were minute compared with those of the thirteen colonies to the south. The largest quantity was sent from Nova Scotia—83,000 feet of a total of 28,591,233 feet imported into the British West Indies in 1773. The percentage of fish was slightly greater, but even the loss of this trade would not have been greatly felt by the islands. In 1772 the sugar

Table 1.9. Jamaican imports from America and Canada, 1768–74

Year	Lumber (ft)	Shingles & staves	Oil (bbl)	Pitch (bbl)	Hoops	Hhds	Onions (bdl)	Butter (firkins)
1768	3,168,539	8,311,069	387	1,564	11,800	595	13,818	38
1769	4,173,894	8,879,810	863	2,527	2,237	12,000	32,668	53
1770	3,406,598	6,918,202	698	1,561	28,925	2,051	36,220	303
1771	3,368,570	6,405,282	368	2,005	107,150	2,203	19,350	301
1772	4,031,105	12,398,282	616	1,881	118,975	2,231	10,710	200
1773	5,245,562	13,980,641	780	1,995	168,230	3,234	41,600	497
1774	4,181,000	11,752,000	480	1,131	70,700	—	36,643	400
Canada (1768–72)								
	136,175	180,500	40	15	—	—	—	—
Newfoundland (1768–72)								
	Masts							
	300	28						

Year	Flour & bread (bags)	Biscuit (bbl)	Rice (bbl)	Fish (hhd)	Fish (bbl)	Meat (bbl)	Horses	Candles (boxes)	Grain (bu)
1768	30,442	2,258	4,211	2,211	2,980	4,781	135	1,832	55,475
1769	38,924	2,468	4,862	3,340	8,028	5,894	1,149	385	38,853
1770	38,645	4,527	15,475	1,607	9,228	5,225	536	2,026	37,753
1771	36,255	3,858	5,744	2,414	9,673	3,360	548	2,217	37,120
1772	29,589	5,208	3,084	2,587	12,575	3,505	263	2,292	24,870
1773	40,245	5,111	5,219	4,152	12,801	2,811	648	2,761	42,315
1774	31,142	4,638	6,898	2,733	12,179	9,152	499	1,215	52,470
Canada (1768–72)									
	163	—	—	37	—	—	—	—	—
Newfoundland (1768–72)									
	439								

Source: "Imports of Listed Articles into Jamaica from America including Canada and Newfoundland, n.d.," PRO, CO 137/85, fol. 239; "Imports from Canada and Nova Scotia into Jamaica," n.d.; Add. MSS 12,404, fol. 146; Add. MSS 38,347, fols. 336–37; PRO, CO 318/2.

colonies imported 21,185 hogsheads, 17,750 barrels, 10,954 quintals, and 1,358 kegs of fish from all the American colonies. Canada, Newfoundland, and Nova Scotia sent 1,569 hogsheads, 203 barrels, 4,893 quintals, and 195 kegs.[33]

The reason for the failure of these colonies to compete with their southern neighbours is quite clear. Canada, acquired by the British from the French by the Treaty of Paris of 1763, was mainly a fur-trading society. The white population, chiefly French-speaking, was small, and these new British subjects had very few economic or social ties with the British islands. Most of the agriculture carried on in Canada was at the subsistence level. In short, the economy of none of these colonies was geared to compete with or to replace that of the thirteen American Colonies. Even the Newfoundland and Nova Scotia fisheries were controlled and provisioned by the New England merchants, who received from the Newfoundland fishermen part of their catch in exchange for rum and other West Indian products. Most of this fish was considered unsuitable for the New-foundland trade but was reexported to the West Indies as food for slaves. Bryan Edwards, Jamaican planter and historian, called the economic performance of Canada and Nova Scotia very poor. For example, of the 1,208 cargoes of lumber and provision imported from North America into the British sugar colonies in 1773, only seven were from Canada and Nova Scotia, and of 701 topsail vessels and 1,681 sloops that were cleared outwards from North America to the British and foreign West Indies, only two topsail vessels and eleven sloops were from those provinces. In the years before the outbreak of the American War, wrote Edwards, the volume of goods supplied by Canada, Nova Scotia, and New-foundland, in terms of the whole consumption of the British Caribbean colonies, was not "worthy of national attention."[34]

These points are demonstrated in table 1.10, giving imports from North America into the West Indies. When compared with the thirteen colonies, it was inconceivable that within a decade the Canadian provinces could have developed an agricultural base sufficient to meet the demands of an expanding British West Indian economy.

In the commerce between the sugar islands and the mainland colonies, the American traders usually received a significant part of their payment in rum. Consequently, before the war the consumption of that product was increasing in America, and its sale paid nearly all the contingent charges arising in the islands, except the purchase of new slaves.[35] American imports of British plantation rum advanced annually between 1768 and 1774 (see table 1.11). Although the figures show a slight decline in 1771 and 1773, this seems to reflect a drop in production rather than a loss of sales. Rum exports to America averaged 2,800,000 gallons per year, and rose from 2,060,726 gallons in 1768 to 4,783,825 gallons in 1774. The largest quantities went to Pennsylvania, New York, Virginia, and the New England colonies, and before the Revolution the British West Indian monopoly of supplying the American markets with rum was never threatened by the foreign islands. The French planters manufactured very little rum;

Table 1.10. British West Indian imports from America, 1770–73

Goods	Unit	1770 America	1771–73 America	1771–73 Nova Scotia	1771–73 Newfoundland & Canada
Boards	ft	35,922,627	76,767,695	232,040	2,000
Shingles		—	59,586,193	185,000	—
Hoops		3,817,899	4,712,005	16,250	9,000
Grain	bu	402,958	1,204,398	24	—
Peas & beans	bu	49,337	64,006	1,017	—
Bread & flour	bbl	23,449	396,329	991	—
	kegs	—	3,009	—	
Rice	bbl	40,003	39,912	—	—
	t/ce	8,200	21,777	—	—
Fish	hhd	—	51,344	449	2,507
	bbl	29,582	47,686	664	202
	quint	206,081	21,500	2,958	11,764
	kegs	—	3,304	609	—
Beef & pork	bbl	2,870	44,782	170	24
Poultry	doz	2,615	2,739	10	—
Horses		6,691	7,130	28	—
Cattle & oxen		3,184	3,647	—	—
Sheep & hogs		12,797	13,815	—	—
Oil	bbl	—	3,189	139	118
Cheese	lb	55,447	—	—	—
Butter	lb	167,313	—	—	—
Tar & pitch	bbl	1,807	17,024	—	—
Spars		—	3,074	—	—
Shook casks		62,099	53,857	30	—
Soap & candles	boxes	—	20,475	40	141
Oxbows & yokes		—	1,540	—	—
House frames		163	620	—	—
Iron	tons	13	399	—	—
Oats, meal	bu	25,868	—	—	—
Potatoes	bu	3,382	—	—	—
Shoes	pairs	3,149	—	—	—

Source: Macpherson, *Annals,* vol. 3, 571–72; Edwards, *History,* 2:398; BL, Add. MSS 12,431, fol. 170.

that distilled by the Dutch and Danish colonies of Demerara and St. Croix was of inferior quality, and although a small quantity of Dutch rum was clandestinely imported into the continent, there was no danger to the British islands.[36]

Table 1.11. Sugar and rum exports to America, 1768–75

Year	Sugar (cwt)	Rum (gal)
1768	19,750	2,060,726
1769	49,020	2,718,923
1770	65,489	3,250,060
1771	46,994	2,180,060
1772	44,456	3,332,750
1773	39,365	3,049,298
1774	76,071	—
	8,520,000 lb	4,783,680
1775	75,880	—
	8,498,671 lb	4,783,825

Sources: "An Account of the Quantity of rum and sugar Imported into North America from the British West Indies . . . 1768–1773, 1 February, 1786." PRO, BT 6/84, fols. 297, 299; James Allen, *Considerations,* 38; "General Account of Sugar, Rum . . . Exported from the West Indies in 1773 and 1774," n.d., PRO, BT 6/83, pt. 2, fols. 40, 54.

From the inception of American–West Indian commercial relations, sugar imports into the continent from the British Islands were not large. These increased from 19,750 hundredweight in 1768 to 65,447 in 1770. The quantity decreased steadily after that year to 39,354 in 1773, because of weather conditions in the British islands between 1769 and 1772. In 1770 the mainland colonies imported £949,656 worth of West Indian products; of this amount, the value of sugar was only £116,231.[37] In 1775 the £45,780 worth of sugar taken from Jamaica was only a quarter of that island's total exports of £178,675 to the thirteen colonies. On the other hand, the value of the rum taken from Jamaica was £116,425. This led Edward Long to estimate that if the Americans refused to take Jamaica's sugar, the deficit in trade against that island, as for the other islands, would be the value of the sugar which had to be paid for in bills of exchange drawn upon merchants in Britain. There was never enough money in the islands to meet the deficit. "If on the other hand," he wrote, "the Americans should continue to take this Quantity of Sugar, no Balance [would] remain to be paid by [Jamaica]. But there would be a mutual equal liquidation of commodities, without any blame on either side—The island would not make less remittance to Britain; for the ampler the demand upon it for sugar, would operate as a premium to improving its plantations and [would] greatly increase the annual product."[38]

Between 1770 and 1775 the other West Indian staples—coffee, ginger, cocoa—either had greater exports to America than in the previous five years or remained about the same. Exports of Jamaican coffee to America (see table 1.12) increased almost fivefold from 1768 to 1774. Not much molasses was exported to the continent, and even that small amount decreased substantially between 1770 and 1773. Given the numerous distilleries emerging on the mainland and the extensive commerce carried on with cheap American rum, the importation of molasses was of immense importance, and most of it came from the French West Indies. Exports from the British islands to America (see table 1.13) fell by more than half between 1770 and 1773, mainly because rum production in the sugar colonies, proving profitable, was rising. For their part, the French produced very little rum, preferring to sell their molasses to the Americans.

In 1770 the total value of imports into America from the foreign and British West Indies was estimated at £949,656. Rum imports from the British islands amounted to approximately 45 percent of this. Molasses was the next most

Table 1.12. Jamaican exports to America, 1768–74

Year	Vessels	Rum (pun)	Coffee (casks)	Molasses (casks)	Sugar (hhd)
1768	84	1,039	589	626	902
1769	140	4,443	971	2,265	1,407
1770	170	4,513	1,223	1,021	1,958
1771	141	2,545	1,020	938	1,421
1772	143	4,294	1,331	753	1,513
1773	184	7,438	1,001	1,003	1,513
1774	—	8,660	2,816	902	1,811

Source: "Account of the Sugar, Rum, Molasses and Coffee Exported from Jamaica to America for the Years indicated," n.d., PRO, CO 137/85, fol. 239.

Table 1.13. Exports of minor staples and molasses to America, 1770–73

Year	Coffee (cwt)	Cocoa (lb)	Ginger (cwt)	Cotton (lb)	Molasses (gal)
1770	4,031	120,988	607	138,600	220,450
1771	2,305	146,857	302	129,744	101,717
1772	4,222	126,794	230	68,171	106,032
1773	4,097	131,539	268	112,181	105,432

Source: "Account of the Quantity of British plantation coffee, molasses . . . Imported into the Continent of America . . . between 5 January 1770 and 5 January 1774," BL, Add. MSS 38,342, fol. 51.

valuable article, at slightly over £181,800, but only 7 percent of it was taken from the British islands. The sugar imported from the Caribbean was valued at £165,641; all but £49,070 came from the British islands. Of the coffee, valued at approximately £15,259, all but £44 worth was taken from the British colonies. Rum, molasses, and sugar made up the greater part of the imports from the West Indies, and more than two-thirds came from the British West Indies.[39] The value of British West Indian products bought by the Americans was slightly under that of British West Indian imports from America. In some years, however, when natural disasters such as drought or repeated hurricanes forced the planters to import greater quantities of American provisions and lumber, the British islands had a sizeable trade deficit. In 1774 Jamaica had a trade deficit of £17,532 on imports of £177,746.[40] But this imbalance in trade, rather small, occurred at a time of instability in Anglo-American relations.

To lessen the perceived dependence of the British sugar islands on America and to halt the perceived drain of specie from Jamaica, Long suggested the adoption of an orthodox mercantilist plan which recommended that the planters import "from Britain and Ireland many of the commodities with which the North Americans supply . . . [the West Indies]; and, by good management, providing many others of them within our own island[s]." Long had not offered the planters any meaningful change, or even a feasible alternative. In effect, his plan called for Britain to monopolise the provision and lumber trades to the islands in the place of America. His scheme would have increased the cost of production and pushed the West Indian planters into greater debt. Another Jamaican, with whom he later agreed, argued to Long that the West Indian dependence on America for supplies was of immense benefit to the islands— "that it cannot be lessened in any considerable degree without diminishing the growth of the Staple commodities Rum and Sugar."[41]

Any imbalance of trade between America and the British West Indies occurred chiefly after 1769. In Jamaica, successive bad crops from 1769 to 1772 led to an annual decline of approximately £250,000 in the island's exports, and the planters were forced to import larger quantities of provisions from the mainland colonies. Another reason for the growing unfavourable trade was the high prices of many articles produced in the British West Indies. The Americans were therefore forced to go to the foreign islands, where their profits on the goods imported into America were increased to 18 percent, or 6 percent more than they made on British West Indian products.[42] The question that emerges is: Did the trade between the foreign islands and America really affect the West Indian planters? It does not appear that the British colonies lost anything by the trade between America and the foreign islands. In fact, they stood to gain in the long run. Edward Long, who wrote extensively about the loss of specie from Jamaica, placed the situation in its proper perspective. Writing on the effect of paying the Americans with money, he said: "When the Americans prefer our money, it goes in the reduction of a certain amount of the debt we owe them, & we have in the place of it, just so much more of the produce of the Island which enables us to draw more Bills, or is applied to [the] discharge of Debt incurred ... with factors or merchants [in Britain]."[43]

The blame for the drain of specie from the British sugar colonies is not attributable to the Americans alone, but also to the West Indian merchants who traded with the foreign islands.[44] In fact, the West Indians gained by giving cash or bills of exchange to the American traders, as they received continental products at reduced rates. Richard Pares has examined the American documents and concluded that the accusations of the British planters that the Americans were exporting money to the French islands were greatly exaggerated. He wrote that "in the correspondence of the northern merchants there is little trace of either of these practices; but on the few occasions when the export of money to the West Indies is mentioned it is usually the foreign islands that the writer had in mind."[45] Furthermore, merchants who carried light coin to the French islands were faced with the prospect of having their money confiscated, and this deterred them.

As for the northernmost colonies, imports by Canada, Newfoundland, and Nova Scotia from the West Indies were, like their exports, inconsiderable when compared with those of the thirteen colonies (see table 1.14). In the early 1770s

Table 1.14. Exports to Canada, 1768–73

Year	Sugar (cwt)	Rum (gal)
1768	376	50,340
1769	116	4,840
1770	462	41,290
1771	369	42,820
1772	726	42,756
1773	312	64,610

Source: PRO, BT 6/84, fols. 297, 299.

the Canadian colonies took an average of less than 50,000 gallons of rum a year. Sugar imports were also inconsequential and appear to have been declining, from 462 hundredweight in 1770 to 312 in 1773. The majority of this went to Newfoundland.

Some of the reasons for the small quantities imported into the Canadian colonies have already been discussed. In addition, by 1775 the New England merchants had completely monopolised the continental carrying trade. This is best illustrated by the quantity of British West Indian rum sent from the thirteen colonies to Canada, Newfoundland, and Nova Scotia. Although most of the rum imported into the thirteen continental colonies was for domestic consumption, a small quantity was reexported to the new colonies; this averaged about 47,000 gallons annually between 1770 and 1773.[46] Table 1.14 gives further support to the contention that the Canadian colonies offered no external markets for tropical products.

This detailed study of British West Indian commercial connections in the years 1770 to 1775 has established two main facts. First, by 1775 the American mainland trade, including the Canadian portion, was totally interwoven with that of the British West Indies. Second, together they formed part of a North Atlantic commercial system that encompassed the entire British and foreign West Indian islands, North America, the foreign mainland colonies, and Britain. But the American markets were growing rapidly. As their expansion exceeded the supply requirements—and the supply capabilities—of the British West Indies, it was imperative that the Americans expand their trade to the French islands. There is very little evidence that the British sugar colonies were in any serious state of decline up to 1775. Since Edward Long wrote most widely about the West Indies, and Jamaica in particular, it is perhaps fitting to indicate in his own words that his greatest fear was not the agricultural decline of the British islands but the overproduction of sugar. In his opinion, there was a point beyond which the consumption of sugar in Britain and North America could not be increased. "If, for example," he wrote, "by vigorous industry of the settlers in the newly Ceded Islands, together with the unrelaxed endeavours of those in our older colonies, the whole importation in the course of some years should be raised to 2,000,000 hhds, an event that will probably happen before the expiration of the next ten years, this will cause a glut at the British market, and reduce the price one fourth, or to about 26s 3d per cwt."[47]

Since Westminster had relinquished its control over the intercolonial trade, the colonists set about developing a very successfully integrated economy which enabled the British sugar planters to depend on a cheap, steady, and reliable supply of lumber and provisions from the continent, and to concentrate on utilizing most of their land to grow cane. During the pre–Revolutionary War period there were no fears of mass death among slaves because of starvation or crop failure. There were times of distress over which the colonists had no control. But even when these disasters occurred, the planters were always able to rely on the appearance of an American trading vessel with lumber and provisions.

The trade between America and the British West Indies was an intrinsic factor in the structure of British commerce and the functioning of the plantation system. Any interruption of that trade threatened the commerce of the empire and the continuance of the British West Indies as viable and profitable sugar-producing areas. The prospect of a war with the American colonies seemed certain to ruin the planters. Between the years 1770 and 1775, the disputes between Britain and America had only minimal effect on the British Caribbean colonies, and they continued to receive the fundamental necessities of a plantation economy—labourers, adequate shipping to good markets, and a plentiful supply of cheap provisions and lumber—insomuch that during these years the planters prospered. No contemporary writer made a better assessment of the West Indies in the last quarter of the eighteenth century than Long when he wrote: "The years 1774, 1775 & 1776 were remarkable for the greatest Importation that had ever come from our Islands, and at that period which ended at the commencement of the American War they may with truth be said to have obtained the highest point of Cultivation & Improvement, not that they were capable of, but that they had ever arrived at."[48]

∽ 2 ∾

The American War
and the British Caribbean Economy

From the outset of the dispute between Britain and the American colonists, the situation on the continent alarmed many officials. The concern of the Earl of Dartmouth, Secretary of State for the colonies, over the deteriorating relations, for example, conveys the fears and hopes of the colonists. "The State of Affairs in North America and particularly in the New England Colonies," he wrote, "had become very serious. It is to be hoped however that nothing will happen to obstruct the Commerce that for the mutual interest of both ought to be cherished on both sides."[1] Yet Britain and America adopted a policy of commercial warfare; restrictions followed restrictions. In reaction to rebellious activities at Boston, including the Boston Tea Party, Britain passed the Boston Port Bill, which closed the port in 1774; it passed two Restraining Acts in the following year and adopted the Prohibitory Act at the end of December 1775.

The enforcement of the Prohibitory Act early in 1776 caused a virtual cessation of American exports except for a trickle from the free ports of the foreign governments and from the illegal trade with the Americans in the ports of the foreign and neutral islands. Following on the heels of the prohibition of American trade was a series of natural disasters in the Caribbean, which destroyed locally grown provisions and compounded the already delicate economic situation. Together, the closure of American markets, natural disasters, and the war reduced the importation of captive Africans to a trickle, limited sugar production, and seriously threatened the security and preeminent position of the West Indies in the Atlantic economic system.[2]

In response to the threat of war between Britain and the colonies, a petition presented to Parliament in 1775 by the West India interests forecast disaster and the death of several thousand enslaved workers. Even in Jamaica and the Ceded Islands, where arable land was available for growing provisions, the planters were expected to suffer heavy losses. Richard Glover in his evidence to Parliament spoke of graver conditions for Barbados and the Leeward Islands with an enslaved population in excess of 100,000.[3] The evidence was disregarded by the British ministry, which discussed the claims of the planters and merchants. In the colonies, officials held that British policy had little impact on the flow of provisions and lumber to the sugar islands, and they pointed to low prices as indicative of the continued large importation of American goods.[4] Governor Edward Hay of Barbados wrote: "no bad effects have been felt in this island hitherto from the disturbances in the Northern Colonies . . . as many vessels with their provisions and Stores have arrived from there as usual."[5]

Even some planters were lulled into a false state of security and believed that rebel merchants would defy Congress to retain their commercial relations with the islands.[6] They expected the colonists' self-interest to operate against their nationalist struggles. Sugar was the basis of the prosperity of the Caribbean islands and its production demanded the coordinated labour of a large number of enslaved labourers. This necessitated ever increasing importation of provisions, as the landowners preferred to concentrate on the more profitable tropical exports. The political crisis thus called for a change in supply sources and greater dependence on local products, but the emphasis in the beginning was on a new source of imported goods.

In what emerged as a frantic search for new suppliers, West Indian assemblies first enacted legislation giving bounties to importers of foodstuffs. It was some time before measures were adopted to encourage the production of local food.[7] The Assembly of Jamaica appointed a nine-man committee in November 1775 to consider ways to prevent a scarcity of foodstuffs and lumber, to encourage the cultivation of all types of grains, and to implement the production of lumber. On its recommendation, an embargo was imposed on the export of provisions in the following January, and measures were taken for its continuation by proclamation when the house was in recess.[8] The Receiver-General on order of the Assembly purchased all foodstuffs. They were sold to the planters at cost, and trading vessels were allowed only enough supplies for the voyage.

Besides restricting Jamaica's export trade, the Assembly considered stimulating local production of food. Acting on another recommendation, it awarded £150 currency to any planter in St. Andrew who produced for sale not less than one thousand bushels of Indian or Guinea corn, rice, peas, or beans between 1 December 1776 and 31 March 1776; for seven hundred bushels the award was £100, while £50 went to the producer of five hundred bushels of grain. The awards were later extended to planters throughout the island. In November 1778 the legislature prohibited the theft or destruction of sheep, goats, and cattle, and in 1779 William Harvey was appointed to purchase and quarter cattle for the troops at 7½d per pound. This latter measure greatly encouraged cattle production, and the population almost doubled from 135,750 head in 1768 to 224,500 in 1780.[9]

In addition, botanic gardens were established in Jamaica and St. Vincent, and several well-known plants were introduced into the West Indies because of the American War. The most important was the breadfruit tree. In 1772 Valentine Morris, plantation owner of Antigua who became governor of St. Vincent, wrote to Joseph Banks, who was aware of the food value of breadfruit from his expedition with Captain Cook, and suggested that the plant be imported into the sugar colonies to feed the slaves. On Morris's recommendation, the West India Committee voted to award £150 sterling to anyone importing a healthy plant into England. With food shortages worsening in the West Indies, a subcommittee was appointed to examine a report by John Ellis, agent for Dominica, and to study ways of introducing breadfruit trees into the British islands. Very little was accomplished, and in February 1777 the West India Committee of Merchants and Planters again took up the issue, establishing a fund to reward importers of the trees.[10] A decade later, food shortages in the West Indies continued despite the termination of the war, and the project now received the backing of the British government. In 1789 the first attempt was undertaken to supply the British West Indies with breadfruit plants when Captain William Bligh sailed in the *Bounty* to the South Seas.[11] The expedition ran into trouble. Trees were eventually imported into the West Indies in 1794, and breadfruit has been a source of food ever since.

Despite efforts to develop local sources of provisions, only small quantities were produced. The items commonly grown prior to the American Revolution were still planted. But local provisions never adequately met the islands' needs. Two major factors that restricted food production were limited acreage and the unwillingness of planters to take slaves out of cane cultivation. American sources for provisions and lumber were extremely difficult to replace. Hence the question: Did enough food reach the British West Indies during this period for adequate levels of sustenance among all classes of inhabitants, especially the slaves?

In some islands, accounts are conflicting.[12] The case of Barbados is of particular interest. When Hay contradicted early reports of impending disaster, the Assembly reacted by restricting the governor's administrative power, petitioning the king, and making declarations similar to those by the Americans. Clearly, true economic conditions can be difficult to determine in times of such political controversy, when even official dispatches are contradictory.

Hay's first impression of the impact of the dispute on supplies to Barbados was recorded in April 1775: "I think there is little to fear from any ill Consequences to this Island." At this time, there was no prohibition on West Indian–American trade and, despite the restrictive economic policies of Congress and Parliament, American shipments to the islands continued uninterrupted. Shortly afterwards, however, Hay embargoed the export of two thousand barrels of flour to England because supplies of American provisions were uncertain "unless from those Colonies who have not sent Deputies to the Congress."[13]

His statements betray a lack of knowledge of the logistics of sugar production in the British colonies, and a failure to appreciate West Indian dependence on American supplies.[14] In spite of warnings to the contrary, he remained committed to his initial view that Barbados had little to fear. And despite his prohibiting the export of the flour, he wrote: "Some people have been apprehensive of the North American shutting up their Ports, and withholding their Provisions and lumber. Hitherto as many ships as usual have come here from North America. For my own part, I am more apprehensive of the effects of a dry Year, than of any Distress from the North Americans." Even when conditions worsened after the beginning of 1776, Hay maintained that the islands could "be supplied from places not mentioned in the Act" and he suggested that lumber be imported from northern Europe.[15] Yet from the commencement of the Prohibitory Act, supplies to the islands caused grave alarm. The Barbados Assembly's inventory of provision stocks in the warehouses at Bridgetown showed six weeks' supplies.[16] Similarly, a report compiled by the merchants of Antigua confirmed fears that supplies there were greatly depleted.[17]

It was at this critical time that Captain Benjamin Payne of the Royal Irish Regiment arrived in the West Indies in quest of provisions. Over the objections of the merchants and planters of Barbados, Hay permitted Payne to purchase a quantity of beef, pork, oatmeal, rice, and rum. Some members of the public, assemblymen, and councillors criticised Hay and members of the Council for selling the island's scanty supplies.[18] The Assembly heeded the public outcry. It accused Hay of being insensitive to the interests of the colony and blamed his policy for a rapid increase in prices. It then sent an address to the king, outlining the crisis that had befallen the island since the American War.[19] Hay responded with an optimistic report to Lord George Germain in which he acknowledged some shortages but claimed that there were adequate supplies of livestock and of British and Irish provisions. He blamed the merchants for maintaining high prices and discounted the Assembly's claims of imminent famine: "Upon the whole, I must say it is wicked to talk of Famine in the most plentiful Island of all the West Indies, and where I, who have no plantations, and must buy all the provisions for my Table, can assure your Lordship that scarcely any One Article of provisions and livestock of the Island has raised in price for near these three years."[20]

David Makinson, who has examined this issue, writes that Hay was unwilling "to acknowledge any distress on the island regardless of the circumstances or causes," but concludes that the governor had assessed "the condition of his colony far more accurately than his antagonists in the Assembly, as there is no documentary proof, beyond a rise in prices, to substantiate the claims of either the Assembly or the Barbados agent."[21] On the contrary, Payne's correspondence supports the Assembly's claims of severe food shortages. He reported that the Council had unanimously met his needs. "Indeed they went further; they have not left a single cask of salt Provisions on the Island," he wrote, and, on conditions in the West Indies generally, "all accounts agree and indeed I have had some proof of it, that the islands in general in the West Indies are in the greatest want of . . . provisions."[22]

Further evidence indicates severe hardship throughout the West Indies. William Dickson, secretary to Hay, wrote that the complacency of many planters and Governor Hay had led to disaster: "no supplies were brought out to the island from England; famine began and though the dry season was in progress, everyone planted crops which withered immediately. People were dying in the streets, or silently pining and expiring in their cottages. Labour was in great measure suspended."[23] The attorneys of Codrington plantation reported miseries on many estates because of the "dreadful scarcity of grain." These conditions were confirmed by a Barbadian planter, and by Rear-Admiral Barrington, who found no food on the island and reported that the enslaved workers were fed with rum.[24]

There is little doubt that Hay's reports of plenty were exaggerated. He admitted in a confidential letter to Germain three years later that the inhabitants were "in a desponding way," that their debts were considerable, that the small crops for several years were insufficient to meet the annual cost of the estates, and that "Creditors became solicitous to recover their Debts. Two planters have lately run away and have left their estates to be broken up by their Creditors. Many are much involved."[25]

The cessation of West Indian–American trade had indeed caused a widespread shortage of provisions. This so alarmed Governor Hay that in March 1776 he applied to Vice-Admiral James Young for relief. First, he requested passports for Barbadian vessels carrying American provisions to exempt them from seizure and asked that American prizes be sent to Barbados where prices were high. Young agreed, but did not favour giving licences indiscriminately to individuals, so Hay and Young established a company headed by several members of the Council. However, the limited scheme of two hundred shares at £20 currency each for a total capitalisation of £3,000 sterling failed because of restricted membership and lack of subscription.[26] In another attempt to supply Barbados, Hay seized two ships bound for other islands—one en route to Jamaica from Liverpool with provisions, the other headed for Antigua—and forced them to sell their cargoes in Barbados.[27]

The Leeward Islands too were subject to extreme hardships. However, it appears that the initial impact of the American War on supplies was not as immediate as in Barbados. Their proximity to foreign islands enabled the merchants to trade illegally with the rebels. The Dutch island of St. Eustatius lay some eight miles to the northwest of the Leewards. Northward, a few miles farther away, lay the French island of St. Barthélemy; St. Croix, a Danish island, was but a little more remote; and beyond, at no great distance, lay St. Thomas and the Spanish colony of Puerto Rico. To the south lay the rich French islands of Guadeloupe, Martinique and St. Lucia. Most prizes captured by British warships and noncommissioned vessels were carried to the Leeward Islands first.[28] As the war intensified, however, several factors led to a worsening of conditions. The number of captured rebel merchantmen decreased with the vastly improved sailing ability of the ships and because they flew French, Dutch, and even British colours. After September 1777 the Leeward Islands experienced periods of severe shortage, and the several councils and assemblies petitioned Governor Burt for relief.[29] Both houses of the legislature of Montserrat, for example, called for the importation of provisions from the foreign islands in British ships.[30] This appeal stemmed from a genuine fear among the whites of slave uprisings.[31]

At the end of 1777 shortages worsened. There was no bread in Montserrat and Nevis for several days. In Antigua and St. Kitts, conditions were only marginally better. In the following year, very small quantities of foodstuffs reached the Leeward Islands. Of the situation in Nevis, Pinney wrote: "You have no idea of the distressed and unhappy state of this country."[32] According to Francis Farley, Clement Tudway's manager in Antigua, there were reported periods of prolonged scarcity. At times there was no corn, and many planters were without other supplies for their slaves—"nor," added Main Swete Walrond, "do we know whence any is to be bought St. Eustatius excepted, where there are only a few hundred Bushels of Beans, and a Gentleman is gone to purchase them. . . . A great many Slaves have died."[33]

Food shortages continued with tragic results. Despite efforts by Walrond to provide adequate rations, deaths among the slaves on the estates caused alarm. He wrote, "You have buried seventeen Negroes since 24th July, fifteen of whom you will find have died since my last letter. You now have many sick, some very ill, and God knows where our losses in Slaves will end."[34]

Conditions were similar in Nevis, judging from Pinney's letters: "Our present crop is very bad—the Island will make one-third less than it did after the hurricane of 1772. What will become of us? The unhappy contest with America, united with our internal distressed situation is truly alarming, and will, I am afraid cause the ruin of . . . every individual." A month later, he wrote in the same vein to his uncle and added: "What with . . . the low ebb of West India credit, united with our present unhappy contest . . . Provisions and all plantations necessaries are so excessively dear, that the expense of supporting our slaves and keeping up our Estates in a proper condition, swallows up the greatest part of the produce. For these reasons, I want to contract my concerns here and fix a fund in England—not solely to depend upon estates subject to every calamity."[35]

To alleviate the problem, the Antigua legislature appealed directly to Admiral Young for "letters of Protection" for vessels going to America for provisions.[36] He agreed not to seize those trading with the neutral islands. Governor Burt also allowed the importation of provisions and lumber in vessels with certificates signed by at least two merchants that the cargo was not the property of the rebels. The lumber and foodstuffs purchased in the neutral islands were certainly from America, and Burt was therefore forced to sanction an illegal trade in the foreign ports. To exonerate himself from charges of contravening

British commercial laws, he told Germain: "This mode my lord is attended with an injury, it takes from the Dutch and French American produce; but my Lord the Injury on the other side would be greater. In this dilemma of two Evils, I shall be under a Necessity of chusing the least and by giving every aid so far as possible to the distressed loyal Planter and Merchant keep their minds easy, and . . . happy."[37]

Supplies from all sources, including direct importation from Britain and Ireland, were only drops in the bucket. The problem of feeding the slaves was further compounded when in 1778 the Americans embargoed food supplies to the foreign islands. Burt immediately renewed his appeal for help, warning that "unless . . . Ships are sent, the Ground and Colonial provisions will not half supply the islands," and "should there be a Hurricane God only knows what may be the Event." He requested four ships with supplies—two for St. Kitts and Nevis, and one each for Antigua and Montserrat. A year later the Treasury dispatched a quantity of provisions for the Leeward Islands, but only after the Antigua legislature had borrowed $20,000 to pay for them, and "notwithstanding these Reliefs," many slaves died of diseases caused by malnutrition.[38]

In Jamaica the prohibition of American trade was at first as worrisome as in Barbados and the Leeward Islands, but became less so as the war continued. The island contained a greater number of provision gardens; more slaves were employed in food production; there was a larger population of free coloured, who cultivated local provisions; and the Assembly awarded bounties to develop local supplies.[39] Although the increase in the acreage allotted to provision crops was limited by the planters' ideological views on the island's economic development, some improvement was evident in local crop production.

However, from the middle of 1776 the essential articles of food for the slaves became scarce, and prices more than doubled.[40] By the end of the year, the scarcity of provisions and lumber caused grave concern among many planters, especially when convoys from Britain and Ireland were delayed.[41] Although conditions improved slightly by the end of the war, they were markedly worse than in 1775. Captain Pasley's comment on leaving the island is indicative of conditions there in 1782: "I rejoice for this time I am tired of Jamaica. Very different from the place I knew only four years ago. Fowls 15s a couple, poor and bad: Turkeys 30s and every thing in proportion—tis impossible to live."[42]

The impact of the Revolution on the Windward Islands varied from colony to colony. But on the whole they had fresh arable land which was cultivated in local provisions. For example, Grenada experienced a moderate setback. The increased cultivation of foodstuffs had averted severe shortages, but the production of sugar and rum declined appreciably, as evidenced by the shipping from that island. Governor Lord Macartney estimated that the number of ships from Grenada to Britain in 1777 was 107; this had decreased to 27 in 1778. In the following year Grenada produced one of its largest crops, valued above £700,000 sterling. Yet the war had retarded the island's economic growth. By the time of its capture in 1779, most provisions were scarce and expensive and, as in the other colonies, no more were expected from England before 1780.[43]

Dominica experienced severe shortages from early in 1776. There was but little relief from captured American vessels and from the operations of the Prohibitory Act itself.[44] The act had allowed the British sugar islands to trade freely with those places in America that came under the control of the British army. Shortages of food throughout the islands continued despite the illegal trade.[45] After France entered the war, a greater strain was put on the already scant supplies. From 1779 to 1782 there was increased demand for provisions because of the larger number of British troops in the West Indies. Scarcity in Britain and Ireland exacerbated scarcity in the colonies. For example, in 1780 the troops in Canada, as in the West Indies, received no rations from the contractors. Reduced British shipping to the sugar colonies also increased the shortages, and "it was only the end of the War in 1783 that saved the British forces abroad from a major provision crisis," wrote one historian.[46]

Reduced supplies meant higher prices, and the cost of operating the estates became a severe burden for a majority of planters. The average price of lumber, for example, increased by 650 percent in Barbados; in the Leeward Islands it more than doubled, while Jamaica saw increases of 150 percent and more. In the Leeward Islands draft horses used for mill work increased in price from £25.15s before the American war to £85 during the war years. In Barbados the price of American horses doubled in one year. Beef, pork, and flour went up by at least half, as did salt fish and herring, while corn, the principal staple in the slave's diet, advanced in excess of 100 percent on average in the Leeward Islands and by 400 percent in Barbados. Tables 2.1 and 2.2 give the average and market quotation prices in Barbados.

Pinney's account books reveal the frightening increase in the price of plantation stores in Nevis. Planks and boards, which were sold at 100s in 1775, were purchased at 405–440s in 1779, at 840s in 1781, and at 528–700s in 1782. White oak staves increased from 216s in 1772 to prices varying from 440s to 660s in 1778–83. Flour, purchased at 24s per barrel in 1768–73, advanced to 54s in 1776, 60s in 1779, and 63s in 1783. Indian corn, which sold for 5s 8d per bushel in 1774, fetched

Table 2.1. Average prices in Barbados, 1775–84

Commodity	Unit	Prewar price	Postwar price	% increase
Lumber	m ft	80s	600s	650.0
Horses (Br.)	head	1,000s	1,800s	80.0
Horses (Am.)	head	400s	800s	100.0
Cattle	head	100s	300s	200.0
Rice	cwt	12s 6d	30s	140.0
Corn	bu	2s 6d	12s 6d	400.0
Beef	bbl	50s	75s	50.0
Pork	bbl	65s	100s	53.8

Sources: "A state of the prices of provisions and the value of sugar and rum in the years 1775 and 1776, 8 September 1776," PRO, CO 28/56, fol. 76; "Comparative Prices for provisions and other articles, 28 December 1784," PRO, CO 28/60., fols. 183, 226, 243, 312.

Note: Where prices are reported as a range, the midpoint is used.

Table 2.2. Market quotations in Barbados, 1774–76

Commodity	Unit	1774–75	1776	% change
Flour	100lb	20s	33s 9d	+68.8
Corn	bu	3s 1½d	11s 6d	+368.0
Salt fish	quin	18s 9d	35s	+86.7
Beef	bbl	65s	110s	+69.2
Pork	bbl	85s	125s	+47.1
Herring	bbl	31s 3d	50s	+60.0
Butter	lb	9d	1s 6¾d	+108.3
Sugar (muscovado)	cwt	27s 6d	21s 10⅓d	-20.5
Sugar (clay)	cwt	41s 3d	31s 3d	-24.2
Rum	gal	2s	1s 3d	-37.5

Sources: George Walker to Lord George Germain, 1 September 1776, PRO, CO 28/56, fols. 75–76; Ragatz, *Fall,* 113.

Note: Only sugar and rum declined in price.

as much as 16s 6d in 1777 and as high as 20s 7½d in 1782.[47] Table 2.3 demonstrates further the high cost of provisions and lumber in the Leeward Islands.

The available statistics on prices of provisions and lumber in Jamaica reveal that, although they increased to a lesser extent than in other islands, they too rose steeply (see tables 2.4 and 2.5). William Smelling provided firsthand information of these conditions: "Everything is at present extravagantly dear. Beef sells at £10 per barrel and other articles in proportion. Lumber we cannot afford to purchase any. If the unfortunate War in America is not soon ended we shall suffer greatly. This country Corn is now 5s to 12s 6d—and should our own provisions fail we must starve of which we had a specimen last year."[48]

In Dominica, the overall increase seems to have been less than in the other small islands. For example, "in 1776, 1777 and 1778 the average price of lumber was double that of former years. Horses, Horned Cattle and live stock rose

Table 2.3 Average prices in Leeward Islands, 1775–84

Commodity	Unit	Prewar price	Postwar price	% increase
Rice	bu	6s	14s 3d	137.5
Beer	bbl	65s	130s	100.0
Pork	bbl	75s	165s	120.0
Flour	cwt	25s	58s	132.0
Corn	bu	6s	14s 3d	237.5
Boards/planks	m ft	230s	500s	117.4
Shingles	m ft	24s	113s	370.8
Staves/headings	m ft	170s	600s	252.9
Staves, red oak	m ft	125s	495s	296.0
Horses	ea	515s	1,700s	230.1
Cattle	head	363s	830s	128.7
Livestock	doz	40s	214s 6d	436.3

Sources: "The Average Prices of Lumber and Provisions before and after the War, 1 January 1785," PRO, CO 152/64; "An account of the Prices of Lumber and Provisions in the Leeward Islands. Heads of Inquiry with Annuals to the Annexed, No. 1 in Thomas Sheby to Lord Sydney, 7 September 1785," PRO, CO 152/64. No. 115; Ragatz, *Fall,* 154.

Table 2.4. Prices of American goods in Jamaica, prewar and wartime

Commodity	Unit	Prewar prices	Postwar prices	% increase
Rice	bu	16s 10½d	60s	255.6
Maize	bu	4s 4½d	12s 1½d	177.1
Flour, common	cwt	17s 6d	35s	100.0
Flour, super fine	cwt	12s 9d	43s 9d	243.1
Boards, common	m ft	160s	400s	150.0
Boards, pitch pine	m ft	200s	500s	150.0
Shingles	m ft	33s 9d	110s	225.9
Staves, white oak	m ft	280s	700s	150.0
Staves, red oak	m ft	180s	—	—

Source: "Answers to Several Heads of Enquiry" 1st Querie, 11 November 1784, PRO, CO 137/85; Ragatz, *Fall,* 153; "Prices of Sundries in Jamaica in the years 1776, 1777, 1778, 1779, 1780 in Jamaican Currency," Add. MSS 12,412, fol. 22d.

Table 2.5. Market prices in Jamaica, 1775–76

Commodity	Unit	1775	1776	% increase
Staves, hogshead	m ft	180s	700s	288.9
Staves, puncheon	m ft	260s	1,000s	284.6
Flour	cwt	27s	77s 6d	187.0
Rice	cwt	23s	36s	56.5
Butter	lb	10d	1s 8d	100.0
Herring	bbl	35s	62s 6d	78.6
Mess beef	bbl	85s	150s	76.5

Source: "Comparative Prices and Changes attending the Jamaica Planters at and since Commencement of the War extracted from actual accounts," BL, Add. MSS 12,413, fol. 45.

Table 2.6. Prices in St. Vincent, 1770–84

Commodity	Unit	1770–74	1778–84	% increase
Staves, white oak	m ft	132s	660s	400.0
Staves, red oak	m ft	100s	400s	300.0
Horses	ea	600s	1,000s	66.7
[Horned] cattle	ea	360s	530s	47.2
Sheep	ea	34s 6d	83s	140.6
Geese/turkeys	ea	12s	29s	141.7
Fowl	doz	3s	72s	100.0
Salt fish	100 lb	15s	60s	300.0
Rice	100 lb	16s	85s	431.3
Pork (Am.)	bbl	83s	—	—
Corn	bu	10s 3d	24s 9d	141.5

Source: "The Prices of Lumber, Horned Cattle, Livestock and Indian Corn . . . in Edward Lincoln to Lord Sydney, 8 January 1785," PRO, CO 260/7, no. 14; "Extract of Letter from planter in St. Vincent to Merchant in London . . . ," n.d., PRO, BT 6/77, 208.

about 50 percent. Beef and pork about 25 percent." After the French captured the island, the prices of most articles rose another 100 percent between 1778 and 1781; those of lumber, flour, beef, and pork trebled. Prices in Grenada too increased progressively after 1775 until the island's capture in 1779. Similarly, in St. Vincent price increases ranged from 47 percent for cattle to 431 percent for rice. Higher prices reflected the inflationary impact of the American War on the West Indian economy.[49] The available statistics (see table 2.6) show the marked rise in prices of all classes of supplies between 1774 and 1784.

Although there was a gradual increase in the prices of rum and sugar sold locally, this did not compensate for the high costs of provisions and lumber. In

1776 rum fetched 1s 3d per gallon in Barbados. Between 1777 and 1783 the average price doubled. In St. Kitts rum prices advanced from 2s 6d in 1777–78 to 3s in 1779 and 3s 6d in 1780 and 1781. St. Vincent rum increased by an average of only 33 percent from 2s 3d per gallon in 1775 to 3s from 1776 to 1779. In Jamaica too, the increase in rum prices was minimal and averaged only 5 to 10 percent.[50]

The loss of the American market for West Indian rum made it essential that rum consumption and prices be high in Britain, but after the initial increase in prices at the beginning of 1776, there was a slump. For example, decreasing sales led to a decline in the price to 2s per gallon in June of that year. The fall in demand for rum continued throughout the war, and although prices rose periodically, most planters in the smaller islands received an average price of slightly more than 2s 3d per gallon. Jamaica rum consistently fetched the highest prices; in 1780 it sold in Scotland for 4s 6d per gallon, mainly because of its high quality.[51] Cargoes of rum, cotton, and even sugar remained in the storehouses for months. Houston and Company wrote: "Rum is at present and has been for several months a perfect drug." Other information carried the same message "no Sale for Rum here, is become a drug."[52]

Sugar prices increased at the beginning of 1776, but declined and remained low for the rest of the year. Speculators, who had forced up prices at the commencement of hostilities by buying all the sugar, had left the market stagnated. At times, much of the sugar was unsold, and throughout the war the market remained unpredictable.[53] In 1777 prices of sugar increased from 40s to 50s for most of the year except in December, when they reached 67s 6d for St. Vincent and an average price of 56s 6d per hundredweight for St. Kitts, while Jamaica and Grenada sugars fetched 58s to 60s. After the first quarter of 1778, these prices declined markedly. The market quotations for sugar in London in 1778 show that Jamaica brown sold for 44s to 46s, with prices as low as 40s for lesser grades and 46s to 52s for sugar of higher quality. On occasion, several hogsheads fetched as much as 48s per hundredweight.[54] Those from Antigua and St. Kitts sold for 51s and 57s respectively.[55]

After France entered the fighting, the demand for British refined sugar declined and was reflected in the sale of sugar on the London market.[56] Prices increased later, but the impact on the planters was uneven and much depended on finding prompt transport and sale. The overall benefits were minimal because of heavy crop losses, the high rates of freight and insurance, the rising costs of operating estates owing to the dearness of lumber and provisions, and the declining labour force from falling slave imports and deaths among the seasoned slaves.[57] Furthermore, although the increase in the prices was substantial, most sugars fetched the lowest prices. In addition, the loss of the American trade had cut off the flow of money into Britain. Only on a few occasions did sugar prices exceed 69s 6d per hundredweight.[58] Table 2.7 gives the prices of

Table 2.7. Market quotations in Scotland and London, 1776–81

Year	Sugar		Cotton		Rum	
	Low	High	Low	High	Low	High
1776						
March	30s	42s	19d	22d	2s 2d	3s 3d
June	—	—	18d	22d	2s	—
October	30s	43s	18d	21d	1s 6d	2s 6d
December	35s	46s	—	—	2s 6d	2s 9d
1777						
January	42s	50s	—	—	2s 9d	3s
February	40s	48s	18d	21d	2s	2s 10d
July	37s	40s	17d	19d	2s	—
September	40s	50s	16d	19d	1s 10d	2s 4d
December	58s	65s	16d	19d	2s 3d	2s 4d
1778						
January	35s	40s	Unsaleable		Unsaleable	
April	53s	55s	13d	15d	2s	—
June	40s	48s	Unsaleable		Unsaleable	
July	45s	50s	11d	13d	—	—
October	40s	45s	13d	14½d	No demand	
December	44s	56s	—	—	2s	2s 2d
1779						
March	40s	45s	1s	15d		Losing article
June	48s 9d	58s	—	—	—	—
August	58s	60s	14d	15d	2s	3s
1780						
January	—	—	18d	20d	2s 6d	3s 4d
June	53s	63s	—	—	—	—
August	50s	54s	18d	20d	3s	4s 6d
December	56s	57s 6d	—	—	—	—
1781						
January	53s	54s 6d	—	—	—	—
March	54s 6d	65s	—	—	—	—
April	58s 6d	69s 6d	—	—	—	–

Sources: "Market Quotations in Scotland and London taken from the Letter Books of Houston and Company," NLS, MSS 8,793–94; NLS, MSS 5,464, 61–63, 65–68, 70–72, 102–8.

Note: Quotations on sugar are per cwt., on cotton per pound, on rum per gallon.

West Indian commodities sold in Scotland, mainly Edinburgh, for almost the entire period of the war. The fluctuation in price levels is remarkable, and at times cotton and rum were unsaleable. Houston and Company claimed that Scottish prices for sugar were roughly 4s higher than on the London market.

In view of the fact that sugar prices in 1781 were double those of 1776—sugar fetched from 30s to 42s in the earlier year and went as high as 58s 6d to 69s 6d in the latter—did the British West Indian planters make a profit? The question is a difficult one to resolve. Other things being equal, high returns should lead automatically to higher profits. Normally, planters made marked gain during previous wars, but conditions then were significantly different. In the American War, the cost of provisions was astronomically high, and the loss of continental markets for rum was catastrophic to the sugar economy. Rum sales to America usually paid for the contingent expenses of the estates, more or less. In addition to the loss of revenue from this source, operating and staffing costs rose during the war. The salaries of white bookkeepers, overseers, distillers, and carpenters, for example, increased by an average of 50 percent in Jamaica. Other evidence shows that the wages for some bookkeepers advanced by 40 to 100 percent; those for skilled labourers doubled. Wages for carpenters, estimated at £50 annually, increased to £70 and £80 for ordinary ones and as high as £100 for highly skilled tradesmen, while distillers' salaries rose from £20 to £30 annually. Similarly, the cost of hiring slaves, a practice that was gaining ground in the islands, increased significantly, from under 1s 10d to an average of 2s 3d and as high as 2s 6d daily.[59] Table 2.8 gives a clear picture of the increases the planters were forced to endure during the period. Many of these charges would have varied from estate to estate, and these are probably very conservative.

Other charges relating to the sugar industry also rose steeply. In addition to the local costs of production, estimated by Long at something over 14s per hundredweight at the outbreak of the war (see table 2.9), the increased freight, insurance, interests, duties, port charges, and commission during the war added, by Long's calculation, another 33s to the planters' total cost of marketing sugar. In arriving at the total expenses of shipping one hundredweight of sugar in 1781 (table 2.10), Long breaks down the charges into seven categories, omitting such minor ones as warehousing, rent, cooperage, and interest on duties. Adding the result to a rounded-down 14s for production, he cites 47s as the total cost of landing one hundredweight of sugar in England.

Long's figures can be supported. Another account, from the Chisholme family, gives a detailed listing (see table 2.11) of the charges on thirty casks of sugar,

Table 2.8. Some contingent costs on Jamaican estates, 1763–94

Salaries/wages	1763–73	1773–83	1783–89	1789–94
Head overseer's first bookkeeper	£70–100	£70–100 (100–150)[a]	£100–120	£100–150
Distiller	£21–28	£28–35 (32–42)[a]	£35–43	£43–45
Junior bookkeeper	£17–20	£20–30 (25–30)[a]	£20–22	£22–25
Carpenter	£50	£70–100	—	—
Hired slave labour (field hand) per diem	22d	27–30d	—	—

Sources: Van Keelen to Barham, September 9, 1782. Bodl., Barham Papers 357/1; "Report from the Committee on the Trade with India Colonies," *Parliamentary Papers* (IUP), 2:32; "Comparative Prices and Charges Attending the Jamaica Planter at and since the Commencement of the War Extracted from Actual Comments," n.d., BL, Add. MSS 12,413, fol. 45.

a. Estimates given by Edward Long and by the manager of Sir Joseph Foster Barham's estate, Mr. Van Keelen, placed the increases during this period at 40–100 percent.

Table 2.9. Production costs of sugar in Jamaica

	Cost in currency	Cost in sterling
Holding/planting/clearing	£7 10s	£5 7s 1¾d
Cutting/boiling/curing	£7 10s	£5 7s 1¾d
Carriage, 10 miles	15s	10s 8½d
Wharfage	2s 6d	1s 9½d
Filling/heading/cooperage	3s 6d	2s 6d
Cost per hogshead	£16 1s	£11 9s 3½d
Cost per cwt	£1 6s 9d	11s 9¼d
Cost when line 2 is £4	£1 11d	14s 11¼d[a]

Source: Long Papers, BL, Add. MSS 12,413, fol. 67.

a. Though the actual figure is 14s 11¼d, Long chooses to call it 14s to compensate for any errors in his estimates.

or 262 hundredweight, imported into England in 1781. Missing is the cost of insurance, which can be supplied by using Long's figures for the same year: the rate was 25 guineas per hundred pounds sterling, and most hogsheads of 12 hundredweight were valued at £25 for insurance purposes.[60] Long's total is the lower by 9d, which can be explained by his omission of several of the listed charges, such as warehouse rent, cooperage, primage, pierage, and trade. Long

Table 2.10. Shipping costs per hundredweight of sugar

Duties	11s 8½d
Wastage	3½d
Insurance	10s 9d
Interest	4½d
Freight	8s
Port charges	8d
Brokerage/commission	1s 2½d
Total	£1 13s

Source: "Charges on 1 cwt Sugar," [1781], BL, Add. MSS 12,413, fol. 44.
Note: Costs are quoted in sterling.

Table 2.11. Itemised charges on 262 hundredweight of sugar

Charge

Duty on 269 2 qtr 12 lb[a]	£158 8s
Bill money/landwaiters' fees	14s 6d
Freight at 8s per cwt	£107 16s 10d
Primage/pierage/trade	£1 8s 9d
Lighterage/wharfage/landing/housing/weighing	£3 10s
Cooperage at 6d per cask	15s
Rent, 8 weeks at 3d per week per cask	£3
Brokerage at {fr}1/2{fr} per cent	£4 1s 4d
Commission at 2{fr}1/2{fr} per cent	£20 6s 7d
Interest on £158 8s for 80 days	£1 14s 4d
Total charges on 262 cwt[a]	£301 15s 4d
Charges on cwt	23s
Insurance	10s 9d
Total cost of 1 cwt	33s 9d

Source: "Sales of 30 Casks of Sugar by the *George* and *Savannah,*" 6 April 1792, NLS, MSS 188:75, fol. 61; see similar accounts in fols. 61, 63, 65, 68, 102, 108.

a. In most instances, between 10 and 12 percent of the gross weight was deducted as tare weight. The total weight of sugar here was 196 cwt, though the Chisholmes, who were selling it, were paid for only 62 cwt 1 qtr 8 lb.

conservatively gave 47s as the cost of landing a hundredweight of sugar in England, and the Chisholme accounts confirm the accuracy of his estimates.

Although the cost of producing a hundredweight of sugar was as high as 47s, the price for sugar was at times also high.[61] It is therefore likely that the largest planters who were able to ship their sugar to Britain made significant profits, but on the whole, when one considers the increase in so many charges, most planters made little or no profit.[62] The overall profit was put at less than 3 percent for the period.

The small margin of profit, if any, for the majority of planters made them even more dependent on good yearly crops, large exports to Britain and Ireland, and the possibility of higher prices. However, imports of West Indian staples into Britain decreased, being subject to the same market conditions as in peacetime.[63] The decline, beginning in 1777, was attributable to the American War, to prolonged dry seasons in some islands, and to the hurricanes of 1780 and 1781. Extant statistics underline the extent of the decline in the West Indies. Between March 1774 and March 1775, Jamaica sent 51,218 casks of sugar to England. In the 1777–78 production year, this fell to 33,856 casks, and after the hurricanes of 1780 and 1781 Jamaica exported only 30,282 casks of sugar between March 1782 and March 1783.

The figures for Antigua and Barbados were also sharply down. Sugar imports from the former declined from 21,125 casks in the first year to only 3,204 casks in March 1780 to March 1781. Similarly, during the 1774–75 season, Barbados sent 6,929 casks of sugar to England; in the production year ending in March 1779 this fell to 2,804 casks.[64] More detailed examination of exports to England for the years 1774–82 shows a similar drop in sugar production in the remaining British West Indian islands. The total imports of muscovado sugar for the years 1776–79, when there were no hurricanes, show a decrease of some 1,494,497 hundredweight from the aggregate 7,684,585 sent in the preceding four years. The further decrease for the years 1780–83 exceeded 2,250,600 hundredweight, or about 30 percent.[65] Table 2.12 gives the state of sugar imports to Britain from 1772 to 1783.

Rum imports into Britain show the same trend. From 1770 to 1773, the British West Indies exported to Britain and America in excess of 5,500,000 gallons annually. In 1772, for example, of the 5,635,641 gallons exported, the continental colonies took 3,351,378 gallons; the remainder went to Britain.[66] In 1776 rum imports into Britain increased by 1,236,000 gallons over the 1775 figures; imports then declined from 3,341,025 in that year to 1,562,327 gallons in 1782. This failure of Britain to take larger quantities of rum from the West Indies is particularly significant because the continental market was prohibited to them.

Imports of other staples fell sharply. Cocoa dropped from 6,536 hundredweight in 1776 to 1,000 in 1782, and colonial-grown coffee from 54,937 hundred-

Table 2.12. Sugar exports to Britain, 1772–83

Year	Sugar (cwt)	Four-year total	Year (March–March)	Casks of sugar
1772	1,829,721		1772–73	112,305
1773	1,804,080		1773–74	106,745
1774	2,029,725		1774–75	131,778
1775	2,021,059	7,684,585	1775–76	115,511
1776	1,726,507		1776–77	100,302
1777	1,416,291		1777–78	76,700
1778	1,521,457		1778–79	83,257
1779	1,525,833	6,190,088	1779–80	90,051
1780	1,394,559		1780–81	80,867
1781	1,080,848		1781–82	72,866
1782	1,374,269		1782–83	74,976
1783	1,584,275	5,433,951		

Sources: West India Committee Records: Minutes of the West Indian Planters and Merchants, 1st ser.: vol. 1, fols. 9, 18, 28, 47, 61, 76, 85, 115, 147, 149, 174; Second series: vol. 2, fols. 30, 58, 92, 58d, 92d, 112d; see also CO 137/91 fol. 58.

Table 2.13. Exports of minor commodities to England, 1775–83

Year	Rum (gal)	Coffee (cwt)	Cocoa (cwt)	Pimento (lb)
1775	2,305,808	54,937	5,334	2,522,256
1776	3,341,025	51,833	6,536	1,589,145
1777	2,068,756	48,636	4,080	1,418,471
1778	2,456,572	38,801	3,494	2,498,192
1779	2,143,055	25,295	2,932	613,247
1780	1,615,841	8,568	1,908	676,976
1781	1,207,421	6,305	1,235	951,262
1782	1,562,327	12,118	605	451,880
1783	1,873,029	19,933	2,853	901,597

Sources: "An Account of the Quantity of British Sugar Imported into England between 1772 and 1791," BL Add. MSS 12,432, fol. 18; Ragatz, *Fall,* 189n.1; Schumpeter, *Overseas Trade,* 22; "Imports and Exports between England and the British West Indies 1773–83," T38/269; Sheridan, *Sugar,* 495; *Parliamentary Papers: Report on the Committee of Trade* (IUP), 2:78; Pares, *War and Trade,* 471; Young, *Common-Place Book,* 26; Dookhan, *Trade,* 34.

weight in 1775 to a mere 6,305 in 1781.[67] The export of coffee mainly from Jamaica had fallen off by almost 90 percent by 1781. A slight recovery took place in the next two years. Table 2.13 gives the quantities of some tropical staples, including rum, imported into Britain between 1775 and 1783.

Conditions in 1781 forced the West India Committee to go along with the importation of sugar from the conquered Dutch colonies of Essequibo and Demerara at British plantation duties, in British or neutral vessels. Passports were issued to British ships to allow them to trade with the captured colonies, and British warships and privateers were prohibited from capturing merchant-men en route to the United Kingdom with foreign colonial products.[68] The relaxation of the Navigation Acts, apart from demonstrating the readiness of the government to abandon its colonial policy when the interest of the West Indian planters clashed with those of the home industries and consumers, had a twofold effect on the producers. First, it enabled foreign merchants to export their sugar to Britain, increasing the supply and thus depressing prices. Second, by the admission of neutral ships in British colonial trade, it permitted a large part of the British merchant fleet to go to the foreign Caribbean islands, creating further serious shortages of shipping in the colonies.

A committee of the Assembly of Jamaica investigated the effects of the new regulations on the island's economy. In its report, it stated that "while French sugars were triumphantly sailing onto the ports of Great Britain, under impe-rial colours, uncharged either by enormous freight or enormous insurance," Jamaican sugar rotted on the wharves.[69] In a joint petition, both houses charged that British policy, "[w]hile it limits the trade of the colonies, gives them in return a kind of exclusive preference at the home market by the great duties which were therein imposed upon foreign West-India produce; but the . . . laws in question, while they take away this preference have carefully preserved all the limitations."[70]

Between 1779 and 1783, not only did British policy fail to give priority to the West Indian planters' interest, but it also burdened their commodities with higher duties to defray the cost of the war. In 1779 Parliament imposed a tax of 5 percent on the Customs and Excise duties on colonial products imported into Britain; the extra charges raised the duty on a hundredweight of sugar from approximately 6s 4d in 1775 to 6s 8d in 1779. In 1780 5d were added to the duty, and in 1781 it was increased by a further 4s 8d to approximately 11s 8½d. A year later, another tax of 5 percent raised the duty on sugar to 12s 3d per hundred-weight.[71]

The general result of the duty on West Indian staples was the restriction of sugarcane cultivation and the retardation of the islands' economic development.[72] The planters were forced to pay the total cost of the duty on their sugar even before it was sold. On most occasions, their commission agents advanced the money—and charged them interest on it. Figure 2.1 illustrates the steady growth in the duty on sugar during and after this period.

Between 1776 and 1782 the Leeward Islands suffered from severe dry weather, which destroyed the ground provisions and the cane fields. Antigua was the worst hit; Burt likened the island to the "desert of Arabia." On 3 October 1780 a hurricane and tidal wave extensively damaged Westmoreland, Hanover, St. James, and St. Elizabeth in Jamaica. At least a thousand slaves were killed; buildings were demolished, ground provisions damaged, trees blown down, and thousands of cattle and livestock lost. A committee appointed to evaluate the damages estimated that the losses in Westmoreland alone exceeded £950,000 currency. More than 50 whites and 150 enslaved workers were killed in Westmoreland and Hanover, and a quarter of all property was destroyed.[73]

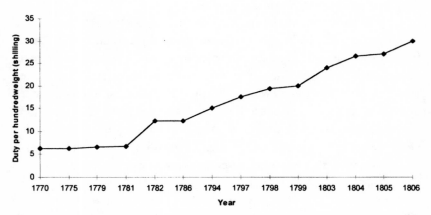

Fig. 2.1. Duties payable on West Indian sugar. In 1806 the duty on British West Indian sugar was put at 30s, with the provision that if the average market price of muscovado in bond, exclusive of duty, fell below 48s per hundredweight in the four-month period preceding 5 January, 5 May, or 5 September, the Lords of the Treasury might remit 1s per hundredweight. If the price fell below 48s and not below 47s, they might remit 2s; if below 47s, they might remit 3s. Irrespective of the price afterward, the rate was not decreased. The fact that the duty remained at the level of 27s until May 1810 shows the level the market price had reached. *Sources:* Deerr, *The History of Sugar,* vol. 2; Ragatz, *Statistics,* tables 6, 7; "Sugar Quantities Retained for Home Consumption and Net Revenue," Dalhousie Papers, NAS, GD 47/7/5.

A week later, Barbados was flattened by a hurricane. A government investigation placed the total losses at 2,033 enslaved persons, 211 horses, and 6,606 head of cattle; the estimated damages exceeded £1,300,000. Of this destruction Admiral Rodney wrote: "the whole country appears one entire ruin and the most beautiful island in the world has the appearance of a country laid waste by fire and sword and appeals to the imagination more dreadful than it is possible ... to find."[74]

In 1781 Jamaica was again struck by a hurricane. While damage was less catastrophic than in 1780, the destruction of plantain trees and corn caused suffering among the enslaved population. Previously, such disasters were countered by increased importation of foodstuffs and lumber from the American colonies, but the unavailability of this source worsened the problem of subsistence for the slaves and led to a general decline of the population of the islands. By 1783, for example, the slave population of Barbados had fallen to 57,434, from 68,548 in 1768.

Planters were forced to use their enslaved labourers to plant corn instead of cane, and then to hire extra hands to regain lost time.[75] Even so, most estate managers had difficulty feeding their people. Malnutrition among the enslaved population was widespread, causing disease and death. Of the 167 slaves between the ages of thirty and forty on Barham's estate in Jamaica, only a few were fit to work; the remainder suffered from diseases because of malnutrition. Death among the slaves was also common in the Leeward Islands, and the high incidence of malnutrition caused many managers to reduce their workload. Antigua alone lost one thousand by March 1778. Montserrat lost nearly twelve hundred. There were also numerous deaths in Jamaica from repeated hurricanes and the lack of food. In Barbados the agent for the Assembly, John Brathwaite, estimated that between 1780 and 1781 the slave population declined from 78,874 to 63,248; the population is listed as 61,808 in 1784.[76]

So disheartening was the economic condition of the islands that the future for their continued prosperity and preeminent position within the British Empire seemed bleak. In the Leeward Islands, Grenada, and Barbados, several planters abandoned their estates and immigrated to the foreign islands with their slaves to avoid litigation for debt.[77] Others liquidated their plantations at public auction for less than their market value in order to pay their creditors.[78]

Throughout the British West Indies, the governments faced financial crises. Local treasuries were near bankruptcy and most assemblies refused to tax an overburdened people. By 1782 the government of Barbados, for example, had accumulated a debt of some £30,000. The shortage of money in St. Kitts in 1779 forced the legislature to set up a committee to raise £5,000 by public subscription to cover the expenses of the troops stationed there; the Assembly pledged the next year's poll tax as security.[79] To ease the situation in Jamaica Governor Dalling ordered the Receiver-General to establish a voluntary subscription to raise money; approximately £14,000 was collected. On the next day, the legislature passed an act to borrow £30,000 at 6 percent interest to pay the troops.[80] In Montserrat both houses agreed to borrow £500 at 8 percent interest to purchase food for the poor.[81] Faced with similar problems, the Antigua Assembly passed a bill to draw £20,000 sterling in bills of exchange on the Lords of the Treasury to be repaid by a capitation tax on all slaves.[82] Though the act was without precedent, the British government recommended its acceptance.

The monetary crises in the sugar colonies were complicated by several factors—the exportation of money to the foreign islands to purchase provisions, the loss of the American market for rum, the decay of the barter trade, the drop in the amount of foreign gold carried to the islands to buy bills of exchange, and the large amount of money sent to Britain to pay debts.[83] Many planters on the small islands had incurred large debts for supplies for their estates. From time to time, they had to make direct cash payments to the merchants. In Jamaica the unparalleled scarcity of money was worsened by the decline of the Spanish trade. Jamaican merchants carried on a thriving trade with the Spanish colonies from which the island received much of its money.[84] Though a large portion was sent to England, a part was circulated locally. But "the total Revolution in the usual circuitous Trade of the West Indies occasioned by the Disturbances in America" was given by Lord Macartney as the major reason for the drop in the money supply.[85] To ease the situation, cash was sent from England to pay the troops in the Leeward Islands; those in Jamaica had to be supplied by the British government.[86]

The West Indian agricultural system had several weaknesses that had to be overcome in the years after 1776 if the planters were to produce more of their own food to replace North American supplies. Many tried, and some legislatures adopted measures with little opposition to plan their economies and to encourage local food production, but the results were minimal. The very nature of the British West Indian slave system had virtually prevented the planters from making their estates self-sufficient. Despite the glaring need for food, planters were unwilling to withdraw a significant part of their labour from sugar production. They were trapped in a vicious circle. Those who used slave labour to grow food instead of commercial crops were tampering with the agricultural system, reducing the cultivation of sugarcane, lessening the productivity of their estates, and redirecting their investment in slaves. In spite of the numerous hardships, the planters survived, but at an inordinate cost to themselves, their slaves, and the islands' economies. Many were made insolvent, others formally bankrupt.

Prior to the outbreak of the American War, the economy of the sugar colonies was in a relatively healthy position. Of course, at times natural disasters and other factors common to agricultural societies caused the islands' production of staples to decline. Still, before 1776 any reduction in productivity lasted only a short time. In contrast, the economic experience of the Caribbean colonies during the American War was one of prolonged shortage and astronomical prices. By the end of the war, few planters were able to meet the high costs of sustaining their estates, and the majority were heavily indebted. The loss of the American commercial connections clearly demonstrated that the West Indian economy could not survive without food supplies from the newly created United States, and continuing world demand for sugar and rum. The sugar producers who were accustomed to a system in which they functioned profitably prior to 1776 saw it begin to vanish with the independence of the American colonies.

As substantial investments in slave labour and capital were required for the successful production of sugar, the small and middling producers who planted very little food on their plantations needed unrestricted access to supply markets. This they enjoyed throughout the seventeenth and most of the eighteenth centuries, when the Americans supplied the West Indian plantation system with all the food and lumber it needed. The planters were freed to organise and plan their estate operations around the production of sugar alone. On plantations where the slaves grew any sizeable quantity of their own food, this was indeed a major saving to the estates. However, most were far from self-sufficient, and when the American War broke out and West Indian trade with the continental colonies was prohibited, the planters suffered severe hardships. As we have seen, the slaves, certainly the most crucial prerequisite of the continued prosperity of the plantation economy, suffered from severe malnutrition, and several thousands died between 1776 and 1783. Furthermore, the war greatly reduced the amount of money invested in sugar production and laid the foundation for a general decline in economic growth.

The West Indian planters thus looked forward to a resumption of their traditional relations with the former American colonies. On the termination of the war, several assemblies unilaterally recommended the free admittance of American ships. In most colonies, trade resumed as usual. Many Americans also expected that their commercial relations with the islands would continue unrestricted. But neither the Americans nor the West Indian planters had seriously considered the commercial implications of independence. They were caught off guard when an order-in-council was issued in 1783 regulating trade between the British islands and the United States. It received the full support of Lord Sheffield in his influential work *Observations on the Commerce of the United States*. Sheffield called for the strict imposition of the Navigation Act. In spite of opposition from Adam Smith and later the West Indian interests, the order-in-council was not repealed and formed the basis of British commercial policy which in the long run helped to retard the recovery of the British West Indian plantation economy.

∽ 3 ∾

British Policy, Canadian Preference, and the West Indian Economy, 1783–1810

For the British sugar growers, the single most important question to be resolved at the end of the War of American Independence was: Should the United States be given special commercial privileges in West Indian markets? American provisions were vital to the continuation of the plantation system. As a corollary, United States shipping was vital to the adequate supply of food to the islands. British merchants had little to do with the quantity of foodstuffs reaching the colonies, and British ships which plied mainly between the West Indies and England brought out chiefly manufactured goods and luxury items. Some went to the continental colonies for provisions and lumber when they were assured cargoes of West Indian products for the homeward voyage. However, these were few and had little impact on supplies to the islands. Some wealthy planters also occasionally engaged their ships in a triangular trade involving America, the West Indies, and England, but their annual voyages were unprofitable, and the vessels were an unreliable source of shipping.[1]

Before the war, mainly American merchants had controlled the carrying trade between the thirteen continental colonies and the West Indies. Of the two groups of British merchants involved in the American colonial trade—those resident in Britain and those resident in America—only the latter shared in the carrying trade with the British West Indies. The American monopoly had assured the islands of an adequate and reliable supply of cheap food and lumber, enabling them to concentrate on sugar production. When this situation was terminated by the Revolution, the West Indian planters experienced severe hardships. By the end of the fighting, few were able to meet the costs of running their estates. All needed significant inputs of capital, lumber, and plantation stores in order to maintain, much less increase, sugar production. Thus the recognition of the independence of the American colonies and the subsequent exclusion of the United States from the British commercial system posed worrying problems for the sugar planters.

Their experiences between 1776 and 1782 had convinced the local sugar interests that no significant changes should be made to the old commercial system. Concessions should be given to the Americans to enable the planters to continue the profitable production of sugar. As the return of peace brought prospects of increased trade, both West Indians and Americans looked to a bright future if their countries were allowed to resume their prewar commercial ties. John Adams, the revolutionary leader who became the second president of the United States, expressed the relationship best when he wrote: "The commerce of the West India Islands is a part of the American system of Commerce. They can neither do without us nor we without them. The Creator has placed us upon the globe in such a situation, that we have occasion for each other, and the politicians and artful contrivances cannot separate us."[2]

Similar points of view were coming out of the West Indies. Although Britain was the main market for sugar, the Americans had consumed most of colonial rum and had been an alternative market for the lesser grades of sugar and other staples. As a matter of fact, many West Indian estates could make a profit only when they sold sugar to the Americans, thereby partially minimizing such charges as insurance, custom duties, freight, commission fees, storage, and shipping. A Jamaican planter put it most eloquently: "Jamaica and the other islands will, with the fondness of a child to his parent, naturally cling to the government of America, where is produced every article of husbandry fit for the planter. America, will soon become the theatre of the arts, the seminary of learning and the fragrant abode of luxurious pleasures."[3]

At the conclusion of hostilities in America, the issue of United States trade with the islands received the immediate attention of the local West Indian interests. At the end of 1782, the several Caribbean legislatures urged their respective governors to admit American vessels to a free intercourse. In June 1783, for example, the Council of Jamaica went beyond its legislative authority as far as the British mercantilists were concerned and unanimously resolved that the island's trade relations with the new republic was to be placed on a liberal footing. On its recommendation to Governor Archibald Campbell, United

States vessels were allowed to enter Jamaican ports with lumber and provisions, and to take in return local produce, exempt from duties. The admission of these ships brought immediate relief to the inhabitants, and the planters were everywhere looking forward to the return of economic prosperity. Preparations for repairing plantation buildings destroyed by the hurricane of 1780 and for erecting new still houses were under way. Planters were generally optimistic about their chances of recouping some of their losses with substantial increases in sugar and rum production.[4]

American policymakers were equally desirous of securing a commercial treaty with the British government giving the United States unlimited trade with the sugar colonies. "In addition to the great objects which would become the subjects of discussion, and on which you are fully instructed," wrote Robert Livingston, first Secretary of State for Foreign Affairs in the Congress of the Confederation, "I could wish again to repeat one ... which materially interests us. I mean the procuring of a market for lumber and provisions of every kind in the West Indies." A few days later he penned a similar letter to Benjamin Franklin, and on 12 September 1782 he told John Jay, "If the negotiations go on, let me beg you to use every means for procuring a direct trade with the West Indies. It is an object of the most importance, with us."[5] Early in 1783, Congress appointed a committee to negotiate a commercial treaty with the British government. The three main objectives of any agreement as far as the Americans were concerned were "a direct trade between ... the United States & the West Indies; ... a right of carrying between the latter & other parts of the British Empire; and a right of carrying from the West Indies to all other parts of the world."[6]

The Shelburne administration was not very responsive to a relaxation of the trade restrictions. It initiated policy inimical to the continued profitability of sugar production in the West Indies. The long-accepted reason was that the West Indian planters lost their influence in Parliament. While this may have some truth, it is likely that the emergence of the free trade doctrine in 1776 and the loss of the American colonies inspired British Parliament members to penalize the new United States by restricting trade between the islands and the United States. After Shelburne left office in February 1783, William Pitt the Younger, Chancellor of the Exchequer, introduced a bill that would have admitted United States ships to an unlimited trade with the islands and to a share of the carrying trade between Britain and the West Indies. Opposition to the proposed measure was led by English shipping interests, supported by Lord Sheffield, the loyalists in British North America, and the West India Committee. This latter initially wanted to receive American supplies while excluding United States ships from the carrying trade between Britain and the West Indies, in order to allow its members to monopolise the carrying trade, as well as to encourage the development of British shipbuilding and to maintain a "nursery" for British seamen.[7] The bill was laid aside. Pitt resigned, and on 2 July 1783 the British government issued an order-in-council. It prohibited vessels belonging to the United States from entering British West Indian ports and excluded its salted beef, pork, all dairy products, and fish, reserving this monopoly to Canadian and Irish producers. The West Indians were allowed, however, to import lumber, livestock, grain, flour, and bread from the United States and to export their produce to America, in British vessels.[8]

The exclusion of American shipping from British West Indian ports instantly threatened the continued economic development of the islands. Sugar production was a long, involved process that combined the raising of capital, the purchase and maintenance of large numbers of slaves, the clearing of land, the planting of canes, and the maturing period before harvest. A sugar estate was, according to Richard Pares, "a factory in a field."[9] Since sugar production was more heavily capitalised than any other eighteenth-century commodity-producing business, the planters needed assurances, especially after their recent wartime experiences, that they would realize moderate profits on their investments. Moreover, the order-in-council of 1783 created uncertainty in the minds of the planters, who feared that these restrictions would continue the severe wartime shortages that had plagued the islands and would in the end lead to the decline of the West Indian economy.[10]

High prices were the immediate result of what was termed a "mistaken Proclamation to prevent the Americans from trading with the colonies, and from an absurd Idea that they can be supplied from Canada & Nova Scotia, where cultivation is not known, & where ports are shut up half the year, or rendered nearly inaccessible from the weather."[11]

Upon receipt of the order-in-council in Jamaica, the price of lumber jumped from £10 or £12 to £28 per thousand feet. In the northern part of the island, it went as high as £40, and in Barbados it rose from £7 to £25.[12] A letter from St. Vincent written in 1787 demonstrated that the average price of American products did not fall, as was the trend after previous wars.[13] In the other islands, prices for American products were as high. Furthermore, the order-in-council generated confusion and resentment against British policy. In some islands, misinformation led a majority of the planters to believe that American vessels of small tonnage were not prohibited by the regulations, and some governors sought clarification from London. In Jamaica, for example, members of the Assembly contended that British policy was a device to control American commerce, as it had done before the Revolution. They therefore did not believe "that the Americans were . . . restricted in their Commerce with any of His Majesty's West India Islands, because it was not positively so expressed in the Order of the King in Council." They also argued that since merchants of the United States were foreigners, they were entitled by the Free Port Act to trade with the island as long as their vessels conformed to the regulations.[14] The assemblymen further asked Governor Campbell, a mercantilist and military man, to allow the importation of provisions and lumber, and the exportation of Jamaican products, in United States vessels for nine months. He refused to suspend regulations that, he said, were aimed at promoting the interests of the empire. It seems as though Campbell had written previously to Frederick Haldimand, governor of Quebec, asking for ships with lumber, flour, corn, fish, and horses to relieve shortages in Jamaica.[15]

By excluding United States shipping from the West Indies, the British government had placed the plantation system in a precarious situation, and planters were faced with insuperable problems. There were periods of continuous shortage of provisions and lumber, high prices, fear of famine, and high mortality rates among slaves from hurricane and malnutrition—not to mention the planters' fears of playing a reduced role in the new Atlantic commercial system.

Under such conditions, no planter wanted to invest large sums of money to establish new estates, or to improve existing ones. British policy therefore acted as a deterrent to the continued prosperity of the British West Indies, and marked the beginning of the continuous decline of the sugar colonies. It will be shown that for five years from 1783 to 1787, the Caribbean colonies were forced to rely on the foreign islands for almost every article of food and lumber that had been brought from the continent, sending large sums of money to the French islands rather than trading with the Americans at their own ports. Governor Orde of Dominica summed up the situation resulting from British policy most succinctly: "the difficulties they labour under, in now procuring those supplies with which they formerly abounded, are sensibly felt."[16]

British policy effectively forced the planters to buy American goods from foreign merchants at greatly inflated prices, and thus to cultivate their estates under adverse supply market conditions. A major part of the labour of the slaves had to be redirected to carry on subsistence agriculture as had been done during the war. The West Indian interests were understandably not prepared to accept willingly any change in the commercial intercourse that had made them wealthy and had given them political power in the old colonial system. Long, who seems to have reversed his earlier position on West Indian dependence on America, summed up the feelings of the absentee planters when he wrote: "we cannot understand our situation, nor how far it may benefit our properties. What we fear is, that the Americans, buying much cheaper at the French islands, will take little else from us, than our cash if we have any, & that the French Culture will amount in exact proportion as ours may sink. The people here are actuated by such sordid narrow principles, and such a spirit of monopoly, that no colony can hope to flourish under the system."[17] His observation is particularly interesting since in 1774 he called for a lessening of West Indian reliance on the continental colonies for lumber and provisions.

The restrictions on West Indian–United States commerce after 1783 continued the pattern of trade that had developed between Britain and the sugar colonies during the war: with their cheap and regular supplies of food cut off, the planters were compelled to do most of their buying as well as selling in London. In many cases, orders were not completed, and high prices and severe shortages were generally experienced. This British monopoly of the West Indian trade patently reduced the profitability of the sugar estates.[18] In November 1783, for example, Governor David Parry, in contending that the development of the economy of Barbados was likely to be severely retarded by the new regulations, wrote: "the Exclusion of American lumber and Horses will fall particularly hard upon the Island in its present ruinous conditions." Parry recommended that the planters be allowed a measure of relief, but the British government remained firm in the face of numerous protests in the islands.[19]

The planters now petitioned the Committee of the Privy Council for Trade and Foreign Plantations for special consideration, putting forward a case based on their wartime experiences and their knowledge of the factors necessary for West Indian economic survival. But their arguments could not overcome the conjectural evidence presented by the shipowners and the loyalists purporting to show that Canada was able to supply the islands and that the sugar colonies would not be affected by the new regulations.

Although the war had brought a reversal to the islands' prosperity, their commercial importance remained a major factor against them. They were still the largest commodity suppliers to England and the fifth largest consumer of

British manufactures.[20] The islands' black population continued to be the most important colonial market for cheap foodstuffs. It was this market that the Canadian loyalists, with the support of the British shipping interests and Lord Sheffield, wanted to capture.

British policymakers must have understood that the islands' favourable economic position in the prewar years was dependent on, and resulted from, their commercial relationship with America. It was a mistake of the British government to give primary consideration to the interests of the British North American colonies, when the evidence clearly showed that adequate supplies could not be brought from there.

Indeed, British North America could produce very little of the provisions needed by the West Indian sugar plantations. They had few ships and no experience in the West Indian trade. Even the Newfoundland fisheries were not geared to supply the West India market with low-grade fish for the slaves. For more than a year, between July 1783 and August 1784, no supplies from Canada reached some islands. On 13 August 1783 Governor Orde of Dominica wrote: "Many Vessels have arrived from Africa with Slaves, many also, lately, from Ireland with provisions, but not a Vessel from either Nova Scotia or Canada, with the produce of those colonies"; the following January he commented: "I have been often in Nova Scotia and know it to be more fertile than generally believed—but at the same time that I say this I must acknowledge that I have little hopes of their being able fully to supply our wants for many years—as yet sorry am I to add, not a single vessel with any Article of their produce has arrived here."[21]

Supplies reaching the islands from the continent in British ships could not compensate for the loss of direct trade in American vessels. Several West Indian governors, because of the scarcity of provisions and lumber after 1783 and the high production costs of West Indian staples, recommended changes in British policy as established by the order-in-council. Shirley, who had refused earlier to open ports in the Leeward Islands to United States ships during periods of disaster, recommended in 1784 that small American vessels be allowed to enter British Caribbean ports because the planters were still dependent on the new republic for foodstuffs and lumber.[22] British policy restrictions on United States commerce had led to the resumption of the illegal trade with St. Eustatius that had existed during the war, and it was from this source that the Leeward Islands were supplied.

Governor Parry of Barbados went further. He recommended that the use of

French brandy be discouraged in Britain, that the duty on rum be reduced by 50 percent to encourage its consumption, and that American ships under a hundred tons be allowed to trade directly with the islands, supplying them with lumber, horses, cattle, livestock, rice, and Indian corn for three years, or until the North American colonies were able to furnish these articles. The adoption of Parry's suggestions would pose little or no threat to British shipping. The vessels to be employed in the trade were small, and the articles to be imported could not be brought from Britain, Ireland, or British North America at cheap prices. Stephen Fuller, the Jamaican agent in London, made similar recommendations in the following year, but these were turned down.[23]

By the middle of June 1785, the planters' situation in Barbados had become so serious that Parry wrote a severe critique of British commercial policy. He called for the abandonment of the Navigation Act on these grounds: "The Dismemberment of the American Colonies from the British Empire, leaving them at perfect freedom to exercise their Talents, and to improve the materials with which Nature had supplied them for the purpose of Commerce, has in effect estranged the Objects, and circumscribed the Power of the Navigation Act. The Act ... being no longer capable of enforcing obedience to its restraints over so large a territory as it formerly controlled, the purpose for which it was passed, are in a great measure defeated."[24]

In effect, the functioning of the order-in-council made St. Eustatius, and St. Pierre in Martinique, the entrepots for American products and helped the Americans to evade the restrictions on their trade. Small vessels from the British islands, mainly droghers and crewed chiefly by slaves, went to the foreign colonies and purchased American foodstuffs and lumber for cash.[25] This practice, although it brought a measure of relief to the planters, drained the British islands of their money.[26] The articles purchased from the Americans at near antebellum prices were then retailed to the planters at 50–100 percent profit. Thus, while the buyers were burdened with exorbitant prices, the Americans found nearly the same demand for their products as before the war. One West Indian governor observed that the American trade "is thrown into a new Channel, not destroyed by their separation from the Mother Country."[27]

British vessels by trading with the foreign islands were defeating the principle of the triangular trade as established by British policy. From 1783 to 1787, as during the American War, St. Eustatius remained at the centre of this illegal trade in American products. All efforts to curb it were unsuccessful.[28] Prices for lumber and provisions in the foreign islands made the ventures profitable, and reduced the risks and costs of travelling to the United States. For example, while the foreign colonies were furnished in 1790 "by French and American bottoms, with red oak hogsheads staves at 12, 14 and 16 dollars—with hoops at 14 to 28 dollars—with pine boards at 9 to 16 dollars—with Indian meal at 3½ dollars and with rice at 3 to 3½ dollars per 100 pounds, the British planters in Jamaica were obliged to pay for red oak hogsheads staves, 24, 27 and 31 dollars; for wooden hoops 27, 30, and 36 dollars; for pine boards, 24, 27 and 30 dollars; for Indian meal 4½ to 5¼ dollars; for ship bread the same; and for rice per 100 pounds 3½ to 5¼ dollars."[29] Table 3.1 compares the prices for American lumber and provisions in St. Domingue and in Jamaica.

So extensive was the illegal trade that in 1786 a total of 479 vessels from the foreign islands entered British West Indian ports with American goods.[30] In 1787, 244 foreign ships called at Kingston, more than three-quarters of them American or French.[31] In a comparison of imports into the British islands from the United States, British North America, and the foreign islands in 1786, the quantities of American flour, bread, staves, shingles, horses, and hoops im-

Table 3.1. Prices in dollars in Jamaica and St. Domingue, 1790

Article	Unit	June	October	November
Kingston, Jamaica				
Superfine flour	bbl	10.20–10.50	7.50	7.50–8.25
Common flour	bbl	9.37	9.75	7.12–7.50
Ship bread	bbl	5.25	4.50	4.87
Indian meal	bbl	5.25	4.50	5.25
Rice	cwt	3.37	4.02	4.50–5.25
Pork	cwt	—	14.00	10.00
Hams	lb	.12	.16	.15
Butter	lb	.15	—	.15
Pine boards	m ft	24.00	27.00	30.00
Red oak staves	m ft	31.00	27.00	—
Wooden hoops	m (1000)	30.00	36.00	30.00
Cap François, St. Domingue				
Superfine flour	bbl	10.00	6.50	6.00–6.50
Common flour	bbl	9.00	5.00	5.00–5.45
Ship bread	bbl	3.52	—	—
Indian meal	bbl	3.64	2.50	—
Rice	cwt	3.50	2.91	—
Pork or beef	cwt	6.06	7.00	7.00–8.00

Source: Sheridan, *Sugar and Slavery,* 169–70.

ported through the foreign colonies increased by roughly 50 percent. The number of staves and shingles trebled those imported from Canada, while the lumber, horses, hoops and oxen increased significantly.[32] Available statistics of imports of American products into the British West Indies confirm that the systematic smuggling engendered by British policy had forced many sugar colonies to rely on the foreign islands for most of their supplies. Some islands— Montserrat, St. Kitts, Nevis, St. Vincent—imported most of their American supplies from St. Eustatius.[33]

Table 3.2 shows imports of American goods from the United States, British North America, and the foreign West Indies to the sugar colonies between 1785 and 1787. (The figures for the foreign islands are for 1786–87. Some articles from Canada were reexports; rice, for example, was not produced in that colony.) When the figures for 1785–87 are compared with those for 1771–73 (table 1.10), it is evident that the islands were undersupplied in most articles, and complaints of shortages were legitimate. The deficit in food supplies had to be made up either by imports from Britain or by increased local food production. The evidence shows that only the production of coffee achieved any success.[34]

The illegal circuitous trade through the foreign islands had an effect on the economies of the sugar islands similar to that of the war years. The slave population declined from illnesses related to starvation. In Barbados one account

Table 3.2. American goods imported from the United States, British North America, and foreign islands, 1785–87

Article	Unit	U.S.	BNA	Foreign islands
Lumber	m ft	23,756,816	7,700,000	7,377,043
Staves		61,276,732	10,478,891	20,219,554
Hoops		662,065	103,661	562,208
Corn & peas	bu	562,548	16,925	96,802
Flour	bbl	278,326	12,843	43,193
Bread	bbl	51,729	2,043	2,874
Rice	bbl	21,020	459	1,106
Fish	bbl	482	17,622	25
Beef & pork	bbl	185	1,126	250
Horses		2,464	327	648
Oxen		272	60	300
Onions	bun	101,458	21,203	11,000
Oil	bbl	1,350	1,487	37
Hogsheads		7,561	1,358	1,554

Sources: List of all articles and quantities reaching the British West Indies from all sources, n.d., CO 318/1, fol. 315; see also CO 318/2, fol. 164.

shows the number of slaves falling from 68,270 in 1780 to 62,712 in 1787.[35] Reports from Jamaica in 1786 estimated that 18,000–20,000 would die from starvation; "many hundreds have been killed in robbing provision grounds, many have died of actual hunger, and thousands are now bloated and in Dropsies from the same cause," wrote one planter.[36] Another letter expressed similar horrors and fears: "It is a Truth indispensable as it is horrid, however little it may be known or noticed on your side of the Ocean, that many Thousands of Negroes perished this year in Jamaica by Famine, and as we have had a Hurricane, if a Drowth should follow, as happened after the preceding ones, many thousands more will inevitably perish next year. And this dreadful prospect is greatly aggravated by the knowledge that our Governor's hands are absolutely restrained from opening the ports to let in assistance, however it may be wanted."[37] The extant statistics shown in table 3.3 indicate the effect of war

Table 3.3. Populations of Barbados, Jamaica, and Leeward Islands

Year	Whites	Free blacks	Slaves
Barbados			
1768	16,139	448	66,377
1773	18,532	—	68,548
1783	16,167	838	57,434
1787	16,127	—	64,405
Jamaica			
1768	17,949	—	166,914
1774	12,737	4,093	192,787
1778	18,420	—	205,261
1787	23,000	—	255,780
Antigua			
1774	2,590	—	37,808
1787	—	—	36,000
Montserrat			
1774	1,300	—	10,000
1787	1,000	—	9,500
Nevis			
1774	1,000	—	10,000
1787	1,300	—	8,000
St. Kitts			
1774	1,900	—	23,462
1787	1,912	—	20,435

Sources: Macpherson, *Annals of Commerce,* 3:700, 4:106; *Parliamentary Papers* (HMSO), vol. 84, pt. 3A, no. 15; Pitman, *Development,* 372–73; Ragatz, *Statistics,* p. 5, table 4; Schomburgk, *History of Barbados,* 82–85

and adverse weather conditions on the slave population of most of the older islands. As late as 1787, the slave population had not recovered to its prewar levels, except in Jamaica.

Slave losses by hurricanes and famine were not offset by increased importation. In the colonial period of the United States, when conditions for economic growth in the West Indies were ideal, a steady reinforcement of the slave population with fresh imports of captive Africans was needed, with at least 7 percent annual growth required to maintain production levels and inject new life into the system. The trade peaked in the years immediately preceding the American War, and declined as a result of it.[38] After its termination the slave trade was revived, but then imports declined because there was little economic activity and planters could not afford new slaves. Table 3.4 gives the slaves imported into and exported from the sugar colonies between 1783 and 1791. The larger imports in 1791 resulted from the colonial disorders in the French islands.[39] Note the increase in the number exported in the last four years, 1788–91.

The state of the economies of the West Indian islands can surely be measured by the newly imported captives the planters were purchasing. After a war, the general pattern was for the planters to buy a relatively large number of slaves to restock the plantations. The same trend was evident after the War of American Independence. The decline in overall imports for most of the 1780s and 1790s is indicative of the hardships the planters faced, which probably gave rise to a conscious policy of cutting back. Planters instead introduced a form of amelioration, discussed in chapter 6, to augment their labour force through natural

Table 3.4. Africans imported and exported, 1784–91

Year	Ships	Tonnage	Africans imported	Africans exported	Net imports
1784	93	13,301	28,550	5,263	23,287
1785	73	10,730	21,598	5,018	16,580
1786	67	8,070	19,160	4,317	14,843
1787	85	12,183	21,023	5,366	15,657
Average	80	11,071	22,583	4,991	17,592
1788	98	15,291	24,495	11,212	13,283
1789	92	16,157	21,425	8,764	12,661
1790	97	16,469	21,889	7,542	14,347
1791	128	24,041	30,763	12,866	17,897
Average	104	17,990	24,643	10,096	14,547

Sources: "Account of Negroes Retained in the British West Indies, 1783–1788," PRO, CO 318/1, fol. 141; Edwards, History, 2:53–54; Macpherson, Annals of Commerce, 4:228.

increase. Of course, this policy was effected not because they were becoming "humanitarians" but as a means of reducing plantation costs. While the overall number of new Africans imported into the West Indies increased after 1783, a larger number were reexported, so fewer captives were retained on the islands in the four years 1788–91 than in 1784–87. This can readily be seen from figures 3.1 and 3.2 showing slave imports, exports, and net imports in the West

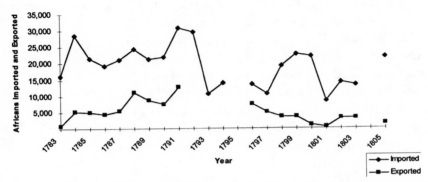

Fig. 3.1. Africans imported and exported, British West Indies, 1783–1805. *Sources:* "Account of Negroes Retained in the British West Indies by Islands, 1783–1788," PRO, CO 318/1, fol. 141; Edwards, *History,* 2:53–54; Macpherson, *Annals of Commerce,* 4:155, 228; *Parliamentary Papers* (IUP), vols. 2, 61; "Slaves Imported into the West Indies, 1790–1800," Dalhousie Papers, NAS, GD 45/7/5, fol. 82 (his figures are higher than most); W. Young, *Common-Place Book,* 5.

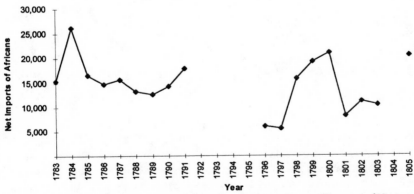

Fig. 3.2. Net imports of Africans, British West Indies, 1783–1805. *Sources:* "Account of Negroes Retained in the British West Indies by Islands, 1783–1788," PRO, CO 318/1, fol. 141; Edwards, *History,* 2:53–54; Macpherson, *Annals of Commerce,* 4:155, 228; *Parliamentary Papers* (IUP), vols. 2, 61; "Slaves Imported into the West Indies, 1790–1800," Dalhousie Papers, NAS, GD 45/7/5, fol. 82; W. Young, *Common-Place Book,* 5.

Indies between 1783 and 1805. It was not until the outbreak of revolution in St. Domingue in 1791 that net imports increased, mainly because of the loss of that valuable market.

A closer look at imports of new Africans into the several islands reflects the broader trend in the West Indies as a whole. In Barbados the high point was reached in 1770, after which imports declined steadily, with minimal resurgences in 1775, 1781, 1788, the later 1790s, and 1803. An important feature of the Barbados case is that a majority of the Africans were reexported. Figure 3.3 shows the Barbados slave trade between 1764 and 1805.

Of the Leeward Islands, Antigua's slave imports (see fig. 3.4) declined markedly after 1775 and remained extremely low until 1782; a measure of recovery then lasted until 1784, after which the trade fell off again and did not recover during the period of this study. Unlike in Barbados, the reexport trade of newly imported Africans was small: the planters were purchasing a larger number. But as in Barbados, the decline of the slave trade in Antigua had already begun before the humanitarian debate got under way.

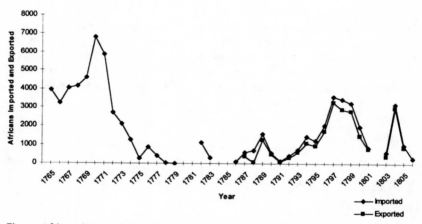

Fig. 3.3. Africans imported and exported, Barbados, 1764–1805. *Sources:* "Account of Negroes Retained in the British West Indies by Islands, 1783–1788," PRO, CO 318/1, fol. 141; "Account of Slaves Imported and Exported in the Island of Barbados since 1788," *Parliamentary Papers related to the slave trade, 1801–1815* (IUP), 61:41; "An Account of the Number of Negroes Imported into, and Exported from, each of the following British West India Islands, and of the shipping employed, 1783–1787," in Macpherson, *Annals of Commerce,* 4:155; "Account of the Number of Slaves returned into the Treasurer's Office, Barbados, 1780–1787, inclusive, 12 May 1780," PRO, CO 28/4, fol. 179; Barbados Census, Melville Papers Barbados 1802, NLS, MS 1711, fols. 75–77; *Parliamentary Papers* (IUP), 61:41, 60–61, 426–27; *Parliamentary Papers* (HMSO), vol. 84, pt. 3A, no. 15.

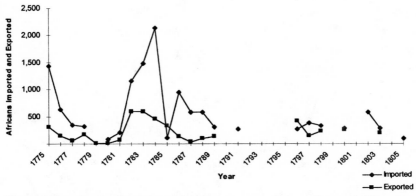

Fig. 3.4. Africans imported and exported, Antigua, 1775–1805. *Sources:* "Account of Slaves Imported and Exported from Antigua from 1770 to 1788," in *Parliamentary Papers* (HMSO), vol. 84: *Accounts and Papers,* vol. 26, no. 646 (12), pp. 50–51; see also no. 646–646A, pp. 37, 39, 44, 45–47; Macpherson, *Annals of Commerce,* 4:155, 228; *Parliamentary Papers* (IUP), 61:60–61, 426–27; *Parliamentary Papers* (HMSO), vol. 87, no. 697, p. 2; "Slaves Imported and Exported from Antigua, 4 December 1788," PRO, CO 152/67; W. Young, *Common-Place Book,* 7–8, 10.

In Dominica, a newly settled British colony, the planters had to buy more slaves to meet their labour needs. However, the trade picture is confused because the island contained two free ports through which merchants were allowed to reexport. In the first period, 1767–79, as figure 3.5 shows, most new Africans imported were retained. Figures are missing for 1779–82, when the French held the island. As in the other colonies discussed, imports of captive Africans into Dominica declined after 1775. Recovery took place immediately after the island was returned to the British in 1783. This growth continued until 1788, after which the number of "saltwater" Africans imported into Dominica dropped off significantly, and remained so until the end of the slave trade. As in Barbados, most of the newly imported Africans were reexported. Thus, even if more Africans were being brought into the islands in the post–American War period, fewer were being retained for the plantations.

Jamaica was the only older sugar colony where it could be said that there was a measure of recovery in the slave trade in the post-1783 period. However, there were only two years, 1784 and 1800, when the imports were greater than in any of the three prewar years, 1774 to 1776. These years marked the height of Jamaican imports of captive Africans. As in Dominica and Barbados, some of the newly imported Africans were reexported. This practice ceased only because the threat to abolish the slave trade arose in the 1790s, and there was a rush to retain more and more Africans. A graphic view of the years 1765–1806 (fig. 3.6)

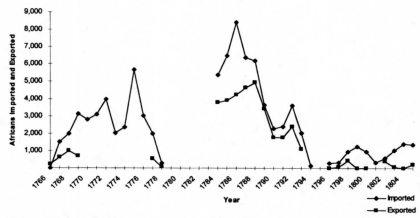

Fig. 3.5. Africans imported and exported, Dominica, 1767–1805. *Sources:* "Account of Negroes Imported and Exported from Dominica, 1788–1804," in *Parliamentary Papers* (HMSO), vol. 84, pt. 3, no. 15: *Accounts and Papers,* vol. 26, supp.; "Account of Negroes Imported into and Exported from Roseau, 1788 to December 1804," PRO, CO 71/38; "Account of the Number of Negroes Imported into Dominica under the Free Port Act of 6 Geo. III C. 49," PRO, CO 318/2, fols. 249, 252; "Answers to Queries," 4 October 1788, PRO, CO 71/14; Liverpool Papers, BL, Add. MSS 38,343, fol. 250; Macpherson, *Annals of Commerce,* 4:155, 228; *Parliamentary Papers* (IUP), 61:37, 426–27, 447.

clearly indicates that the American War had a marked impact on the slave trade to Jamaica.

The smaller number of new captive Africans imported into most of the islands and the reduction of the enslaved population, the greater costs of supplies after 1776, the decline in market prices of West Indian staples, the heavy duties on plantation produce imported into Britain, the loss of rum sales to the United States—all had a deteriorating effect on British Caribbean agriculture. Overall, colonial tropical products reaching Britain did not increase significantly to pre–American War levels between 1783 and 1787 except in 1785, when the 1776 figures were exceeded by less than 50,000 hundredweight. The total imports of muscovado sugar into Britain for the years 1783–87 were less than those for 1772–76. The best postwar year was 1785, when some 2,075,909 hundredweight were imported. Bryan Edwards best sums up this decline when he writes: "the imports of sugar into . . . Britain from all the British West Indies (Jamaica excepted) . . . decreased from 3,762,804 cwt to 2,563,228 cwt. The difference in value at a medium price, cannot be less than £200,000 sterling."[40] Figure 3.7 illustrates the precipitousness of the decline in sugar production after

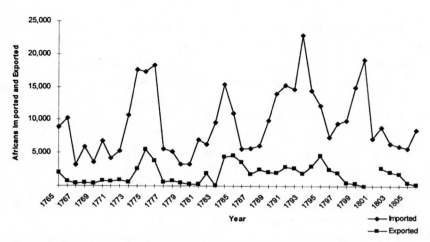

Fig. 3.6. Africans imported and exported, Jamaica, 1765–1806. *Sources:* "Account of Negroes retained in each Island . . . 1783 to 1788," PRO, CO 318/1, fol. 141; Macpherson, *Annals of Commerce,* 4:155, 228; Metcalf, *Royal Government,* app.; "Papers on the Statistics of Jamaica, 1739–1778 (c. 1789)," Long Papers, BL, Add. MSS 12,435, fol. 270; *Parliamentary Papers* (HMSO), vol. 82, no. 622, vol. 87, pp. 497–98; PRO, CO 318/1, fol. 141; *Parliamentary Papers* (IUP), 61:237, 426–27.

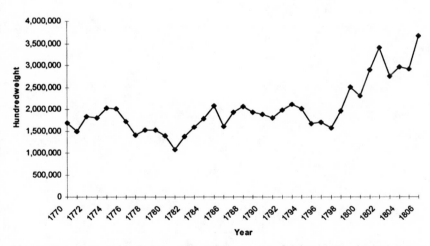

Fig. 3.7. Sugar imports into Britain. *Sources:* "An Account of the Quantity of British Sugar Imported into England between 1772 and 1791," BL, Add. MSS 12,432, fol. 18; Dookhan, "War and Trade," 34; "Imports and Exports," PRO, T 38/269, fols. 1–6; Pares, *War and Trade,* 471; Ragatz, *Fall,* 189n.1; Ragatz, *Statistics,* 22; *Parliamentary Papers* (IUP), 2:75; Schumpeter, *English Overseas Trade,* 60–61; Sheridan, *Sugar and Slavery,* 495; W. Young, *Common-Place Book,* 32.

1776, showing a relatively mild recovery in 1785–88 only. Not until 1799 did sugar exports rise significantly. They remained high until abolition. However, as will be shown, larger sugar exports resulted from the destruction of the St. Domingue sugar industry, and brought lower prices and lower profits for plantation owners. In the decade after 1783, West Indian sugar production as reflected by exports to Britain was in decline.

On the whole, between 1783 and 1807 West Indian rum exports to Britain also did not increase markedly above prewar levels. This was particularly disastrous since, with the profitable American market closed, a large amount of rum remained unsold. Again, 1785 was the best year, with 3,558,380 gallons taken. Rum exports followed the same trend as sugar and, as figure 3.8 shows, they remained static after the pre–Revolutionary War period. The only year in which the 1776 figures were surpassed was 1785, but by barely 200,000 gallons. In view of the higher cost of West Indian rum production, this increase is negligible. Any significant growth in rum exports to Britain came late and as a result of the French Revolutionary and Napoleonic Wars.

The extant statistics on other staples sent to England and Wales between 1783 and 1791 show a similar trend except for cotton. Jamaica accounted for the increase in most exports. Table 3.5 gives British imports of West Indian products including sugar from 1783 to 1791.

British imports of coffee, cocoa, and pimento from 1770 to 1791 show a

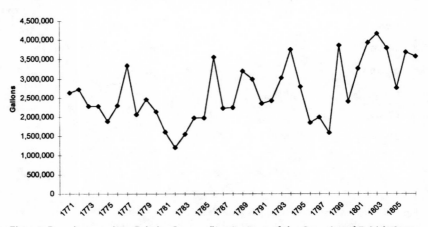

Fig. 3.8. Rum imports into Britain. *Sources:* "An Account of the Quantity of British Sugar Imported into England between 1772 and 1791," BL, Add. MSS 12,432, fol. 18; Dookhan, "War and Trade"; "Imports and Exports," PRO, T 38/269, fols. 1–6; Pares, *War and Trade*, 471; Ragatz, *Fall*, 189n.1; Ragatz, *Statistics*, 22; *Parliamentary Papers* (IUP), 2:73; Schumpeter, *English Overseas Trade*, 60–61; Sheridan, *Sugar and Slavery*, 495; W. Young, *Common-Place Book*, 50.

Table 3.5. Exports of staples to England, 1783–91

Year	Cotton (lb)	Rum (gal)	Coffee (cwt)	Cocoa (cwt)	Pimento (lb)	Sugar (cwt)
1783	9,503,000	1,873,029	19,933	2,853	901,597	1,584,275
1784	11,179,000	1,981,308	41,147	2,586	1,134,254	1,782,386
1785	17,712,000	3,558,380	37,036	5,688	3,258,980	2,075,909
1786	18,560,000	2,229,231	39,032	1,722	1,017,751	1,613,965
1787	21,826,000	2,351,341	30,365	3,954	606,954	1,926,621
1788	9,427,765	3,211,834	32,147	—	—	2,065,847
1789	20,174,000	2,995,856	34,773	—	—	1,936,448
1790	28,580,000	2,361,316	55,691	—	—	1,882,106
1791	12,330,109	2,421,199	40,736	4,301	1,159,134	1,808,950

Sources: "An Account of the Quantity of British Sugar Imported into England between 1772 and 1791," BL Add. MSS 12,432, fol. 18; "Imports and Exports between England and the British West Indies, 1773–83," T38/269; Pares, *War and Trade,* 471; Ragatz, *Fall,* 189n.1; Schumpeter, *Overseas Trade,* 22.

downward trend after 1776. There was a measure of recovery about 1785, and again in 1790 in the case of coffee, but this was only temporary and short-lived. Nearly all of the pimento exported for most of the eighteenth century was sent from Jamaica. Sales to Britain (see fig. 3.9) declined rapidly after 1778 and re-

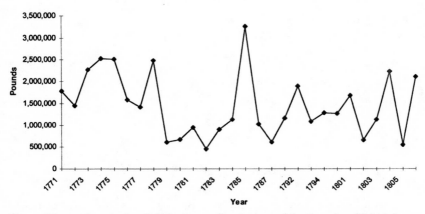

Fig. 3.9. Pimento imports into Britain. *Sources:* "An Account of the Quantity of British Sugar Imported into England between 1772 and 1791," BL, Add. MSS 12,432, fol. 18; Dookhan, "War and Trade," 34; "Imports and Exports," PRO, T 38/269, fols. 1–6; Pares, *War and Trade,* 471; Ragatz, *Fall,* 189n.1; Ragatz, *Statistics,* 22; *Parliamentary Papers* (IUP), 2:78; Schumpeter, *English Overseas Trade,* 60–61; Sheridan, *Sugar and Slavery,* 495; W. Young, *Common-Place Book, 77.*

mained low during the American Revolution and in the following decade. While pimento probably provided an adequate income to some growers, it was not of economic significance to the survival of the plantation system.

Imports of cocoa into Britain (see fig. 3.10) came mainly from the Ceded Islands, with a moderate quantity from Jamaica. While certainly of benefit to individual planters, cocoa production had only minor effects on the economies of the islands. The decline of imports into Britain began in 1776 and continued throughout the War of American Independence and for a decade beyond. It was not until 1794 that imports reached their prewar levels, and they were erratic thereafter.

Coffee was a minor staple for most of the eighteenth century. Only in the mid-1770s was an effort made in Jamaica to improve the island's output as well as the quality of the beans. The War of American Independence virtually killed the industry, which reached its lowest level in 1781. A minor recovery was achieved in the decade after 1783, but the highest prewar level of exports to Britain was not matched until 1794. Coffee then emerged as a major crop, and exports to Britain up to 1806 increased markedly, probably as a result of the destruction of production in Haiti. Figure 3.11 gives coffee imports into Britain from 1770 to 1806.

Even after 1783, the plantation system depended to a great extent on reciprocity of commerce with the United States because it complemented and was never

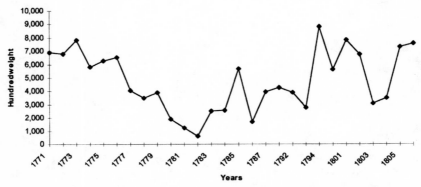

Fig. 3.10. Cocoa imports into Britain. *Sources:* "An Account of the Quantity of British Sugar Imported into England between 1772 and 1791," BL, Add. MSS 12,432, fol. 18; Dookhan, "War and Trade"; "Imports and Exports," PRO, T 38/269, fols. 1–6; Pares, *War and Trade,* 471; Ragatz, *Fall,* 189n.1; Ragatz, *Statistics,* 22; *Parliamentary Papers* (IUP), 2:78; Schumpeter, *English Overseas Trade,* 60–61; Sheridan, *Sugar and Slavery,* 495; W. Young, *Common-Place Book,* 76.

Fig. 3.11. Coffee imports into Britain. *Sources:* "An Account of the Quantity of British Sugar Imported into England between 1772 and 1791," BL, Add. MSS 12,432, fol. 18; Dookhan, "War and Trade," 34; "Imports and Exports," PRO, T 38/269, fols. 1–6; Pares, *War and Trade,* 471; Ragatz, *Fall,* 189n.1; Ragatz, *Statistics,* 22; *Parliamentary Papers* (IUP), 2:73; Schumpeter, *English Overseas Trade,* 60–61; Sheridan, *Sugar and Slavery,* 495; W. Young, *Common-Place Book,* 29.

intended to supplant the trade with Britain. Without the trade the islands' economies would be greatly weakened. Emphasizing the importance of recapturing the American market for rum, Parry wrote: "for want of vent, rum . . . is now a mere Drug upon the hands of the planters, and smuggling from the Dutch Settlements upon the Main, is arisen to such an Height, that they can not sell one third of their rum at home. I need not tell your Lordship, that rum is the ready money of the Planter with which he pays the general expenses of his Plantation."[41]

The discriminatory duties imposed on British West Indian rum entering some American states restricted its sale and spurred the French sugar planters to manufacture rum. Those in St. Domingue, for example, hired expert distillers from Jamaica and began producing rum of a high quality for the American market.[42] Rum production became of such importance in the French colonies that one British West Indian planter jealously complained: "In short we are compelled by the events of War and the rigors of Government to exchange situations with the French; for these materials which they formerly used to throw away, or to vend in an unwrought state, they now manufacture into rum and dispose of more profitably at a price of 2/6 to 2/9 currency per gallon whilst the British Planter, in consequence of the discouragement he labours under will be compelled to discontinue his distillery and to dispose of his raw material as the French did formerly."[43]

Even though rum shipments to Canada increased after 1783, the quantities were small in relation to the production of the islands and did not relieve their problems.[44] Reports in 1784 from Jamaica to absentee planters in England showed that although the price of rum had fallen to 2s 6d per gallon, there were few sales; one letter in March forecast that if the trend continued, most planters would be forced to sell their rum at much lower prices.[45] The glut of rum on the local markets forced down prices to as low as 2s 4d or less per gallon in 1786, and by a further 1d in 1787.[46]

British West Indian exports to British North America were far lower than the loyalists had forecast in their evidence before the Committee of the Privy Council. Sugar imports by these colonies declined quite significantly between 1784 and 1787; rum imports did not show any significant growth given the reduced quantity taken by the Americans. One reason for this rather poor showing was that rum imported into Quebec from Britain was not saddled with a duty, while that from the sugar islands paid a tax as high as 6d per gallon. A comparison of the imports of rum into Quebec in 1786 points up the problem: that province took 138,637 gallons of Jamaica rum, but 207,744 gallons from Britain. The importation for distillation of French molasses at roughly 4d per gallon also reduced the quantity of rum taken from the British Caribbean islands.[47]

Legal imports of British West Indian products into the United States likewise declined. Sugar imports fell from 47,595 hundredweight in 1784 to 19,921 in 1787, while rum imports fell from 2,742,277 gallons in the former year to 1,620,205 gallons in the latter. Table 3.6 offers a comparison of exports of some tropical staples to the United States and British North America in 1770–73 and in 1783–87.

Unlike in the heyday of the political and economic power of the West Indian plantation system, everything seemed to be against the planters' interests, and despite their best efforts they were now unable to influence British policy effectively as they were accustomed to do. Commenting on the operation of imperial commercial policy as it affected the West Indies, John Ehrman writes that "the arrangements were not working well." In 1787 the Committee of Trade therefore resuscitated the old free port system "on a temporary basis and in a limited sense. Listed articles—mostly raw materials, but not imported provisions, sugar or molasses, or exported iron, tobacco or naval stores—could now be carried into specific harbours in four of the British islands by vessels not exceed-

Table 3.6. Exports to the United States and British North America, 1770–73, 1783–87

Year	Cotton (lb)	Rum (gal)	Coffee (cwt)	Cocoa (cwt)	Pimento (lb)	Molasses (cwt)
United States						
1770	65,489	3,250,060	4,031	120,988	34,529	220,450
1771	46,994	2,180,060	2,305	146,837	30,656	101,717
1772	44,456	3,332,750	4,222	126,794	73,530	106,032
1773	39,365	3,049,298	4,097	131,539	91,971	105,432
1783	5,651	679,760	414	55	57,400	63,600
1784	47,595	2,742,271	673	74	169,500	5,800
1785	46,116	2,188,000	1,202	154	54,300	43,800
1786	35,801	1,399,040	1,874	186	16,900	1,800
1787	19,921	1,620,205	3,246	124	6,400	4,200
British North America						
1770	653	38,210	4	200	—	6,418
1771	840	67,588	—	5,500	—	3,078
1772	979	85,715	5	248	3,266	8,935
1773	393	82,505	—	6,352	—	4,296
1783	6,761	564,873	555	136	7,100	135,636
1784	14,744	888,170	454	24	—	54,730
1785	12,214	677,412	786	133	1,000	86,400
1786	18,836	953,743	1,426	79	—	95,260
1787	9,891	874,580	575	81	200	26,300

Sources: "Account of the Number of Ships with Their Tonnage, the Quantity of Produce, Trading to the British Colonies in America and the United States," n.d., *Parliamentary Papers* (HMSO) vol. 84, pt. 4, app. 13, 21; "An Account of the Quantity of British Plantation Produce Imported into America, New foundland, Bahamas and Bermuda," n.d., BL, Add. MSS 38,342, fol. 51; see also Ragatz, *Fall*, 185–86.

Notes: Although Ragatz argues that shipping from Canada to the West Indies increased after 1783, he concludes that shipping costs, as well as the distance of British North America, resulted "in fewer ships and greater charges."

ing seventy tons belonging to the subjects of a European state. The tonnage limit was removed three years later, though the ships had still to be single-deckers; in 1792, the regulations were made permanent, and foreign sugar and coffee were admitted to certain islands; and more ports were added to the list in 1793."[48]

The free ports were extended to ease the plight of the West Indian planters caused by a failed policy and the pressures of the French War, but only some of their demands were met. The extension of the ports also accounts for the significant increase in sugar, rum, and coffee imports by Britain after 1791. The statutes forbidding imports from the foreign islands to the British West Indies were the British government's attempts to close the gaps in its commercial policy,[49] "and the navy and the local courts were told to deal strictly with offenders. But the remedy only nourished another disease." Deprived of a free intercourse with America, the plantation economy never recovered between 1783 and 1787. In addition, "tropical produce was fetching lower prices [on the British markets] as the trade settled down again."[50]

The results of British policy, and of an unprecedented six hurricanes between 1780 and 1786, were frequent and repeated shortages in the sugar islands. The conditions that had existed in the islands during the American Revolution changed very little. The planters were forced to grow provisions, and the colonies were faced with periods of severe scarcity. The aspirations of the British merchants to establish their shipping on a triangular basis were unrealized. British policy did not, in short, achieve its intended results. American produce continued to reach the islands at extremely high prices, but British shipping did not increase to any great extent during the period 1783–87. The West Indian economy did not adjust to the new Atlantic commercial system, and the foundation for its decline was established by this time. The discriminatory duties imposed on West Indian products by the new United States reduced their consumption. The advantages to be derived by the British from a healthy West Indian economy, which were diverse, were lost because of the restrictions on it after 1783. The aim of the British government to bring the Canadian and Caribbean colonies closer together during this period failed, and the sugar islands remained dependent on the United States for their economic survival.

The French and Napoleonic wars handcuffed British commercial policy with regard to the supply of articles of food, such as fish, to the British West Indies. The inability of Canadian merchants to meet the islands' demands for all foodstuffs as allowed by British policy was a constant plaint of most colonists, though at times the merchants involved denied this, with support from some ministers and colonial officials. The level of the shortfall is nowhere more emphatically demonstrated than in the local proclamations, issued by governors normally sympathetic to British preferences, allowing imports from the United States contrary to instructions. On one such occasion Lord Lavington wrote: "the Expectation of the smaller Degree of Supply of Herrings, shads, Mackerel from the British colonies in North America, is a perfectly hopeless speculation, and the most favourable supply of them, which from long uniform Experience can be usually expected from any of the posts of the United Kingdom of Great Britain and Ireland is found to be made too precarious and infinitely too irregular in any respect... to answer the constant and unremitting Demands of the Plantations."[51]

In an effort to shore up British policy and to encourage Canadians to make full use of the preferential trade concessions, some merchants in conjunction with British officials devised a plan to supply the islands with dried fish by initiating a system of bounties.[52] By an order-in-council of 8 March 1806, the British government directed that a bounty in sterling of 2s per quintal be paid on all British North American fish imported into the British West Indies from 1 June 1806; further subsidies would depend on the type of fish (see table 3.7).

To bolster Canada's monopoly exploitation of the sugar islands, the British government ordered the imposition of "a duty on fish imported from the United States of America to countervail any duty which may be payable within those states, on the importation of British fish."[53] Then it called on the governors to include in their recommendations to the assemblies the passage of legislation giving a bounty of a shilling per quintal on all British North American fish. The general perception of this plan was that, although its goal was to force the British West Indian public to support the Canadian fishing industry,[54] the bounty could not bring about the envisioned benefits. As one commentator wrote, "In the reduced state of the British Fisheries the necessary quantities cannot be supplied and the nature and quality of Cod Fish is such as to require great care in the curing of, and great despatch in sending it to Market and even when in the best state of preservation six to twelve weeks is as long as it can be deemed wholesome even for Negroes."[55]

Furthermore, while on the surface the order-in-council allowed importers

Table 3.7. Subsidies on fish

Fish	Subsidy per barrel
Shad	1s 6d
Herring	2s 6d
Mackerel	3s
Salmon	4s

Sources: *Barbados Mercury and Bridgetown Gazette*, n.d., PRO, CO 28/74; see draft letter to Governor Beckwith, 7 May 1807, PRO, CO 260/22.

of fish into the British West Indies to apply to the Treasury for payment of the bounty, in reality the administration had absolutely no intention of honoring such applications except when directed to do so and assured that the colonial treasuries would reimburse such payments. On several occasions, applications for payment of the bounty from agents in England were turned down and the merchants in the colonies were advised to submit their bills to the local authorities.[56]

There was no uniform acceptance of the bounty by West Indian assemblies. The Assembly of Barbados toed the line, passing legislation to grant a bounty of 2s per quintal on salted fish, including cod, imported in British vessels from British North America. In an effort to prevent the merchants from reexporting fish needed to adequately supply the plantations, a fine of 3s per quintal was imposed.[57] The Jamaica Assembly, too, narrowly passed an act awarding a bounty on Canadian fish closely approximating that proposed in the order-in-council, except for dry or salted cod, which was allowed a higher subsidy of 2s 3d per quintal. The masters of ships had to swear on oath its Canadian origin.[58] However, all money paid as subsidies were to be made on fish imported subsequent to the passage of the act. The Assembly bluntly refused to allow payment of £2,000 for an earlier period, "it being a confessed principle ... never to repay any expenditure made by anticipation of its approbation."[59]

In the Leeward Islands most of the assemblies were reluctant to adopt the bounty system, mainly because of the principle it established. Yet in order to guarantee supplies of fish for their slaves, they went along with a plan to repay the Treasury.[60] In the Windward Islands the assemblies were opposed to the bounty because it could raise the price by 50 percent, though it could not improve shipping conditions or the length of the voyage between Canada and the West Indies. Further, they believed, it would lead to a circumvention of the regulations and the total exclusion of United States fish in order to spark the growth of Canadian fisheries.[61] In some assemblies, opposition to continuation of the bounty was heated. When the governor of St. Vincent appealed for its renewal, the members of the House replied that the subsidy was of no benefit to the interests of the colony and they were unconcerned about its fate.[62] Jamaica, while narrowly renewing its vote to maintain the bounty, resolved "that the attempt of his majesty's Ministers to compel the House to grant a bounty on fish of certain descriptions, by prohibiting the importation of fish in ships or vessels belonging to the subjects of any state [not] in Amity with his Majesty's, whilst the necessity of such an intercourse is recognised as oppressive and unconstitutional; and that nothing but this necessity with the protection and care which we owe to ourselves, whose comforts and lives are wantonly hazarded by this regulation, could induce the house to continue the bounty."[63]

The planters were caught in a bind. Procuring supplies from North America was fundamental to the interests of the plantation. Thus, British officials and Canadian fishing interests could now join hands to force the West Indian planters to identify their needs with those of Canada and to see the granting of the bounty as of great importance to the development of the two sets of colonies through the significant benefits to be derived from the trade between them.[64] But in spite of the efforts to develop West Indian reliance on Canada, local interests were not disposed to replace the United States with Canada. They all opposed a countervailing duty on United States fish imports as unconstitutional and because it "would operate as a Discouragement, and eventually deprive us of a continuance of that assistance from which we have already experienced considerable Benefit."[65] One assembly, in refusing to pay the bounty and in rejecting a countervailing duty on United States fish, did so on the grounds that it did not wish to increase the public debt and that market conditions were enough to encourage the Canadian fisheries. Furthermore, there was no reciprocal action where rum was concerned. The development of Canada, they felt, should not be at the expense of the rest of the empire, especially since "the Price of Salt Fish and every other article both from Europe and from America necessary for the cultivation of a West India Plantation is much more than doubled within these fifteen years and that on the other hand the Price of Sugar or rather the Nett Revenue eventually accruing to the Planter after all his labor and Expense have constantly declined and are diminished to one half of what they were."[66]

Forcing the West Indian planters to trade with Canada through the imposition of bounties increased the cost of feeding the slaves at a time when the planters had embarked on a policy of amelioration and therefore had to supply improved quantities of food to their own slaves and also to those whom they were now hiring to carry out the heavy duty of cane-holing. The contractual arrangements demanded that slaves hired for most plantation tasks be subsisted by the employer. Shortages thus delayed cane-planting operations and increased the cost of plantation operation.

Owning slave labour was becoming a losing proposition at the end of the eighteenth century. The conditions under which the West Indies developed are linked to Weber's model for plantation societies. He argues that three conditions had to be present to guarantee profitability: large landholding and cheap food supply, an unrestricted large cheap supply of labour, and high prices for plantation goods. We have seen that, although the land supply was constant, more labour was needed to make it profitable. The food supply was no longer plentiful and cheap after the American Revolution. Now we must examine the state of the sugar market at the end of the eighteenth century.

❧ 4 ❧

The Sugar Market after 1775

B ritish commercial policy had inexorably forced West Indian sugar producers to rely almost totally on British Empire markets for the sale of their products. Prior to the outbreak of the War of American Independence, Britain tended to consume most of the sugar manufactured in the islands and exported there. In fact, one observer wrote that since the period 1733–36 when Britain exported approximately 23,000 hogsheads per annum, this quantity had declined significantly and very little sugar was "re-exported from Great Britain, except to Ireland which is a home consumption," mainly because the French were able to undersell the British sugar producer in Europe by approximately 20 percent. Consequently, the writer lamented, "The French, our greatest Rivals in the Sugar Trade, supply with their sugars all the before-mentioned Foreign Markets [Hamburg, Holland, Flanders, the Baltick and the Mediterranean Seas] that were used to be supplied by the British Subjects, to the Amount of several Hundred thousand Pounds sterling per Annum, whereby their sugar Plantations are arrived to a most flourishing Condition."[1]

Although increased imports made more sugar available for reexportation, as in the case of Ireland, the American colonies offered the most promising market for reexports. For example, in 1775 Britain sent some 15,000 hogsheads of refined sugar to the American continent, which had already taken some 25,000 hogsheads of raw sugar from the islands, for a total consumption of around 40,000 hogsheads.[2] The islands were not allowed to refine sugar. Partially refined sugar (clayed sugar) had exhorbitant rates of duty. Very few reexports went to Europe during the period 1765–81. It was in this latter year that a drawback or bounty was instituted in order to allow West Indian planters to compete with their French counterparts in the European markets.

Throughout the period, less than 20 percent of West Indian sugar imported into England was reexported, with a peak at 19.45 percent in 1775 just before the outbreak of the American War (see table 4.1). It was probably as a result of this poor showing that the British Parliament standardised its drawback or bounty system in 1791 at 15s per hundredweight. This new policy, whereby the drawback effectively offset the duty on raw sugar imported to England, was intended to enable West Indian planters, who were about to lose their American market, to compete more effectively in Europe. The bounty was enacted by 9 & 10 Wm. chap. 23 for the first time. Both the drawback and the bounty changed progressively during the period but maintained the original goal of giving British muscovado and refined sugars advantages over other sugar imports in Europe.

Although reexports of British-grown sugar in the eighteenth century to

Table 4.1. British sugar imports, consumption, and reexports, 1765–81

Year	Imports (hhds)	Consumption (hhds)	Exports (hhds)	Percentage consumed	Percentage exported
1765	95,861	89,539	6,322	93.41	6.59
1766	124,069	114,373	9,696	92.22	7.78
1767	126,046	109,445	16,601	86.83	13.17
1768	132,597	115,244	17,353	86.91	13.09
1769	121,003	106,911	14,092	88.35	11.65
1770	145,822	131,431	14,391	90.13	9.87
1771	118,973	104,577	14,396	87.90	12.10
1772	144,108	130,818	13,290	90.78	9.22
1773	143,569	130,964	12,605	91.22	8.78
1774	163,516	147,855	15,661	90.42	9.58
1775	161,582	130,152	31,430	80.55	19.45
1776	139,065	117,208	21,857	84.28	15.72
1777	111,272	95,031	16,241	85.40	14.60
1778	117,001	104,760	12,241	89.54	10.46
1779	120,107	112,782	7,325	93.90	6.10
1780	109,876	99,316	10,560	90.39	9.61
1781	85,515	—	—	—	—

Sources: "Quantity of West Indian Sugar Imported into England, with That Consumed at Home and Quantity Left for Export," [1781], BL, Add. MSS 12,413, fol. 42; "British Plantation Sugar Imported into and Exported from England," BL, Add. MSS 18,273, fols. 111–12.

Table 4.2. British sugar imports and consumption, 1789–1806

Year	Imports (cwt)	Consumption (cwt)	Percentage consumed
1789	1,936,448	1,547,107	79.89
1790	1,882,106	1,536,232	81.62
1791	1,808,950	1,403,211	77.57
1792	1,980,973	1,361,592	68.73
1793	2,115,308	1,647,097	77.87
1794	2,009,700	1,489,392	74.11
1795	1,672,774	1,336,230	79.88
1796	1,709,219	1,554,062	90.92
1797	1,577,921	1,373,722	87.06
1798	1,963,922	1,476,552	75.18
1799	2,511,858	2,772,438	110.37
1800	2,312,537	1,506,921	65.16
1801	2,902,737	2,773,995	95.56
1802	3,401,711	2,250,311	66.15
1803	2,759,126	1,492,565	54.10
1804	2,968,590	2,144,369	72.24
1805	2,922,255	2,076,113	71.04
1806	3,673,037	2,801,747	76.28

Sources: "An Account of the Quantity of British Sugar Imported into England between 1772 and 1791," BL, Add. MSS 12,432, fol. 18; Dookhan, "War and Trade," 34; "Imports and Exports," PRO, T 38/269, fols. 1–6; Pares, *War and Trade*, 471; Ragatz, *Fall*, 189n.1; Ragatz, *Statistics*, 22; "Report of the Committee on the Trade with the West India Colonies," *Parliamentary Papers* (IUP), 2:73, 75; Schumpeter, *English Overseas Trade*, 60–61; Sheridan, *Sugar and Slavery*, 495; "Sugar Quantities Retained for Home Consumption and Net Revenue," Dalhousie Papers, NAS, GD 47/7/5; W. Young, *Common-Place Book*, 29.

countries on the European continent were never, even with the drawback, a major part of the sugar imported into Britain, reexports kept the British market buoyant and maintained tolerable price levels at home. The French Revolution, however, restricted the reexport markets. Britain also sought to reduce the drawback or bounty allowed on raw and refined sugar sent to the continent, causing significant fluctuation in the percentage of British West Indian sugar available for reexport. Table 4.2 shows British imports from the sugar islands and home consumption from 1789 onwards.

As for rum and other secondary products, the British market never guaranteed their full consumption, and producers and manufacturers depended to a large extent on the thriving markets of the American colonies. But problems were to arise in both markets, as the independence of the United States led to its exclusion from the colonial trade by the British imposition of its monopolistic commercial policy, and the war in Europe restricted British trade to that continent. Unfortunately, through no fault of their own, the West Indian sugar planters were caught in a web spun from contradicting philosophies. On the one hand, influential interest groups in England were supporting free trade; on the other hand, equally important voices were demanding the maintenance of the monopoly system in United States–West Indian commerce.

Production levels are almost inherently controlled by market demands in any capitalist system. In fact, the market is the cornerstone of capitalist production, and is essential to the emergence, development, and expansion of an economy. In the West Indies, the sugar industry emerged out of the guaranteed markets for sugar that were created in Britain and the American colonies by several legislative measures. The growth of the colonial system regulated by British commercial policy also created, at least in the thinking of the sugar planters, an ideological compact by which West Indian merchants and planters became almost totally dependent on the British market. When the newborn United States was debarred from colonial markets, and the islands lost the most important pillar of the sugar economy, planters rightly looked to Britain to fill the vacuum created by its exclusionist policy. Unfortunately, Britain was unable or, more probably, unwilling to remain the guaranteed outlet for British West Indian sugar. Her own economic problems had created an unstable market for all West Indian products. Prices declined, and sugar production remained flat for a decade and a half after the return of peace in 1783, increasing only in 1799, when more than 2,500,000 hundredweight were exported to Britain.

This chapter seeks to establish that the failure of the British market to consume West Indian products to the same extent as in the years prior to the American Revolution caused decline in the colonies' economy. There emerged severe crises in the 1790s, and even the destruction of the St. Domingue economy did not bring any significant revival, much less expansion, until almost the end of the nineteenth century. By then the die was cast; the clamour for cheap sugar to meet the needs of the British working class had been heeded; prices fell to levels that were unprofitable; influenced by its own sugar interest, the British government took steps to destabilize the West Indian sugar industry. At this time English merchants were virtually excluded from the sugar trade in Europe, reexports were minimal, and stocks piled up in British warehouses. Overproduction coupled with underconsumption, which both had the effect of overstocking the market, provided Britain with the rationale for destroying the slave trade.

Peace between Britain and the United States brought with it grave concern for West Indian sugar planters, who were quite aware that significant changes were at hand. They may not have forecast the exclusion of the Americans and the prohibition of many of their products from British West Indian markets, but they certainly could foresee the further decline of their businesses. Simon Taylor had repeatedly expressed to his brother his fears about investing any more capital in West Indian estates. He preferred to invest in England where he would have been guaranteed an income. The American War had clearly highlighted several fundamental weaknesses in the basically monocultural economy tied so inextricably to slave labour.

Prospects for the sale of West Indian products on the British market seemed to be a problem from as early as 1781, even before the conclusion of the fighting, as the declining ability of the British to consume these products brought declining prices. In its colonial period, United States consumed the largest portion of the rum produced in the sugar colonies. During the war years, rum exports to Britain hardly made a dent in the production of the colonies. As rum had become a drug, factors were advising their correspondents in the West Indies to reduce their stocks by selling them locally. Hibbert Purrier and Company wrote to Nathaniel Phillips of Jamaica: "Whenever you can get a good price for your Rums in Jamaica, we would always recommend your selling them there, as the price of the Cask & the leakage on the voyage are very great drawbacks when sent to this market."[3]

Another consequence of the American War was reduced sugar production on all the islands. This, coupled with the seizure of homeward-bound merchantmen and the French capture of several sugar islands, caused West Indian sugar exports to Britain to fall by almost a million hundredweight, from 2,021,059 in 1775 to 1,080,848 in 1781. The shortfall led to high prices, which reached 106s per hundredweight in 1782.[4] Of course, this could not have lasted long, and with the end of the war, sugar prices fell quickly. The prospects for future sales at moderately good prices seemed very bleak for high-quality products, and worse for ordinary and dark sugars. One company informed a Jamaican planter that peace "had its natural effects upon the Sugar Market in lowering the Prices considerably so that good sugars are now currently sold for 46s. to 56s. per cwt. Ordinary & brown sugars will not be looked at. When we come to consider what a number of untoward circumstances have this year operated against the Planter we cannot wonder at the great & ruinous fall, and we are under apprehensions that it will not be a short time that can produce any alteration for the better unless the War is renew'd. . . . The greater part of two years' crops have lately been imported into France & no doubt much of their sugar has found its way hither by unjustifiable means. Add to this, the total failure of all kinds of fruit & the very alarming failure of the crops of corn by which the poor have been distressed and consequently the consumption of sugar much hurt."[5]

To compound the failure of the fruit industry, which further reduced consumption of sugar and contributed to the general shortage of money in Britain, Parliament had allowed importation of sugar, the produce of the conquered islands of St. Kitts, Nevis, Montserrat, Dominica, St. Vincent, Grenada, and the Grenadines, as well as Tobago and St. Lucia, from Ostend and other European ports into Britain in neutral vessels before 1 April 1783, upon the payment of British plantation duties.[6] Although the measure had been sought by sugar refiners to relieve them from the adverse conditions they claimed threatened their industry, and was supported by the West India merchants, it did significant harm to West Indian planters. One factor wrote that "the great importation of smuggled sugars from the French Islands through the channel of the captured ones . . . , notwithstanding our general bad crop has over stocked the market and reduced the price so much that all bad sugars will do little more than pay their expences. The times are indeed deplorable ones for the planters."[7]

The return of peace and the recognition of the United States as an independent country raised the important question of whether or not the West Indian planters were to be allowed free access to both the British and the American markets as they had prior to 1775. Of course the British policymakers and planter interests adopted conflicting positions. The former, wedded to their old principles of mercantilism, would not relax that policy to allow the latter a continued access to markets that could consume their secondary products. Thus, as in the later period of the American War, producers were finding it difficult to sell their rum. One manager wrote to his absentee owner that "the vent for rum seems every year to grow less & less"; still he was forced "to make Trial of the London Market with a part." Moreover, there were fears that foreign sugar was being surreptitiously carried to Ireland, reducing that island's ability to take off the overflow on the London market.[8]

This inability to procure secure markets for their exports had a dampening effect on the spirits of the West Indian planters. They continued to watch their incomes dwindle. Virtually no plantations made any profits during this period, although prices rose in the 1780s when repeated hurricanes reduced the sugar exports to Britain. The unprofitability was blamed on the higher duties charged during the American War—and these were now imposed on molasses and rum. To add to the planters' woes, Canada and other colonies were erecting distilleries whose products threatened to compete on the London market with rum from the sugar colonies. Efforts to secure total control of the London market for West Indian rum, by displacing French brandy, were further shattered in 1786 when a newly negotiated commercial treaty between France and Britain reduced the duty on brandy. The Assembly of Jamaica in a petition to the king noted that the treaty threatened the vital rum industry in the colonies, and called for "the reduction of the duty on rum" because West Indian producers were unable to compete with "the distillers of British spirits at market on equal terms and a stagnated sale of rum became the natural consequence."[9]

The consequence of British policy, apart from falling profits and distressed conditions for sugar planters, was a continued call for reduced investment in the economy of the islands. Young ambitious planters who had just embarked on careers in the sugar industry were the only ones who continued to be optimistic about the outcome of their investments. Their more pessimistic relatives, many of whom resided in Britain, held out few such hopes. Edward Fuhr, writing about his brother's chances, wondered if he was not too "sanguine a sugar planter" since "[i]t requires large sums to establish sugar Works & ought to be considered very maturely by People of small capital." Edward believed that conditions had to continue as favourable as they were for another year or so if disaster were not to befall him: "The prices at which sugars are now selling will in some measure compensate for the short crop & if Please God you get a good year in 1787 there will be no cause of complaint. The low price of Teas in this country certainly assists the sugars, the consumption of which is increasing daily in Europe."[10]

Certainly high sugar prices would not be allowed to continue for any length of time. The British refiners had given notice on previous occasions that they were the watchdogs of high prices and were prepared to act to reduce them. They were not prepared to allow the planters to make large profits at their expense. When prices were high, the sugar buyers in the outports combined to keep them down. While wishing to maintain the price levels, the planter interests were quite conscious that any intransigence on their part would attract the attention of the government. They certainly wanted to avoid this. Yet the sugar factors were not giving in, and as the buyers also resolved to hold out, there emerged "a temporary contest as usual betwixt buyer & seller, which shall give way." For several months, the planters held their ground while the buyers struggled to reduce the prices. By September 1788 it seemed just a matter of time, as Hibbert, Fuhr & Hibbert noted: "indeed such is the throng of ships in the River that they have not as yet discharged a sufficient quantity to glut the Market."[11]

The stance taken by the planter interests was certainly geared to the preservation of their businesses, yet it hurt them in the long run. The high sugar prices had fatal consequences for the sugar refiners. By the time the market began its downward fall, it was observed that "the Refinery Trade is in a very desponding state & we must now perforce believe, what the sugar Bakers have often told us, that ever since the high Prices of Raw Sugars have forbidden an Export Trade, they have never been able to raise upon the Consumer a price proportionate to what they have paid the planter; but rather than retain large stocks on hand & in hopes of better times have gone on losing money every year. This truth is now evinced by some important failures in this line to more we are told may be look'd for."[12]

The British market was not poised to benefit both planters and sugar refiners at the same time. Throughout the 1780s there was great uncertainty among the planters as to the best markets for their sugar. Those who were accustomed to selling their sugar locally faced innumerable problems, since the Americans were not allowed to take British colonial sugar. But the Americans were procuring large quantities from the foreign islands while the British West Indian planters struggled to find buyers in the colonies. Some estates also sold most of their rum locally, and these faced similar problems. Both sugar and rum had now to be sent to England "to prevent extensive layover for want of a Market." But certain changes were needed to make the rum suitable for British sale, as George Scott, the manager of Duckenfield Hall Estate was told: "What are sent home we desire may be made up strong & even, & tinged to a fine amber colour, all of which is easily done & require nothing but a little care & attention, such generally get a preference here as well as a little extra price."[13]

The standoff between the refining industry and the sugar producers had not come to a satisfactory resolution. In fact, only the fall in prices later in 1788 cooled the atmosphere. The basic claim/charge that the British West Indies produced "dear sugar" remained a major complaint among refiners, sugar bakers, confectioners, even ordinary members of the public. The search had already begun for cheaper sources. Even when the British West Indies were supplied with American lumber and provisions, estimates showed that British plantation sugar was 20 to 30 percent higher than French sugar.[14] The planters offered several plausible reasons. One was the structure of the trade, the monopolistic nature of British commerce. Also, wars and rumours of wars, with their increased duties and other charges, normally raised the price of sugar. Once wartime conditions had passed, the value fell. But after the American War, a number of calamities throughout the islands converged to maintain price levels.[15]

The sugar refiners, however, were resolved to resume the fight for cheaper sugar when the next occasion occurred. The showdown between refiners and planters was not long in coming. The French Revolution had a far-reaching impact on the export of sugar to Europe, and on its production in the French colonies. Revolution broke out in St. Domingue and destroyed the sugar industry there. The future seemed bright for West Indian planters, who began to forecast the return of the glorious days of King Sugar. Prices on the London market were high, ranging from 81s to 84s in January 1792.[16] For a while, it seemed as though excellent prices and great profits would cover up the structural weaknesses of the plantation system. One absentee planter took the opportunity to report to his managers in Jamaica that the British market had been awakened from its protracted slumber, that prices were "better than ever known. Some sugar having sold as high as £4 & rum as high as 5s." He himself, for the best of his sugar, received 76s.[17]

Not all planters could jubilantly announce such high prices for their products; low prices and sales seriously affected some. The sugar buyers were once more refusing to pay. Only rum was being sold readily and, in the opinion of George Turner, West Indian merchant/absentee planter, at a good price of 4s 4d per gallon. Still, Turner informed his manager, "I have not been able to sell Mr. Lawrence Pimento yett, there being no markett. Neither have I sold my sugar . . . as the Markett is now at a stand and its who shall give way—the Merchants or the buyers."[18] The major feature of the British market throughout the 1790s was its fluidity, both in price and in ability to consume the commodities imported.

Sugar prices and sale quantities varied tremendously from lot to lot and from estate to estate. There was no single price, since the quality of the product differed so markedly. Jean Lindsay, writing on the Pennants of Jamaica, pointed out: "Prices varied as much as forty shillings between the highest and lowest .

Table 4.3. Classification and prices of sugar, 1794

Classification	Quality	Price/cwt	Relative price (%)
Fine sugar	Best quality	72s	100
Good colour	Pale colour, little strength	62s	13.89
Middling	Medium strength & colour	55s–56s 6d	21.53–23.61
Strong	Brown	51s	29.17
Dark	Too brown	47–48s	33.33–34.72
Very dark	Brown & moist (too much molasses)	41s	43.06

Source: Fuller to Fuller, 23 August 1794, Dickinson Papers, SomRO, DD/DN 508, fols. 103–46.

. . but each lot of sugar commanded its own price, and on the Penrhyn estates there could be as much as sixteen shillings difference between the highest and the lowest prices."[19]

The price differential is clearly illustrated in table 4.3, which shows that sugar was graded both by colour and by strength (that is, number of granules; buying by sucrose content came only with the twentieth century). Sugars of various qualities varied in price by as much as 31s in this example. Yet they were subject to the same duties and other mercantile charges, such as shipping, freight, insurance, wharfage, commission and brokerage.

Many planters, in spite of disappointments on receiving poor-quality sugars and a poor return, anxiously looked forward to continuing high prices. However, rumblings of dissatisfaction from many quarters about dear West Indian sugar made it obvious to other planters that there would be legislative efforts to reduce prices. George Turner wrote that "from all accounts we have reason to expect a general good crop in all the Islands. Nevertheless, its expected they will sell pretty well this year. But next year its to be all over with the poor planters in the West Indies. Sierra Leone and other parts of Africa, and I suppose from [the East Indies and Mauritius] which is to make it cheaper than ever it was known. But, joking apart, the present people in power seem greatly disposed to forward the growth of Sugar from the East Indies and if pursued the National Purse may do much in aid of the project—which will be kept alive by artfull people here, who to save their own turn will pretend they sell no sugar manufactured by slaves."[20]

With sugar prices on the British market high, the refiners returned to the fray. They attacked the West Indian monopoly and called for lowering duties on foreign sugar from 29s 10d per hundredweight to 18s or 17s. They also proposed the readmission of East India sugar but on the same terms as West Indian sugar, and they demanded the reduction of the drawback and bounty. The British sugar manufacturers once more challenged the promise of good prices and profits for the West Indian planters.

On previous occasions, the contest between planters and refiners had come to a tolerable solution when prices on the British market fell sufficiently to meet partially the demands of the latter. In the last dispute, the matter stopped short of being brought to Parliament. This time, however, legislation was secured to prevent the excessive exportation of sugar. The drawback and bounties, which were very helpful in allowing reexports of sugar to Europe, were adjusted downwards. In 1791 the entire duty was returned on reexports, but with the enactment of 32 Geo. III chap. 43 the drawback would end in July 1792 if the price of sugar exceeded 60s per hundredweight, in October if the prices were higher than 55s, and afterwards if sugar sold for more than 50s. During the suspension of the drawback, West Indian merchants were forbidden to export sugar directly to Europe as allowed by the Act of 1739.[21]

The new policy on the drawback was erratic. By 1796 when the duty reached 17s 6d per hundredweight, the drawback was fixed at 13s 6d. The duty went up in 1798 to 19s 4d, yet the drawback remained unchanged. In the following year, the duty was hiked to 20s per hundredweight but the drawback reduced to 11s. A committee of the Jamaica House of Assembly examined the policy the British government had adopted. Their report concluded that every effort was made to manipulate sugar prices by adjusting the drawback. They argued: "The 41st Geo. III Chap. 44 first fixed the price at 58s as the highest at which the duties should be given back, and established a scale by which a part was to be retained, increasing progressively until the price arrived at 70s when the whole duty is kept.... By the 49th Geo. III Chap. 98, all Customs on sugar were repealed, and a new permanent duty was imposed of 20s 6d and a war duty of 9s 6d including... the contingent duty of 3s. A drawback is given of 22s when the price is below 40s, 21s when it does not exceed 45s, from the last mentioned price to 58s, 20s is to be drawn back; when the price exceeds 58s and does not exceed 60s the drawback is 18s.... [At] 70s ... no part of the duty is restored."[22]

Bounties suffered a similar fate. In 1791 they amounted to 15s per hundredweight for bastards, broken loaves, and powdered sugar, while 26s per hundredweight was awarded on complete single-refined loaves and double-refined sugar. In 1796 the bounties were reduced to 13s 6d and 23s respectively. Three years later, they fell further to 11s and 19s.[23] Upon application of the grocers and refiners, in 1791 a limited quantity of East India sugar was imported into England at a duty of £37 16s 3d per £100 of gross sales. Such high duties met with demands from the East India sugar interest for its importation at British plantation rates. On East India sugar, the duty was levied *ad valorem,* while on West Indian sugar it was paid by the quantity. Hence, as the value of sugar declined, the protection for the latter also decreased. From about 1801, however, the duty on East India sugar was calculated on the same basis as West Indian. In this year the duty on East India sugar was set at 22s per hundredweight, which amounted to a marginal difference of 10 percent and virtually destroyed the preference. But the competition was not seriously felt during the French Revolution because prices were high. Nor had the East India Company developed its sugar industry to the point where it was able to flood the British market to the destruction of British West Indian plantation sugar.[24]

The British policy of admitting East India sugar pleased the sugar refiners and grocers, as expensive West Indian sugar could be replaced by the cheaper Bengal sugar. India also offered a much larger market for consumer goods than the sugar colonies. Furthermore, the act allowed British vessels to import into England foreign-produced sugar and coffee to be warehoused and then reexported without paying duty.[25] All these measures pointed to the ultimate goal of the British government to lessen the preference given to West Indian sugar throughout the seventeenth and eighteenth centuries and thereby to reduce the price by forcing it to compete in its home market.

The impact of the British legislation was not lost on anyone. In Liverpool the mayor called a public meeting of merchants, tradesmen, and townspeople to adopt resolutions demanding their participation in the Indian trade.[26] Those involved in the West Indian trade did not duplicate this support. A deputation of West India merchants and planters, having met with the Chancellor of the Exchequer, presented to Prime Minister William Pitt and Secretary of War Henry Dundas a document charging that Britain, by opening its markets to foreign sugar and coffee suppliers, had broken the compact guaranteeing a mutual monopoly.[27] The agents of the various West Indian colonies also petitioned Pitt, contending that his government's policy had destroyed the two fundamental principles in the relationship between Britain and her colonies. The sugar islands provided exclusive trade and navigation to British ships and seamen. The former was bound to the exclusive supply of Britain by sugar produced in the islands, with a free exportation of surplus to foreign markets. The agents warned that the imposition of East India sugar at such lower duties would ultimately ruin the sugar colonies, without guaranteeing profits to British investors.[28]

Two years after the passage of the act, and the adoption of the policy of destabilizing the sugar industry in the West Indies, the merchants and planters reiterated that it was "the height of Impolicy" on the part of the British government to adopt measures that forced the old sugar planters to compete with areas of "the East Indies which was by no means under the command of Great Britain" and whose sole purpose was the undermining of the West Indian economy since "the comparative duty levied under the present Regulations and mode of collecting upon sugar imported from the East Indies will be found at Current prices of that article inadequate as an encouragement to the British Colonies labouring under Restrictions of Cultivation and Commerce to which our Possessions in the East are not subjected."[29]

These supplications fell on deaf ears. The British government had since the Declaratory Act of 1767 established its right to legislate for the colonies. Most West Indians had accepted this, insofar as trade was concerned. In their communiqué to Pitt and Dundas, the West India planters and merchants drew attention to the compact on which relations between the mother country and the colonies were based: "this compact, the spirit of which completely pervades our colony-laws, was for a mutual monopoly; a decided preference being given, *on each side* in the market of the other, with a complete power vested in the British Legislature, in addition, to regulate the colony-trade for the general benefit."[30]

British ministers may have wondered why all the complaints. After all, they had sought to regulate the British sugar market to preserve its sugar manufacturing industry and to afford its consumers access to cheap sugar. Thomas Plummer in a letter to Sir Joseph Foster Barham notified him of the immediate decline in sugar prices by 4s per hundredweight, and that the merchants had called a meeting. He accurately summed up the outcome of the various protests when he wrote, "but it is to be feared that no circumstances of theirs will occasion an abandonment of this measure.[31]

Opposition to British policy was also expressed in the colonies. The Jamaica House of Assembly was most vociferous. Since the steep rise in prices was not due to any act of the West Indian planters, the House believed that regulation of the market should have been left to capitalist forces and not government interference. The assemblymen opposed "having the nature of their principal staple limited in a mode most unprecedented and unjustifiable, depriving them thereby of the advantages of a rise in foreign markets, which alone could have enabled them to pay off the debts contracted during a long series of public Calamities, without holding forth a compensation in cases of unprofitable crops, and in addition to these heavy grievances, every species of Calumny continues to be sanctioned by some of His Majesty's principal ministers of State to render his Majesty's loyal subjects in the West Indies odious in the eyes of their fellow subjects in Great Britain."[32]

At the beginning of the social upheaval in St. Domingue, the prospect of a buoyant market had gripped the imagination of the sugar planters and rekindled their spirits with the same desires as in the olden days. As we have seen, however, their dreams were shattered by the adoption of British legis-lation whose ultimate goal was the destabilization of the sugar economy, coupled with the inability of the Europeans to consume sugar because of their distressed economy. One report as early as September 1792 noted that "the failure of the crops in Saint Domingue appears not to have had the Effect upon the price in Europe which was expected. The distress of the people in France has I suppose in a great measure put a stop to the consumption of it in that Kingdom. In this, the brown sugars, I mean the coarsest kind of mus-covado, which if the common people found themselves unable to purchase better, would be what one must suppose they would consume, is absolutely unsaleable—nobody would bid anything for it. This kind was generally manu-factured into coarse lumps for exportation but it seems that Branch of the manufacture seems at a stand, and [in] Holland there are no less than 40,000 casks stored in that Country."[33]

Compounding the economic depression and lack of money in most coun-tries, there was a consensus among British West Indian merchants and planters that war in Europe was inevitable. This would reduce further the export market, and would depress the local market in Britain to such an extent that sugar would be virtually unsaleable. Dickinson and Dickinson, absentee planters, wrote to attorney/manager Thomas Shekoo Salmon: "The General opinion here is that we shall have a war with France. We see no good to accrue to this country or her West India Colonies by that Event; but we believe it is unavoidable; the French certainly will, and perhaps the Americans may under French colours fit out great number of Privateers; it will be a War therefore very injurious to our Trade."[34]

The advent of the Anglo-French War indeed had mixed blessings for the sugar industry. Most of the plantation records do not tell of a brisk and thriving market, but report dull market conditions with marked price fluctuations for most of the period. At times the difference between the low and high price was as much as 40s, as the war in Europe seriously affected the British market. The drop could be so precipitous that many sugar factors refrained from giving planters quotations lest the price fall even lower than quoted.

If local British demand could not consume the large quantity of sugar imported, the industry could not make any profits. As Thomas Plummer of the firm Plummer and Barham wrote to Barham, "our only hope respecting an advance in sugar or indeed preserving its present standard is a demand for exportation—but the spread of the French arms on the Continent leaves us far less to expect than last year."[35] The reports for the rest of the year were no better. For example, Rose Fuller, a doctor and MP, wrote in a letter to his brother Stephen Fuller, an agent for Jamaica, "The sugar market is very dull & getting lower everyday, from the largeness of the quantity arrived & the little demand for Home Consumption or exportation:—The general opinion is it will become lower."[36]

Earlier forecasts of a bumper market in Britain for West Indian products with the destruction of the French sugar industry were only partially and temporarily accurate. After an early rise, prices were not sustained at significantly high levels. Managers and planters who were bearing the brunt of the failure of the sugar market in Britain felt that the buyers had misread conditions in the West Indies, where British forces had captured Guadeloupe but could not command the full cooperation of the island's French planters. Thus estate owner and manager Walter Nisbet wrote to the Reverend William Shipley, the absentee owner for the Nevis estate, "The sudden & unexpected fall in the price of Sugars, added to so bad a crop, must be severely felt by most Planters. I am indeed at a loss to assign the Cause—if the price has been reduced, on a supposition that the Market would be loaded with French Sugars, Buyers as well as Sellers, will find themselves equally mistaken; the poor British Planter will be the only sufferer. The fact is that few French sugars have been shipt; nor do I apprehend from the present situation of those Islands, that many Hhds will reach England this year."[37]

Some managers searching for solutions to the unhealthy state of the British market and the resulting decline of the West Indian economy proposed in 1794 that they be allowed to retain a quantity of sugar in the colony until the end of that year in the hope that prices would rise again through regulating the supply. Another recommendation was to open the ports to the North Americans by allowing United States ships to furnish them with goods and to take West Indian products including sugar in exchange. One manager wrote that in his opinion "the most favourable thing that can possibly happen to these colonies would be a general Peace and the American Trade continued."[38]

The practice of allowing United States traders to take sugar for their products was resumed throughout the West Indies, but it did not have the desired effect. The statistical information does not show significant sugar exports to that country. Furthermore, the United States government imposed an embargo on trade with the West Indies in retaliation for the Royal Navy's practice of impressing American seamen and capturing American ships.[39] Even without a large share of British West Indian commodity exports, the United States emerged as the major carrier of tropical products to Europe, flooding that market to the detriment of the British reexport trade and consequent stagnation at home.

British market prospects for West Indian products seemed no better in 1795. In fact, lower prices and sales loomed on the horizon with the expected arrival of large quantities of East Indian sugar. With their whole economic future seemingly doomed, towards the end of 1795 the West Indian merchants pressed for the repeal of the act reducing the drawback and bounty, but the measure remained in force. Conditions continued dull especially for sugar of middling and inferior colour and quality, of which the market was full. Plummer decided to sell Barham's sugar since, as he told him, "there is no prospect of advance at present and contemplating the probable arrival of the second fleet in a few days I have judged it for your interest to continue sales & hope for your approbation."[40]

Briefly in 1797 life was breathed into the market. Reports indicate that it had become brisk, with prices roughly 5s per hundredweight higher than those of the previous year. Most factors took the opportunity to unload some of their sugars warehoused in Britain. Unfortunately, the market could not sustain the sales or prices for the 1797 crop for all the various qualities of sugar produced in the British West Indies. The finest sugar had always commanded very high prices and quick sales, and continued to do so. But by far the largest part of British West Indian sugar fell in the low-to-middling range. As Plummer wrote to Barham, "Our sugar Market has been very steady in point of price since my last advices—but with the exception of a day or two has had little briskness in it. Fine sugars, which are extremely scarce, are enormously high 93/ 94/ and one board last week sold at 95s. Middling & low sugars the market is full of—and I am sorry to remark that your Mesopotamia sugars this year are more brown than usual."[41]

Sales were so poor that many sugar factors had no money to pay the duties on their consignments. When Thomas Plummer fell into this cash-flow problem, Barham accepted two drafts to help him survive for a while longer. After duties were paid up front, the sugars remained unsold for months, sometimes a year, in packed warehouses, with the market in England worsened by the activities of the French in Europe. In 1798, probably for the last time in the period of this study, sales were reported as being brisk for another brief period. Several orders for export had enlivened the London market for about a "week for those first landed." Plummer sold seventy-six hogsheads, of which twenty belonged to Barham, at prices ranging from 80s to 86s per hundredweight. But by the end of 1798, sales had virtually come to a halt, and West Indian sugar once again began piling up in London warehouses.[42]

One of the interesting issues with which an analysis of this period has to deal is whether or not the British market was overstocked. It was Eric Williams in *Capitalism and Slavery* who wrote that "overproduction in 1807 demanded abolition" of the slave trade and that "overproduction in 1833 demanded emancipation." Seymour Drescher contends, to the contrary, that the reexport market was consuming all excess West Indian sugar, and he rejects the claims of overproduction.[43] Interestingly, Williams never had the opportunity to examine the wealth of plantation papers that can help us to resolve the matter; Seymour Drescher had the opportunity but seems never to have read any. In the final analysis, Williams's claim of overproduction seems to be the right conclusion. A careful examination of the plantation papers and their information on the state of the British market shows a vast majority claiming that, for the most part, after 1792 only limited sales were made. The market for West Indian sugar continued to be severely affected by the Napoleonic Wars.[44]

As early as 1796 Thomas Plummer informed Barham of the "dull" state of the market, which was "full" of brown sugar, and we have seen that it remained depressed for the next two years or so. In 1799 conditions worsened, and in August 1799 Plummer returned to the topic: "From the best information I can obtain the sales of sugar do not amount as yet to one half of the import of the Leeward Island fleet—of Jamaica sugar very little has yet been sold—and indeed if the Leeward Island sugar which now occupys the warehouses does not meet more rapid sales, the landing of the Jamaica must be impeded."[45]

Because an extraordinarily large quantity of sugar had arrived in Ireland

from foreign sources, and because demand on the Hamburg market was declining, prices had fallen in both Ireland and Britain.[46] One factor informed his
planter that "the influx of Foreign sugar is a serious injury to the old Colonies—
the Danish sugars are now forced upon the Market by Public sales and our own
remains in consequence without demand."[47] In London the price fell to 52s,
with some sold at 58s.[48] In fact sugar imports had taken a significant rise. The
quantity brought into London rose by 63.5 percent, from 104,877 hundredweight in 1798 to 170,277 in 1799. However, the state of the British market for
sugar was too depressed to allow for any increase in consumption.

A committee of West Indian merchants undertook an investigation into the
state of the British sugar market. The findings were no surprise to anyone. They
asserted that the Americans had flooded the Hamburg market with sugar imported directly from the non-English-speaking Caribbean islands, greatly reducing the foreign demand for British sugar. The situation was compounded by
the removal of the drawback. A restoration of the old drawback system was
requested in some circles to relieve the planters, but it was the Bank of England
that, to bail them out, "agreed to advance to the Holders of West India produce
which will prevent any depreciation of Markets from Their necessitys."[49] The
situation continued without any relief in sight. Some agents resorted to dodg-
ing planter clients because of poor news. "I have deferred writing for some
time," admitted Robert Johnson, "that I might be able to acquaint you with what
is going forward in regard to sales. The uncommon events that have agitated the
sugar market have made it very difficult to do business regularly."[50]

Even a restoration of the drawback and bounty was not expected to have
any immediate impact in generating reexports. Plummer wrote that "the large
quality is so much against an advance that even should a demand for Export
present itself—which from the great quantity at Hamburg is not expected &
from the numerous failures we should be at a loss who to trust till the present
Commercial disrangement is subsided." By the end of November 1799, prices
had dropped to 46s 6d per hundredweight—less than the production and
marketing costs. With lower prices, a stagnated market, and full warehouses,
the British government enacted legislation to allow distillers to use sugar in
their business. This raised hopes among the planters and merchants that the
distillers would take a large quantity of brown sugar out of the market and
thus rejuvenate it. The experiment achieved partial success, but by 1800 an
estimated 76,000 hogsheads remained unsold, with that year's crop yet to
arrive in England.[51]

The piling up of sugar continued in the warehouses in England and Scotland. In London alone, the quantity stored had reached 100,000 hogsheads by the spring of 1801 and was sufficient to meet that year's demand. Compounding the problem were the increased imports from Demerara and Surinam, which, according to one opinion, had "sadly interfered with those from Jamaica."[52] West Indian planters were caught at the centre of a struggle for control of the sugar industry. Their notions of their rights to the British market based on an outdated compact served them ill. By the turn of the nineteenth century, British West Indian planters were being asked to operate in an emerging free market economy where capitalist modes of production dictated the prices of their commodities. Unprepared, they found themselves forced to unload their sugar below cost in order to recoup something.[53]

By 1802 there was no improvement to the London sugar market, which continued to be overstocked. Though the distillers had brought a measure of relief, most sugar agents were looking to peace to put the British market on the road to recovery. Plummer wrote to Barham: "We are looking for large orders from France to follow the signature of the definitive Treaty but the quantity on hand is larger than any probable demand—Without such orders I fear we shall not maintain the prices now current. There was 84,000 hhds left at Xmas—about 20,000 fine but the two fleets from Jamaica and the Leeward Islands being arrived 20,000 more so that we have in London four score Thousand hhds of old sugars—and in consequence of Peace new sugars are expected in May."[54]

Overproduction worldwide and underconsumption in Britain continued to be a source of worry. Whole cargoes remained unsold, and talk of the imminent renewal of grain distillation heightened the fears of West Indian planters and their agents. The expected treaty raised hopes in some quarters; in others the sugar factors were more pessimistic. In this latter mood Davidson and Graham told Lord Penrhyn: "The unlucky rumour of Peace has withheld orders for sugar from the continent, & has so impressed People in this country with an idea that such an Event maybe in agitation—that our prospect at present is rather gloomy & shows us so strongly the slender foundation upon which the market is supported. Thus situated, we honestly confess to your Lordship that our cash is not over abundant, & if you can conveniently relieve us from the payment of £5400 due the 30th March, it will be an accommodation to us."[55]

Peace did not spark the market into any lively activity. The history of the sugar trade shows that it never does. It was nevertheless a short-lived affair, and preparations for war were under way even before the ink on the treaty had dried.

High expectations were pinned on these new hostilities; the most hopeful were the sugar traders.[56] But the market remained dull for most of 1803, with no export or home sales because of yet another dispute "between the Buyers and Sellers as to Taxes."[57] It was not until shortly before Christmas that the market took an upturn, and as on previous occasions this was brief. Reports for 1804 indicate that, while that year's hurricane in the West Indies boosted the market for a few days, it quickly returned to its former state when for weeks no sugar could be sold.[58]

Probably as a result of the stimulus to sugar production caused by the early high prices and of course the destruction of the French sugar industry, larger quantities began reaching Britain from the West Indies after 1798. These were significantly higher than in any previous year in the last quarter of the eighteenth century. With sugar from the captured islands and other areas in the Caribbean, from India, Mauritius, and Java, and from countries such as Brazil, unusually large quantities of sugar poured into England. "Together with the decline in the English markets" and the lack of exports of manufactured goods, they converged to restrict the sale of West Indian goods.[59]

While sugar was the core product of the British West Indies economy, for profitability the other plantation activities—penns (cattle estates in Jamaica), pimento walks—were relevant and at times of major importance. So it is important to examine the British market in relationship to the consumption of other crops. The role of rum in the eighteenth- and early-nineteenth-century West Indian plantation economy is little understood, but its sale was vital to the system's survival. All the islands produced their independent brands of rum, and they sold to different markets. For most of the eighteenth century, Britain was the principal outlet for Jamaican rum, while the other islands serviced the American market.[60] The loss of the American trade thus called for larger exports to Britain.

Even the American Revolution did not completely halt trade between the islands and the rebels. Rum sales in the West Indies also seem to have been more profitable than if that item were taken to London. So planters continued recommending the sale of rum locally when prices were good.[61] Only the rum that could not be sold to the North Americans was to be sent to England, and it was to be specially distilled "strong & even, & tinged to a fine colour."[62]

As Britain tightened its exclusionist policy against the United States trade in colonial markets, some states retaliated with discriminatory measures of their own. With less and less British West Indian rum being imported into the United

States, rum from all the British islands now had to depend on the British market.[63] Initially, with rebellion erupting in St. Domingue, the London market responded to the rum trade in almost the same way as to sugar. Prices for rum reached as much as 4s 4d per gallon, to the gratification of the planters. However, they then followed the same downward trend, ranging between 2s 6d and 3s 6d by July 1797. The market could not consume the quantity available, and prices declined further as stocks piled up in warehouses. The majority sold for 2s 4d per gallon; only the finest quality fetched the higher price of 3s.[64]

While the British market was performing badly for rum, some West Indian markets were not. Rum prices in the Leeward Islands escalated to 6s in 1795 and 7s in 1799. Yet these good prices did not guarantee the planters any security, because rum could "not command either Cash or Bills of Exchange. The fact that owing to the Restriction on the American trade previous to the War, they got into the habit of distilling molasses & Corn Spirits which, with large quantities of Gin and Brandy they imported, almost drove our Rum out of their Market; & whenever that happens it is very difficult to regain it."[65]

The statistics on rum sales to the United States clearly indicate that British policy had effectively lost the United States market for West Indian rum. The British and Irish markets were overstocked, and prices were "much lower than it would be advisable to sell the rums."[66] Then the British government imposed an additional duty on rum in 1803 to help pay the cost of the war, virtually destroying an already tenuous market. As Plummer wrote to Barham, "Mr. Addington has put a most complete extinguisher on the Rum Market by his heavy additional duty—not a puncheon can be sold and unless a navy contract relieves us ... this article will remain on hand. The public cannot afford to drink Rum at a Guinea per Gallon."[67]

By 1807, conditions in the West Indies had become extremely precarious. Much of their rum had no market. Britain had never consumed more than a small part, and the main market, the United States, had established its own distilling industry as well as purchasing from other supply centres. Managers, in spite of their reluctance, were forced to draw bills on their planters in England to make up the deficit from rum sales and pay the contingencies of their estates.[68] The traditional role of rum in the economy of the plantations could not be maintained during the period of this study, given the insecurity of the markets. Merchants dealing in West Indian commodities had grown weary of taking risks, as one wrote with regard to West Indian managers drawing bills on his agency: "We undoubtedly agree in the propriety of your wish to have as few Bills drawn for as possible for reasons which must be obvious. The difficulties at present of selling the rum in the Country is great, but if every Estate follows the same plan of sending to England, little can be expected from it; we should therefore think it advisable to recommend putting off drawing as much as possible & if interest must be paid for a short time, it would show an unwillingness which might check the attorneys' readiness to draw upon all occasions; some estates have thought it well to abide by the first loss & sell their rum for what it would fetch in the islands."[69]

More critical was that the influx of foreign and other sugar into Britain and Ireland had a devastating impact on sales, which in turn led to a drastic reduction in prices. One writer, assessing the relation between rising West Indian sugar prices, the slave rebellion and destruction of the sugar industry in St. Domingue, and the passage of the Sugar Act of 1792, pointed out to Lord Hawkesbury that there was absolutely no justification for attempting to reduce the prices of West Indian commodities by legislative means. Market conditions had caused the rise, which matched the general growth in all prices and costs of services in England, and in North America. In his opinion, the government's action was political, aimed at satisfying the demands of sugar refiners and buyers: "the temper of the public mind respecting the high price of sugars might make it politic in his Majesty's Ministers to pass the bill in question; the price of that commodity has not risen more in proportion than that of meat, butter, cheese and a variety of other articles of the first necessity. The freight of all heavy Articles from England to the Islands has been very considerably augmented and the North American produce is twice as high as it used to be."[70]

There were no runaway sugar prices at either the lowest or the highest levels. I have already shown that the price was not dependent on the supply factor alone, but more on the quality, and West Indian sugar faced a major crisis at this time. Most exports were classified "middling and brown" or lower, being too strong and too dark. A contributory factor seems to have been the introduction of the Otaheite cane, which had two major negative features: it produced more sugar per acre (thus reducing prices in Britain), and the quality was inferior. It is therefore important to understand that only those sugar estates that maintained a high quality during the period received consistently high prices. This was particularly true of Amity Hall, belonging to Henry Goulburn. Quotations for his sugar ranged during 1798 between 76s and 120s per hundredweight when the lowest price on the London market was 59s and the highest reached only 83s.

This shows the fluidity of prices on the market and how they were linked to quality.

It is also important to observe that the prices quoted for sugar in the plantation records diverge to some extent from those quoted in many published sources. Furthermore, even if sugar prices seemed high at the end of the eighteenth century, to the planters and merchants they were hardly high enough to match the rising costs of production and marketing, as well as the interest on borrowed capital, and still provide them with annual incomes.

An assessment of published prices shows that they rose significantly overall in 1792 above the previous year's. The advance at the lower level in 1792 was only 2 percent; at the highest it was 17 percent over the 1791 prices. From then until 1795, prices fluctuated but never regained the levels of 1792. Again, there was uneven growth in prices from 1796 through 1799. During this period, the lowest price went as high as 61s and the highest to 87s. Most estate records indicate that the turning point when overall prices of West Indian sugar fell consistently was 1800. For most of the period 1800–1807, they were lower than during the War of American Independence.

Sugar prices taken from the plantation papers seem higher. In some cases, the prices varied markedly as quality came into focus. Published sources tended to standardise the quotations. Estate prices depended on the commitment of factors who were prepared to wait for the best prices. After 1800, prices for sugar remained relatively low at both ends of the scale, hardly rising above 75s per hundredweight. By 1807, planters were happy to get almost anything; the 45s per hundredweight that Penrhyn received for his sugar was considered an excellent price in view of the fact "that sugars don't sell so very well."[71] Sugars now had to be of the highest quality in both colour and density. Davidson and Graham pointed out to Lord Penrhyn: "We regret to observe also, that these sugars are of very light weights—they will not neat above 12 cwt. per Cask, nor will they produce £7 per hhd."[72]

The lack of sales for West Indian sugar and rum continued right down to the abolition of the slave trade and afterwards. There were many who blamed the conditions of the British market and the state of the West Indian sugar industry on politics. In 1805 one writer reported that "the transaction of the political world has caused a total stagnation in the sugar market."[73] The situation was indeed calamitous. There were business failures throughout England and Scotland.

In addition, the West Indian sugar interest was facing a "universal distress for money" caused by political decisions that placed "the commerce of the country ... in a state unprecedented hitherto, threatens the existence of manufacturers & Mercantile Houses so generally, that confidence is almost annihilated with the Bank & Bankers, and accommodation in money matters ... is nearly vanished." The writers, Davidson and Graham, recommended that the practice of drawing bills on commodity shipments be terminated because there was no guarantee that agencies could recoup their advances for sales, given the dullness of the British market. This they viewed as "a principle" that was "extremely critical to ... credit."[74]

Throughout the period, the West Indian economy became the target for high taxation. Additional duties were repeatedly placed on sugar between 1791 and 1806, when they reached 27s per hundredweight. One manager quipped: "if their duties are to be continued, they will be a prohibition to sugar making. The planters had better give up their Estates to government for in fact they are getting no compensation for their labor." British taxation was another of the destabilizing measures that formed the policy to weaken the West Indian plantation. This overall view was not lost on some managers and planters. One fittingly summed up in 1807 the state of the West Indies when dejectedly he wrote: "It is too late now for the ministers to do something in the rum & sugar market. We have been apprised on all sides. We have become the Martyrs of oppressive taxation. When they had in their power to take off our brown sugars in the distilleries, they were encouraging of grain from other countries that were immediately under the control of our enemy; our Rums were a mere drug in the markets, not paying as scarcely the expences of the Distilleries that are annually incurred for carrying on the process. These circumstances did not require a very slight glance to discover that we were labouring under heavy misfortunes, but to all of which they were callous."[75]

Several fundamental unquestionable observations can be gleaned from an assessment of the British market for West Indian products in the period 1775 to 1807. It could not consume the increased quantity of products that reached it, and prices were therefore quite low. When increased imports from the West Indies were added to those from other areas, the supply had certainly exceeded the demand. There was also hardly any likelihood of increasing local demand in British and Irish markets without regaining and increasing the export trade. However, the North Americans, at prices the West Indian islands could not match without destroying the sugar industry, adequately supplied the important European markets. The removal of the drawback and bounty that had served the export trade so well made West Indian sugar uncompetitive, and it would have required excessively large subsidies to return colonial sugar to its former competitiveness. This would have maintained West Indian monopoly beyond the point to which the British government was prepared to go.

Some relief leading to a growth in home consumption was expected from the introduction of sugar into the distilleries, but this was a temporary measure whose effectiveness depended on increased exports. The steps taken by the British government were perceived as having only a limited effect in stimulating the market, as Barham noted: "The distilleries may perhaps take off 10,000 hhds & the breweries (if these points can be carried) a little more but what is this to the immense glut in the market, which is now supplied by East India sugar (chiefly from Java) imported by the Americans to which I am told is added a large increase of produce from Cuba."[76]

Prices were also affected by the declining quality of West Indian sugar with the introduction of the Otaheite cane. The new cane helped to overstock the British market, and it brought no gain to the planters since the inferior musco-vado it produced brought poor prices. All the evidence I have found indicates that the British market was overstocked with sugar by the end of the eighteenth century. One estimate placed West Indian production alone as exceeding "the home consumption by one third."[77] Overproduction had certainly led to re-duced prices, and again claims that sugar prices were markedly high after 1791 are certainly inaccurate. There were times when prices were high, but these were overshadowed by the many more times when they were low and by the insecu-rity of the market. During the period, because of the failure of the British market and the understandably low prices there, compounded by high duties and the substantial reduction in the drawback and bounty, West Indian sugar proprietors were losing money, and losing heavily. The die was cast, and the complexity of the fluctuating economic conditions put the islands in a contin-ued state of decline.

~ 5 ~

Debt, Decline, and the Sugar Industry, 1775–1810

O ver the last years of the twentieth century, it has become fashionable to talk about a debt crisis, a crisis with which most Third World countries—including the Caribbean—are faced. The obvious question that arises is, Why have these countries, which were hubs of trade in the seventeenth and eighteenth century, descended into virtually impoverished areas? They remain tied to international lending agencies such as the International Monetary Fund, the World Bank, and the Inter-American Development Bank. This work is an attempt to examine the reasons why West Indian plantations, which were major sources of capital for the economic development of Britain throughout the seventeenth and most of the eighteenth century,[1] came to be seriously indebted to British merchants at the end of the eighteenth century.

To understand the factors that gave rise to debt, one must fully understand the nature of the plantation system. It then becomes apparent that the major cause of debt lay in the West Indian economic system itself.[2] Not only were the colonies allowed to develop monocultural economies; these were strictly controlled by the Navigation Acts which channelled the trade in commodities and all financial arrangements into a bilateral system favouring the mother country. The acts required all colonial goods to be shipped in British vessels directly to Britain. They also protected merchant-creditors trading to the colonies and made it difficult for colonials to tap alternative sources of capital and credit. One minor amendment in 1773 permitted foreigners to lend capital to planters on the security of their West Indian estates.[3] But it was hardly likely that many foreigners or West Indians made use of this measure, because by that time most plantations were committed to credit and trade connections that could not be easily changed.

In spite of the benefits to be gained from many of these regulations, the West Indian planters were dissatisfied with the emergence of a British sugar cartel that controlled prices on the London market.[4] They also perceived the commercial system as one in which British creditors, because of their monopoly, were able to extort undue profits from the islands. The lenders of course felt that, as the operation of the West Indian plantations called for large inputs of capital, those who invested their money were entitled to a fair return.

The source of capital used in the development of the sugar industry has been a bone of contention among some historians. Sheridan writes that the Dutch and a group of wealthy London merchants were instrumental in setting up the sugar plantations. He contends that some immigrant capital was also invested in the embryonic stage but, although this was important, the initial capital came mainly from the merchant class interested in trade with the islands.[5]

Pares's earlier view credits the West Indian planters with a greater role in the formation of the plantation system. They were, he contends, the chief source of the vast sums of money invested in its development at all stages:

> The money came in the last resort from the planters themselves. The factors charged them high interest, even, on occasion, compound interest. They paid it to themselves on the planter's behalf, without any order from him, and they made sure of having it, whoever else went short. The money which was received from one planter was lent again, either to him or to another planter. . . . Thus, it was the planter who was paying, so to speak, for his own enslavement. The profits of the plantation were the source which fed the indebtedness charged upon the plantations themselves. In this sense Adam Smith was wrong; the wealth of the British West Indies did not all proceed from the mother country: after some initial loans in the earliest period which merely primed the pump, the wealth of the West Indies was created out of the profits of the West Indies themselves, and, with some assistance from the British taxpayer, much of it found a permanent home in Great Britain.[6]

The structure and functions of West Indian plantations called for a high level of capital investment and, as a corollary, a high rate of capital depreciation. But capital investment was long-term debt bearing 6 percent interest annually and was normally held by mortgage, which in many instances could not be repaid.

It was believed that heavy capital input led ultimately to a lower unit cost of production. The purchase price of an average-sized plantation of about 300 acres in 1773 exceeded £14,000. This included the acreage, enslaved labour, mules and steers, mill, dwellings, hothouses, corn houses, other buildings and offices, and implements and utensils for packaging and shipping sugar. The largest single item was the enslaved workers.[7] Edward Long estimates that such an estate would have cost more than £19,500 in 1775.[8] Queenhithe Estate in the parish of St. Ann, Jamaica, which consisted of 1,284 acres worked by 125 Africans, was valued at £35,009. The cost of the workers alone amounted to £8,750, or a quarter of the total cost.[9]

A sugar plantation was indeed a form of enslavement. Once it was established, the owner lived in the hope of recovering his investment with every crop. Even when the crop failed repeatedly, the planter continued in hopeful expectation, and the commitment tied the planters' hands. The case of Rooke Clarke is an interesting example. After spending a large sum on his estate, he wrote to his brothers: "But as I have gone through this far in the Grand attempt it must not now be given up or let go back for want of a little support this would be certain ruin."[10] Therefore, instead of abandoning the estates, the planters and their attorneys continued to draw bills of exchange or to increase the deficits in their accounts current, and to sink further and further into debt, believing that the sugar crop would "come right" and everything would be well again.

"Accounts current" began initially as short-term debts and were normally established for recording the sale of West Indian commodities to offset the purchase of British goods and services. These were held by merchants or factors, locally and in Britain. As the islands declined, they were not readily paid off, as earlier, but grew into large sums, which were transferred into mortgages. As the planters became more indebted, it became increasingly difficult to raise money either locally or from factors in Britain, as Clarke pointed out: "Raising moneys . . . brings a great loss with Fatigue & Expence in frequent journeys to and from Town. What I am not equal to. As the price of produce have been could I have shipt & drawn it would have been a great saving. A bad crop . . . puts me past paying any part of my Debt to my Friend, Mr. Da Costa who I owe £600 to. He with a Doctor Barretto the Jew physician as good a character as ever lived having loaned me money without a penny advantage nay for three or five months without interest. I am bound to pay him & Da Costa from Capital. . . . my Debts here are within two thousand pounds, had my sugar crop been as usual I should not have owed £500. . . . Disappointments in crops [are] with my Thoughts & Mind dayly."[11]

These disappointments were certainly an element of life in the West Indian plantation economy in the late eighteenth century. Throughout his lifetime, Rooke Clarke wrote optimistically of retiring his debt, which stood at £19,997 sterling in 1789.[12] The performance of the estate had not improved in sixteen years, and in 1791 conditions were very much as previously, as evidenced by a letter written by his widow, Mary: "at present, the sugar crop falls short of their expectations. The pimento is at present promising, but is so uncertain an article to make a dependence upon. . . . I do not wish to stay if they would make me a present of the best estate on this island."[13]

Many other encumbrances remained millstones around the necks of the estates years after the original planter or merchant-investor had died. These included the extravagant lifestyles of some owners, or of their children. For example, while Rooke Clarke agonised over the debts owed by his estate, his daughter ran up her own debt, which he had to retire. He wrote: "I am very uneasy not making Mr. Grayes a payment and have at a venture drawn for £30 sterling—pimento to overpay which & a like sum may [be] drawn for in favour Mr. Best is in hand to ship on first vessel with some coffee to pay whatever debt may appear against Nance. She having 16 pairs of shoes in so short a time. Some are I hope for her mother who has only one pair and them ½ worn."[14]

Besides individual instances of extravagance, excessive annuities appear repeatedly as reasons for planter indebtedness. Mount Alexander Estate in Grenada, owned by Dr. Alexander Wilson, had annuities totalling £1,979.[15] These pushed the estate further into debt, as did high interest and the costs of absenteeism, including persistent mismanagement. However, these factors do not always account for the growth of West Indian indebtedness towards the end of the eighteenth century.

Establishing a plantation called for a heavy outlay of capital for unskilled slave labour and equipment. Africans and their descendants alone accounted for a quarter, in some cases as much as 40 percent, of the total expenditure. Fixed capital items for the sugar works and distilleries including the mills, coppers, buildings, and other equipment cost from 20 to 30 percent. The investment in land and its preparation for cane cultivation was estimated at from 30 to 45 percent. Finally the livestock, mainly cattle, horses, and mules, accounted for 5 to 15 percent of the total investment.

Both the "animate and inanimate" objects on a West Indian plantation were subject to inordinately high levels of "wear and tear" and had to be replaced at high cost. The replacement of slaves who died or who were too old to do field labour was among the heaviest annual charges, exceeding 5 percent in some islands.[16] In addition, climatic and weather conditions, along with heavy usage and the constant heat to the coppers, severely damaged the utensils and implements. The use of wood as a fuel for boiling sugar contributed to the destruction of the coppers, as the intense concentration of heat burned holes in these vessels.[17] Towards the end of the century, iron boilers replaced them, but they too corroded and were destroyed. Since most of the buildings were constructed of imported lumber, the wood was particularly susceptible to termite infestation and had to be replaced regularly. And frequent natural disasters took a heavy toll on the buildings, animals, and enslaved population.[18]

Under normal conditions, these repeated costs were part of the annual contingencies, which were paid from the sale of rum and other secondary crops. There was also a group of late investors in whom the sugar industry still raised hopes of making profits. For example, Rooke Clarke undertook on Queenhithe Estate extensive repairs to the buildings, and he purchased utensils and other equipment in the early 1770s when plantation life was still full of optimistic investors. He apparently belonged to a group of latecomers to the sugar industry, men who ventured into the planting business believing that they could make it pay. Yet he was startled by the high costs and wrote to his brothers: "I could not have thought the Buildings etc. so heavy of Expensive as I find they be. I send you particulars of the Masons works in the Buildings. Due to heavy costs, it may be wise to sell the property on his death. Besides the money out of my pocket to Workmen & for Utensils as Coppers or rather Iron Boilers, Mills, Mill cases, Tyler Bricks, Nails, Locks, Hinges. Cash which without charges of Workmen is full £1500 sterling there is to be added the labour of my Negroes. Self and three or four white people on Wages, getting Timber for my Buildings & planting canes."[19]

The estate debt was never paid off before Clarke's death. When George Turner assumed the management of the estate in the late 1780s, Mary Clarke observed: "I hope Mr. Turner will be well pay'd for his trouble in time, hear is a fine Property, but their are heavy debts. . . . if please God to bless him with Health for a few years will make all his own free of debts."[20] But what with termites and weather and misuse, the annual charges for supplies were a heavy drain on the estates, as Rooke Clarke had noted: "My supplys the coming year wanting a new sugar mill must be had with a great additional supply of tools.

Oznaburgh Rolls, Herrings, etc. having Cumings Negroes With linen wanted for House Use and Wearing apparel for Mrs. Clarke & myself who are indiscreetly bear as is the House."[21]

Numerous other charges that had to be met out of working capital, especially late in the eighteenth century, added to the impoverishment of the planter class. These included the care of sick slaves; the wages of white overseers, coopers, ploughmen, blacksmiths, and other artisans; and commissions ranging from 6 to 7 percent to their attorneys. Then there were the ancillary expenses such as quitrents, taxes on the slaves and houses, and customs duties. In the Leeward Islands and Barbados, a 4½ percent duty imposed further grave financial burden on the planters at the end of the century.

Perhaps the most debilitating annual expense, which sent planter debts escalating, was that incurred in purchasing new captive Africans. Though the planters felt compelled to own their labour force, it is not clear from their accounts or other records whether or not they maintained a clear-cut long-term evaluation of their labour needs and how slave purchases were to be made, based on their financial position and crop prospects. There is ample evidence in the correspondence that planters did not include this expenditure as a recurrent item in their budgets. In fact, it is clear that new captives were purchased quite irregularly for most of the period, and had "a direct but lagged relationship to changes" in planters' "gross receipts from sugar shipments to England."[22]

Generally, the cost of new Africans appears more as an emergency outlay of capital: bills were drawn on merchants and factors or, in a majority of cases, new Africans were purchased from the proceeds of the previous year's rum sales. "Yet every normal plantation needed new slaves all the time; for slaves could not be treated merely as an investment of capital which would enlarge the scale or increase the intensity of production; this investment was subject to a terrible depreciation allowance for the slave population did not maintain itself."[23]

From the beginning of slavery in the British West Indies, planters purchased their slaves on credit from the Company of Royal Adventurers Trading to Africa, which by 1665 was in severe financial difficulties because it owed some £100,000 to its English creditors. Much of this vast debt was money owed by West Indian planters. When the Royal African Company entered into the slave trade, it assumed only some of the debts. As the slave trade developed, the planters contracted additional debts for the purchase of new Africans on four or six months' credit or more, as they struggled to maintain their workforce. In addition, the planters owed permanent debts, which they were either unwilling or unable to pay when they fell due. "The total debt owing to the Royal African Company from the West Indies was put at £120,000 in 1680, £136,000 in 1684 and £170,000 in 1690."[24]

Most of this large debt was created because slavery itself led to a high level of expectation during the "golden years" of the British West Indian sugar industry. During these years, planters were always "over-sanguine." Optimism was the hallmark of West Indian agriculture. Every succeeding crop was expected to surpass the previous one, and to arrive at an improved market. This is quite clear in John Shickle's letters to John Pennant. Just before the 1773 sugar crop, Shickle estimated production at 400 to 450 hogsheads from 120 acres in new canes and 350 in ratoons. Two years later, the production of Pennant's estates was estimated to be in the vicinity of 1,000 hogsheads, and Shickle made this evaluation: "Estates are reckoned more valuable than they used to be. It is plain that lands is dearer, Negroes & Stock Double & in course makes the Estates of more value." The reality fell short of Shickle's projections, and in September 1776 he wrote to John Pennant: "The *Olivia* comes with the convoy & brings the last of your bad crops as at foot & the next I wish may not be worse. I don't expect to make 100 hhds at Denbigh next crop & the Mountains is all bad. . . . I wish for better times and seasons."[25]

The problem of indebtedness in the West Indian plantation system resulted from the belief of planters that they should own their labour force. It soon became overworked and undernourished, and as it was initially male-oriented, it failed to increase by natural means and shrank by 1.5 to 3 percent annually, in spite of some births on the estates. Throughout the early years of slavery the planters thus amassed a mountain of debts, which "were never entirely reduced but were increased."[26] In the beginning of the sugar industry, planters could support such practices. But as time went on and commodity prices went down, the planters had to forego some of their earlier liberality. By the late eighteenth century they were embarking on measures to ameliorate the conditions of their slaves and so increase the population by natural means.

At this point, however, a series of events occurred that frustrated their plans. The first, which spelled disaster and greatly added to the planters' indebtedness, was the American War of Independence, which was the most severe blow of the century to the economy of the British West Indies. Indeed it marked the watershed in the history of sugar production in the British colonies.

Restrictions on the admission of United States products severely affected the labour force in the islands after 1776. Parts of chapter 2 have detailed how devastating was the impact of the prohibition of American trade. On some estates, only a portion of the large slave population was healthy enough to work. Most of the slaves suffered from diseases caused by malnutrition, and they died off with great regularity. For planters faced with the need to replace them, labour costs were inordinately heavy. The plantation papers are replete with examples.

The American War seriously undercut the prosperity of the British West Indies. The lack of United States supplies greatly increased the cost of production, and began a period of instability that finally culminated in the abolition of the African slave trade in 1807.[27] In addition, the debt load repelled prospective new planters. These—the attorneys, estate managers, overseers, storekeepers, and merchants who were previously prepared to take the plunge, believing they still had the magic to make profits at this late stage of the sugar industry—no longer were itching or could even afford to buy property. In fact, on all islands, plantations were being abandoned, or confiscated for debts. In Jamaica "in the course of twenty years, one hundred and seventy-seven estates have been sold for the payments of debts; fifty-five estates have been thrown up; and ninety-two are still in the hands of creditors."[28]

The American War had brought West Indian planters to a crossroads. Many factors who advanced credit in earlier years were now reluctant to do so. One heavily involved Scottish company warned its agents in the West Indies that "trade of every kind seems to be at a perfect stand owing to a most uncommonly great & general scarcity of money over all the three kingdoms, where it will terminate God knows, but we have never known the like before—in such circumstances we must therefore intreat & request of you to make us as large remittance this year as possible & on no account whatever to draw us into new engagements, for we assure you it is not in our power to extend further, we must rather endeavour to contract our business by every proper opportunity."[29]

So disheartening to these quasi-capitalists were the economic conditions of the islands that their continued economic growth and preeminence within the empire seemed at an end. While many West Indian planters abandoned their plantations and immigrated to the foreign islands with their enslaved people to avoid litigation for debt, others helplessly witnessed the sale of their plantations and belongings at public auction for nonpayment of debts below existing market value. Moreover, as we have seen, throughout the British West Indies the governments faced financial crises. Local treasuries were virtually empty and some assemblies were reluctant to tax an overburdened planter class. By

1782 the government of Barbados had a debt of approximately £30,000. The local government in St. Kitts owed the British government some £37,609; the Assembly agreed to pay it off at £10,000 annually. The Jamaica government, already heavily indebted, incurred a further public debt estimated in 1803 at £231,000 for waging the Last Maroon War. These public debts were most often owed to local merchants and were mainly for supplies sold to the government for public works such as forts and fortifications. The construction and maintenance of these had become particularly burdensome during the wars at the end of the eighteenth century.[30]

West Indian planters could avoid debt only under certain conditions: that their commodity products fetch high prices; that production levels remain very high; that the labour force have a low mortality rate; that production and shipping costs, including freight, insurance, and duties, be kept low; and that they continue to receive cheap food and lumber, paying in rum and sugar rather than currency. The American War changed the basic way of doing business in the West Indies. It removed several features of plantation life that had enabled the system to operate profitably. First, it ended the unrestricted commerce that had existed between these out-regions of the empire, whereby planters were supplied with cheap "adequate" food, lumber, and some plantation stores. Second, the practice of paying the North Americans with sugar and rum, which absolved the planters of drawing bills on their factors in Britain, was virtually discontinued.[31]

From the shortages of the war, planters advocated a shift in the supplying of the enslaved population to reduce the heavy costs of imports from Ireland and British North America. One planter asked his attorney to plant guinea grass on one of his sugar estates. He wanted to rear large numbers of cattle for the mills and for transportation, as well as for food for the Negroes instead of expensive Irish salt beef. Of course, experience had led him to conclude that cattle raising at the end of the eighteenth century was no longer just an adjunct to sugar production. It had become "as profitable to raise & sell cattle, as it is to sell sugar. Sugar could be very dear, that has [been] raised by the death, or illness—of negroes—or cattle."[32] Another planter decided that intransigent slaves should be sent to the United States "where provisions are of little value"; keeping them in St. Kitts only led to further indebtedness, since they were "not worth taxes and maintenance."[33]

Indebtedness was a considerably greater burden on the planters after the American Revolution than before. During the years 1745–75, normally considered the "golden age" of sugar, the economies of the West Indian islands had thrived. Imports of new captive Africans almost doubled, and sugar output increased by nearly 250 percent. A long list of would-be investors were waiting in the wings to go into debt to become sugar planters. After 1776 wartime conditions and British mercantilist policies had psychologically scarred the sugar planters. The mood that had propelled them headlong into sugar planting and debt was lost. Trade restrictions coupled with vastly increased duties had so reduced the net value and raised the debts of West Indian estates that one planter deemed it "unprofitable for us to carry on their culture; for our expenses are certain and enormous; & ... our profits very much the reverse." He observed: "This country seems to care little about us, or our remonstrances, as long as a certain revenue is raised. Tis true, it may last for a short time, but, like the Dog in the Fable, they are likely to lose the whole, by grasping at too much. It is a melancholy, but a just picture, and what adds to the gloominess of the prospect, is the little chance we have of relief from the present distressed and confused situation of this country. Our fate therefore, seems to be involved in uncertainty."[34]

One way out of the situation into which West Indian planters had invariably fallen was to sell off the estates and liquidate their debts. Some chose this course. Others chose to sell portions of their vast holdings, and to apply a part of the proceeds to the accounts current in order to meet their annual expenses. However, few prospective planters were rushing to purchase sugar lands, so planters established the principle of letting the buyer pay "one half of the purchase" at the time of the sale; "the other half may be paid in two years."[35]

"The terms of sale & prices" did not encourage purchasers; those who bought did so at vastly reduced prices. In less than a generation, the West Indies had become a buyer's market for sugar estates. Land sales to pay contingencies and commission charges, and so prevent his attorneys from submitting bills on his London account, did not materialise, and Penrhyn's attorney wrote to him: "In consequence of not making sales of the lands, I must be under the necessity of drawing on your Lordship the annual installment you are pleased to mention on account of Mr. Falconer's estate as Mr. Smith is very pressing and desirous to fulfil some instructions of the Gentleman's Will."[36]

The net proceeds from annual production shipped to Britain were inadequate to meet the debts and other charges incurred there. With exports to both Britain and the United States declining, and the costs of supplies and annual contingencies rising, the profitability of West Indian estates had all but disappeared at the end of the eighteenth century. The net proceeds on West Indian sugar stood at £14 8s per hogshead. One computation of the value of West Indian properties in 1773 and in 1800 held that they had depreciated in the interval by roughly 19 percent.[37]

By 1807, the year of the abolition of the slave trade, the net return to the West Indian planter on sugar sales averaged around £7 per hogshead.[38] Conditions were so poor that John Robley and Company wrote a series of letters to Sir William Young, governor of Tobago and sugar planter, informing him of the declining conditions and holding out no better prospects for the future: "We sincerely wish it was in our power to inform you of some favourable change in the prices of sugar, but the market still continues in the same dull state and the demand very small—nor is there any appearance of its soon turning more Considerable."[39]

Throughout the eighteenth century, the profitability of West Indian estates was predicated on the production and export of staple commodities to guaranteed markets at good prices. Planters entered into debt arrangements because they were nearly always certain of exporting their sugar to Britain and most of their rum to the American colonies. With the adoption of a restricted economic policy, the United States market was greatly reduced, and rum accumulated in all the island colonies. This gave the North Americans the upper hand, enabling them to refuse to pay cash for rum and also to extract higher rates of exchange for their goods against rum.

Planters were forced to turn to the United Kingdom and the rest of the British Empire against their "better judgement." Rum prices were low but, according to one planter, "they needed to raise money to pay taxes and other contingent charges, for we cannot sell rum here for cash. We can only get rid of it by way of barter for any American articles such as lumber, corn, flour, etc." The economies were in such dire straits that the practice of using one year's crop to pay the previous year's debt had emerged as a standard feature of plantation life.[40] Still, it was not that simple. Surviving accounts current show that, in some cases, planter accounts fluctuated from debt to credit.

The financial costs continued to haunt them long after the resumption of peace. Some estate owners were affected physically, by being captured. In St. Kitts planters were forced to pay the cost of the defence of the island, for which they were charged a special fixed sum. Unfortunately, reduced crops resulting from poor weather conditions and from insect infestation, as in the case of the borer in the Leeward Islands, made it difficult for them to pay these special taxes, and they became a part of the estate's external debt. Of this, Robert Thomson wrote to Lady Stapleton: "The demand against the Estate for the last payment of the losses sustained during the siege amounting to nearly £230 sterling, will fall due the 15 July next, and I shall not have rum enough to pay it. I must be obliged to draw a Bill upon Messrs Neave but I will continue the bill payable at 12 months sight, and by that means they will have a great part of the ensuing crop of sugar in their hands before it become due."[41]

Similarly, estates in Grenada and St. Vincent were under severe losses and further indebtedness as a result of rebellion in the former and the Carib War in the latter. For example, the insurrection in St. Vincent in 1795 increased Sir William Young's debt by roughly £60,000. Added to this, drought in Antigua between 1795 and 1797 increased the costs of maintaining his enslaved population and compounded his debt problem to the point where he could not pay the interest. Assessing his debt accumulation, he wrote: "From the date of the Churac's War, 1795 I ought to have retrenched every domestic expence beyond what was necessary to decent subsistence. Now for a time—for too long a time indeed!—I neglected such duty of economy and management."[42]

Sugar was the product that gave the British West Indies its importance in the world economy of the eighteenth century. Any interference with production that reduced output automatically pushed the planter class further into debt. On some islands production fell off by 20 or 25 percent, and planters began to experiment with other crops, such as coffee in Jamaica and cotton in the Leeward Islands and Barbados. The income from sugar was not enough even to defray the plantation expenses, which in the case of Walter Nisbet amounted to £4000 currency for the upkeep of four to five hundred Negroes on his Nevis estate. Nisbet had to rely on his British creditors to maintain him during this period, and the deficit on his account current rose by 444 percent in one year, from £594 sterling in 1777 to £2,635 the following year. After recommending "a considerable remittance," Houston and Company told him that conditions would worsen because "money still continues amazingly scarce in this country, we never knew the like before—& we fear it will have the effect of keeping down the price of sugar . . . for speculation is perfectly damped."[43]

The decline in production levels and the consequent increase in the indebtedness of planters were compounded by a general rise in cost of all items necessary to plantation life and sugar production, and some services—this at a time when British commercial policy prohibiting United States–West Indian trade had taken away the lifeline of the plantation system. In 1781, at the height of crisis in the British West Indies, Rooke Clarke surveyed the conditions of the planters and wrote: "the losses, Disappointments & Embarrassments that has long attended my Concerns have been and are such that I am all wonder that I have thus far stood them. Being unfortunate crops not only puts me past paying long standing Debts, but it does paying wages to them without whose help all must be at a stand, this to a feeling Mind gives pain inexpressible its what makes me truly wretched and I can't remedy it."[44]

The situation had not changed a decade later; at the outbreak of the French Revolution, production remained at pre–American Revolution levels, and losses to planters remained quite substantial. Walter Nisbet reported: "In the last four, I have experienced a yearly deficiency of 200 hhds from the average …of the former fifteen years—In all full 800 hhds—a sum not short of twenty thousand Guineas—and I may say, with great truth, that your own losses have not been much inferior. Such is the glorious uncertainty of our specious properties in this country. They indeed require no additional taxes. I most hastily wish I could dispose of mine on terms the most moderate—the Gewgaw part of life is now over, and moderate things, with peace of mind, and little trouble, I should infinitely prefer to the largest income here."[45]

The single most important item of capital investment was the large black population. Acquiring and maintaining slave labourers was also the cause of great indebtedness because the population on almost all West Indian plantations was subject to such high rates of mortality and depreciation. Yet annual purchases of new captive Africans were necessary in order to maintain production levels. The care and supervision of the Negroes was thus a very important aspect of plantation management. Nevertheless, it was neglected on many West Indian plantations, and in the years prior to 1775 it would appear that the life of a slave was not a matter of great concern because planters were able quite readily to replace those who died.

There emerged the vicious circle of large investment in captive Africans, high mortality rates, high depreciation costs, high replacement charges, and rising debts—a vicious circle arising from the nature of the investment. In order to realize a profit, enslaved workers were subjected to unduly long hours of work, excessively harsh discipline, and poor diets including too much alcohol and salt. Slaves on sugar plantations were the worst treated, even when compared with those of jobbers. Some jobbers made it possible for their Negroes to do light work; they "had days off for growing their own provisions which they sold to buy their own clothes. But, Negroes on sugar estates generally have no days allowed them."[46]

Frequent outbreaks of fever and dysentery caused by bacterial or viral "infections which flourished in the unsanitary conditions under which the slaves lived" decimated the slave population.[47] Chronic diseases such as yaws, cocobays, and gonorrhea regularly debilitated enslaved Africans and their descendants. In addition, hurricanes took a heavy toll on the Negroes and increased the indebtedness of several estates.[48] The years of the American War of Independence witnessed excessively severe losses in the slave population from malnutrition, disease, and natural disaster. In order to reduce both the heavy recurrent expenses for the purchase of "saltwater" Africans and the high costs of food, many planters took the decision to cut back on imports. John Shickle reported: "I have not bought any new Negroes as you ordered, and if you had not forbid it I could not have thought of it while Provisions are so scarce."[49]

The policy of reducing debts by deferring purchases of new captive Africans continued through the remainder of the century. In 1781 when Shickle again raised the question, Richard Pennant, although tempering his objection, advised him to "buy as few negroes as is possible—till we have some prospects of trade or till our national affairs wear to more favourable appearance. At present they look very gloomy." A further request the following year was greeted with a much more emphatic denial: "these are bad times, to buy more negroes than are absolutely necessary."[50]

The decade of the 1780s represented another watershed period. Estate lands could not be worked without labourers in the plantation system of the eighteenth-century West Indies, and even if economic conditions militated against new purchases, many planters were aware that their restrictive policies hampered work on their estates. Hence, towards the end of the decade, they attempted to find a middle ground. They permitted the purchase of new Africans as long as the money was derived from the sale of rum, from the profits gained from the penns, and from the sale of estate lands. They refused, however, to make new purchases if the Africans were, in the words of Richard Pennant, "to be paid for by Bills drawn upon me here. For I am really tired of laying out money on an estate that makes no returns—the estate having cleared me nothing for these six years past."[51] Sir Joseph Foster Barham adopted a similar stance, informing his attorneys Wedderburn and Graham of his "not sending money to the West Indies to purchase slaves."[52]

The probability that the slave trade would be abolished had brought the West Indian planters to the crossroads of plantation life. Could they have maintained the policy of not buying new Africans? Some continued in the hope of solving their indebtedness by making the estates profitable again. Others expected better conditions and terms because of heightened economic activity. George Turner of Queenhithe had this to say on the subject: "If the abolition takes place I certainly ought to have more Negroes bought (especially young wenches) for the benefit of the whole, but when I look at the large sum of money, I have already advanced out of my private fortune, the heavy engagement I am under, & the precarious situation of things . . . makes me unwilling to buy more till things have worked themselves a little sound."[53]

The fear of the abolition of the slave trade, as a first step to the abolition of slavery itself, was ever present in the minds of owners of chattel property. How could they resolve their several contradictory positions? On the one hand, they could not purchase new Africans for a host of reasons: their indebtedness; the unprofitability of estates owing to the loss of North America as a market for rum and as a source of cheap plantation food and supplies; the low prices of West Indian products. Even when these advanced, the high costs of production negated any profits. On the other hand, the planters had to maintain, even increase, commodity production, and guard against the termination of slavery.

The best solution, they decided, was to encourage natural increase by purchasing a larger number of female than male Africans. They believed that the passage of a bill ending the slave trade would lead in the end to general abolition. As early as December 1782 Richard Pennant, now Lord Penrhyn, had perceived this change in the nature of the investment in slave property as the new direction plantation owners should adopt. At that time, his major concern was to cut down the rising costs of sugar production. He wrote to his attorney: "In order to keep up the number of negroes upon an estate—I should think it . . . right to have a greater proportion of women than men—and to give rewards to such mothers as took the most care of their children—or brought up the greatest number."[54] A decade later George Turner recommended to his manager: "If therefore you should see it prudent to buy, young wenches should be your object and I recommend great Care to be paid to those allready on the Estate who are young enough to have children by giving little rewards to them who can be persuaded to be steady to their connexions."[55]

The preference for acquiring females on West Indian plantations continued from after the American War right down to the passage of the Abolition Bill. The purchase of captive Africans, it seems, was no longer made solely to increase sugar production but rather as part of a long-term restructuring of the slave system to keep it in existence. One attorney writing to his absentee owner boasted: "I have purchased from Messrs Boyle Jopp & Co. 25 very fine young Eboe girls about 17 to 18 years of age, 10 are at Coates, 15 are at Thomas River."[56]

Although these new acquisitions suggest that the planters were pushed further into debt to maintain a system whose future was uncertain, the slaves themselves met some of the costs of these new Africans. On West Indian plantations, towards the end of the eighteenth century, some owners had begun manumitting slaves who requested and had the money to pay for it or whose freedom was sought by overseers or attorneys. This was by no means a burst of altruism on the part of the planters. They reinvested the money in fresh Africans. Lord Penrhyn, writing to his attorney, emphasised: "The money . . . received from the present manumissions will buy 10 or 12 new negroes."[57]

While cutting back on Africans purchased, and then buying more women, might have seemed to advance the planters' immediate aim of not increasing their debts when plantations were in decline, they now added to their indebtedness by hiring gangs of labourers, as discussed in chapter 7.[58] The hiring of labour was meant to ensure that the workers lived longer and bred little "slavelets" who would be reared to maintain slavery. It was hardly the view expressed by Lord Penrhyn to Hering, who had requested hired labour to reduce the work of the estates' labour force: "I certainly do not wish to push em hard. I wish em to live comfortably & happily & I rather pay some hired labour—than to press them too much."[59]

As the estates sank deeper into debt, the planters' ready acceptance of employing jobbers waned. Requests by attorneys for authorization now brought detailed questions, including how the cost was to be met. By 1804, when most plantations were in the throes of decline and few were making profits, planters firmly objected to jobbing: "there is a very heavy enormous charge (much too great) for hired jobbers labour which I don't approve of at all—I wish to put an end to jobbing—and only to put in as many canes which my own people can do—and as you have limited the plant to 100 acres it will not be necessary and as I wish you to reunite the two estates the work of the Estate can be done without hired labour."[60]

In the 1790s, the destruction of the French sugar industry had revived hopes among British West Indian planters that prosperity would return and they would be able to pay off much of their debt. At first commodity prices, especially for sugar, rose very high. Planters, once more sanguine about the prospects of the sugar industry, incurred larger debts on accounts current. But this view of prosperity was illusory. High insurance and freight rates and increased duty charges offset any higher prices.[61] Consequently, better prices did not bring debt relief to the planters.

As early as 1792, the bottom fell out of the sugar market and prices fell by approximately 10s per hundredweight. British capitalists were reluctant to invest any more money in the West Indies; they even objected to bills of exchange secured solely by West Indian commodities. Richard Neave observed that the produce of the estates "would not be sufficient to pay the annual interest consistent with such yearly reduction we require to be made of our debt."[62] During the French Revolutionary War period, which some historians cite as a profitable one for West Indian plantations,[63] the sugar estates were plagued by high debts and declining profits. In 1796 Neave again wrote: "there is no hope of procuring money on West Indian security while 10 percent can be made at home by purchasing Exchequer bills."[64]

The overall general rise in commodity prices did not solve the problems of West Indian debt in the two and a half decades from 1790 to 1815. Although prices increased from 1794 to 1798 or so, the benefits were short-lived and many planters "were outraged by discovering . . . large debit balances where they had expected credits."[65] But deficit spending was a feature of late-eighteenth-century plantation life. The practice of drawing bills of exchange on, or increasing deficits of, accounts current was fast coming to an end. West Indian sugar had lost its starring role in Britain–West Indian commerce and as a source of great profits for producers, agents, factors, and manufacturers. Table 5.1 gives a view of the returns to planters from sugar sales in Britain between 1785 and 1804.

The available statistics show that the sums credited to the planters' accounts declined significantly after 1791. They varied from 66 to 73 percent of the value of the sale of their sugars until about 1796; then charges increased, and returns ranged between 45 and 58 percent, hardly topping 50 percent after 1800. That is, at times the net returns to the planters, after deducting only the charges for shipping and landing sugar in Britain, were lower than those very charges. When production costs in the West Indies are deducted from the returns, it is evident that most planters suffered net losses on sugar at the end of the century. Formerly these would have been offset by the sale of rum to America, but with British government restrictions negating this, the planters' debts mounted, as can be seen from an assessment of the Houston letter books and doubtless other sources.

The worsening situation of the planters was due mainly to the lack of exports to the continent. Hence, the expected arrival in Britain of a relatively large

Table 5.1. Gross income, charges, and net returns on sugar exports to Britain, 1785–1804

Year	Gross income (A)	Charges (B)	Net return (C)	B - C	B ÷ A (%)	C ÷ A (%)
1785	1,276	540	736	+196	42.3	57.7
1789	496	179	317	+138	36.1	63.9
1790	684	207	477	+270	30.3	69.7
1791	1,168	318	850	+532	27.2	72.8
1794	2,184	724	1,460	+736	33.2	66.8
1795	480	165	315	+150	34.4	65.6
1796	815	262	553	+291	32.1	67.9
1800	1,081	454	627	+173	42.0	58.0
1801	1,825	983	842	-141	-53.9	46.1
1802	491	263	228	-35	53.6	46.4
1803	1,440	716	724	+8	49.7	50.3
1804	1,018	471	547	+76	46.3	53.7

Sources: "Account of Sale of Several Hogsheads Sugar," Chisholme Papers, NLS, MSS 5464, fols. 24, 58, 83, 100, 102, 108, 116, 120, 166, 176, 185, 203, 285; "Sugar Sales of the Estate of Lady Stapleton by Richard Neave," UWB, Stapleton-Cotton MSS 6.

Note: Income, charges, and returns are expressed in £.

quantity of sugar did not bring the "ease & comfort" to merchants and factors that it once had. On the contrary, "arrivals only offer additional weight to the inconvenience which the trade labours under—not a cask of sugar can we offer for sale which does not first put us into an advance of £21 per hhd, in Duty Freight and other charges, besides seamen's wages—while we are suffering most cruelly by an Impeded Export, without any foreign demand and a Glutted Market, with only miserable prices,—for the Home consumption will be too trifling in quantity, & too tardy in its operation to produce the relief so necessary to the Trade."[66]

After 1800 underconsumption of sugar in Britain continued to bring poor prices and increased debts for West Indian planters. Capitalist economies thrive on active markets, bustling with activity, where goods are bought and sold and where investors speculate without fear or restrictions. The West Indian economy in this period was hindered by a series of restrictions both economic and political. The failure to move the sugar from the warehouses forced the merchants to initiate changes in their credit arrangements with the planters. By abolishing the practice of drawing bills on commodity shipments, they were striving to safeguard their own position, knowing full well that the failure of the West Indian economy could jeopardise their own credit standing. On this issue, Davidson and Graham told Lord Penrhyn: "if any unforseen circumstances at a Crisis so alarming, should disappoint your Lordship with Remittance you intend making us, as a provision for your Bills, it may prove injurious to our Credit, when every means of assisting ourselves rest entirely on the Sale of Produce, under the very irksome state in which we have already represented our Market to be, and which the most desponding imagination could not have suggested at the time we first had the Honor of being introduced to your Lordship."[67]

Yes, the British West Indian economy had lost the charm it once held for British merchants and sugar factors who in the "golden years" had received substantial incomes from commissions on West Indian exports and from interest on accounts current.[68] Some of these accounts now showed large deficits. One was Lord Penrhyn's, as Henry Davidson of Davidson and Graham observed: "Our cash payments since 31st May last for your Lordship have been £9,300 and our present acceptances amount to £48,000, whilst the great Bulk of our importation remains unsaleable. Our cash Receipts have for the same Period been £3500."[69] No merchant or factor could carry this backlog.

The lack of sales certainly caused a cash flow problem, which was compounded by additional duties on West Indian sugar. The imposition of a further 3s per hundredweight in 1806 brought contrasting responses. One planter in the Leeward Islands saw them as the latest obstacle in her struggle to pay the debts on her estate: "I am very anxious to have my Dear husband's debts paid and till they are I shall not take anything from the Estates." Another was more pointed: "If these duties are to be continued they will be a prohibition to sugar making. The planters had better give up their Estates to government for in fact they are getting no compensation for their labor."[70] While the Napoleonic Wars continued, the higher prices, although negated by equally high costs and duties, kept the planters struggling to maintain the plantation system in spite of their indebtedness. However, Pares writes: "After Waterloo the high costs remained and the high prices disappeared; they came down, in fact, to the prices of the 1760s. It was this which finished the British West India sugar industry as a paying concern, and brought nearly all the plantations into the hands of the merchants at home."[71]

The plantation system in the West Indies was the mechanism through which large amounts of capital flowed out of the West Indies to Britain and the United States in the eighteenth century. The external debt of the British West Indies during the eighteenth century was basically a collection of varying sums of money owed to different merchant-creditors or factors in Britain. The colonial governments themselves were from time to time indebted, but their debts were most often owed to local merchants and were retired periodically by the imposition of special taxes, which placed added burdens on the already indebted planter class.

Why did the planters who created large amounts of wealth fall into such a severe state of indebtedness? First, because the restrictive British mercantilist system did not permit them to establish a manufacturing base. The plantations were maintained as producers of raw material and consumers of high-cost manufactured goods. They sold raw sugar and other commodities cheaply and purchased manufactured goods—machinery, implements, utensils for rum and sugar production, clothes, lumber, processed food, and even refined sugar—at much higher prices.

The acquisition of sugar estates, especially in the second half of the eighteenth century, was attended with extremely high costs. Planters who settled the Ceded Islands or who established new plantations in the older colonies were heavily in debt from the beginning, and the operation of the estates sank them deeper and deeper.

Another reason for indebtedness was that the planters held on to a slave labour system that entailed a heavy initial outlay and a high rate of capital depreciation. Because the enslaved workforce did not maintain or increase its numbers by natural means, the planters had to make continuous annual purchases of new captive Africans at high prices.

Debts also arose and grew because the prices of West Indian commodities fluctuated markedly on the British market and at times were much less than the costs of production. Towards the end of the eighteenth century, large quantities of sugar and other commodities accumulated in warehouses throughout Britain. And there were no alternative markets.

Alternative sources of supply were closed too, by the imposition of restrictions on imports from the United States after the American War. The plantations could not survive these, and the independence of the United States emerged as the most momentous single event in the eighteenth century for the West Indian economy. Debts that began as small balances in accounts current around the outbreak of the American War mushroomed into large deficits, which called for mortgage security. The respite brought to the West Indian plantations by the destruction of the French sugar industry was short-lived. Though prices remained higher in the 1790s than during the previous decade, returns were minimal and, for most planters, nonexistent. The estates sank deeper and deeper into debt, which in the end led either to loss by public sale or to confiscation and management reorganization by the creditors in England.

Throughout the seventeenth and eighteenth centuries, merchants in Britain provided large amounts of credit capital to the West Indian planters, for three main reasons, depending on the period. In the beginning, many planters were friends or relatives of the merchants and were treated as such; an example is the relationship between Sir William Young (to his great detriment) and John Robley and Company. Once the sugar industry got under way, the merchants or factors kept the wheels of the sugar mills turning by greasing the cogs and fuelling the fires in order to safeguard the commissions on which their survival depended. And with the decline of the British West Indian economy at the end of the eighteenth century, the planters were still loaned money, as their debts were now an important source of income through the interest they generated. While the planters did not worry about debts for most of the eighteenth century, by the end of that period, indebtedness had become an issue of major concern.

⁓ 6 ⁓

New Management Techniques and Planter Reforms

One of the key issues facing all West Indian planters at the end of the eighteenth century—at probably the most difficult juncture in the existence of the plantation system—was the management of the estates. At the end of the American War, they had to recognize that an in-depth restructuring of their estate operations was needed. The structure on which they had been nourished for more than a century had been significantly curtailed. There was a new policy towards the newly independent United States, excluding her ships and some of her products from the British West Indian trade. And economic decline had necessitated other adjustments, to the management of the slave population as well as to the cultivation of canes.

The Jamaica planter Edward Long recommended the employment of managers who had been weaned on local conditions. He proposed, for all the islands, the use of residents who because of their "long ... service ... and who, by having charge of a number of estates, differently situated" had "gained that knowledge from habitual observation and experience."[1] One of the chief factors that limited the training of planters and their managers for most of the seventeenth and eighteenth centuries was the lack of written material on Caribbean agriculture. There were no schools, and techniques were acquired in diverse ways that did not always ensure their correctness. It was not until 1767 that a group dedicated to extending agriculture in the West Indies was established, and publications related to the culture of crops began to appear. An early beneficiary was coffee cultivation and production in Jamaica in the 1770s. Planters made every effort to acquire the best guidelines for growing and processing coffee beans. The

Assembly, indeed, was foremost in the dispersion of information pertaining to the production of coffee. Jethro Tull's work on agriculture was cited by Edward Long as the genesis of the new trend in plantation agriculture, one that supported experimentation as a fundamental aspect of good husbandry.

Overseeing the functioning of the whole agricultural system in the British Caribbean was a class of managers or attorneys. During the eighteenth century absenteeism had become entrenched. In 1774 Edward Long estimated the number of nonresident proprietors and annuitants from Jamaica at 2,000. Of the 775 sugar estates on that island in 1775, some 234 were held by 180 absentees, minors, or incompetents. Just under fifty years later, one writer reported that absentees amounted to seven-eighths of the planters. The situation did not change significantly by 1832, when absentees, minors, and incompetents owned 540 of the 646 sugar estates.[2] In the other West Indian colonies, absenteeism was also a feature of plantation life, with the managerial class gaining a firm foothold.

The selection of these attorney-managers had little to do with their competence and training as agriculturists. Only a limited number possessed any knowledge of plantership. Managers were normally employed through informal arrangements with families and friends. Many were planters; others were merchants and professionals, including members of the clergy. Attorneys were at times in control of several contiguous estates, and many were well placed in their relations with the merchant class, both in the colonies and in England. The power that they wielded as a group caused them to be held in "reverential awe" by the overseers and bookkeepers and certainly, by extension, by the slaves.[3]

In the days when the sugar industry flourished, many planters employed two attorneys, perceiving this to be to their advantage. One was the "planting attorney," the other the commissary factor or "mercantile attorney." At the height of the sugar industry, both managers were paid commissions of 5–6 percent of the gross value of the produce of their plantations. In some cases, this system of double attorneys worked against the well-being of the estates, as the two pursued "separate interest and clashed with each other."[4]

In addition to their commission, some attorneys received "from half a guinea to a guinea for every hogshead of sugar" that they shipped. And in other ways, managerial positions were very lucrative. Employees used their positions to defraud their employers. They produced on their owners' estates "all kinds of stock suitable to our markets which they feed principally with the grain etc. belonging to the estate on which they live; they also grow exotics as well as the vegetables natural to the climate; and, to complete the system, they employ the slaves to vend such produce." The wives of the managers were in charge of these operations. The overall income was so exorbitant that one observer coined the adage "Fat managers and lean employers." Managers of estates of nonresidents fared better than their owners, "the first receiving benefits without the least risque."[5]

The operation of the managerial system was seriously affecting the plantation economy. The high expenditure of money outside the British Caribbean on planters' children in England and their being resident there did not help the cause of West Indian agriculture. The employment of Europeans as overseers or managers was equally disastrous. Many were not "fully qualified to judge when they are acting right, or when wrong, copying merely from their neighbor, who may happen to know little more of the business than themselves, and obliged to follow the employment several years before they can obtain a sufficient degree of general information." Under the old plantation system, many estates were judiciously cultivated. Cane cultivation was extended beyond the capacity of the land to yield significant returns. The enslaved population and livestock were overworked without any greater profits—whereupon managers introduced jobbing to compensate, thus increasing the cost of operating the estates. Increased disbursements for local production and the immense cost of all kinds of imported goods from Britain forced the planter "to borrow money, not only for his own support, but to pay off the debts of his ill-managed and unproductive lands."[6]

Hence, changes in the management of estates were instituted to ensure the survival of the plantation system. Of this, one planter-attorney wrote: "A West India estate may be properly compared to a manufacture; the profits of which depend entirely on the knowledge, experience, and without these necessary requisites in a manager, it becomes the most unprofitable of all estates, and literally, a sinking-fund."[7]

There was little or no consensus on estate management. A new appointee attempted to undo the perceived mistakes of his predecessor by instituting his own plans "often without ability to perform what he has engaged. Many of them simply substituted new and undigested plans, without understanding what the issue will be, and without much adverting to the welfare of his employer who was at times reduced to the very brink of ruin, by knavery, ignorance, obstinacy." In the final analysis attorneys blamed one another for the indebtedness of the estates, for increased costs, and for overdrawing on accounts.[8]

The downside of absentee estate management was not so much high salaries. In most of the Leeward Islands, managers received only £80–100 sterling per annum. In some cases, they were paid commissions ranging from 10s 5d to 21s per hogshead of sugar exported to Britain. This income was inadequate to maintain families in the West Indies, where the cost of living was considerably higher than in London. Yet attorneys lived conspicuously well by exploiting their positions on the estates to produce consumer items for the local markets. Conflict of interest was a major problem with a declining slave economy where new techniques were needed to boost sugar production. In short, the system of management had to be restructured.

An initial change was the recruitment of better qualified attorneys who were paid larger annual incomes and who were expected to exercise greater professionalism in the operation of the estates. Most owners fixed their attorneys' salaries at £200–250 per annum without commission.[9] After many years' experience, salaries increased to as much as £400 sterling. In a few cases, in addition to an annual fee of £200, attorneys were given a 6 percent commission on the net profits of the penn.[10] While planters were well aware that the commission system was fraught with difficulties, they were equally conscious that their interests would not have been adequately served without adding incentives in the form of commissions to managers' wages, based on the maxim "Mankind are chiefly govern'd by Rewards & punishments, rather than the mere force of principle."[11]

In spite of the failure of the old system of management, planters retained certain features. For example, Joseph Foster Barham retained the model of joint responsibility to ensure accountability. To reduce the common occurrence of overruns in expenditures, both managers signed all accounts and bills. Having two managers aimed to reduce the contingencies of productivity in light of the declining British sugar market and the high duties and low prices that had left only "a triffling ballance to the proprietor." Joint management practices also ensured continuity upon the sudden departure of a manager, so as to prevent "the estate [from] coming into the hands of strangers.[12]

While the chief cause of the plantations' decline at the end of the eighteenth century was mismanagement, there were other factors—severe dry or wet weather, hurricanes, shortages of food and high prices caused by the American Revolution, British policy towards the United States, high internal taxes resulting from repeated declarations of martial law—that bore heavily on the plantation system. The decline was thus beyond managers' and even resident planters' control. The drop in the slave population cut into production. In addition, commodity prices fell significantly with the end of the fighting in America at a time when estates needed to restock their labour force. Of this, Simon Taylor wrote to his brother: "I know Negroes will be wanted for all of them. The buildings and contingencies, exclusive of the Lawsuit, will Eat up not only the whole of last years crop but the Ensuing one and was it not for Lyssons you would have nothing to subsist on, there would be at least 200 Negroes wanted for all the Estates and if Lookout is purchased about 50 more; also provision lands to be purchased. It will be therefore necessary for you to live as frugally as possible."[13]

Since trade restrictions constituted the most immediate threat to the plantation system, Simon's prescription that his brother should return to the West Indies to manage his estates was not a guaranteed remedy. Restructuring of operations was a more likely solution. And one of the first changes was in the treatment of the enslaved population.

There was a commonly held belief that planters purchased captured Africans and then worked them to death from sunrise to sunset under the burning sun or in pouring rain. Under these cruel conditions, they worked in gangs under the constant fear of the driver's whip whenever they gave the slightest sign of relaxation from their task. There was no regard for illness or inability, age or sex.[14] Consequently, many Africans were "daily wearing out and dropping into the grave." In light of the heavy losses of the capital invested in Africans, managers had to play a greater role in the lives of the enslaved people. They had to support the "stock, encourage healthy propagation, lessen their propensity to vice, cabalistic or obeah arts, induce them to receive Christianity, not to excite their hatred or jealousy."[15]

These became the most important features of the new management strategy, designed to protect the most valuable capital investment on the estate. When Richard Pennant (later Lord Penrhyn) inherited his father's extensive plantations in Jamaica, his first attention was to the treatment of the enslaved workers. He called for efficiency at all levels. He recommended the training of local personnel to replace skilled indentured workers from England. Barham did likewise. He wrote the attorneys of Island Estate recommending the immediate removal of the slave huts from their unhealthy surroundings. He emphasised: "In my mind there is no advantage on earth which could justify any unnecessary severity towards them or unreasonable exaction of their labour. I know that the general opinion of the country was that humanity was the best policy; but I carry my ideas a little farther than many on this subject & think myself obliged to seek not only their help but their happiness & I beg to let this principle have its utmost extent in practice."[16]

In an early indication that the wind of change was blowing, Thomas Thistlewood broke with general policy in the 1760s and exempted pregnant slaves from physical labour six weeks before and after delivery. J. R. Ward writes that this form of amelioration was the planters' attempt to reform conditions for their enslaved labourers in order to lower labour costs, increase profits, and thus arrest the decline of the economy.[17] Towards the end of the eighteenth century, "planter amelioration" was a policy that sought to safeguard the security of the islands by having a population of contented slaves. Several planters opted like Thistlewood for more lenient treatment. Barham too ordered his managers to give "the utmost care & attention to the negroes, & I do this not in any doubt of your thinking. *In every respect their comfort* & their happiness [may result] in some diminution of profit. I shall not consider it a loss, & if I did I shall not be dissatisfied. The first thing I always look at is the increase & decrease of negroes."[18]

Central to the new management drive was the growth of the enslaved population by natural increase. Creoles—meaning those born in the New World, now in some places meaning of mixed ancestry—were perceived as more loyal and tractable than Africans, who in any case were "far too expensive." Nearly all the planters exhorted their attorneys to make natural increase the major feature of their management policy; Barham told Webb and White, "In the management of the estate as by far the principal object I consider the utmost attention to the welfare & happiness of the negroes in every mode & at any price. If anything occurs to you in furtherance of this object you will please to suggest it. From the acct. of taxes . . . I collect that they are again on the decrease. If by any mode of treatment, encouragement of breeding or care of children this can be obviated I shall deem it a greater gain than the largest crop."[19]

The commission system and rewards for increased production had led to the misuse of enslaved labour on many estates. In fact they worked against the interests of the planters, since overproduction led not only to high mortality among the workers but to lower prices. With the possible termination of the slave trade, all these issues converged to increase the anxieties of absentee owners. Compounding the problem, the slave lists showed few births. In Barham's mind, the failure of the large population of women to procreate was "contrary to the course of nature." Probably more vexing than the small birthrate was that, in spite of his efforts, the mortality rate remained high. Some planters concluded that, if they could not raise the birthrate, they would have to abandon the estates.[20]

In order to safeguard their interests, the old practice of buying new Africans virtually on demand was stopped. So was the purchase of plantation supplies and other items from London in quantities that led to waste and spoilage. Most managers now had to make do with their own resources and to practise the strictest austerity possible without hurting the capital in enslaved people. Thus they adopted the principle "It is not what may be convenient or desirable but what is indispensible."[21]

While the planters' amelioration policy, aimed at preserving and increasing their capital in enslaved workers, does not place most of them among the ranks of late-eighteenth-century humanitarians, some exhibited a measure of humanity to their slaves. However, their austerity programme resulted from the fact that the estates were losing money. Reducing purchases was an important first step. Lord Penrhyn laid down guidelines for the treatment of his enslaved personnel: "They should not be overworked. . . . They should be treated with tenderness when they are ill and with Humanity and attention, at all times. That the women be treated with indulgence at those times especially when their situation calls for it. That the children may not be put to hardships that their strength is not equal to. That the Negroes may have provisions."[22]

The worsening economic conditions in the West Indies, which were certainly deepened by the destabilization of the sugar industry, created tension between attorneys and absentee owners over the management of their plantations. The emphasis on preservation, even increase, of the capital in enslaved Africans reduced inputs of labour, and production fell. Those managers who depended on commissions to top up their incomes suffered from the new policy. They chafed at the incessant criticisms and prodding of proprietors. Many did not share the feelings of humanity and saw the enslaved Africans as mere units of labour. One told his absentee owner: "Be assured, Sir, it has ever been my wish to have the plans strictly adopted and pursued that you have from time to time recommended as far as weather and other circumstances would allow always studying ease to your people and stock. . . . But as it strikes me from the displeasure of your last, that I am not managing altogether agreeable to your wishes as your attorney. Perhaps, I might answer better as a second, which I would most readily agree to rather than you should suffer any longer from my mismanagement, which in turn might be the means from losing your good and worthy friendship, and rather than that, I would forfeit my Existence."[23]

While some planters attempted privately to ameliorate the conditions of their labourers, and while they expressed grave concern about the decrease of the slave capital, some colonial governments had forced the planters to implement a more humane approach to the management of the enslaved population. In 1782 the Assembly of Jamaica initiated the adoption of Melioration Acts. It had failed in the 1760s and again in 1774 to limit the number of new Africans brought into Jamaica. The opening up of coffee plantations had greatly increased demands for labour. The Assembly, concerned about the growing number of newly imported older African captives in the colony, passed a bill prohibiting for three years the importation of all Negroes over thirty years of age. The African traders opposed the measure at the Board of Trade, and the act was disallowed. Imported Africans were seen as more likely to cause slave revolts. Hence, since many planters considered Creoles more tractable, the 1782 Melioration Acts must be seen as seeking to reduce the incidence of slave rebellions.[24]

The legislation did not have any significant impact on the lives of the slaves. Many planters abandoned superannuated slaves in public areas, creating problems for vestries throughout the island. Hence, the Assembly passed a new Consolidated Slave Law in 1787 "for the better Order and Government of Slaves." The measure required owners to provide slaves with "good and wholesome provisions, proper and sufficient clothing" as well as adequate land and the time to cultivate it. These Negro grounds were enumerated in the censuses. In addition, every master or attorney had to plant one acre of provisions for every ten slaves. Planters had to maintain the slaves who became old or ill. The Assembly amended the law the following year, establishing annual holidays and specifying the duration of mealtimes. In 1792 it once more revised the law, to regulate the severity of penalties. Failure to comply with the regulations drew a fine of £50.[25]

In response to a resolution of the House of Commons imploring colonial assemblies to adopt legislation to improve the conditions of enslaved workers in the hope of increasing their propagation, the Leeward Islands legislature passed a law with heavy penalties forcing planters and managers to give their workers better rations. This experimental measure immediately increased by more than one-third the annual cost of provisions purchased by most estates in the Leeward Islands. More important, the act became a weapon of the assemblies in their struggle with the British government to permit the American trade. Whenever the assemblies and councils wished to force the governors' hands to open the ports to American goods and shipping, they highlighted the heavy penalties the planters had to pay for noncompliance with the act. Amelioration measures in the Leeward Islands were certainly not adopted from humanitarian motives. The long-term goal was to secure an increase in the number of enslaved Creoles by giving them more and better food and by relieving young girls and pregnant women of excessive labour.[26]

Although Jamaica had pioneered legislation to improve conditions for slaves, it was the Grenada Assembly that ushered in a period of revolutionary reform with the adoption of the Guardian Act in 1794. This measure restricted planters' notion of and exercise of absolute power over their slaves, mandated adequate food and clothing, and barred excessive labour or night work except during the manufacturing period. Planters were to instruct the Africans in the principles of Christianity to prepare them for baptism. Furthermore, the law forbade the clergy to take fees for the sacrament or for visiting slaves during illness. The most significant and innovative contribution of the act was its establishment of the office of Guardian of Slaves. Each parish had three who were to enforce the act.

While the ultimate aims of the legislative measures were identical to those of many planters, in most islands amelioration was adopted on a plantation-by-plantation basis. Each owner directed his managers as to what was acceptable to him. Owners gave special allowances and rewards to women who bore large numbers of children. Emphasis was placed on the well-being of the African child.[27] On the Jamaica estate of Nathaniel Phillips, all black children were thoroughly examined every Sunday morning to ensure that they were free of vermin, yaws, and worms. Their meals, along with those of the infirm and aged, were prepared in a common kitchen by selected superannuated female slaves.[28] Cases of special concern resulted from the loss of parents. When this occurred, especially if the parents were in the active service of the estate, the management made an effort to rear the children under the watchful eye of the overseer.[29] Still, these ameliorative policies were adopted less for humanitarian than for economic reasons. One writer noted: "the statements and evidence in the Parliamentary Report of July 1807, on the commercial state of the West Indian colonies, furnishes the deplorable chronicle, every article of which is a proof of the general proposition established above, chiefly on other grounds—a proof that the slave trade has ruined the sugar colonies—irretrievably ruined them."[30]

In order to achieve an increase in the enslaved population by natural means, certain changes in the system were needed. One area that certainly cried out for improvement was food—not only an increase in quantities, as the Leeward Islands act had legislated, but changes in the diet as well. The food allowances of the slaves were hardly likely to enable them to work very hard. Then, they were required to prepare their own meals and to cultivate their plots of land. They had to perform all these duties on a staple diet of corn, with small amounts of "half-rotten herrings" which when "unfit for white people, . . . were purchased in bulk by the planters for their slaves."[31] The worst fed, the field hands, were allowed local ground provisions instead of corn only on rare occasions; this was mainly in Antigua and Barbados.[32] In cases where they were on hire, they preferred to be paid three bits (something over a shilling) per week. House slaves usually ate from their masters' tables and are believed to have been better nourished. The bulk of the enslaved population received no fresh meat, butter, or other fresh animal products except on rare occasions, as when planters and managers in Barbados provided flying fish.[33] To get some variety in their diet, the workers bartered or sold the corn they received, or bought food with money earned from the sale of their livestock or from other independent economic activities. One lamented: "Me no like for have him Guinea Corn always! Massa gib me Guinea corn too much! Me no like him Guinea corn—him Guinea corn no good for gnyman."[34]

Whatever changes emerged came out of the general feeling among planters and managers that the importation of slaves not only was much too costly but would be restricted soon. Their altruistic attitude towards the enslaved population, seemingly founded on humanity and justice, emanated more from a desire to retain both their workforce and a measure of profitability. The Jamaican planters who obeyed the Consolidated Slave Act of the 1790s did so in the belief that bettering the conditions of the slaves would increase their life expectancy, would encourage black women to produce children, and would thereby maintain the system of slavery. In this light, many planters wrote of the limited changes as linked to the "progress of mankind." Yet the black man's "progress" in their vision was to be firmly and forever rooted in slavery. As long as "the slaves were humanely treated, their consciences were not troubled."[35]

The American War had certainly disrupted provisions and nearly all other plantation supplies for the enslaved workers. British exclusionist policy continued this hardship. Having lost the supply market for nearly every staple in their slaves' diets, most planters sought to increase production of some articles on their own estates. Of course, such a policy conflicted with the traditional functioning of the plantation system, which never relied on its own food production. Though the slaves were allotted plots of land on which they grew food and raised animals, this fell within their independent economic activities, and planters respected this right of property, allowing them to dispose of their produce as they saw fit. Besides, supplying them helped to create dependency on, and attachment to, the master. Planters therefore continued to supply food and clothing, regardless of its inadequacy. Some even questioned the nutritional value of the foods that made up the labourers' diets. Unfortunately, inherent prejudices and doubts about the humanness of the enslaved Africans clouded the debate.[36]

The restricted diet to which many slaves were subjected made them susceptible to a host of diseases, which wreaked havoc among the black population. The brother of one absentee planter took an interest in this matter. He wrote informing the master that his servants' diet consisted of "seven quarts of guinea corn . . . little enough for the weekly subsistence of a worker. The simple consideration of what one would order to be given to a horse after riding him a ten mile stage will help one in deciding in favour or against this miserable allotment." On some estates workers were required to subsist on their own resources for a part of the year, but these were inadequate, given the limited amount of land provided for "Negro grounds." One plantation set aside only "a detached strip along the river of about one acre—one half of which was reserved for the supply of vegetables to the overseer's house—all this for the subsistence of two hundred & fifty negroes for a space of five months."[37] To compound the excessive hours of toil, the Africans were plagued by infectious diseases such as dysentery, fevers, yaws, and cocobay which flourished in their unsanitary and crowded environment.[38]

To remedy these ills, some managers and owners recommended withdrawing lands from sugar cultivation in order to plant food, or to establish pens. This would accomplish two goals. Sugar exports would be reduced, though still adequate to the demand, leading to better prices in Britain. Similarly, increased production of local beef would mean reduced imports of salt beef from England, as well as a better quality of meat for the workers, as recommended by Lord Penrhyn.[39] Within the general scheme of amelioration, some estate owners favored giving slaves Saturday afternoons to cultivate their provision grounds.[40] On some estates, import substitution was also initiated. One absentee stipulated that "nothing that can be raised as a substitute . . . in the island" was to be imported.[41] Though signs of success were limited, absentee owners implored their managers to hold fast. Catherine Stapleton wrote: "Patience is required & perseverance highly necessary. The more obstacles & disappointments, the more we should give our minds & exertions to the cause—The Tide has been so many years against us its turning I *will not* believe *can* be far distant."[42]

The policy of amelioration was a costly one to planters, who somehow felt that Africans were animals and could exist in conditions intolerable to humans. Those who viewed their mission as having long-term goals that would improve their profits recognized the need for the new policies, as one wrote: "The expence is rather considerable but the object of their comfort great."[43] There was probably no worse discomfort for enslaved Africans than the condition of the huts in which they lived. Most were worse than the stables in which the planters' thoroughbred horses were kept. A description of them stated that "the architecture . . . is so rudimentary as it is simple. A roof of plantain-leaves with a few rough boards, nailed to the coarse pillars which support it, form the whole building." These huts required annual repairs; after a couple of years, new ones had to be built. Towards the end of the century in Barbados, some were upgraded. They were now constructed as wooden cabins and covered with shingles, and they were placed within a common yard in order to allow good ventilation and easy access to the common kitchen. The aim was to develop congenial ties among the black families on the estate. These alterations, although rare, were indeed necessary if conditions were to lend themselves to the natural increase of the black population.[44]

Improving the diet and the housing were only parts of the changes required if the quality of life were to undergo any marked advancement. The ill-treatment meted out to Africans was brutal. There are numerous eyewitness accounts of the flogging and disfiguring of blacks for the most minor offences. In most islands, willfully killing slaves was punishable only by fines. And of course, many planters or their managers killed their chattel property by lack of care and ill usage.[45] Corporal punishment was common and brutal. Yet most Europeans cared little because they had lost all sensitivity to the agonised groans of slaves who would cry out under the whips: "*Oh Massa, Massa—God a'mighty God bless you, Massa! I beg your pardon! I beg your pardon! Oh! Massa, oh! I beg your pardon! Oh! God a'mighty—God bless you!*" These protestations elicited no mercy in most cases, no compassion, no feeling that the human body was incapable of absorbing such pain and abuse. Even women showed no concern. On seeing this abuse, one reportedly responded: "Aha, it will do him good," or "Ay, it is very necessary."[46]

Not only men but slave women were subjected to the brutalising effect of the whip: "At one spot, in the coarse of our ride, we had our attention arrested by a party of four, almost naked females working in a cane field. They were labouring with the hoe preparatory to the planting of sugar, and that a stout robust-looking man, apparently white, was following holding a whip at their backs."[47] The wounds caused by these senseless beatings led to death in many cases. Planters were beginning to realize that, even though they controlled the labour of their slaves, their productivity was severely retarded by ill-treatment. Consequently, amelioration processes called for terminating abuse. Some of the more lenient owners ordered their managers to desist from using the whip on their estates. In a couple of cases, managers were supported for dismissing overseers who flogged the slaves and, when admonished, promised to continue the practice.[48] No one's interest, least of all that of the planters, was being served by the wanton destruction of capital, even if that capital were human and regarded as private property. The slaves still constituted the highest investment in the plantation system. It was certainly senseless to destroy them by excessive labour or physical brutality. A slave was unusual property, subject to human frailties and death without the planter gaining anything from the investment.

For most of the eighteenth century, the sugar planters were able to replace their enslaved workers without much drain on their incomes because rum production was adequate to meet contingency costs. It was considered profitable to push the workers as hard as possible, regardless of the unnatural severity of the labour or the mortality that accompanied it. Late in the century, management not only removed some of the harsh punishment, but it also sought to provide better treatment and social life. From the beginning of slavery, marriage as an institution had not been encouraged. The new thinking saw such alliances as providing a family atmosphere conducive to natural increase. One attorney, satisfied with his experiment in this area, informed his absentee planter: "one of the New Negroe Girls at Coates who has got intermarried with one of the men at the Penn is in a thriving way; everything is going on to my satisfaction."[49] Reports about slave life in Barbados indicated that new Africans, when introduced onto the plantations, were "designated with appropriate appellations, each having the name assigned to him placed round his neck written upon a card, or piece of wood. Commonly the christening and marriage form but a ceremony—the men being desired to choose their wives at the time they were named; and are joined accordingly."[50]

Linked to the encouragement of marriage was the acceptance by some planters that religious teaching was not incompatible with slavery. In Antigua, owners allowed baptism but the parents met the cost. They also allowed the Moravians and the Methodists to operate freely among the black population. Reports show that their meetings were "crowded . . . and to [the] discourses they listen with seeming attention."[51] The missionaries' role was to make the rigid conditions of slavery, the inferiority, the whippings, and the ill-treatment, the poor diets and strenuous labour acceptable to the blacks. Life on earth did not matter because there was heaven. African beliefs in "transformation" were subjugated to those of white Christianity. Barham's manager wrote: "I heartily approve of the Intention adopted by the Gentlemen concern'd of sending over Missionaries, for good morals are certainly the strongest foundation for good Order in a political view, independent of the advantages they themselves derive from the undertaking." Missionaries thus emerged as the new force in plantation management's efforts to keep the black workers loyal and submissive. Barham assured his attorneys that "they teach no other doctrines to the negroes than what lead to order and submission."[52] Hence they were provided with supplies, as other white persons, on the accounts of estates.[53]

Another area in which the slave system sought to make adjustments from both social and economic perspectives was in the matter of manumissions. These were not encouraged for most of the eighteenth century, chiefly because such a policy meant a loss of labour and possibly good breeding stock. Furthermore, in 1774 the Assembly of Jamaica passed legislation compelling planters to pay an annuity of £5 to the churchwardens for every enslaved person manumitted. There were three basic ways by which slaves were freed. Some were rewarded for loyal service to the plantation, usually according to the wishes of the owners in their wills. Normally, provision was made for the worker freed in this way to subsist without becoming a burden on the state. A second group was rewarded for loyalty to the state in times of crisis. In such cases, the Assembly recompensed the planters for their losses. The most common method, however, at the end of the eighteenth century was for enslaved persons to purchase their own freedom. In some cases, white employers secured the freedom of their mulatto children or the women with whom they had special relationships, for fees.

Although enslaved workers, attorneys, or concomitants purchased their freedom or that of their women from time to time, this was grudgingly allowed. At times, the planters entered into the agreement to demonstrate friendship between the attorneys and themselves, as when Barham told one of his managers: "I have to confess very strong objections to sell any slave in whatever case— but I should be sorry to let the opportunity escape of expressing my regard for you and opinion of your services."[54] This practice resulted in and from the growth of a mulatto class in the enslaved population and was viewed as detrimental to the continued existence of slavery. When the opportunity arose, managers were encouraged to sell or free such persons and to replace them with prime field hands.[55] The practice of manumission continued in spite of the threat to the slave trade. These arrangements also had economic benefits for the estates. The money acquired from manumissions was set aside to purchase younger Africans. In one case, the £200 sterling received for Elizabeth Williams immediately went to buy two young men.[56] On some plantations, this practice had developed into a lucrative business, which earned enough money in one year to purchase several new captives. This reduced significantly the amount of money that the estate itself had to expend in a given year. The established Africans and Creoles embraced this strategy of achieving freedom. Owners and slaves seemed to have worked out mutually agreeable arrangements, as indicated by Lord Penrhyn: "I have no objection to the two women and girl being manumitted. . . . You will buy some new negroes."[57]

After the American War and the severe losses it brought to West Indian plantations, one of the first areas to be cut back was the purchase of new Africans. No one wanted to buy more than was absolutely necessary.[58] The difficulties created by British policy with regard to plantation supplies from the United States made the care and health of the black population of greater concern to management. In all valuations, slaves accounted for the largest share, sometimes as much as four times the value of the land, as in Barbados around 1786. Furthermore, personal property was estimated as a fraction of the total value of slave capital. It was vital that the black population not be allowed to waste away.

The labour force, it is generally held, had a disproportionate number of men to women. In the early years and for most of the eighteenth century, plantation administrators preferred men because of the heavy labour required on the estates. This disproportion would have contributed significantly, to low birthrates in all the colonies—although, as we have seen, other factors including excessive labour, poor diet, and unhealthy living conditions also played their part.[59] It must be noted, however, that on the plantations there were normally more enslaved females than males, but it was also true that more women than men were unhealthy and incapable of procreating. With the loss of the American market for rum which was the chief fund for purchasing new Africans, the planters needed to rear their own labour by changing the ratio of women to men, as Lord Penrhyn wrote: "In order to keep up the number of negroes upon an estate—I should think it ... right to have a greater proportion of women than men."[60]

The new direction the planters and their attorneys took was certainly linked to their perception that the slave trade would be abolished. If Penrhyn's view of the fate of the slave trade was a bit early, by 1792 other absentees did not doubt that the day of that trade was fast coming to an end, as far as Britain was concerned. George Turner clearly identified the issues on the minds of his associates: "Situated as I am I hardly know what to write on the subject. If the abolition takes place I certainly ought to have more Negroes bought (especially young wenches) for the benefit of the whole, but when I look at the large sum of Money, I have allready advanced out of my private fortune, the heavy engagement I am under & the precarious situation of things, while this dangerous subject is under discussion, makes me very unwilling to buy more till things have worked themselves a little sound. Yett, I apprehend in the course of a few months, it will be the last time to buy. . . . As I wrote before we must take prudence for our guide and be governed by events and our resources—as the estates should certainly now work for themselves. If therefore you should see it prudent to buy, young wenches should be your object."[61]

The trend throughout the eighteenth century had been to import Africans. Planters had no time to wait until their young ones reached the age, about fourteen years, when they were productive. Most "saltwater" Africans were already at an employable age. Now some planters went full steam ahead with measures to maintain the slave population by natural increase. However, by the time this decision was made, the existing plantation women were not of the optimal age and health for childbearing. One planter interested in this scheme therefore suggested that "all new slaves purchased were to be young females." Another wrote: "I also gave my opinion with respect to the purchase of slaves which you might be inclined to make which is this to purchase females in preference to males until the number of each are equal as it is by this means alone that we shall be able to keep up our stock without diminution which is now become, in consequence of the bill now pending in Parliament an object of ruinous consideration to all persons who have West India Property." Lord

Penrhyn's attorney Fearon had already initiated such a policy when he purchased "from Messrs Boyle Jopp & Co. [of] 25 very fine Eboe girls about 17 to 18 years of age," dispersed between two of his estates, ten to Coates and the remainder to Thomas River.[62]

Simon Taylor, equally conscious of the urgent need to restructure his estates, formulated plans for a large one-time purchase of an estimated 160 to 200 young boys and girls in the spring of 1799. From this group he hoped to maintain his labour requirements.[63] Unfortunately, not even the best-laid plans bore fruit on all estates. Success was rare at best; only one report from the Leeward Islands claimed any increase through such schemes. Of this, the manager wrote in satisfaction: "I believe that you are sensible that any disposition leads me to make the gang of negroes as happy & comfortable as their situation admits & I have no small degree of pleasure in being able to state to you that from the effects of such treatment they have been gradually increasing in their number for several years past."[64]

Purchasing new Africans was the first step in securing a labour force. Maintaining it was the hard part. Inherent weaknesses in the plantation system negated growth within its labour force. Some planters sadly bemoaned the fact that, even with increased purchases of women, the birthrates on their plantations had not grown as expected. Some became frustrated. Barham's impatience was conveyed in a letter to his managers expressing his disappointment that his large population of enslaved women had "only six births."[65]

Of course, there were causes for the problems of the planters. Any attempt to rationalize the labour force demanded changes in the system of slavery. Barham had correctly pinpointed one as men's "unwillingness to get out of old habits."[66] On many estates, the feeding of the enslaved workers had not changed for more than a century; they were expected both to work hard and to produce children on a diet that consisted mainly of starch. Not only were the meals poor in food value, they were hopelessly insufficient. The standard weekly supplies consisted of four or six pints of horse beans or Indian corn, rice, and four or six herrings. At times, about two pounds of salt beef or pork replaced the herrings.[67] On some estates, the slaves supplemented their supplies with small quantities of ground provisions from their gardens. However, the majority of their produce was sold in the Sunday markets to earn money for their own items of luxury, or for their freedom.[68] Even after the slave trade was abolished and there was a greater need to keep the birthrate high, the food allowances remained limited, as Robert Goulburn reported.[69]

Of course, food supplies continued to be a major problem, with the United States' ships and some of its products excluded from the West Indian trade. Also, even though each slave above the age of fourteen was given a small plot of land on which to grow food, very few were cultivated. Labourers who worked twenty hours a day during crop time had no time to cultivate gardens. Several observers contended that "slaves in general were too hard worked to breed."[70]

The decline of the economy gave the policy of amelioration a measure of respectability throughout the British West Indies. One observer reported that "if the African slave trade is abolished, and if slavery is still continued, some wholesome laws will be absolutely necessary, for the population will not increase under the disadvantages of hard labor, and indifferent food. . . . if these people were well fed, and treated in such a manner as human beings ought to be treated, the stock of negroes already on the island would be sufficient for all its purposes, without any further supplies from Africa."[71]

Most commentators believed that enslaved Africans could maintain their numbers under the right conditions. The governor of Barbados in his report on slavery showed that the adoption of new techniques of management by some planters had positive results. He singled out an estate on which there were 288 enslaved persons—90 men, 82 women, 56 boys, and 60 girls. Under the old management system there were fifty-seven deaths and only fifteen births in the year 1780–81. With new management, the whips were abolished, arbitrary punishments were terminated, and all offences were heard and sentences passed by a "Negro court" composed of slaves. The change was dramatic. In a four-year period, there were forty-four births and only forty-one deaths, of which ten were elderly. The most striking claim was that under the new system the net annual clearance of the estate increased by over 300 percent in more than a decade.[72] There were other such instances where lenient and humane overseers produced more sugar with fewer hands. In fact, the evidence overwhelmingly shows greater productivity on estates where there was greater humanity.[73]

Of course, those planters who against their better financial judgment continued to purchase costly new captive Africans with no guarantee of returns, much less profit on their investment, had to ensure that their policies were put into effect. The happiness, health, and numerical increase of the enslaved population were recommended as the major goals of the planters, so that the capital in humans might be preserved and increased. To achieve this, Barham sent his attorneys a list of regulations. The blacks were not to be worked on Sundays except when absolutely necessary, such as during crop time or emergencies. All extra activities were voluntary. Those who refused to work on Sundays were still entitled to their food allowances. Those carrying on independent economic activities were free to pursue them on that day. All slaves desiring plots for cultivating provisions would receive them. Sufficient time, on the estate's account, was to be given to these gardeners, and their produce was for their own private use or gain. All pregnant women were exempted from field labour. Those who produced live births were to be given pecuniary rewards in that year. Annual distinctions were provided for mothers with three or more living children. In families with five or six children, the women were entitled to maintain animals on estate lands. They could transfer this right to others. Similarly, where there were Christian marriages, the women in families having seven or more children were exempted from all estate work, and their husbands were entitled to tether animals on estate lands. They too could transfer this right.[74]

Over the years covered by this study, beginning almost from the day that he assumed responsibility for his estates, Barham had envisaged and sought to put in place a system that would encourage births and promote the safe rearing of children. Penrhyn was of the same persuasion. George Turner joined the ranks of absentees who rewarded their slaves. He wrote that "great Ease was to be paid to those allready on the Estate who are young enough to have children by giving little rewards to those who can be persuaded to be steady to their connexions. . . . where proper care has been taken . . . Estates so managed have not bought Negroes for Twenty Years & have increased in number."[75]

Such rewards extended to monetary gifts to the young mothers and to the midwives whose services were of immense importance if the project of increasing the birthrate on estates were to be successful.[76] However, the whole scheme was dependent on the women, who had rejected the very thought of bringing children into the world as slaves. Thus, when everything else failed and abolition of the slave trade was pending, some absentees encouraged their managers to reward the overseers £20 for any "increase . . . in the annual balance."[77]

Changes were also being instituted in the duties and tasks given to young females. Absentee owners prohibited their carrying "the trash from the mill in which a position they have to stoop a good deal." This was considered "injurious to their breeding—and the trash might be carried out in little high carts or on asses or on mules." Objections on similar grounds were made to "women feeding the mills." These functions were now to be performed by men of all ages or by old women.[78] Managers did not always readily adopt such indulgences for young women. It was generally accepted that pregnant women were to be given light duties, such as hoeing, which kept them erect and posed little or no risk to childbearing.

Explanations for the low birthrate, the abortions and miscarriages, and the high percentage of infant mortality are largely to be found in a managerial class that neither understood nor had resolved their racial attitudes to African people and their descendants. Managers and overseers who ill-treated their pregnant women—some were reported to have flogged them while they lay stretched out over holes in the ground bored for their bellies—continued to assure absentee owners that there was "no want of care in their pregnancy." One manager ascribed the problem to loose morals: "It is impossible to confine Negroes in their choice of concubines. This plurality of wives constituting their greatest luxury arising from natural habits and constituted by general usage among them. In this country, promiscuous intercourse is being carried beyond all bounds of licentiousness known in Europe. They are not satisfied to confine their intercourse at home but carried on abroad on neighbouring Estates that they may have less interruption at home and less jealousy abroad. . . . There is much difficulty to keep the Negroes Women at home while forward in pregnancy or at any labour."[79]

Such statements reflect the traditional racist beliefs of a managerial class that sought to maintain Africans in a position of inferiority. Associations were indeed occurring on an interplantation basis, to avoid inbreeding among the Africans on one plantation. Many women travelled long distances at night to be with their partners. Evidence given to the Committee of the House of Commons on the Slave Trade and Slavery in the British West Indies pinpoints different reasons for the failure of any policy aimed at raising the birthrate. Few managers wanted to have children on the estate. They would rather the infants "die than live." Furthermore, the frequent abortions were the result of overwork, poor diet, and excessive maltreatment. The buildings in which many babies were born were open and damp. There was no bedding, and the newborn children lay on the bare boards or on "bass mats." After birth, infants were immediately taken away and were not allowed to nurse at their mothers' breasts until after the eighth day. This explains why births were not registered and included in the slave lists until the ninth day. During this period, mothers who had children four or five months old nursed the young babies. These mothers were themselves unsuited for this function. Hence, most babies "convulsed" and died by the eighth day. Many children suffered from an endemic childhood illness called lockjaw, or tetanus. On the other hand, babies born in healthy surroundings and treated properly lived. Mothers themselves were not treated correctly. After childbirth, in most cases, the only food they were given was a bottle of rum and about three pounds of salted meat.[80]

Many planters took steps to stamp out these abuses. All births were registered immediately. Conditions of nurseries were improved. Mothers were given better diets and less work, and were not flogged. The care of the children was brought under the responsibility of the management. Many owners now demanded annual reports on births and the treatment of women. They evinced a determination to find out the causes of "so small a pregnancy—few children being born and raised."[81]

As most efforts to increase the number of labourers on the estate by natural means failed, planters included the enslaved women in their monetary reward programmes. "Deserving mothers" were given "either on the birth or careful rearing of their children" a sum of money, gifts, or other privileges.[82] African traditions were discarded in the interests of planter profits. Women were encouraged to have children as frequently as possible. The habit of nursing children for long periods was discouraged because it was believed to retard conception. As one manager explained his approach to the scheme, "as soon as the month is out every mother comes to me with her child, and I gives her two dollars in money, with some other little gift for the child, I also give Granda, or Midwife, two dollars, for in this country I have observed that a good deal depends upon her attention & good visit."[83]

While not achieving their intended goals, these policy changes showed that there were attempts to ameliorate the conditions of enslaved workers in order to protect the capital normally invested in new Africans. Only a few planters reported a continuous increase in the slave population on their estates.[84] Describing the hubbub within the residential compound of one progressive plantation, a visitor to Barbados wrote: "The picture is further enlivened by groups of black children; some running and skipping about; some seated playing before the doors, in Nature's ebony trees, and some, unable to walk, attempting little excursions upon their hands and feet."[85]

But the plantation system operated under slavery did not give rise to many such successes. While Lord Penrhyn could write with a measure of satisfaction, "I am glad to see so many pregnant women," Barham was the more typical when

he wrote dejectedly, "I collect that they are again on the decrease. If by any mode
... this can be obviated I shall deem it a greater gain than the largest crop."[86]

Many of the changes resulted from the threat to the whole system. Planters,
as we have seen, were aware of the commercial value of good care of the enslaved
population, so they supported amelioration policies. Better houses were built,
with more humane and healthier surroundings. A spirit of family life was now
allowed on progressive estates. Greater care was shown to the infant slaves. They
were fed collectively under the watchful eyes of older people. On a few estates
one pound of fresh beef was allowed to each child less than ten years. While this
last seems as a very altruistic act, its goal was to help "the penn interest" maintain
its economic viability.[87] Other measures were adopted to save both children and
adults by inoculating them against contagious diseases. Among diseases ram-
pant on estates, smallpox was listed as one of the chief killers of children. Some
doctors feared the programme of inoculation developed throughout the West
Indies was not as effective as they had envisaged, mainly because of "the difficulty of procuring matter for any considerable number of persons."[88]

One of the more innovative changes was to select young slaves, from the old
established families or from those whose behaviour was exemplary, for apprenticeship in the various trades. This was expected not only to save the plantations
the cost of bringing out white artisans but also to create among the blacks a
belief that acceptance of the system of slavery could mean advancement into a
higher class. Young Creoles were trained to replace white skilled personnel in
several areas—as coopers, carpenters, masons, millwrights, and, with the reintroduction of the plough, as ploughmen. By training their own slaves, estates
were able to do away with hired labour, as we shall discuss in the next chapter.
Reports indicate overwhelming satisfaction with the progress of many of the
black population in these areas of employment. However, while the training of
slaves as skilled workers proved advantageous to the estates in the long run,
initially it brought increased cost to plantation management. There was a severe
reduction in field hands, who had to be replaced by purchasing new captive
Africans.[89]

Indeed, this brave new policy of training slaves as artisans was just one of
many decisions that faced plantations owners in a time of rapid technological
change. They adopted innovations only when they were cost-effective or when
the decision was the lesser of the evils open to them. A prime example was the
plough. Despite its high cost, the plough was readopted in order to arrest the
high mortality rate among the slaves and to facilitate natural increase. Other

labour-saving devices also sought to reduce the burdensome costs both of jobbing and of purchasing new Africans.[90]

The most costly technological innovation to emerge at the end of the eighteenth century was the steam engine. From the beginning, Jamaican planters
showed interest. There were two basic uses to which the steam engine could be
put. It could be used to irrigate the cane fields, and so enhance production, or
it could be used to power the mills for grinding cane. On both counts, its operation was very costly and unsatisfactory. On most islands, the water supply
was too limited to allow for the establishment of a major irrigation system. The
sinking of wells proved ineffective. On many estates, the soil prevented the wells
from serving as reservoirs. Furthermore, irrigating the fields called for extensive
quantities of expensive guttering tubes, at a time when the plantations were
struggling to remain profitable. Also, because of the topography of several of
the islands, irrigation led to soil erosion, so planters called on their managers to
be cautious in implementing it.[91]

The soil was becoming infertile. Consequently, the method of cane-holing
that had been practised in Barbados was now adopted in Jamaica. Extensive
manuring was also carried out to ensure healthy ratoons. These were advisable
practices, since not ploughing the soil protected it from extensive exposure to
sunlight and thus the loss of nutrients. Both methods were costly, and the planters embarked upon them only when the alternative seemed worse.[92]

Almost from its inception, the steam engine was adapted to grind cane,
producing approximately 25 hogsheads per week. James Mitchell of Moreland
Estate in the parish of Vere was probably the first planter to establish a large-
scale milling operation using steam. Lord Penrhyn too had employed the process to grind his cane. However, coal was the major fuel and had to be imported
from England at extravagant expense, so the mills were adapted to the use of
bagasse mixed with coal.[93] These early attempts did not prove very successful.
Trained personnel to operate and service the mills had to be brought out from
England. Many of the early mills using steam were taken out of production,
replaced with refurbished wind or water mills, which produced at the same level
of 25 hogsheads per week.[94]

Other innovations were also being introduced into the sugar industry to
reduce costs. Coppers that were destroyed with great regularity by the intense
heat of the wood fires were replaced by iron ones. Barham stressed the need to
continue this policy: "I observed in the former list articles of considerable
expence for the boiling house ordered in copper which Mr. Wedderburn told

me on their estates were ordered in iron of which the expence was inconsiderable. The reason to be assigned for this unnecessary expence was that it had been usual at Mesopotamia to have them in copper. Surely if any unnecessary expence has been usual at Mesopotamia it should be reformed at a time when the profit of the estate did not amount to the expence of a [tache]."[95]

It is clear that the planter class made calculated decisions in implementing changes in the management of their estates, including the labour force, in order to rationalize the sugar industry at this time of evident decline. Most of the changes they attempted resulted in increased cost. The amelioration of the conditions of the enslaved population was very costly, as was technological innovation. The introduction of the steam engine forced the planters to abandon their good working equipment for modernization with no guarantee of increasing either cane input or muscovado output. And it raised the cost of production because it consumed expensive coal. Furthermore, the 1790s marked the beginning of a very unstable period for the sugar industry. Prices were never high for long enough periods to reward the planters fully. Rum sales were virtually lost with the restrictions on the United States market. And Parliament had begun a policy of destabilizing the West Indian sugar industry with the importation of sugar from India and foreign countries for processing and reexport. There was also the cutback on the drawback and bounty.

Operating West Indian estates undoubtedly had brought greater financial hardships, and the new management trend demanded greater accountability from manager-attorneys as well as implementation of austerity measures. Some attorneys likewise asked owners to refrain from taking annual incomes until the estates' profitability was reestablished.[96] Merchant factors in England also made changes to safeguard their financial interests. The drawing of large sums of money on commodity trading was proving an unsatisfactory way to do business in a developing capitalist society where credit institutions were no longer reliant on this practice for their security. Thus firms that in the seventeenth century had initiated credit facilities to underpin their West Indian commission businesses now wanted to abandon them. One firm emphasised that they had "no reason to alter our opinion on the necessity of some alteration in the arrangements of your Nevis Estate but on the contrary the considerable sums drawn this year for disbursements afford the strongest grounds to confirm our ideas of expensive management of a property."[97]

As a result of decisions adopted by many factors and merchant houses, financing West Indian estates necessitated a reversal of the traditional trend and now called for the investment of large sums of money both in England and the West Indies. Throughout most of the eighteenth century, the profits from the penns and rum production, with an additional sum averaging about £500 sterling by one estimate, were enough to pay the contingencies, even meeting a part of capital expenditure. According to Barham's sugar factor, "the contrary, however, has lately happened & the bills have increased" to the point where he was required to send out cash to the plantations to pay the "large drafts for contingencys."[98] Other absentees were equally bewildered, even frustrated, by the unprofitability of many of their estates. In several cases, there were heavy losses. Reports indicate that numerous estates "produced nothing" for long periods at the end of the eighteenth century. Instead, the owners were pushed deeper into debt, estimated in one case at more than £3000 in a quick time. Penrhyn lost £500 in 1786. The trend was expected to continue on his estate. As a result, he adamantly opposed investing any more money in purchasing new captive Africans.[99] The same trend was occurring on many other West Indian estates. For example, Barham was emphatic in his opposition to investing "further capital in a situation when it is likely to make no return." He called for more detailed changes in management. Continued consolidation of estates was recommended, and in some cases planters were encouraged to sell or let the land "for what it will fetch."[100]

Another estimate illustrated that estates that produced 200 hogsheads of sugar and 100 puncheons of rum earned approximately £5,000 sterling. Annual charges amounted to £2,000 for English supplies and at least £2,143 sterling for island contingencies.[101] Not much was left for the planter. This calculation did not consider expenses on capital items. The falloff in colonial prosperity was certainly quite clear to creditors and owners alike. According to one estimate, "an estate which 105 years ago did with a capital of less than £10,000 in slaves produce an average income of above £5000 per annum does with a capital of about 3 times that number not produce £3000.... During this period the profits of land have been at least trebled."[102]

The most effective way to arrest this trend of unprofitability in the view of many absentees was to implement management changes and to adopt policies that ensured "a certain degree of economy." Crop production was to be kept at the same level or reduced. Failing this, Barham noted that it was probably better to give the total income of his estates "to his attorneys for their management." He continued: "It gives me great pain to write in a stile of dissatisfaction but if you will suppose yourselves in my situation you would doubtless do the same—

That from the circumstances of the time W.I. property must be unprofitable is true. But I hold it also to be true that when any kind of property under any circumstances become permanently worst than nothing it is a bad scheme of management."[103]

Pegging the blame for the ills affecting the plantation system on management did not go down well with the attorneys. Most responded aggressively, threatening to sever their relationships with the estates and their owners, and laying the blame on other factors inherent in tropical agriculture and the structure and operation of the plantation system. The tension between owners and management was in no one's best interest.[104]

Several approaches were suggested for dealing with the declining conditions in which the sugar economy was now operating. The preservation of the capital investment in slaves remained the primary policy objective throughout the period of this study. By adopting the method of claying, a finer quality of sugar was to be manufactured to receive higher prices on the London market. Those who wished the islands to move beyond the production of base muscovado pointed out that the duty was the same on coarse as on fine sugar, that there would be less carriage to the ship, less freight to pay, and proportionately less waste. All these advantages of fine sugar over coarse were expected to revive the sugar industry.[105] The quantity of sugar produced was also to be lowered, so the reduced supply would force up prices in England. To reduce freight charges, larger casks with lighter headings were recommended. In rum production, the distillation of overproof rum, a sort of alcohol concentrate, was suggested. This was expected to bring about savings on freight, on the number of casks, and on local transportation. But probably the most significant idea was the call for diversification of estate production away from sugar to indigo, or to cotton, which was envisaged as the major source of Britain's wealth in the early nineteenth century.[106] Coffee was under cultivation, especially in Jamaica, and several estates were making significant progress. Penns were also seen as replacements for the sugar industry, but the local market was too small and there was no guaranteed export market.

The question of management in the sugar industry entered a new phase with the abolition of the slave trade in 1807. One manager noted that "the planter must now adopt measures, to be satisfied with less produce and make the labour of the negroes more easy" in order to maintain, even increase, the enslaved population.[107] On some estates, alteration to the composition of the gangs and the work that they performed resulted from the end of the slave trade. Men were separated from women. The former were to carry out all laborious tasks, while women were given lighter work in the hope of effecting greater procreation. This focus on natural increase continued in the decades after 1807 as the main plank in the planters' efforts to continue slavery on their internal population resources.

The managerial system was always a feature of the plantation economy in the West Indies. It began on a limited scale towards the end of the seventeenth century and increased in the eighteenth, as the islands grew affluent and the original planters either retired to England or died and their sons and daughters inherited the sugar estates. By the end of the eighteenth century, two factors emerged to force changes in the structure of the managerial class and in the performance of its functions. The majority of West Indian planters were absentees, living mainly in Britain; several, although residents, lived in towns or on other estates some distance away from their plantations. Then, the British West Indian economy was declining markedly after the American Revolution. Consequently, new management policies were adopted, with owners keeping closer watch over their managers to ensure that their directives were implemented.

The overriding goal of the new management approach was the maintenance of the enslaved population in conditions that allowed for its growth through natural increase. Hence the planters initiated amelioration, such as insisting on reduced and easier work, allowing pregnant women time off, and giving rewards for the successful birth and rearing of children. Some outlawed flogging and placed women in separate gangs in an effort to stimulate their family consciousness. On many islands, planters introduced or permitted the teaching of the Christian religion to the enslaved population, as well as allowing a limited form of marriage.

As a result of the new management thrust, black skilled labour began to replace whites, and these positions were handed down through the generations in the most long-serving and trusted slave families in order to foster the belief that loyalty to the system had its rewards. From this perspective, the system began to break down the notion that Africans were incapable of undertaking technical roles, as more and more assumed the positions formerly held by whites. The period marked the formative years of amelioration, which colonial assemblies, with the exception of Barbados, were quick to formalise with legislative measures although with few serious attempts to implement the policy. The most far-reaching was the Guardian Act of Grenada.

Why were these efforts made to adopt new measures? The decline of the West Indian economy called for reduced importation of captive Africans, so owners now emphasised breeding their own labour force. While one may be tempted to relate these changes to the white humanitarian impulses towards the African slaves, it is an incontrovertible fact that amelioration, which was the main feature of the new management policy, was more concerned with arresting the decline of the plantations and less with humaneness to the enslaved population.

∽ 7 ∾

Hired Slave Labour

In a society in which the planter class owned its own labour force—one in which captive Africans and Creoles were available for purchase with few restrictions but market forces—a system of hiring enslaved labour in both urban and rural sectors of the British West Indian economy developed as an integral part of labour procurement practices. This practice emerged almost from the inception of slavery in the Caribbean. However, it had its greatest impact after the middle of the eighteenth century. The existence of hiring allowed all free persons to acquire slave labour as they desired, without the requisite capital to purchase the workers. Hence, all were psychologically attached to slavery, all could be engaged in it.

Barry Higman has identified several areas of the colonial economy in which slaves were hired independently. They were the main component of crews on ships trading to America; indeed, customs officers occasionally refused to clear out these vessels as they had no white personnel. Other hired slaves in the transport business were boatmen and porters. In rural areas autonomously employed slaves performed independent task-work, while plantation workers were required to labour for an entire day. Although Higman has failed to deal with the structure of the self-hire system, he argues that enslaved workers in both rural and urban settings preferred self-employment because it removed them from the direct supervision and punishment of the white managerial class. This practice also afforded them incomes with which they could purchase luxuries or a better diet, or their freedom. With independent incomes, enslaved workers could now make rational decisions about the consumption or disposal of their acquired resources.[1]

Sarah S. Hughes in "Slaves for Hire" considers the organization, structure, and overall significance of hiring slaves in Elizabeth County, Virginia. This form of labour procurement was not unique to that area but was general throughout Virginia and the rest of the South. Slavery in the West Indies provided many of the same opportunities for slaves to embark upon autonomous economic activities in both rural and urban areas. Howard Johnson in *The Bahamas in Slavery and Freedom* examines the self-hire system in the Bahamas. Since this colony was not a true plantation economy, he concludes that slaves had a fair amount of leisure, which they employed profitably in earning independent incomes.

A system of hired labour also developed in true plantation economies, and this method of purchasing labour according to the immediate or long-term needs of management illustrates that the plantation system had become flexible in accessing labour during periods of financial stringency. Hiring allowed adjustments to be made at times when planters were not able to meet the high cost of acquiring and maintaining a labour force in a declining economy in which capital resources were severely depleted and where the available investment capital was being attracted to other areas. Planters thus made the rational decision to hire labour in spite of several disadvantages.[2]

There were two main categories of labour for hire. Of these, jobbing slaves were basically predial workers employed primarily in agriculture. Their masters hired them out under varying arrangements. In most cases, the slaves travelled around the plantations performing specific tasks. Jobbers—here meaning slaves hired out by the job, though the word could equally signify the owners who supplied them—were also skilled slaves employed either by contract or on a daily basis to perform a single piece of work such as constructing a building or a mill structure.[3] (In the agricultural sector, there was a unique group of slaves belonging to settlers known as "ten acres men." These landholders purchased slaves, but because their holdings were small and they could not utilize all their slaves' time, they entered into special self-hire arrangements with the slaves, who raised provisions on small plots called "places," making cash payments to their owners. These blacks made significant contributions to the food supply on all the islands, especially in Barbados.)[4]

The second category of hired slave labourers were mainly employed in urban centres, and mainly longer-term. Among these could be found tradespeople, seamen, and a host of other skilled and semiskilled workers. On occasion, masters hired out their slaves and received all emoluments directly. But other slaves had established a relationship with their masters by which they were permitted to operate their own self-hire businesses.[5]

Hiring enslaved labour varied from estate to estate and from colony to colony. However, certain features were common to all the islands. Slaves were hired on three main bases—some employed by the day, others by the job, and still others on lease for varying periods of time, more than a year in some cases.

Slaves who worked by the day were hired singly or in gangs. For gangs, the charge was computed upon the aggregate number at a daily rate. The digging of cane holes, however, was not treated as day work but was normally contracted out to jobbers by the acre. When jobbers undertook any piece of work, the employer usually had to provide living facilities and to subsist them in accordance with the standard daily rates.[6]

Jobbing gangs were also referred to as task gangs. Their main employment was holing cane lands—an assignment that, in terms of time and task, and even acceptance of the undertaking or not, depended to a large extent on the work conditions and the hardness or softness of the soil. The size of the gangs varied between twenty-five and sixty, but the best size was reckoned by a Barbadian planter to be twenty-eight, the number sufficient to dig an acre of cane holes in one day. There, a cane hole measured 4¼ feet square by 2 feet deep, and there were 2,412 cane holes per statute acre.[7] Some managers were prepared to accept larger gangs, but they recognized the drawbacks, as explained by Thomas Samson: "There is severall reasons for not having too many negroes in one gang 60 is as much as can be wrought to advantage digging and planting canes. They have often to be drawn off and the larger the gang the greater the loss to the Estate."[8]

In addition to cane-holing, jobbers carried out a variety of activities on an estate. At times of restructuring, when planters wished to expand the areas under cultivation, jobbers were used in an effort to save the energy and lives of the estate slaves. Of course, all jobbing exercises on estates added further cost to the planters and/or managers, but they were undertaken in the hope that the plantations would survive. Writing to Sir John Hugh Smyth, the firm of Hibbert, Stephens & Raester reported that all outstanding jobs on his Jamaica plantation were expected to be "expensive, and indeed when you consider the strength which the Estate has been deprived of within these few years, without being replaced, and the loss of French's moiety of sixteen negroes you must see the necessity we are under of hireing strength to keep up the Estate which we assure you has been no easy Task; and be reconciled to be without Remittances till we can recover from our Losses and the Estate is established."[9]

Jobbers were employed in such other tasks as clearing mountain land for coffee estates or planting grass in the establishment of penns. Apart from the agricultural sector, jobbers worked in skilled areas such as in the construction business. They were hired to do roofing, or to frame and build houses, including those connected with sugar and rum production. Normally, jobbers on skilled projects such as building lime kilns or installing and repairing sugar production equipment were associated with a white artisan. In nearly all cases, these jobbers were employed because the projects were beyond the physical and mental capacity of the estates' own skilled gangs.[10]

When slave gangs were leased for extended periods, the contract always stipulated their appraised value as well as the conditions under which they were leased. All charges and expenses were usually borne by the lessee and were carefully listed in the agreement. Generally, a reappraisal of the slaves was to occur at its expiration. If their value had risen, the owner paid the lessee the monetary difference. Contrariwise, the lessee made good any fall in value. This covenant safeguarded the capital investment of the slave owner, while at the same time it guaranteed to the lessee monetary rewards for good treatment and care of the slaves. One report noted: "that the effects intended by that Covenant are usually produced is very Apparent from the Balance of Re-appraisements rarely falling otherwise than against the original Proprietors."[11]

On occasion, when a gang of young slaves was leased, larger annual fees were charged "in proportion to the expectation of their becoming more valuable at the end of the Lease." Also leased were tradesmen, domestic servants, and slaves engaged in various other occupations. These were hired out, on a monthly basis or for many years, on such terms and conditions as their services would bring or their skills deserved. They remained in the employ of their lessees during the term of the contract "at the risque of the Proprietors, but subsisted by the Person who hires them."[12]

The practice of hiring out slaves in all categories of employment is extremely interesting in assessing the adequacy of labour within the plantation. It demonstrated flexibility in the plantation system and made labour available to all who could afford it. The widespread use of hired labour indicates that plantation labour was short on many estates, which at this time had more land than personnel to work it. With jobbing on the increase in the West Indies, "every overseer or white man who had money or credit, purchased some new negroes in order to job for them on account of the great profit arising therefrom."[13]

From haphazard origins, renting slaves had developed into a business by the second half of the eighteenth century. Many managers, attorneys, and even overseers, although having no land, acquired gangs of slaves that they hired out to large plantations unable to keep up their workforce. Most of these owners of hired labour were categorised as "overseers and jobbers" or "pen-keepers and jobbers" or "coffee planters and jobbers." Others were skilled individuals such as millwrights, carpenters, and midwives. In St. James, in Jamaica, they were listed as belonging to the second class of settlers, the first being the sugar planters. Some operations was quite large, with an individual owning as many as 120 slaves. A few companies undertook jobbing tasks, while women were also listed as jobbers. For example, I. and Sarah Mowat of St. James owned 34 slaves. Rebecca Chambers of the same parish listed her occupation as "pen-keeper and jobber."[14]

West Indian plantations, in spite of their large capital investment in slaves especially in the last half of the eighteenth century, did not have full control of their labour needs. This placed them at the mercy of a managerial class that "without being owners of any land at all contrived to raise gangs of Negroes, as their own property almost sufficient to supply (upon hire) the deficiency of the labour on their masters' half ruined estates—ruined by accumulated arrears of servants' wages, and half hired labour."[15]

With the growth of absenteeism and the rise of the managerial class, hired labour became a prominent feature of the plantation system. Most absentee owners were convinced that their estates could not be operated without it. They were loath to reject the recommendation of the attorney-manager and then be told that production was delayed or diminished by the labour shortage. Here is Sir Joseph Foster Barham to his managers in Jamaica: "I quite agree however objectionable hired labour may be in general that under the present circumstances it will be advisable to avail ourselves of it as far as is proper as one would not be willing to let the crop down on account of the high prices."[16]

Also, at the end of the eighteenth century, attitudes towards plantation slaves were changing, as we saw in the previous chapter. Individual planters were taking greater interest in the daily lives of their slaves, including the nature of their work and their ability to perform the various tasks on the estates.[17] In fact, several factors had converged to encourage absentee planters to allow their managers to employ hired labour. Few West Indian estates maintained their slave population by natural increase. In addition, the slaves were generally sickly, judging from their stated condition on the slave lists.

The rumblings of the abolitionists had created uncertainty in the minds of slave owners about their future labour supply, and most planters were prepared to shift the emphasis for their female slaves from labouring to procreating. But overall, in their plantation accounting, some planters were more aware of their slaves as capital than as human beings. This inclined them to use hired labour for the most laborious jobs, as Barham indicated: "I quite approve of your intention to have the mountain ground cleared by hired labour as it produced freshness among our own negroes for there is nothing which can tend to their health, comfort & increase which I shall think ill bestowed & do not earnestly recommend you to adopt."[18]

Lord Penrhyn, chairman of the West India Committee, was equally well disposed to the humane treatment of his slaves. In keeping with his general policy of amelioration, Penrhyn was willing to use "expensive" hired labour to relieve his people of burdensome tasks and so preserve his capital. He wrote to his attorney, Mr. Hering: "You say the negroes are hard pushed to do the work of the estate I certainly do not wish to push 'em hard—I wish 'em to live comfortably and Happily—and I rather pay some hired labour than to press them too much."[19]

It is probably accurate to characterize the last quarter of the eighteenth century as the period of introduction of the amelioration process in many of the British West Indian Islands.[20] As this emerged both from the need to maintain the capital investments in humans and from a limited humanitarian impulse, the perspective changed. Illness among the slaves was seen more as symptomatic of overwork and less as malingering.[21] Absentees on the whole accepted two basic premises: first, the enslaved population was quickly worn out by excessive labour, and second, its declining strength necessitated the increased use of hired labour. In order to maintain work on the plantations and eke out some measure of profit, they even went along with managers' requests to employ hired labour in such secondary tasks as "to assist in cleaning the canes."[22] Though the planters, who were buckling under accumulated debts, felt that light tasks like weeding did not call for large outlays on hired labour, they initially preferred to let their attorneys be the final judges. Yet they were ever mindful of, and many were quick to suggest, the adoption of old and tried, as well as innovative, labour-saving methods on their estates. Thus Bernard and William Dickinson, the owners of Appleton Estate in Jamaica, told their attorney, Thomas S. Salmon: "We are fully sensible our strength at this estate is not such as to make very great exertions without the assistance of hired labour, all of which is left entirely at your discretion.... During

Marshals time the Plough was tried with very great success, and Marshall was a convert to its utility: we hope it is still continued, it certainly must save labour; if we can persuade the overseer to think so there can be no doubt of its utility."[23]

Not all planters shared the same enthusiasm for hired labour. Some opposed the high charges. In a letter to George Scott, the manager of Duckenfield Hall Estate in Jamaica, the owners wrote: "We have for a long time observed a vast expence the estate is put to for job work. We suppose this is found necessary from the insufficiency of our own Gang; to remedy this part, you have our full liberty to purchase from 15 to 20 or 30 Negroes as you see good opportunity, and that they can be employed to the benefit of the Estate; female negroes are immediately useful, but if first are bought, hope you will be careful to purchase from healthy cargoes, and think the above number of Negroes should not be put on at once."[24]

Planters were quick to pick up discrepancies between the aggregate of slaves on the slave lists and their managers' repeated requests for increased hired labour. There was no contradiction in many cases, because an examination of those slave lists shows a considerable number unsuited to plantation labour. On Barham's estate, for example, at the turn of the nineteenth century, of the 167 slaves between the ages of thirty and forty, only a few were fit to work. Most suffered from malnutrition caused by the severe dislocation of supplies.[25]

On the slave lists of Spring Estate in Jamaica, a high percentage were categorised as weakly, sickly, useless, old and weak—in short, hardly suited for plantation agriculture. Women were in the majority, but when the aged and infirm were deducted, the males were more fit for field work. Since George Ottley, attorney to Clement Tudway, was extolling the gains in the slave population during his management of the estate, Tudway expressed surprise when the question of hired labour arose, because he had been led to believe the number of slaves was "considerable."[26]

Using slaves on a lend-a-hand basis became common practice towards the end of the eighteenth century and was a direct attempt by managers to meet their labour requirements without incurring additional costs. In a letter to Mrs. Catherine Shipley, Robert Thomson, manager of her estate, assured her of his efforts to reduce expenses: "I have been obliged to now hang a set of your coppers which proves an extra Expence but in doing it I have gone the cheapest way to work, by employing your own Tradesmen, & borrowing others for which I am to make a return in labour, so that there will be little more money to be paid than for the purchase of the lime, Curbing Tiles etc."[27]

Estates that were jointly owned faced severe problems in maintaining their labour force either on the sale of a moiety of the shares of the land and slaves or on the death of a partner. In both cases the remaining partners, to maintain continuity and harmonious relations and to allow the work of the estate to progress smoothly, hired the slaves who were not listed in the mortgage. Normally, new owners negotiated the employment of the affected slaves "at a moderate hire" for as long as the former partners were prepared to leave them on the estate. This was more difficult on the death of a partner, as stipulations in wills had to be met. Usually the slaves were divided up into shares. The remaining partners were charged the cost of hire, negotiated as contingency expenses to the general account of the estate. When disputes arose, arbitration was used to settle all questions pertaining to "the hire of the negroes."[28]

The British West Indian public service also depended to a great extent on the hiring of slaves, when requisitioning failed, for the heavy labour of some institutions such as the regiment. These hired slaves performed tasks that included the digging of trenches and the building of edifices. Slaves were also hired for jobs "where brute force was needed," as in the transportation of equipment and material for the construction of forts and fortifications. On many islands, the Negroes required for the state were requisitioned by the assembly and cost the government only their provisions. Still, government was finding it extremely costly to maintain slaves under its jurisdiction. One governor reported that "at the rate of nine pence Currency Each per day . . . it has been found impossible to afford them food of sufficient nourishment & Quality, considering the very great labour & fatigue, the appearance of the times made it necessary for them to undergo."[29] In Jamaica in 1792, when war in the West Indies seemed imminent and troops were sent there, the initial plan was to hire slaves to serve the regiments. But the cost of hiring and maintaining them was so high that the Colonial Office recommended to the governor that the island purchase its own slaves.[30]

Who were the owners of slaves for hire? It is not possible to identify all the groups who owned slaves and hired them out. Lesser members of the plantation system and proprietors of small estates established jobbing businesses in which they hired out enslaved persons. On some islands there were coloured female slaveowners living in towns who kept slaves for rent. Some merchants and storekeepers in the towns kept slaves for rent. White artisans also acquired small gangs of slaves with whom they worked in the building trades.[31]

Self hire was also an important feature of hiring out. Slaves paid a portion of their wages to their owners for the privilege of working independently. On occasion, these sums negotiated were very large, and independent workers earned less than the payments they were required to make. This was particularly the case with slaves who were prostitutes. The owners selected them for their beauty and thus their perceived earning power, "as it is expected they will be taken into keeping by white or free persons."[32] Hostesses in taverns doubled as prostitutes. They were given "the food they eat, the hard bed they sleep on and the few loose clothes that are hung upon them." Many purchased their freedom with their savings. One writer noted that "it is so common a resource among them, that neither shame nor disgrace is attached to it."[33] When these prostitutes failed to give their owners the large sums expected, they were beaten mercilessly. Nonpayment of agreed sums by hired slaves because of a shortfall in income or because they felt they had earned the money was also common in all colonies and among all categories of hired labour.[34]

Slaves who could not earn the agreed income resorted to theft and other illegal activities to make up the deficit. Some stole grass, which they sold in the towns for "one or two dogs, according to the quantity and demand for it."[35] Predial slaves were pushed exceedingly hard to fulfil their financial arrangements, and were accused of carrying out depredations upon plantations. Many were thus "chopped and maimed by watchmen and taken up as runaways and sent to goal" or the workhouses.[36] As a result of such incidents, in 1794 a Tobago law prohibited owners from allowing their slaves to hire themselves out in any category of employment. Those who flouted the law paid a fine of £10. They also had to register with the police and obtain copper badges, which the slaves wore. A similar registration policy was adopted in British Guiana.[37]

Suppliers of hired labour seem to have been very efficient and businesslike in their operations—probably because the demand for their services was so constant. One attorney wrote to his absentee planter: "We began a fortnight ago on both Estates to hole for the fall plants with jobbers. I have engaged Mr. Lumden's gang to work on P. Hill and McEachern's for Phil[d] but such is the demand for jobbers that they are raising their prices dearly."[38]

Notices giving details of slaves for hire were carried in the newspapers.[39] These advertisements gave information on the gangs including the various tasks that they undertook. However, because of the problem of travel, slaves for hire normally came from within the immediate vicinity of the plantations. Estate administrators knew these gangs, and had preferences based on their work habits. Of course, some managers had their own gangs, kept within easy reach of the plantations. Witness this letter from John Kelly, manager of Duck-enfield Hall estate in Jamaica, complaining about the poor treatment of Ne-groes on Jamaican estates and emphasising the care with which his slaves were maintained: "they are very different circumstanced from those of sugar estates. The few of them that occasionally are sent out to job, never keep spell . . . it not being customary for jobbers to do so. . . . Negroes on sugar estates generally have no days allowed them and certainly not regularly allowed them [during the Crop time]."[40]

Hired labour was certainly not peripheral to the plantation system. It was an important feature of slavery when the plantations could not meet their labour needs. Extra help for the difficult tasks, the ones that caused high mortality rates among their own workers, safeguarded their human capital.[41] And though most of the workers were not free, plantation management still engaged in a market-oriented labour system when they rented slaves. Here, estate administrators dealt with free labour trends such as supply and demand, and their correlation and impact upon the price of labour.

If the practice of hiring slaves for certain aspects of estate work developed during the most profitable years of slavery, when the cost was not burden-some,[42] it became so towards the end of the eighteenth century, when the British West Indian economy was in decline and investment in plantation slaves was a less profitable exercise. Two contradictory positions emerged. On the one hand, attorneys and managers continued to press the need for more hired labour to meet the shortfall. On the other hand, absentee owners were unwilling to give carte blanche for hiring, and preferred to reduce sugarcane cultivation.

Beginning with the American War, when the planters had to produce more local food, many managers withdrew sizeable portions of their slave gangs to plant provisions. This necessitated hiring slaves to make up the lost work on the main functions of the estates.[43] The excessively large number of deaths among the slaves, as reflected in population statistics for some islands, likewise forced managers and planters to continue to hire slaves during the American War and afterwards. And during wars, large gangs of slaves were requisitioned from estates to perform public service, which also seriously reduced all activities on the plantations.

With the decline of the British West Indies in the third quarter of the eigh-teenth century, many planters refused to lay out large amounts of capital on new slaves. Others around this time were hiring jobbers for the heaviest work so as to improve the conditions of their own slaves. Two groups therefore relied on hired labour to maintain production levels. Since planters throughout slavery had been unable to maintain their slave population by natural increase, and were now unable or unwilling to supplement it by purchase, many managers and attorneys were forced to use hired labour to do plantation work.[44] The constant request for increased purchases of slaves to avoid the unprofitable use of hired labour is well documented in the plantation papers. In most cases, hiring slaves was viewed as a stopgap.[45]

The lack of an adequate labour force on many plantations, coupled with an increasing difficulty in hiring slaves beginning around the end of the American War, only added to the sugar industry's instability. One manager pointed out: "we have not strength to put in a plant from which anything capital can be expected."[46] The inadequacy of the labour force continued right down to the abolition of the slave trade, and the continued reliance on hired labour greatly nullified plantation profitability. One manager, commenting on the general condition of the sugar estates in his area of Jamaica, wrote that he could have safely said "that 40 Estates out of 41 are in want of Recruits, thus circumstanced they gradually decrease in negroes in a few years, the loss of which reduces the Crops allmost to Nothing. If a sugar estate is necessitated to engage annually much hired Labor, and to purchase all Mules & Cattle it requires, and if sugar bears a low price, the expences will far exceed the profits."[47]

The absolute necessity of retaining on estates an adequate number of slaves to produce sugar efficiently and profitably was not lost on either the planter class or its managerial group. Yet the economics of the times had forced many to avoid slave purchases, even though the increased reliance on hired slaves was fast becoming a burden. As with the purchase of mules, there was "an absolute necessity to hire negroes to take off the crop otherwise the Estate would be ruined and there is certain contingencies that cannot be avoided upon all West Indian Estates annually whether they make good or bad crops but a good Rum crop goes a good way in Paying them off."[48]

The significant advances in the price of sugar on the British market as a result of the slave revolt in St. Domingue led to increased acreage under cultivation throughout the West Indies, which in turn called for an increased labour force. This, according to one manager, they could not have accomplished "without the assistance of Hired labour."[49] Many managers continued to urge the practice so as to sustain the production level on which the incomes of many were calcu-lated. But they had to balance self-interest gainst their employers' interests. One manager wrote: "Notwithstanding I am sensible of your wish to go to as little expence as possible. I should have gone the length of £500 or £600 in hired labour for the Estate could I have got a Jobber in that neighbourhood but as no such thing is to be had there which will lessen the Crops of 1796 and 1797—The plantation people are busy getting what fall plant is possible and I am well convinced that £200 laid out on that account would have increased our crop at least 15 or 30 hhds sugar."[50]

The need for hiring slave labour continued throughout the rest of the eighteenth century and into the nineteenth. British policy had forced many planters to take their slaves out of cultivation of export crops and to put them into local food production. On some islands, managers lamented: "Yams are planted in our best lands and though it be injurious to them I wish to continue the practice while provisions are at so high a rate. If we were to plant them in inferior soil we should get no crop."[51] This had begun during the American War, and it continued in spite of the rising cost and difficulty of employing jobbing.

Owners and managers found it more and more difficult to procure enough slaves for all their businesses. In addition to the increase in subsistence agriculture at the end of the eighteenth century, the cultivation of secondary crops, chiefly coffee and cotton, posed new challenges to the sugar industry, and put added pressures on a labour force already stretched too thin.[52]

Although the practice of hiring slaves had become very widespread by the end of the eighteenth century, there was no consensus among planters and their managers that it was a great success in all its functions. It is quite noticeable, however, that as the cost of slaves increased significantly in the middle of the 1790s, jobbing gangs were difficult to procure even though their numbers were not significantly reduced. This shortage of employable gangs is unsurprising. Jobbing slaves, the most unfortunate of workers, were hired to carry out the hardest tasks which even plantation slaves were not allowed to do, and as the planter class placed more emphasis on improving their slaves' life expectancy— many owners now did "not if possible allow them to dig cane holes"[53]—the demand for jobbers escalated. So it is perhaps equally unsurprising that the jobber owners were becoming reluctant to allow their gangs to perform all the strenuous work of the estates, as they once did.

The comprehensive use of hired labour resulted more from a shortage of plantation slaves than from any suitability to plantation production. Many managers were quite prepared to use hired slaves for tasks that they considered too dangerous to the health of their own slaves. They were less willing, although forced to make concessions at times, to employ hired slaves widely in the manufacturing end of sugar production. Of this, one planter wrote: "I have been obliged to hire negroes to assist in taking off the crop but they seldom answer so well as if they were belonging to the Estate."[54] But as long as plantation slaves failed to increase naturally and were abnormally costly to replace, the plantation economy had to rely to a great extent on hired labour. At the beginning of the nineteenth century, one manager reported that new slaves were sold "out of the ship...this week at £120 each and I do not think they will ever be lower again, there is so many new coffee plantations settling."[55]

Hired slaves thus became an even more necessary component of the labour supply right down to the end of slavery and the adoption of a free labour system. Indeed, in the postemancipation period, the roving gangs would give continuity to the system of hired labour for particular tasks. Most planters and their managers were made dependent on the system of hired slave labour, and it was tolerated because "nothing but accidental prices" had allowed the estates to sustain such contingencies.[56] But jobbing was an extraordinarily expensive exercise; according to one manager, "its what ought to be avoided, it has cost me within these 4 years 500£ ster. for the hire of as many negroes only, as that sum would have bought at first but in carrying on an Estate 'not to advance is to recede.'"[57]

The prices and conditions of hiring slaves were as varied as the number of West Indian islands. In nearly all the islands, the cost of hiring slave labour depended largely on the season of the year and the type of soil the slaves had to work. In Barbados the price ranged from ten to twenty pence per day, and slaves were "fed at the expence of the person" for whom they laboured.[58] This was an increase of at least 50 percent over earlier prices, and resulted from the general decrease of slaves employed for field work on nearly all West Indian sugar plantations after 1775. In Barbados the enslaved population fell from 71,874 in 1774 to 63,557 in 1788. In Antigua the number of slaves declined by nearly 2,000 in the same period, and fell even further to 30,283 in 1807.

The islands of Nevis and Montserrat confirm the trend of declining slave populations. In 1774 the number of slaves was averaged as being 10,000 each; in 1788 the figures were given as 8,420 in the former island and 8,285 in the latter. In 1807 there was a further falling off in Nevis to some 8,000, as compared with 9,000 in Montserrat. The Grenada population statistics also show declining figures, from 35,118 slaves in 1777 to only 29,942 in 1807. This trend was slightly reversed in St. Vincent and Jamaica. The number of slaves quoted for the former was 11,853 in 1787, advancing to more than 14,000 in 1807, while Jamaica's figures were 205,261 in 1778, 258,700 in 1784, 256,000 in 1788, and 308,000 in 1807.[59]

The ordinary price for rented labourers employed by the day ranged from "seven pence half penny to ten pence, with the ordinary allowance of Food i.e. from a pint and a half to two pints of Corn (computed at a penny per pint) and sometimes (according to their work) a dram with molasses which makes the average here in money and in food, amount to, from Eleven pence half penny per day. . . . The negroes hired to hole at sixty shillings per Acre, earn for their Owners, more than double the medium price of day labour including the douceur of a dram of Rum and Melasses every day, worth about three half pence more than the medium."[60] This is corroborated in the work of William Dickson, whose source material seemed to have been the papers of Joshua Steele, a prominent Barbadian planter.

In most of the Leeward Islands prices for hired slaves appear to have been greater than in Barbados and were to some extent dependent on the category of slave employed. Those working by the day cost about 13½ pence sterling each, plus the normal subsistence by the employer. For the most part, the food supplied to jobbing gangs was inadequate for the rigorous tasks they did. But this was general throughout the plantation system, and the life of a jobbing gang hardly exceeded seven years.[61] The owners of slaves employed to job on such tasks as digging cane holes were paid £3–4 sterling per acre, depending on the type of soil and hence the intensity of the work. These slaves too were subsisted by the employers.

When slaves were leased for long periods—normally at least a year, in some cases as much as three[62]—the charges for leasing were from 10 to 12 percent, and on rare occasions as high as 15 percent, of the appraised value of the slaves. The lessee bore all expenses for insurance, medical costs, food, clothing, and other subsistence charges. The conditions of reevaluation were also stipulated.[63]

The principle upon which slaves were leased seems to have been standard throughout the region; the major difference was the cost. In Montserrat, the charge for holing cane lands was £5 per acre as against 1s 6d to 2s currency for a day's work. Charges in Grenada were also based on the category of slave and the type of work. Owners of slaves rented by the day earned approximately 3s currency, amounting to "one & 20 Pence St." The masters of jobbing gangs apparently preferred to subsist their slaves. This might have meant the owners wished to ensure that their slaves received an adequate diet, or simply that the owners made more money by feeding them themselves. It is likely that in Grenada very few slaves were employed in task work or jobbing gangs, since no price quotations seem to exist for this category. Slaves leased in groups or individually for a year or more earned £12 to £15 per year for individual field hands.

In Dominica, charges for field labour were higher than in Barbados, but as in Grenada the owners subsisted their own gangs on day work. The conditions on leasing appear to have been similar throughout the West Indies as to valuation assessments. In all cases the leased slaves, field hands or skilled workers were well insured and properly maintained by the lessee.[64] When gangs were leased before they were fully of age, the annual charges were higher "in proportion to the expectation of their becoming more valuable at the end of the lease."

In St. Vincent, charges for day labour were about the same as in Grenada, 3s currency. Annual charges varied more than in other islands, ranging from £12 to £16.[65] The practice of hiring slaves was not very widespread in St. Vincent. The chief category rented in that colony was the skilled worker. During the period of employment, they remained at the risk of their proprietors, who were responsible for their insurance and such other charges. Employers met their subsistence.

Some managers encouraged the investment of capital to purchase skilled tradesmen, especially masons, carpenters, and coopers, from Barbados. These workers were to earn an income for the estate through jobbing. Reports indicate that skilled slaves earned significant profits for their owners after repaying their original cost. Though the rates paid to these workers varied according to the value placed on their skills, they were never paid as much as white employees. One manager wrote to his absentee owner: "I have employed a white carpenter and 5 Negroes for 6 months. He is at the rate of £200 per annum and the Negroes £30 each."[66]

Of the skilled slaves, the cooper was at the lowest level, earning up to 90s per month; at the top of the range, an efficient, well-trained, and experienced mason or carpenter could earn as much as £6 12s per month. The owners of domestic servants who were commonly rented were paid a monthly fee of 30s. The least well paid of the hired slaves, but certainly the hardest working, was a field hand. The annual charge for his services generally amounted to only £10–15 with supplies. The incomes of self-hired slaves are not quite clear. Observers hint that all categories of these employees—porters, boatmen, fishermen, drivers, boilers, watchmen, mechanics, domestics, prostitutes—were expected to earn good wages of "between 3 and 4 bits per day."[67]

West Indian plantation papers refer often to the cost of hired labour, but this information mostly concerns field hands. From the evidence relative to skilled labour, we can glean that charges increased towards the end of the eighteenth century for all categories of rented slaves, mainly because of the rising costs of new Africans and the demand for hired labour stemming from the shortage of plantation slaves.[68] By the middle of the 1780s, the planters had been caught in a web of expenses.

With the decline of the British West Indian economy, some planters and their attorneys refused to purchase new Africans. This worked to the great detriment of the estates by restricting plantation activities and lessening production while increasing the incidence of hired labour. The costs actually wound up being higher, as one firm of managers explained: "We have long been with concern the great Expence to which the Spring has been put for want of Negroes. We have often begged Mr. Hall, the attorney, for the other Proprietors of that estate to purchase with us a few new Negroes, but he has constantly objected to it under the Plan that Negroes were dear. There has been however little alteration in their Price these two years, and indeed let their Price be what it may, it cannot be so expensive as jobbing since the jobber receives near 25 percent of his capital."[69]

The dilemma of purchasing new Africans or hiring labour continued to plague planters throughout the 1780s when British restrictions on West Indian trade enhanced the downward trend of the economy, reduced supplies, and forced up production costs. Planters adopted a wait-and-see game attitude to maintaining their labour force, purchasing slaves only when unavoidable. Many managers abhorred this approach. However, they had no choice but to go along with the use of "hired labour, until slaves can be purchased," as one attorney wrote. In his opinion, "the latter mode" was preferable, and he was prepared to "take the first opportunity of making the purchases" that were imperative to the survival of the estates.[70]

The shortage of capital for slave purchases was compounded by the continuous severe shortage of food for the slaves caused by British policy towards the United States. Planters had first to plant provisions before they could purchase slaves. Given this added problem of subsistence, many managers were reluctant to continue the process of seasoning slaves, and hiring was the next best alternative.[71]

Reliance on hired labour was maintained through the 1790s. Demand, and with it cost, was pushed up by the needs of the new coffee and cotton estates, while the use of jobbers on the sugar estates continued to rise. James Craggs, attorney, told Mrs. Henry Goulburn: "The price of hired labour is now in demand from the great number of new coffee plantations now settling. I shall be obliged to hire about 20 Negroes to take off the next crop. Our strength on the estate is so low."[72] By the 1790s, some agricultural activities were performed chiefly by rented labour. For example, of the 90 acres on Nathaniel Phillips's Jamaica estate to be put into cane holes, 80 acres were undertaken by jobbers at the rate of £7 10s per acre, which, according to the attorney, Thomas Barritt, "came to a large amount jobbing last year, and with the £287 due the Factors Dec. last, & the heavy taxes this year, we are now about £700 in their debt and do suppose with the supplies there will be required by the 31 Dec. next, we shall be 10 or £1200 in debt." The price quoted was 10s per acre higher than what Barritt had paid to cane-hole another area of the estate, Boxford Lodge, a year earlier.[73] It seems, however, that attorneys remained reluctant to use hired labour in the manufacturing end of sugar production because of the high cost and unreliable supply.[74]

As the shortage of plantation slaves became more acute, and as conditions on the sugar estates worsened, the cost of hired labour escalated until charges for clearing and fencing an area and planting it with grass, normally considered light plantation work, reached the astounding price of £12 per acre in 1797.[75] Although the price of hired labour by task seemed to have fallen in the following year, the deteriorating conditions on the estate led one attorney to write: "I am afraid my appointment as Yr. atty has been in an unfavourable time, when expences of all kinds accumulate & the price of produce has fallen very low indeed. The accot. for jobbing labor to 1st May 1800 (1 Year) I have reduced on Mesopotamia 70 or 80£ less than the year ending 1 May 1799 but still the taxes have increased the same sum."[76]

The accounts of West Indian estates indicate that large sums were paid annually to a variety of people for hired labour, as the falling slave population could not cope with the sheer quantity of work. However, the records cover only a small part of the estates' existence, and hardly reflect the full cost of the activities undertaken. In 1789, for example, Duckenfield Hall Estate's account with Turney & Jameson, probably the factors or owners of jobbing slaves, shows a charge for Negro hire of £1,090. In the following year, the charges for jobbing amounted to only £141, payable to George Scott, the attorney. Scott's charges for hired labour almost doubled in 1791 to £273. The cost of hiring slaves in the Duckenfield Hall account with MacBean and Bagnold topped £1,000 in 1793. In 1794 the estate's expenses for hired labour in an account current held with

Sandford Peacocke exceeded £2,500.[77] It seems most likely that these charges reflect only a small part of the total cost of rented labour on Duckenfield Hall Estate in any given year.

The Grand Bras Estates in Grenada also expended large sums of money on hiring slaves. The amount claimed by J. C. Hughes in 1804, exclusive of that for the 1st December, exceeded £2,500. The next year, the charge fell significantly but was still high at £1,600 currency. As slaves retained on the estates declined, judging from the smaller overall number kept on the islands from imports, and as the need for rented labour remained high, payments by the Grand Bras Estates in 1806 rose again above the earlier figures.[78]

Many absentee planters became alarmed at the high costs incurred under this heading by their attorneys. They claimed that they could not understand the contradictions inherent in the West Indian slave labour system. On the one hand, they were slave owners with, in their opinion, an adequate number of Negroes to work their estates; some were even constantly pressured to make annual purchases of Africans. On the other hand, their accounts showed high charges for hired labour. In one case when the owner raised objections, the attorney replied: "You mention that as your number of negroes is considerable, you often wonder that others are hired to do part of the plantation work. This I must beg leave to observe has never been the case since my residence here."[79] Others accepted the inadequacy of their labour force and were persuaded to leave decisions about hiring slaves to the attorneys on the spot. Several planters believed that the reintroduction of labour-saving devices would ease the problem on their estates. On Appleton Estate in Jamaica the plough had been used successfully earlier, and the owners, the Dickinsons, recommended its reintroduction.[80]

One absentee, Phillips, took decisive steps to impose a limit of £300 each for jobbing work on both of his estates, Pleasant Hill and Phillipsfield.[81] Barham was equally concerned about his estates' finances. Their decline in production was a major disappointment in light of the continued large expenditure on slave hire. Since Barham was convinced that improved production was not the solution to West Indian problems, he stressed the urgent need for reducing expenses: "Certainly nothing but accidental prices could have enabled the estate to sustain such contingencies as those of last year which (particularly in hired labor) much exceeded what has been the usual standard tho' I am not saying that this was not under circumstances proper which you who are on the spot are unquestionably the best judge."[82]

Such liberality by some absentees in permitting their managers to make crucial money decisions could continue only if the sugar industry was profitable. To the contrary, however, after the initial period of high prices and great profits as a result of the St. Domingue slave revolt, the British policy of destabilizing the industry through various parliamentary measures brought them down significantly by the end of the 1790s. While prices continued high, Barham's liberality prevailed, but he sounded a warning bell that it might not last: "Hired labour I find has amounted to a sum which nothing but the present prices could have borne, & I much fear that they may not continue long."[83]

It was obvious that once prices had receded to any marked degree, most planters would move to limit or even curtail hiring labour to a significant degree. While Barham tended to consent to his managers' use of hired labour, he was always conscious that the practice was unprofitable in the long run. He wrote to his attorneys that the choice of labour for his estates must always be decisively advantageous to his interest. Given the falling profitability of his estates, he observed, the use of hired labour made "sugar . . . too dear & in the present fluctuation of affairs expence is [best] avoided unless the advantage be clear & important."[84]

Compounding the problem was the loss of the United States market for rum—the commodity that, for most of the eighteenth century, had not only served as currency in the American trade but had covered nearly all of the contingent charges on the estates. When British commercial policy after the American Revolution vitually ended rum sales to the United States, it also virtually ended the planters' ability to meet their bills. The lost source of revenue had helped to pay, among other things, the cost of their labour. So now, even when attorneys were allowed to purchase new Africans or to hire slaves, the revenue from rum sales was inadequate to meet the costs of contingent expenses.

The history of master-slave relations is fraught with contradictions. Of course, planters were in the business to make profits, and at a time when they were expending large sums of money with little return, it is unreasonable to expect them not to have been concerned about their capital investments. Hired labour was an attempt by some owners to maintain their capital investment in their slaves by not working them excessively. This is vividly described in a letter from Henry Goulburn to his attorney, Thomas Samson: "The charge also for digging two cane pieces seems very considerable. With a view to avoid the recurrence of such charges as the last & to which the labor of the negroes which I fear tends to the annual decrease of their number I certainly can have no difficulty in authorising a purchase whenever one can be conveniently made."[85]

Nearly all planters who wished to cease renting slaves were conscious that this would place immense stress on their own population. They concluded that the best course was to reduce the cultivation of sugarcane. This would keep down expenses and would reduce the supply on the sugar market, leading to better prices. But cutting back on cultivation had another function. It would reduce the workload of the slaves, as Barham pointed out to his attorneys: "If the negroes are unequal to the present work, the plant must be diminished. Hired labor cannot be afforded unless it be for some good exigency."[86] Yet a sense of great humanity motivated the actions and decisions of Barham. His directives are always couched in language that had some consideration for his slaves. In spite of his losses, when he asked Wedderburn and Company to cut back on his expenses quite markedly, he took care to write: "with regard to hired labour I must leave it to your discretion. You must best know what will pay in point of profit & what is requisite to care for my own slaves which latter point I hope will never be out of mind."[87]

The slipping financial position of the planters brought changes in the labour practices on their estates. Previously, slaves were hired to do much of the plantation work, especially the tasks considered too demanding for their own slaves. Now most requests for hired labour were disallowed. While some planters continued to accede to the recommendations of their employees, other absentees were not so indulgent. An application to Lord Penrhyn for permission to hire a gang of slaves met with this retort: "But will you first of all inform me—a gang of how many workers will be wanted to make 200 hogsheads—How many acres could such a gang of workers, in May or June or time enough to put in Plants sufficient to make that quantity of sugar—and to be paid for by instalments in June 89, June 90, June 91—When you have furnished me with answers to these questions I will write further to you on this topic."[88]

The above approach not having deterred his managers from engaging hired labour, Lord Penrhyn took a more direct line to stamp it out. Yet he remained sympathetic to the plight of his slaves and was concerned that despite the large number of women, totalling 229, there were only 11 children. His concern must be seen in light of the general state of the sugar industry. His humanity towards his slaves must also be seen primarily as an attempt to preserve his capital investment. This is why Penrhyn adopted a policy similar to Barham's, opting for decreased cane cultivation and sugar production rather than increased hired labour. In response to Penhryn's orders to Fearon to terminate hired labour on his estates, Fearon assured him that he planned to train estate enslaved persons to replace the hired cooper who had been employed by his predecessor.[89]

Another move afoot was in the area of hired skilled labour. The cost of this category of worker was extremely high, ranging from £4 10s to more than £6 per month.[90] Since all estates needed at least one cooper, some managers had already adopted the policy of training personnel from among the well-established and tractable plantation Negro families to ply this trade, as well as other skills. Other managers recommended the purchase of various classes of skilled workers to be employed in pressing cases on their own estates, but mainly to be rented out as jobbers.[91]

By the last quarter of the eighteenth century the policy of hiring slaves had been well established within the plantation system. The decline of the British West Indian economy had restricted its unlimited development. However, it is quite possible that this activity became more entrenched within the slave system after the termination of the slave trade. Hired labour grew out of the decline of the plantations' slave populations. Attorneys, managers, and overseers used the emoluments they received from the estates to purchase small plots of land adjoining the estates on which they were employed. Here they kept their slaves whom they hired out to their masters.

In many cases, the system engendered conflicts of interests, as in the case of Thomas Samson who, when he was appointed attorney, was allowed to keep the slaves he had owned as an overseer. He was also permitted to hire them out to the estate on which he was manager.[92] In Barbados, planters complained of the fraudulent practices of their attorneys who owned slaves that they employed on the estates over which they had control.[93] Many ills originated from such a system. The manager of Barham's estate claimed that, under the system of rented labour, the "attention & industry of the overseers are too often lessened by the hope of hired labour & exertion is at an end. The field canes is extended beyond the possibility of being properly cleaned by the Estate negroes; a partial distribution of labour upon a large surface cannot be so beneficial as when confined to a smaller space, added to all this, is the longer carriage of the Canes to the Mill by which in wet weather the Estate suffers prodigiously."[94]

Even though hired labour, as a system, allowed for flexibility in labour practices during slavery, it retarded the adoption and expansion of technological innovation.[95] Writers who have considered this issue blame the existence of slaves for the failure of the plantation system to adopt such devices as the plough. None of the documents that I have examined makes this charge. However, one nineteenth-century observer of West Indian plantation life saw the incompatibility in the economic interests of the planters and of their managers and attorneys. Since the hiring of slaves for the holing and planting of cane lands was such an entrenched practice in the British West Indies, especially in Jamaica, most managers who held slaves found it extremely convenient and profitable to let out the slaves to their employers "for the purpose of holing and planting his ground by the laborious method of the hoe."[96] It was simply in their interests to maintain the status quo and prevent the implementation of change.

The quality of work by hired labour was not always of the best. One Barbadian planter, Joshua Steele, initiated the practice of using his enslaved force to undertake all jobbing exercises on his estate. This was voluntary on the part of the slaves, who were paid "a small pecuniary reward over and above their usual allowance, to do the extra work performed by jobbers. His slaves did the holing ... for less than a fourth part of the stated price to the jobbers."[97]

When using hired labour, employers had to pay market rates. In fact, within slavery there was created an entire service industry, in which people who owned slave labour that was not committed to any plantation sold it on terms dictated by market demands. Slaves could be hired for all categories of work. The owners, while making substantial incomes, could avoid the cost of maintaining their workers, as the employers generally fed and housed them. Hired labour was a form of capital investment that, through the exploitation of others' labour, allowed owners to maximise the earnings of all categories of workers, including children. It is particularly interesting that the practice became so profitable at a time when the plantations themselves were in crisis and the value of the major British West Indian crops, especially sugar, was falling. It is also interesting that even when skilled labour could be procured from among blacks, at reasonable rates, it appears that most employers provided white supervision, which maintained the image of the black skilled worker as dependent and reliant. On the whole, however, even though hiring slaves had weakened the paternalistic ties between slaves and masters, it developed stronger capitalist ones.

By the end of the eighteenth century, the practice of hiring slaves had become entrenched in the British West Indies in all areas of the economy. In the rural communities, with the decline of the field hands and the inability to invest large amounts of capital in slave purchases, the estates had to rely on hiring slaves for all aspects of plantation work. In the towns, the rising number of slaves whose time could not be fully employed by their owners, coupled with these owners' desire for sources of cash, developed a system of self-hire that covered most economic activities on land and water. In fact, prostitution became a way for white managers and planters to deal with cash shortfalls. Among slaves, serving as hired labour created a sense of independence and assured them that they could survive on their own. The predial slaves who cultivated their "places" realized significant success in this activity, as their crops found a ready market among all free classes on the islands. Thus began the transition from chattel slave to peasant and wage earner. In the towns, the skilled slaves who performed many of the jobs were allowed to travel freely within the island. Even prostitutes worked independently, and many were later able to purchase their freedom from their earnings. Others who did remain enslaved did so in order to safeguard the children born from these relationships.

In the agricultural sector, the system of hired labour continued into the postemancipation period with the "roving gangs." The rates of pay of these gangs were much lower than during slavery, as the exploitation of labour continued. Hired labour had provided many slaves with satisfactory incomes, which enabled them to participate in the market economy. Furthermore, it showed up all the contradictions in the traditional arguments defending slavery. It is quite obvious that slaves entered into contracts both with their masters and with employers. As income earners and consumers, they influenced the markets, but they continued to be legally restricted and considered chattel. Many ills also emerged from the system of self-hire. Slaves were forced into stealing in order to meet their commitments, and many black women became prostitutes to satisfy the monetary greed of a "pimpish" planter/managerial class. But for good or ill, hired slave labour was indeed a fundamental and integral part of the system of slavery.

8

British Caribbean Slavery and Abolition

The end of the eighteenth century was one of the most significant periods in the continuation of the plantation system. Supplies from the United States were restricted and its shipping was excluded. Many planters were forced to initiate changes in their systems of management to meet the hardships wrought by Britain's United States policy and the decline of the West Indian economy. Compounding this was the rise of the free trade movement, which appealed to the self-interest of Englishmen. Free trade was posited as the alternative to the system of monopoly on which the British West Indian sugar industry had been developed and maintained. Exclusivity in each other's markets, for slaves on the one hand and sugar on the other, was a compact between the mother country and its colonies. The arrangement had nurtured the sugar industry, which in turn consumed large numbers of Africans and which had also given British financial institutions and the fledging industrial sector guaranteed markets in which they emerged and matured during the seventeenth and eighteenth centuries.

Secure in their productive and marketing capacity, and emboldened by the free trade arguments enshrined in Adam Smith's *The Wealth of Nations,* opponents of monopoly for the sugar industry moved for its dismantling through a direct attack on the slave trade and British West Indian slavery. British society did not initially seek the abolition of slavery on humanitarian grounds. Yet it was clear at the end of the eighteenth century that the destruction of the slave trade was the first step in the termination of slavery, for both reasons. The West Indian plantation force was not maintained by natural increase—although several individual plantations had kept up their slave population through amelioration—so if there were no new imported Africans, the policy adopted by the British government would ultimately end slavery as the primary form of labour.

The question of the slave trade was actively debated in the West Indies even before the apparent decline of the economy and certainly before the advent of British humanitarianism. In Barbados, non-slaveholding residents favoured its ending. They fervently believed that the island would gain from such action.[1] Still, no serious effort was made by the government of Barbados to interfere with the trade. In Jamaica, however, as a result of the slave revolt in 1763, two attempts were made to restrict the slave trade. The 1774 legislation limiting the age of new slaves was disallowed by the Board of Trade because of opposition from the merchants of Liverpool and Bristol. The Assembly of Jamaica opposed the Board's decision on grounds of justice and humanity. To this charge the Earl of Dartmouth, the Board's president, emphatically stated: "We cannot allow the Colonies to check & discourage in any degree, a traffic, so beneficial to the nation."[2]

So the wishes of the colonists were overridden by British mercantile interests. There were double standards in European society about the slave trade and slavery. In response to Lord Mansfield's decision in the Somerset case, which ruled that slavery could not exist on English soil, Benjamin Franklin mocked British hypocrisy, "which encourages such a detestable commerce by laws for promoting the Guinea Trade; while it piqued itself on its virtue, love of liberty, and the equality of its courts in setting free a single negro."[3]

Though hailed as monumental, Mansfield's decision had little or no impact on the trade, which increased from the middle of the eighteenth century to the outbreak of the American War of Independence in 1776. Although important to the continued operation of the plantation system, the slave trade was increasingly perceived as damaging to the economic interests of the planter class. One anonymous writer observed that the trade held out to planters' agents in the islands opportunities for "speculation which ruinously direct them from the employers business—which offer them temptation that hardly leaves it in their power to be honest—and above all it furnishes the means of producing a greater quantity of sugar than the market can bear, thereby reducing the whole mass of W.I. property of like value."[4]

In spite of attempts in the colonies to restrict the slave trade because of its threat to destroy the society by rebellion and because it drained the financial resources of the planter class, the commerce continued unabated with ruinous effect on the African population and heightened potential for the destruction of plantation society in the Caribbean. William Wilberforce, the spokesman for the abolitionists, began his attack on the trade by identifying its numerous ills, among which he listed the wanton and senseless dispersion of the African population and the destruction of family life through the subjugation of a people, the merciless exploitation of their labour, and the violation of their persons. Estimates suggest that for every African imported into the West Indies alive, another two or three were either killed or maimed in the raids conducted to capture them. The slave traders destroyed their villages without remorse. "All these proceedings" occurred in a country in which, according to Wilberforce, the inhabitants were "an honest, peaceable, cheerful, social set of Beings." Then they were taken into the British slave system, which he believed was more barbarous "than that of any other European nation."[5]

The growth of the slave trade to the British West Indies occurred at a phenomenal rate in the eighteenth century, according to statistics on Africans imported after 1750 (see table 8.1).[6] This accounted in part for the measures

Table 8.1. Slave trade in Jamaica, 1750–1806

Year	Africans imported	Africans exported	Africans retained	Percentage retained	Triennial mean export percentage
1750	3,587	721	2,866	79.90	
1751	4,840	718	4,122	85.17	
1752	6,117	1,038	5,079	83.03	17.30
1753	7,661	902	6,759	88.23	
1754	9,551	1,592	7,959	83.33	
1755	12,723	598	12,125	95.30	11.05
1756	11,166	1,902	9,264	82.97	
1757	7,935	943	6,992	88.12	
1758	3,405	411	2,994	87.93	13.66
1759	5,212	681	4,531	86.93	
1760	7,573	2,368	5,205	68.73	
1761	6,480	642	5,838	90.09	18.08
1762	6,279	232	6,047	96.31	
1763	10,079	1,582	8,497	84.30	
1764	10,213	2,639	7,574	74.16	15.08
1765	8,931	2,006	6,925	77.54	
1766	10,208	672	9,536	93.42	
1767	3,248	375	2,873	88.45	13.53
1768	5,950	485	5,465	91.85	
1769	3,575	420	3,155	88.25	
1770	6,824	836	5,988	87.75	10.72
1771	4,183	671	3,512	83.96	
1772	5,278	923	4,355	82.51	

Year	Africans imported	Africans exported	Africans retained	Percentage retained	Triennial mean export percentage
1773	9,676	800	8,876	91.73	13.93
1774	18,448	2,511	15,937	86.39	
1775	9,292	1,629	7,663	82.47	
1776	18,400	3,384	15,016	81.61	16.51
1777	5,607	588	5,019	89.51	
1778	5,191	772	4,419	85.13	
1779	3,348	484	2,864	85.54	13.27
1780	3,267	252	3,015	92.29	
1781	7,049	294	6,755	95.83	
1782	6,291	1,868	4,423	70.31	13.86
1783	9,644	64	9,580	99.34	
1784	15,468	4,635	10,833	70.03	
1785	11,046	4,667	6,379	57.75	24.29
1786	5,655	3,658	1,997	35.31	
1787	5,976	2,083	3,893	65.14	
1788	3,287	2,530	757	23.03	58.84
1789	9,808	2,030	7,778	79.30	
1790	14,063	1,976	12,087	85.95	
1791	15,900	4,092	11,808	74.26	20.15
1792	14,761	2,663	12,098	81.96	
1793	23,018	1,915	21,103	91.68	
1794	14,590	3,041	11,549	79.16	15.73
1795	12,291	4,649	7,642	62.17	
1796	7,409	2,490	4,919	66.39	
1797	9,587	2,045	7,542	78.67	31.06
1798	9,926	489	9,437	95.07	
1799	15,047	412	14,635	97.26	
1800	19,311	5	19,306	99.97	2.57
1801[a]	7,200	—	7,200	100.00	
1802	8,933	2,712	6,221	69.64	
1803	6,391	2,092	4,299	67.27	20.03
1804	5,979	1,811	4,168	69.71	
1805	5,684	515	5,169	90.94	
1806	8,487	166	8,321	98.04	13.77

Sources: "Account of Negroes Retained in Each Island ... 1783 to 1788," PRO, CO 318/1, fo. 141; "An Account of Slaves Imported and Exported from Jamaica," *Journals of the Assembly of Jamaica,* 10:369; Macpherson, *Annals of Commerce,* 4:155; Metcalf, *Royal Government,* app.; "Negroes Imported from Africa into Jamaica and Exported from the Said Island, 1750 to 1775," BL, Add. MSS 12,431; "Papers on the Statistics of Jamaica 1739–1778," BL, Add. MSS 12,435, fol. 270; *Parliamentary Papers* (HMSO), vol. 82, no. 622, and vol. 87, pp. 497–98; *Parliamentary Papers* (IUP), 61:237, 426–27; see also Add. MSS 12,435, fols. 16, 30, 37d.

Note: Figures for 1801 are for only half the year.

adopted by the Assembly of Jamaica to restrict the importation of slaves over thirty years old. It was one thing to have an adequate labour force, but it was difficult and risky to attempt to enslave adults of this age. One of the most significant features of the statistics is the number of slaves retained on the islands. In Jamaica, more than 80 percent of the Africans imported were retained. Between 1750 and the early 1770s, because of increased activity, the sugar plantations bought the largest portion. New sugar estates were established and old ones were expanded. The period also witnessed the development of the coffee industry, which accounted for a large share of imports, especially in the last quarter of the century when the sugar industry was in crisis and the coffee producers increased their operations.[7]

Several trends can be identified in table 8.1. After 1750, there is a significant growth in the number of captive Africans imported annually. The years immediately preceding wars witness some of the largest imports. Peaks are evident in 1754–56, again in 1774–76, and in 1790–1793. The years of war show a decline, which is followed by recovery in the immediate postwar years, as in the periods 1763–66 and 1783–85. There was no significant period of peace between the French Revolution and the Napoleonic Wars. However, the decade 1790–1800 was influenced by the threat of abolition. The market was thus pressured into taking more new Africans than usual.

While imports tell a story, the number of Africans purchased for local use had a greater impact on the economy. From 1750 right up to 1783, more than 86 percent of imported captives were retained. Until this time, apart from wars, there were no threats to the plantation system. The American War and then British policy towards the United States changed this trend, as did the rapid economic development of the foreign West Indian islands, especially St. Domingue and Cuba, which also consumed a large number of slaves. After the order-in-council of 2 July 1783, the percentage of new Africans reexported increased. In fact, between 1783 and 1785, approximately 26 percent of the Africans imported were sold on. In the next three years, 1786–88, over 50 percent of the captive Africans brought to Jamaica were reexported. There was no significant period of peace between the French Revolution and the Napoleonic wars. The decade 1790–1800 was also influenced by rebellion in St. Domingue and the threat of abolition. Because of the latter, the market was pressured into taking more captive Africans than would normally have been the case.

A similar upward trend is noticeable in reexports from other islands after 1784 (table 8.2). The statistics for 1784–1806 show that in Dominica, Barbados,

Table 8.2. Percentages of Africans reexported from sugar islands listed, 1784–1806

Year	Antigua	Barbados	Dominica	Grenada	Jamaica	St. Vincent	Sugar colonies generally
1784	21.5	0.0	70.5	17.3	30.0	42.3	18.43
1785	300.9	0.0	59.9	18.1	42.3	65.3	23.23
1786	14.3	62.5	50.5	9.5	64.7	41.7	22.53
1787	6.5	12.0	73.9	15.5	34.9	0.3	25.52
1788	16.6	80.1	79.9	34.2	77.0	25.1	45.77
1789	45.0	89.1	93.6	66.9	20.7	35.5	40.91
1790	—	69.5	77.6	79.6	14.0	44.7	34.45
1791	—	72.8	73.6	74.2	25.7	30.3	41.82
1792	—	79.4	65.8	71.9	18.0	—	—
1793	—	76.9	54.9	70.8	8.3	—	—
1794	—	77.4	—	67.8	20.8	—	—
1795	—	83.9	—	150.0	38.2	60.1	—
1796	150.4	91.5	10.0	137.8	33.6	179.1	55.20
1797	38.7	83.6	17.2	226.7	21.3	16.8	47.26
1798	68.2	85.8	43.9	46.3	4.9	11.4	18.26
1799	—	75.7	36.9	34.8	2.7	20.2	15.51
1800	92.9	95.2	0.9	69.9	0.0	108.2	4.86
1801	—	—	—	52.1	—	51.6	4.09
1802	—	65.8	65.3	14.0	30.4	—	21.33
1803	69.2	78.6	6.4	70.5	32.7	—	22.55
1804	—	85.5	0.0	60.7	30.3	—	—
1805	0.0	0.0	16.7	—	9.1	—	0.69
1806	—	—	—	—	2.0	—	—

Sources: "Abstract of the Number & Value of Slaves Imported and Exported at St. George's, Grenada between 1 April 1784 and 1 November 1792," BL, Add. MSS 38,228, fol. 231; "Account of Negroes Imported and Exported from the British West India Islands, 1783–1788," PRO, CO 318/1, fol. 141; "Account of Negroes Imported into and Exported from Roseau 1788 to December 1804," PRO, CO 71/28; "An Account of Slaves Imported and Exported from Jamaica," *Journals of the Assembly of Jamaica,* 9:369; "An Account of the Number of Slaves in Barbados, 1780 to 1789, Inclusive," PRO, CO 28/62, fol. 262; "An Account of the Slaves Imported into and Exported from St. Vincent 1784–1789," 25 July 1789, PRO, CO 260/9, and see 16 July 1789–20 September 1791, CO 260/73; "Answers to Queries," 4 October 1788, PRO, CO 71/14; Barbados Census, Melville Papers, NLS, MS 1711, fols. 75–77; Macpherson, *Annals of Commerce,* 4:155, 228; Metcalf, *Royal Government,* app.; "Papers on the Statistics of Jamaica 1739–1778," BL, Add. MSS 12,435, fol. 270; *Parliamentary Papers* (HMSO), vol. 82, no. 622; vol. 84, *Accounts and Papers,* vol. 26: supp. to no. 15, app. 31; vol. 87, pp. 497–98; "Slaves Imported and Exported from Antigua," 4 December 1788, PRO, CO 152/67; "Slaves Imported into the West Indies, 1790–1800," Dalhousie Papers, NAS, GD 45/7/5, fol. 82; W. Young, *Common-Place Book.*

Grenada, and St. Vincent, while a number of "saltwater" Africans were retained, most were reexported. Some years, there was even an excess of exports over imports.

The older colonies of Antigua and Barbados had become centres for reexports. In Barbados the plantations met most of their needs through natural increase. In the debate in Parliament over the motion to abolish the slave trade, William Pitt the Younger as prime minister informed the House that Barbados had not imported a slave for nine years.[8] The credit squeeze on that island had greatly impeded the purchase of new Africans, whose prices stood above £50 sterling in 1785. Dominica was by no means a true sugar colony. It was far too hilly and rainy to produce high-quality sugarcane. The major crop was coffee, which required many fewer slaves than sugar. Under the Free Port Act, a large number of new captives was reexported annually, though the figures dropped after 1796. Contrariwise, in Barbados and Grenada the trend of high reexports was maintained throughout the period. Jamaica and St. Vincent were considered frontier colonies, with significant quantities of undeveloped land, so more "saltwater" Africans were retained.

The ending of the American War brought a flurry of activity. Planters moved quickly to restructure/rationalize the sugar industry in the wake of their severe losses in both production and personnel. After wars, it was the normal practice to increase imports of new Africans into the islands in order to regain lost ground—and because planters tended to prosper in wartime. During the American War, however, they had suffered heavily, from the loss of markets, the loss of supply sources, and the loss of large numbers of their slaves owing to food shortages, disease, violence, overwork, accidents, and natural causes. The war had also cut into slave imports and the enslaved population. The need to retain new captive Africans in the colonies was now particularly pressing, but British policy greatly restricted this. It restricted the rum trade too, forcing planters to reduce their purchases of Africans because of a shortfall in income.

The consequence of the American War and British policy was the decline of the slave trade to the British West Indies at the end of the eighteenth century, as table 8.3 illustrates. In Barbados, for example, few new Africans were imported after the relatively good imports between 1764 and 1772. The figures for 1773–76 show a decline to 2,844; imports all but disappeared in 1777–80 when only 41 new Africans were taken. There were recoveries in 1781–92, with a slight increase in the middle years 1785–88. A significant feature of the trade was the rapid growth in imports into Barbados after 1793. In fact, the number of imports in

1792–96 was almost triple that for 1773–76, and it was even higher in 1797–1800. A possible explanation for this growth in imports has virtually nothing to do with the sugar industry. As have been shown, reexports from Barbados were very high for the entire last quarter of the eighteenth century, and particularly so in the years 1792–1800 when they ranged between 75.7 and 95.2 percent of imports.

Table 8.3. Africans imported into Antigua, Barbados, Dominica, and Jamaica, 1773–1800

Year	Barbados		Dominica		Jamaica		Antigua	
1773	1,269		2,011		10,729		—	
1774	289		2,349		17,687		—	
1775	879		5,687		17,364		1,431	
1776	407	2,844	3,032	13,079	18,400	64,180	630	2,061
1777	34		1,996		5,607		345	
1778	7		305		5,191		321	
1779	—		—		3,348		—	
1780	—	41	—	2,301	3,267	17,413	81	747
1781	1,138		—		7,049		210	
1782	303		—		6,291		1,164	
1783	—		—		9,644		1,491	
1784	—	1,441	5,371	5,371	15,468	38,452	2,146	5,011
1785	120		6,254		11,046		112	
1786	606		8,407		5,645		952	
1787	713		6,383		5,682		582	
1788	1,585	3,024	6,203	27,247	6,131	28,504	580	2,226
1789	556		3,647		9,898		311	
1790	131		2,271		14,063		—	
1791	426		2,390		15,343		268	
1792	744	1,857	3,632	11,940	14,761	54,065	—	579
1793	1,438		2,037		23,018		—	
1794	1,218		150		14,590		—	
1795	2,059		—		12,291		—	
1796	3,582	8,297	299	2,486	7,409	57,308	278	278
1797	3,461		349		9,587		380	
1798	3,244		972		9,926		337	
1799	1,968		1,241		15,047		—	
1800	830	9,503	962	3,524	19,311	53,871	283	1,000

Sources: Same as table 8.2.

Dominica showed little growth in imports of Africans after the years 1773–76 except for 1785–88. It is quite noticeable that reexports were also high, ranging roughly from 50 to 80 percent. The number of new Africans brought into the island fell off consistently between 1789 and 1797. In Antigua the trade in new Africans was virtually terminated after 1775, except for the four-year period 1781–84 which was mostly wartime.

The island that allows us to look most analytically at the performance of the slave trade and subsequently slavery in the British West Indies during the years 1773–1800 is certainly Jamaica. This island, because of its vast new lands and its propensity for diversification of its agriculture, was perceived as a frontier colony with the capacity to increase production in most West Indian commodities as well as to grow significant quantities of provisions. Imports of Africans showed a general decline after the period 1773–76 when 64,180 new captives were imported. This number fell markedly from 1777 to 1788 except for 1784, the first year of peace after the American war, then recovered between 1789 and 1800. Yet it must be noted that no four-year span 1777–1800 equaled or exceeded that from 1773 to 1776. Outside the table, the four years 1790–94 exceeded 1773–76 by over 3,500 captive Africans, a result of the loss ot re-exports to St. Domingue.

The smaller imports of Africans at the end of the eighteenth century posed a crucial labour problem for West Indian planters. Natural increase did not maintain population levels, and most members of the workforce were now growing old and infirm. The large numbers on the slave lists did not always reflect the true situation, as Barham was informed: "From the state of the list of slaves now sent, you will be enabled to form … a just conclusion of their effective strength which allowing for sickness, casualties etc. seldom admits one day with another both of working and able negroes more than fifty to sixty workers which from your knowledge are perfectly inadequate to the ends of the property … and without the addition of further assistance must even with every humanity and attention ultimately impair its present powers."[9]

The strains on the already depleted labour force had worried several managers who were directed, in the name of amelioration, to employ "3 negroes to do the labour of 2." In reality, such practices could not be adopted because of the reduced strength of the gangs and the laborious nature of cane cultivation. One way to resolve this dilemma was to hire slaves on contract or by the job, and most managers did so, but it deepened the indebtedness of the planters. Overall, planters and managers worried continuously about the decreasing size and health of their labour force as they witnessed the dissipation of their capital and the erosion of the profitable returns needed to keep up their estates.[10] The problem of an inadequate supply of field hands, despite long slave lists, persisted throughout the period and was attested to by the managers who wrote: "considering at present that there are near 100 children not yet capable of labour and 100 employed as Tradesmen, Watchmen for the pen, Invalids etc—so that effective strength for field work is very small."[11]

At the end of the eighteenth century there were simply too many infirm or sickly people among the slave population.[12] As imports decreased, mortality through overwork, malnutrition, and disease remained high. The workforce was inadequate to provide satisfactory labour on the plantations, and too old and diseased to reproduce.[13] Death, infertility, poor diets, inadequate housing, stress, diseases, abortions, miscarriages, and the resolve among slave women not to bring children into a world of harsh labour, brutality, and the denigration of black people continued to plague West Indian plantations. The link between overwork and deaths was obvious because mortality rose during periods of high production. Also, slaves on cotton and coffee plantations, where labour was less severe, lived longer and increased naturally. Hence, there were many calls for the reduction of labour on "sugar estates so far as to put the negroes on an equal footing with their counterparts on other plantations."[14]

The reduction of imported foodstuffs from the United States increased malnutrition and conjoined with other factors to initiate the most severe period of illness and death among the Caribbean slaves in the eighteenth century. From as early as the middle of 1785, attorneys complained of the disastrous effect of the persistent scarcity of provisions. After 1780, hurricanes worsened matters by destroying provision grounds. Jamaica was probably the most severely affected. A series of hurricanes in the 1780s was followed by one on 1 September 1790, called the worst for a decade, that flattened buildings and provision grounds, including plantain walks. Herds of roving cattle added to the devastation. Estates were purchasing new Africans without adequate supplies of provisions, which increased the mortality rate in the seasoning period. On one estate, some forty-nine new Africans were suffering from such entrenched malnutrition that they had to be fed specially. Of these, thirty were described as "either Meagre, Bloated taken to eating dirt or with most dreadful ulcers." Under such conditions the estate doctor felt that his services were useless and that the Africans needed "the best generous nourishment." Their value fell below £30 per head.[15]

Food supplies from Britain, Ireland, and Canada were inadequate to satisfy West Indian demands. The shortage of United States supplies perpetuated the practice adopted during the American War of employing slaves to plant provisions. Yams were now cultivated on sugar lands, though the yam crop reportedly damaged the soil and, overall, the operation was much more costly than the "cheaper supply of American articles" would have been. The dilemma for the managers worsened when the yam crop failed.[16] The problems of feeding the slaves continued, with serious consequences for plantation production. At best the quantity of provisions raised was minimal. Throughout the French Revolutionary Wars, estates experienced shortages, as one reported: "The fall corn crop at Pepper Having totally Failed all that could be spared from Barton Isles was sent there but it will be greatly insufficient. . . . The Watchwell People are totally without any sort."[17]

Poor diets added to unhealthy living and working conditions inevitably increased the occurrence of disease. Not only did the slave population contain a high percentage of old, sickly, and invalid people, but many others were listed as physically handicapped by ailments such as yaws, sores, or lameness.[18] An examination of the slave lists and reports from attorneys affords an interesting assessment of the health of the various classes of enslaved people. Most of the skilled Negroes, the drivers, carpenters, and other artisans were listed as "able." Coopers, probably from the rigours of their job, were "weakly" to "very weakly." While field workers were categorised for the most part as "able" or "healthy," many were considered "weakly." The majority of young boys were "healthy." Infants too young to work were normally in good health, although many had yaws. A high proportion of the women were listed as "healthy." However, a significant number were either "weakly" or "sickly." Like the boys, the young girls were generally "healthy." Overall, on most slave lists, there were more women than men, but more of the former were cited as unhealthy. There were also more women listed as field hands on many plantations.

Viewed as statements of capital investment in humans, these slave lists contain too many invalids or unhealthy workers. Large sums of money were lost annually by purchasing new Africans who were quickly worn out. Decreasing imports at the end of the eighteenth century resulted in plantation lists containing a high percentage of "very old & superannuated" workers. The incidence of disease compounded the problem, and the field hands available for work on sugar plantations were reduced, according to one report, "to a very small number not half of the whole—with so weak a gang much Revenue cannot be expected."[19]

There were also periodic and seasonal diseases after prolonged rains, hurricanes, or other natural calamities. These illnesses were different from the chronic ones among the slave population; they included the common cold, fevers, whooping cough, pleurisy, measles, and chicken pox. Many became endemic on plantations throughout the Caribbean. Children were particularly susceptible, with high mortality rates. Even though some of these ailments were considered minor and "readily yielded to medicines," they caused many deaths primarily because the victims were in such poor physical condition.[20] The fall of 1787 was adjudged one of the sickliest in memory. High fevers had reached epidemic level in the Leeward Islands. One planter wrote that "many both of the white inhabitants & Negroes have died. In some estates the number sick at one time has been astonishingly great, even so many as to amount to one half of their Gangs. You have been more fortunate, as I never had above twenty at any one time. In the course of the year we have lost six people."[21] In 1790 an outbreak of pleurisy in Antigua led to heavy losses. "One plantation alone lost 9."[22]

The flux was one of the most common illnesses, afflicting workers of all ages. It was basically a dietary complaint, which many managers diagnosed as resulting from the consumption of unripe and uncooked fruits and vegetables. One Jamaica absentee planter was informed that forty-six of his slaves were so afflicted.[23] Heavy doses of salt were administered as medicine and may have contributed to complications associated with high salt retention in Africans and their descendants.

At intervals the slave and free populations were ravaged by a rare disease which the doctors and managers called influenza. This was attended with "violent inflammatory fevers."[24] Others associated the attacks with a severe type of pneumonia, which did untold destruction to slave life in a brief time. The full scale of the deaths is never quite clear, because many managers allayed the fears of absentee owners by assuring them that, although casualties were high throughout the island, their estates had escaped with severe illnesses but hardly any deaths.[25]

In 1793 influenza raged throughout the West Indies. Reports from the Leeward Islands showed that the disease decimated the enslaved population in the region.[26] Its effects were severely felt in Jamaica among both ethnic groups. Illnesses lasted in excess of a month. One of the worst-hit parishes was Vere, with Westmoreland and Hanover also heavily affected. A manager described this outbreak as "a kind of influenza" which "amongst the ablest people produced pleurisy. Very few, either white or Black have escaped. We have felt it very severely. This is the fourth week that there has been from 60 to 80 Negroes in the hot house a Doctor almost constantly on the Estate, the overseer or a Bookkeeper attending Night and Day." Within two weeks of this report, the situation had eased: "Conditions had improved vastly; many slaves regained their health and work was resumed."[27]

Episodes of severe illness continued to attack the population in the years of this study. In 1802 prolonged periods of illness reappeared with "the greatest mortality." These were attended with severe food shortages, which left the slaves with "nothing to eat." The outbreak continued into 1803. The major symptoms were soreness of the throat and malignant fevers. On this occasion, the hardest-hit groups were the white plantation employees. One estate reportedly lost some twenty people. Three years later another epidemic, identified by some as whooping cough and by others as influenza, decimated the black population. There were unusually many deaths, and the illness reportedly baffled all medical knowledge on the islands. Then in 1810 an epidemic once more ran through the slave populations of the Caribbean.[28]

Smallpox was another disease that depleted the West Indian population. It was most commonly found among small children, and was well known in America before it became quite endemic in the Caribbean after the middle of the eighteenth century.[29] In 1773 the slaves in Antigua were particularly afflicted by smallpox, which had already reached epidemic levels in Jamaica as early as 1768. It reappeared in the later 1770s and again in 1789. In 1791 and 1792 smallpox ravaged the population on several estates. There were new outbreaks in 1794 and once more in 1801–2. The slave lists for the latter years indicate that several estates suffered what Barham called "considerable loss." He inquired of his managers, "Cannot this be guarded against in future by inoculation or the vaccine treatment?"[30]

Inoculation had been practised in the colonies since the early eighteenth century and was quite commonly used in the West Indies in the 1790s. However, the practice met with mixed reaction. In St. Kitts and Nevis, managers vaccinated the young children against the disease with a certain measure of success. The smallpox epidemic in Jamaica in 1791 sent many managers scurrying around in an effort to procure enough material to inoculate their slaves. Barritt of Phillipsfield succeeded in inoculating 120. Not all managers got good results. Barham's estate lost two children. Reports of death led to opposition to the inoculation of the slaves on some estates. One absentee, William Dickinson, an absentee Jamaican planter, recommended the postponement of the practice, and he called for the dismissal of the doctors if they persisted in promoting "inoculation with a view to their own interest." But the movement could not be resisted. After all, many estates had successfully implemented the practice. Not to follow meant the loss of valuable capital in young slaves at a time when estates were least able to bear any more losses. Since the blacks were inordinately subject to disease and death, any effort that was likely to save lives and to prevent epidemic outbreaks was implemented, if cautiously. Thus, in spite of his opposition, Dickinson wrote to his manager: "with regard to inoculation, if the rage for it cannot be resisted the best way will be to inoculate so as to prevent the danger of infection in the natural way."[31]

Sexually transmitted disease was also a major problem among the slave population. One attorney wrote that he had "given permission to some of the adult slaves to visit some freed slaves who had claimed to cure venereal disease by attention to diet and drink.... I readily granted their request as I have found the good effects of it with other negroes and I hope some of them become useful people instead of sitting in the Negro Houses rejected."[32]

The environment in which the slaves lived provided the right conditions for spawning disease and eventually epidemics. But the illnesses that afflicted the Africans and their descendants explained only a part of the deaths. Medical personnel were employed, but they seemed unable to cope.

Among the problems these practitioners could not control was the infant mortality rate. This was all the more serious in light of the infertility that resulted from numerous reasons already considered—perhaps chief among them the resolve among African women not to bring children into the cruel world of slavery. By the end of the century, all absentee owners and their management had become concerned about the low fertility on the estates. Lord Penrhyn wrote to his attorney Falconer, "I wish the Mothers could be induced to take more care of their children."[33] They were not their children, and white society could not understand this fact of slavery.

In addition, the conditions under which the children were born were dismal. Upon the birth of the child, most mothers died. Those who lived were not allowed to nurse their babies until the eighth day. The young children were given to nannies unfit to feed newborn babies. They were themselves subjected to hard work, poor living conditions, and inadequate diets, and they drank very little more than water. The end result was that the newborn babies died on or about the eighth day. Only the hardiest survived.[34]

There were other causes of infant mortality. On numerous occasions, women aborted during severe punishment. Those in advanced pregnancy were stretched out on the ground with their stomachs in a hole for the assumed protection of the infants or, sometimes, tied to stakes with their hands over their heads and flogged.[35]

Some whites claimed that the root cause of infertility lay in "the premature, promiscuous and unrestrained intercourse between the sexes."[36] Others held that the low birthrate resulted from mothers nursing their children for two to three years. Some managers adopted contentious racist arguments to explain the infertility among slave women: "their natural propensity to night errantry and fond of their Gambling Saturday nights and fetes of dancing attending plays at great distances, exposing themselves to every inclemency of climate and season."[37]

Another major reason for both mortality and infertility among the enslaved women was the planter policy of using slaves as chattels for the payment of debts, irrespective of social and familial ties. When they were torn from their families, friends, and home regions, many languished and died.[38]

Lack of births on the estates became the single most important concern to the planter class, once it was evident that the slave trade would be severely restricted or even abolished. Managers focussed primarily on increasing the black population by incentives and rewards. They also placed greater emphasis on reducing infant mortality, and on some estates the practice of not registering births until the ninth day was terminated. For example, Barham ordered "that every birth be noted in the lists whether they die soon or not," and he blamed management for the prevalence of tetanus among the young children.[39]

The high levels of mortality not only helped to lessen the profitability of the plantations, they also led to calls for the immediate abolition of the slave trade and slavery. Critics of the slave system were demanding explanations for the decline of the population. Was this "owing to little food and too much labour, or to some other exactly equivalent cause?" Who or what was to be blamed for the state of the enslaved population? Was this due to the policy of the planters or overseers, to natural disasters, or to the unhealthy conditions in which they lived?[40]

Planters had repeatedly expressed their opinions on all aspects of plantation life, especially concerning their workers. Many absentees showed great concern for their welfare, health, and well-being. Yet, while a measure of humanity undoubtedly played a part, this concern must also be interpreted as an effort to maintain, even increase, the enslaved population in order to perpetutate the slave system.[41] Barham was not only a slave owner, he was also a student of Caribbean slave systems. With his two estates in Jamaica for examples, he studied the topic during a sixty-year period.

Assessing the decrease of the slave population, Barham contended that disease accounted for only a small part of deaths. He held that medical science should have been able to make those peculiar diseases less fatal. Yet despite all the changes he had recommended, despite all the medical supplies and the availability of doctors, the premature death of his slaves and the low birthrates continued.

Barham also dismissed ill-treatment as a factor. His general policy for the management of his estates was "to make evry other object subordinate to the welfare and happiness of the negroes & to try evry treatment which might conduce to maintain their population." He even initiated religious teaching and marriages on his estates to create family life and stability. Yet he considered his effort a failure. After consultation with other absentees, he concluded that decrease depended not "on the treatment nor on the climate or any similar cause but on the manners & habit of the negroes. These are highly unfavourable to natural increase. The sexes live almost in common together and the females avoid child bearing by evry means in their power. I am informed that what before arose rather from fortuitous practice is now grown into sentiment. The more the existence of their masters depend[s] on their procreation of children the more they seek to defeat it."[42]

On Barham's Island Plantation, where conditions were more inhospitable to childbirth than on Mesopotamia, there was natural increase. Barham believed that this resulted from the more rural conditions and the "domestic environment" there. On Mesopotamia, the enslaved population lived near a populous neighbourhood with "a considerable town." Here they were allowed numerous indulgences associated with their own independent economic activities. Yet their numbers decreased. He ascribed this to an acquired philosophical stance arising from broader political and ideological influences. These enslaved persons had developed the belief that "the proprietor has no control or direct influence" over certain aspects of their lives. Barham wrote that they recognized his "right to their labour but there it ends and any attempt to interfere with other points would be as dangerous as it would be ineffectual."[43]

Arresting decrease, then, was possible only by changing the "political state" of the slaves or by attempting to indoctrinate them "with the examples of men near to their condition whose manners" were different. Barham certainly attempted the latter by his attentiveness to the conditions of the missionaries residing on his estate. When he recognized the autonomy of the enslaved women in the matter of childbearing—a notion other men in the colonies had hinted at many years before—it was a significant admission by a major West Indian planter. In 1802 and again in 1803, Jefferies and Rodgers, Barham's managers, observed that in spite of the measures they had put in place to increase the birthrates, the enslaved women did everything to demonstrate that they controlled this area of their lives.[44] Promiscuity was certainly not a factor in restricting natural increase, while disease certainly had some influence.

Shortly before the abolition of the slave trade and because of the urgent need to encourage slaves to adopt behaviour styles and social norms that were conducive to family life and child rearing, Fearon told Lord Penrhyn of his efforts: "I did attempt to see and endeavour to persuade all my people to intermarry and do away with that rambling at night but I found it a tiresome and arduous task and gave it up as a bad job."[45]

The supposed preference of the planters for male slaves on the plantations, and for purchasing rather than rearing their own labour, seemed to have been discarded towards the end of the century. Planters were now consciously buying more African women and adopting measures that they hoped would encourage natural increase through greater fertility and lower mortality.

A slave was capital, and every addition to the population meant a monetary advantage to the owner. Better yet, Creoles were of higher value than their African-born counterparts. They accepted their condition in life much more readily. They were immune to many of the diseases that decimated the new arrivants. The general view thus emerged that "every infant that a planter can raise on his Estate is worth two he can buy from the Guinea factor."[46]

Whether it was better to purchase slave labour or to rear it depended to a large extent on which expenditure had a net capital advantage to the owner. For most of the eighteenth century, there was a decisive advantage in favour of captive Africans, who cost only one-half to two-thirds as much as Creoles. After seasoning, the price differential disappeared. But the greatest advantage of Africans over Creoles was that the former were able to work immediately.[47] Still, not all planters preferred buying to breeding. For example, Barham rejected this notion as one postulated by philanthropists. He emphasised that he would have dismissed "any overseer or manager ... who had broached such a doctrine."[48]

Slaves were considered most valuable to plantation life between the ages of fourteen and fifty. After that, they were ascribed no value or the nominal sum of £1, since it was claimed that the expense of maintaining them equalled or exceeded the value of their labour. The total cost of rearing a child until he became a labourer (see table 8.4) is calculated at £80. If this cost is taken as the standard for comparison with the price of new Africans, it is possible to evaluate the stated preference of planters at various periods. Strikingly, the emphasis on providing conditions that favoured the procreation of children coincided with a higher import price for Africans; this occurred around 1785, when the price stood at approximately £82. After that year, with very few exceptions, the price of new Africans increased consistently right up to the abolition of the British slave trade.

Table 8.5, giving the prices of enslaved property for the period 1772–1808, provides a reasonably comprehensive data set for the last quarter of the eighteenth century. As it shows, not until 1785 did the prices for newly imported captive Africans exceed £80. They fell below this figure in 1787–88, 1792, 1794, and 1797 but, taken as a whole, prices were high throughout the 1790s. The period also coincided with the planters' demands that their managers refrain from purchasing new slaves because estates were losing money. That is, in spite of an aging and dwindling slave population, owners were reluctant to invest in

Table 8.4. Costs of bearing and rearing child to age fourteen

	£
Loss of mother's labour[a]	10
Medical care and insurance[a]	5
Interest on £15 for 14 years[b]	15
Upkeep of child beyond value of labour	40
Insurance on child	10
Total cost	80

Sources: "Of the Capital," n.d., Bodl., Barham Papers 381/2; see also Barham, *Considerations*, app. 6, p. 79.

a. These figures are computed on the basis of the child dying at birth.

b. Insurance was paid on the mother's life. It seems that this was a part of plantation cost as can be seen in table 9.2. A further £10 was paid to insure the child's life after his birth. Most children died within days of birth. Also note that the planter also held insurance for the loss of the mother's/woman's labour.

new Africans. As early as 1781, many owners refused to purchase "saltwater Africans" except when unavoidable. In justifying his refusal to buy at a later time, Lord Penrhyn cited the losses that he sustained in 1787 and his desire to wait until his estates had regained their profitability.[49]

Table 8.5. Slave prices, 1772–1808

Year	Price (£ currency)	Year	Price (£ currency)
1772	65.00	1791	103.12
1773	58.65	1792	67.42
1774	57.90	1793	90–120, 110–115
1775	54.35	1794	74.40
1776	47.30	1795	82.00
1777	54.30	1796	82.08
1778	—	1797	81.68
1779	—	1798	95–100
1780	—	1799	90–120
1781	—	1800	120
1782	—	1801	120
1783	—	1802	110–115
1784	60.00	1802	160–180
1785	82.00	1803	90.86, 100 (Jam.)
1786	83.33	1804	132 (Dom.)
1787	72.00 (Bar.)	1805	100–105, 150
1788	50–55, 80–100	1806	115–144(Jam.), 150(Dom.)
1789	103.12	1807	70–110, 150
1790	97.92	1808	150

Sources: "An Account of the Average Price of Negroes in the Several Years Under-mentioned," [1799], *Journals of the Assembly of Jamaica* 10:436 (see also 9:149 ff.); "An Annual Account of Sugar Made on Grand Bras Estate Commencing 1775 and Ending with 1805; also an Account of Slaves Bought," n.d., Cooper-Franks MSS, LMA, Acc. 775/953/13; list of slave prices in Barbados, 1773–92, in "Answers to Heads of Enquiry," 13 May 1788, PRO, CO 28/61, fol. 167 (no. 21); John Shickle (Shackle) to John Pennant, 21 December 1772, UWB, Penrhyn MS 1207; extract of letter from Jamaica, 20 February 1793, PRO, CO 137/91, fol. 397; Graham to Barham, 1 January 1793, Bodl., Barham Papers 357/2; William Rodgers to Barham, 31 March 1801, 357/3; Sir John Gay Alleyne to N. T. Senior, 24 June 1785, NLW, Nassau-Senior Papers E64; Thomas Barritt to Nathaniel Phillips, 8 May 1793, NLW, Slebech Papers 8415; Robert Hibbert to John Hugh Smyth, 6 March 1795, BRO, Ac/Wo 16(27) 161; James Craggs to Mrs. Goulburn, 20 November 1798, SurRO, Goulburn Papers 319/53; Craggs to Mrs. Goulburn, 13 February 1801, 319/51; Mair to Henry Goulburn, 10 April 1802, 319/54/3Y; Thomas Samson to Goulburn, 5 March 1802, 319/54/3V; Samson to Mrs. Goulburn, 14 January 1803, 319/53; Samson to Goulburn, 25 January 1805, 319/53.

Note: Double entries are included to assist the reader in understanding the complexity of Caribbean economic history and to show that in some years, when there are many quotations, they show how prices varied on the different islands.

Despite their reluctance to purchase, many sugar factors converged to force the planters to continue to do so: the slaves on a majority of plantations were "old and deceased"; the women were having fewer and fewer children; the threat to the slave trade was gaining momentum. The solution to the pressing problem of maintaining an adequate labour force was to foster natural increase. African women were to fulfil the double role of labourers and breeders. In 1786, Samuel Eliot wrote to Clement Tudway that he was purchasing several women for his plantation because in the long term "women turn out in general better than men."[50] Two years later, Pennant made a similar recommendation for restocking his plantation. Given the costs of captive Africans, planters considered all avenues for restructuring their plantations. As discussed earlier, lighter duties were some of the initial changes recommended.

As the threat of abolition persisted, many planters ordered the purchase of young Africans in order to balance the ratio between the sexes to encourage breeding and greater creolization of the population. This was planter amelioration whose goal was not to prepare the slaves for freedom but to entrench slavery by making it acceptable to them while they looked to heaven for salvation. We must not lose sight of the fact that the planters' ultimate goal was the protection of their capital investment. Throughout the period, slave prices exceeded the local cost of £80 to rear an enslaved child to age fourteen.[51]

Using the example of a Barbados estate, Dickson showed that in the forty years 1743–83 the enslaved population had decreased from 492 to 246, "an 80th part of the original stock" annually, in spite of purchases and births. The rate of decline continued high, "at about 45th part annually of the original stock," in the five years 1778–83. In Dickson's estimation, which was similar to Barham's, the blame lay squarely on mismanagement and the brutality of the system of slavery. He wrote: "the severity of the managers, under the brutal laws of the colony, decreased the stock in 40 yrs by 1¼ percent annually. Since 1778 or so the whole stock of slaves in the island has been decreased, in five years, in the proportion of nearly 2¼ percent per annum."[52]

Statistical information collected by Barham reflected a situation similar to that in Barbados. In spite of the changes in management that he advocated, matters were getting worse. In fact, the enslaved population decreased even more after the abolition of the slave trade, as Barham pointed out: "You will also perceive that the present loss is greater than has ever been before, for it is in the rate of 1 in 44. Whereas the loss in 95 & 96 was only 1 in 47½ & thus 1801, 1802, 1803, 1804 was 1 in 46⅞."[53] The decline in Jamaica seems to have accelerated

Table 8.6. "Diminution" rate of enslaved population

Island	Percentage annually	Fraction
Jamaica	2½	1/40
Dominica	3	1/33
Antigua	1½–2	1/67 to 1/50
Barbados	1¼–1½	1/80 to 1/67

Source: "Diminution," n.d., Long Papers, BL, Add. MSS 18,273, fol. 92d.

closer to the end of the century, when estimates in the Long Papers place it at one in forty, or 2½ percent of the population annually. It was even greater in Dominica, where 3 percent of enslaved population were lost annually. The decline was less in Antigua and Barbados but was still unacceptable, as indicated in table 8.6.

In spite of claims among some historians that planters preferred buying slaves to breeding them, the available information provides a somewhat different picture. On several plantations in Barbados in 1788, of the 3,112 enslaved people, only 429 or approximately 14 percent were African-born. This was typical of the West Indies, where the African-born component of the enslaved population was estimated at only 22 percent.[54]

It certainly escaped the attention of no one that the West Indian plantation economy was at the crossroads of its existence at the end of the eighteenth century. The American War had removed its greatest pillar. Britain's United States policy had firmly imposed British mercantilism on the colonies, while the free trade doctrines of Adam Smith were to be applied to British commerce to the detriment of colonial production and trade. Compounding all of this, the Colonial Office sent out to the islands in 1788 a most comprehensive set of inquiries on the state of the slave trade and slavery. The queries sought to investigate every aspect of the operation of the institution of slavery, as well as the state of cultivation and the production of the estates. The information was requested from the local legislatures to enable their agents or other persons in England "to represent to Parliament the manner in which the Interests of the Islands may be affected by any measures, which may be proposed for the abolishing or restraining the further importation of Negroes, from the coast of Africa."[55]

In response to imperial action, the Assembly of Jamaica established its own committee to report to it on the slave trade and the state of slavery in the colony.

The committee's findings were complementary about the action of Parliament. The committee thus wrote "that the wisdom and authority of Parliament might beneficially be exerted in further regulations of the African commerce, particularly in preventing the purchase of slaves who shall appear to have been kidnapped or deprived of liberty contrary to the usage and custom of Africa and in compelling the said ships to transport an equal number of both sexes and to provide ventilators and sufficient quantity of provisions especially water."[56]

Not all opinion in Jamaica was supportive of the Assembly's resolution. Many believed that abolition of the slave trade would destroy the economy of the islands. Not only was this the immediate reaction of many members of the planter interest in Jamaica, it was also that of other colonists. John Grant, Chief Justice of Jamaica, posed the most salient questions and established the paradigms in which the debate over abolition was to evolve. He wrote that "the wild project of abolishing slavery would deeply wound the trade & revenue of Great Britain, ruin the white inhabitants of the West Indies, and in its consequence be an act of inhumanity to the Negroes themselves. The stopping of further supplies from Africa will in a rapid progression destroy the English sugar colonies."[57]

The planters in England did not react in like manner to those in the West Indies. They repeatedly sent reports on the emerging movement for the abolition of the slave trade. Fuhr of Hibbert, Fuhr & Hibbert drew Nathaniel Phillips's attention to the several petitions sent to the House of Commons. However, he was not unduly worried about their outcome: "These Petitions were set on Foot by the Dissenters and Quakers, but unless they can substitute some better plan for carrying the cultivation of the sugar colonies which produce such an immense Revenue to this country, their request cannot be seriously thought on by [the] Ministry. It seems they do not mean to interfere with Negroes already in the Islands, but prevent any more being carried off the coast of Africa, & that the Sugar Planters must be satisfied with the Increase of their present Flock."[58]

Nor was Fuhr perturbed by the prospect of restricting the slave trade. His chief concern, and probably that of the West Indian interest and officials in England, was that measures be taken to prevent other nations from filling the vacuum left by Britain and thus pursuing the trade with greater determination. He saw no harm to the West Indian colonies by the undertakings "relative to the Slave Trade in the House of Commons" as long as steps were taken to allay the fears and quiet the minds of the public.[59]

On other islands, the reaction by members of the planter class to Parliamentary action did not reflect the utter doom expressed by some in Jamaica. Many supported Parliament's attempt to regulate the trade, which to them was being severely abused by the Guinea merchants. Walter Nisbet in St. Kitts observed: "I confess that I could wish to see proper regulations take place, respecting the African trade; but the total abolition of it is a question of such magnitude to the commercial interests of Great Britain and Her dependencies, that I have no doubt, but our present administration will be above misrepresentation, and will deliberate on the Business with proper wisdom." He was more worried about the British policy that restricted the islands' trade with the United States.[60]

The introduction of the question of the slave trade in Parliament was seen as the forerunner to a general abolition and was certainly of concern to everyone connected with the Atlantic economy, of which the West Indian trade was at the core. Yet this concern was not because of the harm such a measure was likely to do to the sugar industry. It stemmed more from a fear that the Negroes would view abolition of slave imports as the beginning of freedom, and would move to destroy every white person, on the grounds that their king had freed them "but their masters will not suffer it."[61] Many who felt that they could not put their trust in the House of Commons, because it was likely to succumb to "popular delusion," looked to the House of Lords to safeguard the interests of the planter class. After the passage of the bill that sought to regulate the number of captive Africans carried per ton of shipping, nothing else was heard on the issue of abolition for a while, "although members of both parties were pledged to the introduction in Parliament of a bill for the abolition of the trade."[62]

By the time of Wilberforce's motion to table in the House of Commons a bill for the prohibition of the slave trade, there was wide discussion by the West Indian planter interest of the consequences to the colonies of such a measure. When the motion was defeated by a vote of 163 to 88, Lord Grenville wrote to the governors suggesting that, if the failure of the motion led to discontent among the enslaved population on the island, he hoped that this would force the planters "to pay the utmost attention to the great object of endeavouring by mild and gentle treatment of these People to reconcile them as much as possible to their situation."[63]

Barham, the MP for Stockbridge, had no doubt of the motion's ultimate success and wrote to his manager: "The abolition of the slave trade (which there is no doubt will be effected in some shape) must in a great measure alter every person's views in the West Indies."[64] The defeat of the motion did not signal the end of the effort to secure the passage of such a bill. Among members of Parliament who voted against it were many who did not want the trade to continue for an unspecified time. Commenting on the likely success of the movement to abolish the slave trade, Barham pointed to one of the main contradictions inherent in the whole discussion on slavery and abolition. He wrote that "those who give the greatest weight to the apprehension of danger from uplifting the minds of the negroes, cannot be wholly insensible to the danger of adding to their immense superiority of number, by an annual addition of men, who recently reduced into slavery, must be most impatient under it."[65]

By the beginning of the last quarter of the eighteenth century, the slave trade and slavery had served the purposes of the British. Until the administration seriously considered the issue of the slave trade in 1788, there was no moral conviction among the British people that it ought to be abolished. In fact, by this time, they had accepted that the slave trade and slavery were pivotal to the economic development of Europe. Richard and Thomas Neave wrote that they began "to see it with less prejudice than they did, upon a fair investigation of it. We have not the least doubt it being defended upon the principles of humanity, & in a political light the demolition of it goes to the existence of the country, as a commercial nation."[66]

What had changed? What had gone wrong to send shock waves through the hearts of the West Indian interest by 1792? These are questions that have challenged historians for many years. Some accept the argument that the strong moral conviction of the British people was mainly responsible for change; others hold that the independence of the American colonies severed the lifeline of British West Indian slavery and led to its demise. British policy restricting United States–West Indian trade had made slavery an enormously expensive labour system with only small returns to investors in the sugar industry. Slave prices had risen immensely and most of the enslaved Africans died within a short period, which made their labour unprofitable. And there was no natural increase.

Compounding all of these were the shocking revelations of cruelty that emerged in the investigation of the slave trade and slavery. The evidence and reports on the slave trade and the atrocities committed by managers and overseers were without precedent and must have appalled even the most ardent supporters of the slave system. In fact, one absentee planter and merchant remarked: "Mr. Wilberforce & his party would have lost the question but for the

Guinea Captains whose conduct have been a disgrace to human Nature."[67] There were varying opinions with regard to abolition. The committee of the Jamaica House of Assembly argued that some measure of control was needed to regulate the slave trade, which was purely British, owned and funded by British capital. The sugar planters were merely the purchasers and were therefore not responsible for the reported atrocities, though of course they fuelled it through their unlimited purchases.[68] The abolitionists were associated with Tom Paine's "Levelling Principles," and some critics saw the movement as using the abolition of the slave trade to secure parliamentary reform.[69] One point of view held that exports to foreign countries should be restricted. This would be advantageous to the West Indian colonies "in lowering the price of slaves by diminishing the markets & also by discouraging the competition of foreign planters."[70]

The political climate as well as the St. Domingue Revolution made the prospect of abolition quite possible in 1792. Some absentees thus recommended the purchase of Negroes as a precautionary measure. Writing to their attorney in Jamaica, the Dickinsons observed: "After all that has been said about the slave trade we cannot forsee what will be done, many people think nothing."[71] Stephen Fuller, agent for Jamaica, articulated the possibility of violence arising out of the prohibition of the slave trade, which he decidedly opposed. His opposition reflected the ultraconservative West Indian planter interest and sought to associate regulation with violence and destruction of lives. He wrote: "God knows what will be the consequence if the present Bill is passed! The avowed intention of it is to save the lives of a few negroes, but it may end in the destruction of all the whites in Jamaica."[72]

There was general satisfaction in Barbados that such a handsome majority defeated Wilberforce's motion. Expressing the views of the planters, Governor David Parry suggested that the many abuses "in the African trade ... may surely be remedied" without its abolition. According to official information, steps were taken to inform the enslaved population of the debate. Consequently, "everything in the government goes on perfectly quiet, not a slave who is not as mild as a mouse—well and understanding the difference between abolition and emancipation." Efforts to fully indoctrinate the slaves into acceptance of their position in life cleared the way for the further exploitation of African labour. Irrespective of the decision taken by Parliament on the slave trade, the government remained determined not "to weaken the general system of control and subordination" among the black population on West Indian plantations.[73]

In spite of the confidence Parry wished to convey about the peaceable and trustworthy nature of the enslaved population in Barbados, there was in the governor's correspondence a note of uncertainty about their reaction to the passage of a bill abolishing the trade without abolishing slavery. In order to maintain peace, Parry recommended "that Mr. Wilberforce Motion for the abolition of the Slave Trade should lie over for two or three Sessions; or until the commotions in the French Islands shall subside because our slaves will be but too apt to confound that abolition with general emancipation and be perhaps hurried into some excesses."[74]

The fear of sparking slave revolts on all the islands by the passage of Wilberforce's motion in 1792 was vividly expressed throughout the West Indies. Several managers reported that every word spoken in Parliament was generally conveyed to the slaves and had inflamed their minds. The debate had certainly changed the view of the African in slavery in the West Indies.

> Before the agitation of this Question they were a happy contented People more so I am persuaded than any peasantry in Europe for being devoid of all care about making any provision for themselves or families, well knowing that would continue to be afforded them by their Masters whom they were accustomed to look up to as their Protectors. "They performed their duly labour with cheerfulness & either enjoyed sound sleep at night or occasionally passed it in festivity & Mirth—Now, they are taught to view their Condition in a very different light, they are led to consider their masters as Tyrants, that their State of Bondage is insufferable & that the abolition of the Slave Trade is quickly to lead to the abolition of slavery itself—Certain it is they have got the idea that a general Emancipation is soon to take place, & many Attempts of ours to undeceive them are fruitless & vain."[75]

This was the classic case of denial that anything was wrong with slavery. Throughout the discussion, one is certainly informed that there was resistance, even if there were no rebellions in the British islands at this time. Many planters refused to acknowledge the immense threat to the system even with a civil war raging in St. Domingue, a stone's throw away. In spite of their denial, however, their enslaved people knew everything about it, and the possible consequences of a similar rebellion in Jamaica sent ripples throughout the plantations. The Earl of Effingham, then governor, took immediate action to prevent any uprising in the colony. The consensus was that the enslaved blacks in Jamaica were in communication with the rebels in St. Domingue. Adam Williamson, who became lieutenant governor, did not share the often expressed view that the Negroes were unintelligent and "tractable." He wrote: "Many of the slaves here are very inquisitive & intelligent & are immediately informed of every kind of news that arrives. I do not hear of their having shown any signs of revolt tho' they have composed songs of the negroes having made rebellion at Hispaniola with their usual chorus to it, & there are members who are ripe for any mischief."[76]

In addition to the communication between the slaves of St. Domingue and Jamaica, many inhabitants of the French colony had fled the violence there and brought their enslaved people to the English island. Measures were therefore taken to prevent any mixing of the enslaved groups from the two islands. The authorities attempted to restrict entry "to a few females for the care of women with child or young children, but no male."[77]

Throughout the early years of the French Revolutionary War, further measures were taken to restrict contact between foreigners and the British West Indian enslaved population. In Jamaica, the Custodes were required to maintain a "watchful eye throughout the different plantations, and in the towns, that no improper person shall be permitted to reside, who are disposed in any shape to excite insurrections among the slaves."[78] The authorities quickly imposed marital law on 10 December 1791; the frigate *Brune* landed thirty-three soldiers at Morant Bay and the militia was supplied with arms. Were these actions taken mainly from hysteria? In all the colonies there were enslaved groups prepared to undertake rebellion when conditions were right. In Jamaica, according to one report, there was "a body of negroes in Spanish Town who calls themselves the Cat Club." In order to celebrate the events then occurring in England and in St. Domingue, members gathered in Spanish Town "drinking King Wilberforce's health out of a Cat's skull by way of a cup and swearing secrecy to each other, some of them were taken up and put into the work house, but will not divulge the business. In Trelawny . . . some negroes have been detected making up cartridges & fire arms found in their houses."[79]

Rumours were immediately circulated that the slaves intended to cut the throats of their masters at Christmas. Given the tension on all the islands, compounded by their own economic situation and their insecurity about the future, it was quite understandable that several planters and other colonists concluded that the British government was about to cast the islands adrift and that the debate over the abolition of the slave trade was the first step. One planter even recalled that "Lord Hawksbury (when Mr. Jenkinson) once Declared 'that Great Britain wou'd do better without the sugar colonies than with them.' The planters now assert that the measures of the present Minister are so adverse and inimical to these islands that there cannot remain a Doubt of his intention to adopt Lord Hawksbury Opinion, and to shake them."[80]

The uncertainty of the West Indian interest is unsurprising given the general state of affairs. The commencement of hostilities in the Caribbean so soon after the American War rekindled in the minds of the planters fears of economic disaster resulting from the destabilization of the sugar industry, the loss of the United States trade, and possible uprisings among the slave population. Many planters in the Leeward and Windward Islands took the easy way out and simply migrated to the foreign colonies of Trinidad, Demerara, and Puerto Rico. An estimated five hundred proprietors migrated from Grenada, Barbados, and St. Vincent.

The crisis threatening the British West Indies provided the colonists with another opportunity to unite the colonies, as was voiced during the American War. The call originated from St. Vincent. Throughout the Leeward and Windward Islands, daily meetings were held, and circular letters and advertisements were published. Copies were sent to Jamaica but there was no response.[81]

While opposition to British policy continued throughout the war, it remained a verbalization of woes. No steps were taken to pressure the British government into changing its policy. The West Indies were quieted easily with limited concessions that were basically window dressing. Yet it was only natural that a people who had subjugated another for hundreds of years should fear a general revolt, especially when there was an existing example. More than this, however, on all the islands there existed, as the lieutenant governor of Jamaica wrote, "thousands of the slaves who would willingly enter into a rebellion ... not from any oppression or ill usage, but merely with a view of becoming free."[82]

Added to the list of apprehensions was the planters' fear that the free coloureds, particularly in Jamaica, would make serious attempts to wrest control from the whites. In Jamaica these fears arose mainly because of a petition drawn up by the free coloureds and presented to the Assembly. It set forth a number of the grievances about discriminatory practices imposed on them by white planter society, and demanded "the rights of natural free born subjects of Great Britain."[83]

The petitioning was reminiscent of prerevolutionary St. Domingue where the mulattoes were vocal in demanding their rights. In Jamaica the embryonic agitation of the free coloureds coincided more or less with the upheaval in the French colony. These demands thus rekindled the biases that white Jamaicans had nurtured about coloureds and blacks. There were already those who viewed the presence of a coloured group as a threat to slavery. Social relationships between white plantation employees and slaves were frowned upon, and there emerged the belief that the coloureds were internal threats to the system. Hence, towards the end of the eighteenth century, every effort was made to remove mulattoes from estate employment and to replace them with black slaves.[84]

While Jamaicans were certainly concerned about the ever increasing free coloured group, there was little to indicate that it would link up with the slaves in open rebellion. This holds true for Barbados and the Leeward Islands, where the free coloured population was small. Commenting on the attitude of the free coloureds in Barbados to rebellion, Governor Ricketts observed: "I have reason to believe that the free coloured people would cheerfully give their assistance against the common enemy. It has been my endeavour to conciliate them by every prudent indulgence; and I trust this has been done in such a manner as will induce them to attribute it rather to a general and impartial system than any temporary assistance."[85]

In the Leeward Islands, the temper of the free coloureds was gauged similarly. There was worry over what would happen if slavery should continue to exist there while it was abolished in the neighbouring French islands. As a precautionary measure, William Woodley, acting governor, issued a proclamation restraining the admission of mulattoes and free blacks. This was later extended to white people, and was more an attempt to conserve the already short supply of food than a reflection of real fear that the islands were in danger of rebellion. Any belief that St. Domingue would spark rebellions throughout the rest of the West Indies was only temporary, if seriously entertained at all.

The black Jamaican population was well informed of the St. Domingue Revolution, probably even before it occurred. Boukman Dutty, voodoo priest and leader of the rebellion, was a Jamaican. But although they were kept aware of its progress and supported it by their songs commemorating the event, the slaves did not view a revolt in Jamaica as having any chance of dislodging white planter rule. For whatever reasons, the enslaved population throughout the West Indies took no collective action. They remained "loyal." Much of the disquiet expressed by the planter class arose from their own fears and from the debate in Parliament over the slave trade.[86]

The Maroon War of 1795 posed a greater threat to the economy and society of Jamaica than any revolt among the slaves during this period. Not only was a large amount of slave capital lost as a sizeable number of slaves took the opportunity to run away from the estates, but also, at a time when all plantations were on the brink of bankruptcy, a large number of slaves and white employees were conscripted for military duty. Very little work was done on the estates, and the Maroon War cost the Jamaica government an estimated £520,000–580,000.[87] In Barbados, neither the debate in Parliament nor the slave revolt in St. Domingue threatened the peace and quiet of the island, as Governor Parry emphasised. He saw no threat to white society, since there was a greater ratio of whites to blacks than on the other islands. Furthermore, the majority of the enslaved population consisted of Creoles who were "in their general Temper and disposition, mild, tractable and obedient" and attached from birth to their owners and the soil.[88]

At the beginning of the 1790s, the institution of slavery had reached a watershed period. In the British colonies, questions were being asked about the profitability, and thus the continued viability, of a system that could be destroyed by rebellion. In spite of the continued large importation of slaves in the eighteenth century, few colonies had shown any significant growth in their population and none maintained its population level by natural increase. Hard labour, violence, and disease led to the loss of slave capital. For most of the small individually owned plantations, slavery was now proving unprofitable.[89]

The problems of the sugar planters and their impoverishment were exacerbated by the restrictions on United States trade and by North American and British imports of Indian sugar, while the reinvigoration of the sugar industry in Brazil and Cuba brought competition to the West Indians in their home market. By the end of the century, it was estimated that only half of the estates in the British West Indies made profits of 4 or 5 percent. A few estates reported 8 percent, but only because they had bought no new Africans or failed to include interest payments in their accounting. The planter needed a clear gain of 6 percent just to pay the interest on his capital. In real terms, then, the only estates with even minimal profits were those making 8 percent. In England, the business class estimated 12 percent profit as "fair and reasonable," and considered a man's business "not worth carrying on, if he was to gain no more by it than the common interest which is all the planter gets." The West Indian sugar planter had "no room for progressive improvements; nothing left to compensate for the many casualties and heavy losses to which the peculiar circumstances of the climate where his Business is carried on, and the very nature of the business itself subject him."[90]

There emerged the expected argument by contemporaries that slaves "employed on sugar plantations do not and cannot refund the capital sunk on them, and the property which they actuate or render productive."[91] Writing in 1788, Arthur Young expressed the opinion that "the culture of sugar by slaves" was "the dearest specie of labour in the world." His most telling criticism of capital investment in the West Indies was "that the same capital or even one-half of what is so employed, if invested in any specie of domestic agriculture would be attended with abundantly a greater mass of national prosperity—a greater public revenue; more shipping; more seamen; more wealth."[92]

This was a damaging assessment of the sugar industry at a time when the doctrine of free trade was taking hold and when Parliament was collecting information on the state of the slave trade and slavery in the colonies with a view to implementing changes that might include abandoning the slave trade. The Assembly of Jamaica had shown the way in 1763 and again in 1774 with its attempts to limit the trade. And in Barbados, where a bare fifth of the slave population was African-born,[93] there was a popular view that the colony would profit from the termination of the slave trade with Africa. The example of St. Domingue fresh in the minds of white West Indians led some to support the suspension of the slave trade "till the vigilance of the mother country shall be less engaged than it is by a war claiming her efforts in evry part of the world. Would it not under these circumstances be well at least to pause a little than continually to heap fresh fuel which we all fear will at last break forth in an unextinguishable blaze. Let every man calculate with himself the profits which he expects to gain by the purchase of negroes within the two or three next years, let him next calculate what additional security he will have for his whole capital if in this time 200 negroes are . . . imported & see whether he would not to any Common Insurer give for this security a greater price than he expects to gain by this importation."[94]

In the 1790s the West Indian plantations lay in a watershed area of prosperity for several years. Some who supported terminating the slave trade argued that the interests of the islands lay in abolishing it. They pointed out that the prosperity of the colonies had continued with variations until about 1775–76 when in the case of Jamaica its decline "became more rapid and alarming. . . . In the year 1792 insolvency was a constant calamity and it was estimated that in the space of twenty years 177 estates had been lodged in the Provost Marshal's Office for the sum of £22,563,786." In 1804, when the House of Commons first passed a bill to abolish the slave trade, British merchants were foreclosing on hundreds of West Indian plantations. Once they had obtained the decrees, they hesitated to enforce them because they did not wish to become proprietors of unprofitable estates, and many planters now became tenants of British capitalists. Of the state of the West Indian economy in general and of Jamaica in particular at the beginning of the nineteenth century, Hall Pringle wrote: "All kinds of credit are at an end; and if litigation has ceased or diminished, it is not from increased ability to perform contracts, but from confidence having ceased, and no man parting with property; a faithful detail would have the appearance of a frightful caricature."[95]

In Barbados, conditions were equally poor. The islanders were seriously in debt to British merchants and there was very little cash in circulation. Properties valued at more than £500 to £1000 could be sold only by public auction "unless bonds and paper security for some part of the purchase, by instalments for a reasonable length of time, may be legally tendered and accepted instead of prompt payment in cash." Estates were thus broken up and sold in parts in order for creditors to recover as much as they could, which was much less than the market value.[96] By the time the slave trade was abolished in 1807, the sugar colonies were deeply in trouble. The planter class was severely distressed and its problems were worsening with alarming rapidity. A report of the Jamaica House of Assembly claimed that 25 percent of Jamaica estates had recently been sold for debt. It estimated that if the trend continued there was likely to be the "bankruptcy of a much larger part of the community and in the course of a few years that of the whole class of sugar planters."[97]

The abolition of the slave trade took place at a time of grave uncertainty in the plantation system. In the minds of British officials, however, the measure was being adopted when it was likely to distress the islands' economy least. The key argument used by the Colonial Office to justify the government's action/policy was that, with proper care and changes to slavery, the slave population would increase. Judging from the growth performance of the Jamaica slave population from 210,984 in 1787 to 308,000 in 1803, or almost 100,000 in sixteen years, it concluded that population growth was possible throughout the entire West Indies. Thus, it iterated, the abolition of the slave trade was not likely to interfere to any degree with the short-term interests of the sugar colonies, "whilst their ultimate & permanent Interest from the Security which the Prohibition of importing new Negroes would produce would be greatly improved by it."[98]

Abolition was an emotional issue, which excited the anger of British West

Indian planters. Very few looked at it objectively; most argued that it was "destructive to the Colony ultimately, & most certainly fatal to all further Improvement."[99] Of course, there was bound to be disquiet among the owners of enslaved property over the ending of the source of their labour force. It seemed, however, that very few queries, if any, concerned the economic consequences. Most concerned the social and political implications of abolition. Some planters and managers favoured the stationing of regular troops in Jamaica to forestall another St. Domingue. Lord Penrhyn called for unrelenting vigilance to defeat any attempt of the slaves to rebel. He deemed the Abolition Act a "dangerous experiment" not because of the economic implications for his estates but because of its social and political consequences.[100]

In reality, not much occurred in the colonies with the passage of the act abolishing the slave trade. The slaves did not revolt. One attorney commented: "we feel no great impression from the measure."[101] The decision to abolish the slave trade was made over a long period, beginning around 1788, but only after Parliament had made a detailed assessment of the treatment of the slaves, their possible increase by natural means, their work conditions, the extent of hired labour, the susceptibility to disease of Africans and Creoles, and other matters relating to the conditions of Africans in slavery. The long years of war had witnessed the increased unprofitability of the estates through the unsaleability of West Indian sugar. The warehouses in Britain and in the West Indies were overstocked with tropical products, and cheaper and better-quality sugar was now available from India, Cuba, Brazil, and other new sources. The Colonial Office thus contended that to extend cultivation was only "to clog the markets and reduce" prices further. It believed that it had made the right decision in the interests of West Indian planters at a time when the world sugar markets were glutted. Slavery was to be left intact and, it held, the number of enslaved was likely to increase without further importation, given due care through improved management.

9

The Sugar Industry
and Eighteenth-Century Revolutions

In spite of the inherent problems that threatened the destruction of the British West Indian plantation system, the sugar industry remained the cornerstone of further economic development and provided the planters with the rationale for their position in the world economy. It was certainly the foundation on which the Atlantic economy emerged in the seventeenth century as it developed from the bowels of European slave ships and on the backs of enslaved Africans. By the end of the eighteenth century this industry faced severe weaknesses. Probably the most significant was the growth of finance capitalism and the maturing of the British industrial economy based on the principle and doctrines of free trade.

Slavery as a labour system undoubtedly had run its course. It had functioned well under mercantilism in a nascent capitalist society where control by the imperial power guaranteed the development of both sectors of the economy. From a financial standpoint it operated to the benefit of the home merchant class. Eventually, the emerging colonial merchants were effectively controlled by and subjugated to the interests of the imperial power. British merchants and financial interests now controlled those areas of trade and investment once within the sphere of the West Indians. Consequently, venture capital disappeared from the islands and the sugar industry could not be adequately financed at a time when changes, both technical and technological, were occurring fast and furiously.

The British Caribbean sugar industry needed significant amounts of money to stay abreast of these changes and maintain profitable businesses. Even then, the odds of survival were against the planters. Production could no longer be increased through expansion into new fertile areas. To produce an equal quantity of sugar on soils whose fertility was vastly depleted, more labour was needed, and more fertilizer. The modernization of mills with their adaptation to steam necessitated large capital inputs.

In their early period of development the Caribbean colonies became a major source of capital for Britain.[1] The years from 1700 to the beginning of the American Revolution were the golden age of West Indian sugar production. Jamaica showed significant growth. "Slave imports doubled from 4,073 annually in the period 1731–35 to 8,069 annually in the period 1771–5. Sugar output increased from 322,600 cwt in the former period to 879,900 cwt in the latter; and at the same time the index of London sugar prices rose from 100 to 180."[2] This expansion was halted by the American War. The first years of American independence assured policymakers that British interests could be maintained in societies where there was no political control and where injections of capital had a greater impact on exploiting economies and increasing wealth.[3]

The West Indies thus became pawns. Britain was not prepared to relinquish political control because the society was black. British merchants tightened their grip on the islands' economies while seeking to end the colonists' monopoly of the British market in their traditional areas of production. Propaganda was also used to dissipate any sympathy for the planters, or so one contended: "It is a natural conclusion to the minds of the Vulgar that the planters gain immense profits and can well bear great Taxes."[4]

The West Indian planters bore the brunt of British imposition to meet the cost of the American War. The 4½ percent duty had already become odious to those saddled with it. One manager observed resentfully that he had to pay in excess 4 hogsheads of a meagre 127 hogsheads. Besides the duty, local taxes for the war became burdensome to the plantations.[5] But the targeting of the sugar industry as the source of war revenue by the mother country was far worse. During this period, the duty on sugar almost doubled, from approximately 6s 4d per hundredweight in 1776 to 12s 3d in 1782.

After the American War, the sugar planters were down but not out, determined to rejuvenate the industry. If left alone, they might well have done so. In the event, however, Britain imposed its mercantilist policies on commercial relations between the United States and the West Indies, depressing the islands' economies and beginning the process of destabilizing the sugar industry.

West Indies commercial relations were established by the order-in-council of 2 July 1783. Then in 1787 came the passage of 27 Geo. III chap. 7, aimed solely at lessening trade between the British and foreign West Indies and legalising British policy towards the United States. The planters were understandably upset with this new arrangement. Their views found expression in a statement by Nisbet: "With such a calamity and the many other taxes (both natural & created, if I may call them so) heaped on property in this country we really stand in no need of the additional efforts of enthusiastic madness, and party spirit at home, to reduce us to that ruin, which we seem to be tending to very fast." Meanwhile, the war had pointed up chronic weaknesses in the industry. Its revival hinged on increased production and higher prices. At war's end, there were optimistic expectations for the former, as Nisbet told Mrs. Stapleton: "You may depend on 200 hhds from hence, this year—probably, we may surprise you with 250—a circumstance, that cannot give more pleasure to yourself."[6]

Throughout the West Indies, expectations went unmet, and most estates were producing 35 to 40 percent less than forecast. In the Leeward Islands crops were severely hit by the borer, which first appeared there between 1786 and 1787,[7] and a disease called blasts. Walter Nisbet recounts the conditions: "You will only receive between 130 & 40 hhds—The Canes, from the succession of good weather after the hurricane, had a very favourable outward appearance, but when they came to be cut, the damage they had sustain'd was too visible, & the loss in yielding experienced on every Estate."[8]

In Antigua the borer caused similar destruction. Eliot, writing to Clement Tudway, stated: "The Grand-Tierre has been quite laid waste by it, in the course of the last twelve months—some of your pieces of canes, at both Plants, have suffered." It was difficult for planters to assess the real state of the canes while they were young and growing because the affected canes showed little sign of damage. Only when they were cut for the mills did most planters realize the wholesale destruction inflicted on their fields. The newly planted canes were the most seriously affected. Therefore, some planters allowed their estates to continue in ratoons, which showed greater resistance to attacks.[9]

The decline and losses were significant. Production on Stapleton's estate had fallen to approximately fifty hogsheads. Nisbet's own output was less than a third of his normal crop of four to five hundred hogsheads. Several years after the first reports of the borer infestation, the worms continued to ravage the estates. A slight ray of hope appeared in 1789 when there was a falloff in the borer population. However, there was no increase in the productivity of the estates.

In St. Kitts the production for that year was the smallest in the island's history and was estimated at less than 10 percent of the average annual yield.[10]

The problems of the sugar industry continued into the 1790s. Although damage by the borer decreased, the weather was added to the list of woes. And as if natural calamities were not enough to occupy the planters' attention, rumours of conflict between Britain and France deepened the concerns and fears of all the colonists. Confronted with mediocre crops since the outbreak of the American War and plagued by pests, planters voiced their dislike for any "additional calamities, either natural or political to add to the uncertainty of" their "unfortunate properties."[11] The crops continued to be "miserably bad" at the dawn of the outbreak of the upheavals in St. Domingue and the destruction of that island's sugar industry. British plantations were thus in crisis just at the time that the planters were set to make significant gains. While the borer was still a problem, its destruction of the cane had decreased markedly. In August 1793 floods accompanied by high winds did significant damage to estates. This was followed by a severe drought. Then in 1795 the brief and partial respite from the borer ended abruptly, as the worms returned with greater damages.[12]

The borer infestation was general throughout the West Indies. In Barbados and Jamaica, the ravaging of the sugarcane by borer was compounded by blasts, a disease that destroyed the chlorophyll in the leaves of the canes.[13] It seems that the severe attacks began in Grenada in the 1790s. According to one report, the appearances of diseases and "pernicious insects, instead of being incidental for a year or two, as formerly, have become almost habitual for above twenty years past."[14] Not only was the sugarcane susceptible to destruction by worms, the local corn was, too. The plantation papers are replete with letters detailing the impact on the sugar industry of drought, flooding, and devastation by insects; one manager told his absentee planter: "you will again meet with a disappointment in having the old story repeated from every quarter—a bad crop."[15]

The amazing thing about these phenomena was that for the most part one or the other appeared annually. Sustained periods of drought were normally accompanied by a borer infestation. In some years the united destruction was so complete that, wrote one planter, "many people will not even put their mills about." The more fortunate made half crops. After severe floods in 1793, which destroyed thousands of acres of cane, Jamaica was gripped by severe dry weather for several years. Only the remarkable fertility of the soil in some areas made any production possible. In some cases attorneys wrote home pessimistically: "it will be impossible to make anything of a Crop."[16]

In all the sugar colonies the adverse weather conditions slashed the yield, and the ratio of acres in cane to sugar output rose significantly. On some Jamaica estates it took "14 to 16 acres for one Hhd of sugar in place of one Hhd per acre or more." In the Leeward Islands the changes were not as marked, but the ratio of acres to output also worsened between 1778 and 1796. "During the first Period, . . . from 1778 to 1787 inclusive your Estate averaged upwards of two hhds per acre for every acre of land that was annually planted, through a hurricane one year & an excessive Drought another intervened—And from the year 1788 to 1796, the Average has been nearly one hhd and a half per acre while some of the finest Estates in the Island, in point of extent & fertility have not produced above a Third part of their former crop."[17]

The prolonged and severe dry seasons had ripple effects on both the slave and the stock population. For the former, very little local food was produced and, with imports from the United States limited, the situation was always nearly precarious, as the president of the Council of Barbados pointed out: "I should not now take the liberty of intruding on your time did I not conceive it a duty incumbent on me to represent to your Grace the present deplorable situation to which the Island is reduced from the want of almost every article of subsistence owing to the very scanty supplies of provisions we have lately had from the United States of America, a long continued drought, and a most dreadful visitation of worm which has so totally destroyed our crop of corn that many plantations are already destitute of that article so essential to the subsistence of the Negroes—nor can they at any period be supplied with it from Market.[18]

As for the plantation animals, most planters and managers could not secure pasturage for their cattle. Many were sent to other parishes where conditions were not so intolerable. The cost of this sent the annual contingencies skyrocketing. On estates that did not have penns, owners were now urged to clear woodlands and plant guinea grass for the cattle so as to prevent future expenses for this item.[19]

Natural disasters and irregular seasons were always likely to have devastating effects on West Indian plantations. During the 1780s all the West Indian islands were ravaged by one or more hurricanes, beginning with that of 10 October 1780. Six years later, on 20 October 1786, the Leeward Islands were severely hit. The destruction came at a time when resources for the plantations were very low and planter morale virtually broken. The consequences of "these annual visitations have greatly discouraged the Planting Interest here, and rendered small sugar Estates scarce worth holding," so badly had they reduced both quantities and quality.[20]

As early as 1787, Penrhyn drew his attorney's attention to the deterioration of the sugar from that of the previous year. Since a newly adopted system had not raised production and quality, he recommended a return to the old and tried method.[21] This problem seems to have been general throughout the West Indies. Some planters took the view that, while the quantity of sugar remained important, the quality was of greater importance.[22] In Barbados, because of very poor weather conditions, President Bishop reported that "the crop of sugar will not be one sixth of that made in the last year, and the Quality of it so inferior as scarcely to deserve the name of sugar."[23]

Efforts by planters to improve the quality were not always successful.[24] Since the incomes of some managers and overseers were linked to the quantity of the sugar produced, conflict was likely to arise between owner and management— as every absentee involved in efforts to rationalize the sugar industry by restricting production was aware. Barham observed: "This task of reduction is not a pleasant one either to the party employed or to those who are obliged to recommend it, but I fear it will become one that is unavoidable."[25]

Another problem was the shortage of both livestock and labourers to cut the cane, transport it, and operate the mills. In some cases, cane was harvested late and then lay in the fields too long. Fermentation began to occur. In addition, when crops were not reaped until after May, the growth of the ratoons was retarded, lessening both quantity and quality in the following year. And reduced sugar production of course meant the loss of large amounts of revenue not only in the sale of that commodity but also in the output of rum.[26] The short crops occurred at the worst possible time for the sugar colonies "as the Expense of every article for the Estate is nearly double of what it used to be."[27]

Even with the destruction of the sugar industry in St. Domingue, improvement in the financial position of the estates seems more an illusion than a reality. In some cases the indebtedness of the estates worsened. "You will observe, by the Accounts transmitted," wrote one attorney, "that there is at this time, the very considerable Balance of £2,300 currency (about £1300 St.) against the Estate notwithstanding the sale of sugars, for the purpose of paying off the ... demands of last year."[28]

One of the chronic weaknesses of the slave system was that the output of sugar was not proportional to the input of labour. In their attempt to maintain population levels through natural increase, West Indian planters adopted the policy of reducing the workloads. In Jamaica three slaves were expected to produce two hogsheads of sugar (table 9.1). Even this modest quota was not met, and the ratio of sugar to slaves continued to fall as the high mortality rate claimed inordinate amounts of human capital through excessive labour, epidemics and other types of disease, and malnutrition.[29] Alarmed by the decline, many planters including Barham laid down plans to rationalize the sugar industry. Barham solicited the assistance of his attorneys and managers: "You are better judges than I, but this I am sure of, that to us resident here a sugar estate is not worth having unless great alteration shall take place. If this applies to Mesopotamia, an estate which has been generally deemed to be favourably circumstanced I presume others are not better off. There with 200 negroes we make crops of 150 Hhds. But as there is no pen the crops would not defray the charges, if the contingencies were in proportion to those in Mesopotamia. As it is I come there about equally well that is I get little or nothing. Under these circumstances instead of sending good money after bad, I had turned my thoughts to consolidation of the estates by giving up one estate, sending the negroes to the other, & selling or letting the lands for what it will fetch."[30]

Changes were certainly needed to achieve survival of the sugar industry. The plantations had now to exist on their restricted internal resources. During this period the contingencies on many estates were not offset by sales.[31] As the sugar industry expanded into other countries, both within and outside the British empire, and threatened the West Indian monopoly of the home market, there

Table 9.1. Profit/loss on producing sugar

Expenditure

Interest on capital at 6 percent	
3 slaves valued at £50 each	£9
Land employed valued at £300	£18
Insurance on slaves at 5 percent	£7 10s
Feeding of slaves	£5
Total expenditure	£39 10s
Net proceeds from 2 hhds sugar	£24
Loss	£15 10s

Source: Adapted from James Ramsay, "A.M. Reflections to the Abolition of the Slave trade with Answers . . .(London, 1788)," 17–20; see Long, *Jamaica,* 2:437–38.

were numerous complaints of declining profitability and financial losses. The economic viability of the sugar industry called for wholesale changes, from the cultivation of the canes to the manufacture of the sugar.

The establishment of sugar plantations led to the deforestation of the islands. In order to minimise the use of fuel, planters first adopted the Jamaican train, which allowed several pots of cane juice to be processed from the same central fire and widely used for many years as the standard method of processing sugar until the wholesale adoption of steam power. Planters also turned to bagasse as replacement for firewood. This reduced the fodder available to the cattle, but it did not emit the intense heat that destroyed the coppers.[32] Towards the end of the eighteenth century, iron pots replaced copper ones. These could take the intense heat without developing holes.

The invention of the steam engine came at a time when plantations were least able to raise the capital for such costly innovations, especially since individual estates already had adequate mill capacity. Nevertheless, West Indian planters showed interest in its functions. Some planters immediately recognized its utility for irrigating their drought-stricken fields, but here the steam engine's performance was restricted by the water supply. The logistics of using this new invention to power the cane mills made its implementation extremely difficult and costly. Increased coal imports were needed as fuel.[33] This was already very expensive, so the engines were adapted to use a mixture of coal and bagasse. While the cost of fuel was lessened, difficulties emerged in the operation of the furnaces. The estates also had to employ trained personnel who could repair them, and this too was very costly. Some who employed the steam engine for sugar production found that it performed no better than existing mills.[34] Altogether, because of the high cost of operation, the requirement of trained personnel, and the lack of capital, the steam engine was not an early success in the West Indies.

The plough, which was used successfully on some Jamaica plantations before the American War, was reintroduced towards the end of the century to reduce hired labour. The failure of managers to make effective use of the plough is normally blamed by historians on the slaves' unwillingness or inability to adapt to technological changes and to be educated for such skills. In fact, managers and overseers discontinued the use of the plough because management controlled the profitable business of hiring slaves. The readopting of the plough was intended as a slave-labour-saving device to preserve the lives of the workers and to advance natural increase.[35] On the whole, however, this device never had any significant impact on West Indian agriculture because it worked against the interests of the managerial class.

Yet another change that several planters desired to introduce was the claying of West Indian sugar. This was against the interests of the refiners and bakers in Britain, and the high duty charges stifled its adoption. The method would have saved the colonies large sums in freight rates and would have reduced waste through leakage.

The rationalization of the sugar industry saw the adoption of cane-holing in Jamaica. This system originated in Barbados quite early. In Jamaica the cane holes were dug four feet square, about half an inch less than in Barbados, because of prolonged unseasonable weather conditions and because it prevented the rapid runoff of rainwater, reducing soil erosion. The holes were then filled with manure. The parent plant was never able to exhaust all the nutrients, so cane-holing was well suited to ratooning. Above all, it was perceived as a method that saved "a great deal of negroe labour" and protected the soil by retaining moisture.[36] The newly adopted system of cane-holing was also well suited to the planting of the Otaheite cane.

Historians have pronounced the adoption of the Otaheite or Bourbon canes, sometimes called ribbon canes, the most important agricultural innovation to be introduced in the Caribbean at the end of the eighteenth century. According to Galloway, the cane was first imported into the French West Indies around 1780 from Mauritius; by 1793 samples were growing in the botanic garden in St. Vincent. "In 1795, a Jamaican botanist obtained a sample for his island from Santo Domingo, but in the next year Captain Bligh brought some samples directly to Jamaica from the Pacific."[37] The introduction of the cane spread rapidly throughout the West Indies in general, as the planters grabbed at any straw for survival. In the process, most estates abandoned the Creole cane that had been grown since the outset of the sugar industry and was totally acclimatised.

Galloway contends that the decision of the planters was grounded in their belief that the new cane brought three fundamental advantages: it gave better yields of sugar per unit area of cane-piece under cultivation than the Creole; its bagasse produced a better fuel; and the Otaheite matured more rapidly than the Creole cane.[38] Most West Indian planters did succumb to the Otaheite craze mainly because of its reputation for increased yields, as one manager reported: "The South Sea Canes had had several trials and are universally esteemed an acquisition to the island."[39] With the repeated failures of the Creole cane in the

Leeward Islands, the apparent ability of the Otaheite to survive the excessive dry weather was welcomed. The cane did increase the quantity of sugar, but it did so at a time when the British market was overstocked and the price of sugar depressed. The response of most absentees was a demand for reduction in the acreage under cane cultivation. At such a time, increased production became a major drawback of the Otaheite cane.[40]

There were other facets of West Indian plantation economy to which the Otaheite cane did not make a significant contribution. It did not produce adequate fodder for the cattle, and the sugar manufactured from it was of poor quality—two powerful criticisms against it. After the early euphoria over the productive capabilities of the new cane, planters sat down to consider the quality of its sugar. The verdict was unanimous that this was far inferior to that of the Creole cane. The Otaheite made a high proportion of very dark brown sugar, which found little favour on the London market.[41]

The greatest weakness of the new cane was its lesser capacity for producing rum. Summing up the overall performance of the Otaheite cane after about five years of its cultivation, Rodgers concluded: "On very mature consideration, I am very much inclined to think we have not benefited at all by the cultivation of the Bourbon cane, when there was land sufficient for that of the Old Cane—a review of Mesopotamia crops since 1789 . . . speaks pretty plainly for this fact in the article of Rum, and my observation of the loss of our neighbour's stock are convincing that it does not produce the same quantity of food for them—these are two very material points to consider on an Estate, and we propose to put in about 20 acres of the Fall plant with the common cane to preserve the stock of them."[42]

Complaints originating from the Leeward Islands about the performance of the Otaheite cane indicated that the overall results were unsatisfactory. John Pinney, after comparing the quantity and quality of the sugar from the Otaheite with those of the Creole cane, concluded that the former was inferior and that "the sugars of his correspondence, which had been made from the new cane stood the voyage badly and the refiners disliked them.[43] The continued judgment was that there was "no final great advantage" in cultivating the Otaheite cane and that in the interests of the West Indian planters "a good less land in Cane will do."[44]

The West Indian sugar industry did not have the leeway to continue the production of low-grade sugar. In this period, it certainly could not compete with better-quality sugar at lower prices from other areas. Their long experience in the British sugar markets had taught both planters and managers that only high-quality sugar had a chance of doing well. Barham repeatedly stressed the need to produce quality sugar on his estates: "Everything now depends on making good sugar & keeping down expenses Else no estate will clear itself. Quantity is now of comparatively small consequence & nothing would be so beneficial as it would be by general consequence to reduce the crop."[45]

High-quality sugar was sold first, which saved warehousing and other charges, and it received the highest prices. Middling and poor-quality sugars received proportionately much lower prices. They remained in warehouses for longer periods and incurred greater charges and loss from wastage and theft. The production and commercial charges were the same regardless of the quality of the sugar, and so were the duties.

The quality of sugar varied from cane-piece to cane-piece on the same plantation. The difference in value might be 7s to 12s per hundredweight. Some cane-pieces did not produce the same quality sugar two years in succession. But almost universally, newly settled plantations yielded a sugar of the darkest and most unmarketable quality. The difference in value between the best and worst sugars from Jamaica exceeded 20s per hundredweight. Hence, in this period the odds were swinging fast against the continued planting of the Otaheite cane. On islands that were already suffering from soil exhaustion and where the cost of fertilizing the estates was putting great stress on planter finances, it was certainly unwise to add another burden. Pares has reported that correspondence between Pinney and many "experienced planters" condemned "the Otaheite canes for taking too much out of the soil."[46]

In less than a decade in Jamaica, absentee planters observed that their once flourishing estates had declined in production significantly from the introduction of the Otaheite cane. In 1805 Lord Penrhyn told his manager: "The Quantity of sugar made at Denbigh seems so small—only 100 hogsheads."[47] The doubts about the quality and productivity of the Otaheite cane continued right down to the abolition of the slave trade in 1807. In that year Samson wrote to Goulburn: "We had had very fine showers & I have holed and planted 15 acres more, the greatest part of it in ribbon canes & made only 5 hhds. They are a bad yielding cane, tho' a great many of them were planted some years ago. I have only 8 acres of them left which I will dig up next year."[48] The changes introduced in the technical and technological side of the sugar industry did not lead to the level of rationalization envisaged by the planters. The Otaheite cane did not bring about the needed results. In the early years it proved unsatisfactory, and most planters replaced it with the long-serving Creole cane.

Attempts to implement the plough and the steam engine proved unsuccessful, on the whole, because the cost was too high at a time when the plantations were facing serious financial problems and many planters were stressing to their managers "the impropriety of extending concerns in the colonies."[49] Besides, the steam engine did not advance the production of sugar. Most estates were small and were operated as individual units with their own manufacturing equipment, which was adequate to the planters' needs. The steam engine called for an entire reorganization and specialization of the productive factors.

The agricultural sector had to be enlarged and had to produce cane as a commodity whose price was dependent on its quality. The manufacturing sector had to operate on capitalist principles where the labour force was trained and probably free. This was hardly likely in the late-eighteenth- and early-nineteenth-century West Indies. Rationalization along these lines would necessitate the loss of power and control by the planter class. It preferred to hold on to its power and control and to attempt rationalization by greater economy, bringing expenses in line with revenues. Barham was foremost in putting the case: "the crops are not to be complained of but unless means can be devised of keeping the expenses low it is clear the owner can derive no benefits from them. This year the price of produce may be something better but it must be obvious to anyone who compares the present & probable production of sugar with the consumption that till the balance be restored by the ruin of many planters & the consequent diminution of produce that no profits can arise to the owners but by the greatest economy & management." All expenditure including the annual contingencies and any capital investment had to come from the revenue of the estates as their owners vowed not "to send out a shilling for the purpose of improvement" of the industry.[50]

In this attempt, all aspects of plantation life were carefully scrutinized. Excesses were identified and brought to the attention of the attorneys and managers. After examining the invoices of goods ordered out for his Mesopotamia Estate, Barham observed: "Never has there hitherto been any such account, £790 from London only! of which about £470 is for iron work! Luckily my invoices for the Island are not thus conducted, £770 covers the whole. Now the crops are nearly equal, the works are equally to be kept up & the only difference is that you have 130 negroes more. Can this account for excess of £1000 one beyond the other?"[51]

At times tension arose between managerial staff and the absentee planters, especially over hints of misappropriated funds or estate supplies. Witness John Kelly's letter to Jacob Franks: "I am sorry to observe that you appear so much displeased with the list of supplies for next year. With regard to the Gunpowder, the common kind is intended for blasting stones at the quarry to have them to use in doing any necessary work about the buildings, but chiefly to turn arches over the water courses on the estate ... and which water courses in wet weather are very injurious to the Cattle in the carriage of Canes to the Mill. The fine powder was sent for principally to use in making Cartridges, a quantity of which in proportion to each white man on it, the estate is bound by law to provide and which the overseer is obliged to swear to quarterly. It certainly was not sent to shoot with, for the overseer is as little of a sportsman as I am."[52]

Such objections by managers, ostensibly to the reduction of their lists but actually to the imputations in the absentees' letters, were generally met with soothing replies. A dissatisfied managerial class threatened all the efforts of the absentees to rationalize the sugar industry. Thus, when his queries threatened his relationship with Wedderburn and Company, Barham moved quickly to heal the wounds. He explained: "I need not observe to you that on a certain degree of economy it now depends whether a sugar estate gives the owner any return at all. . . . if you calculate an estate that averages 200 hhds & 100 puncheons which now will barely clear to the proprietor £5000 St. & you take out £2000 St. for supplies & £3000 currency for Island contingencies, you will perceive what the balance is."[53]

The difficulty in meeting the contingencies and in balancing the estates' accounts arose not solely from the problems of the sugar industry but to a great extent from those of the rum industry. Rum sales were responsible for the profitability and survival of the system. Throughout the eighteenth century, the estates produced their independent brands of rum. In spite of numerous obstacles, chiefly the restrictions imposed by Britain's commercial policy towards the United States, rum continued to be used as commodity capital in trade with the Americans after the war. A key challenge in rationalizing the sugar industry was to maintain high levels of rum production in the face of falling sugar yields caused by the borer infestations and the repeated irregular weather conditions. On most islands the rum crop was not "sufficient to pay the contingencies of the estate." There were increasingly regular complaints by attorneys and managers showing that the shortfall on yearly expenses amounted to sums in excess of £1,365 because of the inability of the rum crop to meet the demands of the plantations.[54] Yet there was always the optimistic belief that the next year's crop would be better. This was not always the case, as one planter explained: "In the best of times, few things, you well know, are more uncertain than a West Indian crop. Today, the prospect is not favourable, & in a month or two, the reverse. You can therefore reason with no certainty till the sugars are in the boiling house."[55]

Several attorneys expressed their frustration when owners were reluctant to authorise the payment of bills drawn on London agents—a situation that continued beyond the end of this study. The dilemma for managers was that they were expected to administer estates profitably without adequate labour or funds. The long-established practice of paying local debts and other charges from the rum sales was not working effectively. One manager reported: "I am afraid the rum Crop from its low price will not be sufficient to discharge the same. I would wish to know from you whether it would not be better to send the rum home and draw bills for the Contingent Charges. The present price and has been all crop only 2/9 per gallon and when the freight and commissions etc are deducted its positively hardly worth making, the dutys at home are very great, you can inform yourself of this."[56]

With the American market severely limited, West Indian rum accumulated in the colonies. Most of the planters now looked to Britain, Ireland, and Canada with limited success. Like it or not, attorneys were forced to draw bills on their owners' agents in London to pay local taxes, and to purchase provisions and other supplies for the estate.[57] Whatever the objections to drawing bills on sources in Britain, this had emerged as the more secure method to the managers and local planters because, as Walter Nisbet explained, "the destruction that has followed our crops by the Borer, for the last five years has rendered drawing inevitable to myself & every proprietor, if a certain proportion of sugar is not made, it is impossible that the rums can pay Plantation expences."[58]

Growing friction and the threat of war between the United States and Britain further depressed the colonial markets. Americans preferred taking cash instead of West Indian products. Many planters defied British policy to entice the Americans to take their rum.[59] It was the long tradition of commercial relations that enabled West Indian estates to survive as well as they did. The United States remained the best consumer for colonial rum. Canada and Ireland made limited contributions to the economic viability of the islands. The uncertainty of production levels and sales inhibited rationalization of the sugar industry by greater economy. Many attorneys complained that after remitting the trifling quantity of sugar to England, they were left "without a proper fund to pay the current charges of . . . estates for the wages of . . . servants and other incidental expenses."[60]

The difficulty of marketing West Indian commodities was a persistent problem to the planters. The British sugar market could neither consume nor reexport all West Indian sugar, and rum purchases and consumption were equally disappointing. Yet some planters, faced with the choice of producing sugar or rum, supported the latter as being more saleable.[61] The decline of the West Indies sugar industry, under way since the beginning of the American War, had been deepened in the 1780s and early 1790s by British policy. The revolution in St. Domingue seemed a godsend to the planters as it brought significantly higher prices, but these did not last long. When Britain adopted measures to destabilize the sugar industry and reduce prices, West Indian planters rightfully complained that at "the very moment they had some ground of Hope that the scarcity of their produce would augment its price so as to relieve them from the heavy debts they had been obliged to contract, they were subjected to restrictions which rendered their hopes abortive."[62]

Having failed to achieve any significant profitability through the rationalization of the sugar industry, the planters adopted the most direct way. They reduced sugarcane cultivation. One planter stated emphatically that "instead of buying negroes to increase the crew we must come to the resolution of leaving off sugar making."[63] Their experiences during the American War had already brought planters to this conclusion: "Cattle is as very valuable *as sugar* and . . . it is as profitable to raise & sell cattle, as it is to sell sugar. Sugar could be very dear, that has raised by the death, or illness—of negroes—or cattle."[64]

This early suggestion to convert sugar estates into penns was aimed at cutting back on the quantity of sugar sent to the London market. It was hoped that reduced supplies and greater demand would improve prices. The establishment of penns had much to recommend it. They would supply fresh meat to the slaves, improving their diets and health. In addition, the new policy would reduce the harsh labour of the slaves; it would save lives, and even lead to natural increase. Above all, it would allow the estates to regain some profitability. The Dickinsons pointed this out to their agent, Thomas Shekoo Salmon: "The Barton Isles accounts rather prove that the estate will answer better as a penn than a Sugar Work."[65]

The plantation papers abound with directives from absentees advising attorneys to cut back on sugarcane cultivation to reduce production costs and save labour. Barham was particularly emphatic: "I by no means wish at present the crops to be pushed too far which from very laudable motions is sometimes done. Much more do I wish to have the negroes who decrease in some late years tho' not the last I was much concerned to notice, Setting more important considerations aside—the present prices of sugar . . . will ill pay for such losses."[66] Susannah Goulburn, in reply to repeated appeals for more slaves, earlier wrote: "You mention the large crops which you are in hopes of making the next two years. I am truly happy to hear it but let me repeat that caution which I urged so strongly in my last that you do not work the negroes too much as it would be much more advantageous that the property should make smaller crops and preserve the stocks of negroes without diminution than to obtain large crops by overworking the slaves & obliging them to run away that they may obtain a relief from their labour. For the slaves are far the most valuable part of the property & unless they are treated with prudence & humanity the estate can never thrive."[67]

Penns were always central to the profitability of the plantations in Jamaica. Now, many planters viewed them as profitable alternatives to the sugar estates. Establishing penns called for shifting the economy from its dependence on external market sources. Yet, although conversion to penns could not seriously have been carried out under the system of slavery, several sugar estates were transformed by amalgamating the best sugarcane lands in close proximity to the most productive sugar works, then converting the remaining lands into pasture, provision grounds, or indigo or cotton fields.[68]

These changes were features of the rationalization of sugar production. Establishing penns ensured adequate pasturage on land contiguous to the sugar estates for the ready supply of cattle for the mills during crop time. Two factors demanded these changes. The severe dry weather had raised pasturage charges so high that even some managers wrote that the livestock had to be tended on estate lands. The prices of draught animals also pushed the contingent charges very high. Attorneys whose commissions came out of the profits of the penns had an interest in their establishment.[69]

The performance of West Indian estates had shown that greater capitalization did not necessarily bring larger profits. Also, West Indian estates were doing poorly even when some produced larger than normal quantities of sugar and rum. The root cause of lower sugar prices was the overstocking of the London market. But while prices were low, expenses remained high. In such a case, the greater the capital invested, the greater the loss.[70] By the end of the eighteenth century, the prevailing thinking was: Put your capital to work. Capital generated capital because it controlled the inputs into the productive sector, thus regulating the output and in turn the level of capital returned from the investment. This belief rested on the premise that "by addiction to the capital, the present capital would be brought into action. For instance, . . . by doubling the strength, the crops might be doubled, by increasing it still further . . . that might be exceeded, & I suppose by establishing a pen on the waste land, one might gain from that enough to meet the country charges & do away with the Bills—But it is not my wish to send out so large a capital as this would require, & I question If I am likely to find any one possessed of negroes enough, who would be willing to enter into a partnership in the estate."[71]

The plantation system did not hold the same guarantees as manufacturing businesses in England. Probably because penns were widespread in Jamaica, proposals were discussed in the newer and smaller colonies such as Dominica for the conversion of sugar estates into cattle estates and also coffee plantations.[72] However, the most likely successor to sugar in the Leeward Islands and Barbados was cotton. The expansion of the textile industry in England at the end of the eighteenth century opened up a guaranteed market for yet another West Indian commodity. During the American War, the decline of the sugar industry had forced many Barbadian planters to cultivate significant quantities of cotton. The cultivation of this crop led to the invention of a cotton gin. There were probably two types, a handheld one and a windmill model. By 1790 there were several in the Bahamas. Towards the end of the war, some absentee planters looked to cotton as their salvation, and they asked their managers for detailed information on which of their estate lands were most likely to produce a thriving crop. Many recommended securing seeds from St. Domingue, where the best quality cotton was grown.[73]

The Colonial Office also made serious attempts to grow cotton on some islands where a significant number of loyalists had migrated. Lands, seeds, literature on cotton cultivation, and implements were distributed. Furthermore, on several islands the borer infestation caused the withdrawal of some of the land from sugar cultivation and the replacement of cane with cotton.[74] The importance of this changeover in Barbados is reflected in Governor David Parry's private letter to Evan Nepean informing him that the marked decline in revenue from the 4½ percent duty had occurred because cotton had replaced sugar as "the greatest staple of the island."[75] In the end, cotton cultivation lost out to that of the United States. It was only in St. Vincent where the Sea Island cotton grows that the crop has had a lasting impact.

Attempts were also made to introduce the spice industry into the West

Indies. In Jamaica some estate owners flirted with the idea of extending pimento cultivation, but the uncertainty of the crop quickly dashed such ideas.[76] The problems of the sugar industry also led to spice cultivation in St. Vincent. Beginning around 1800 Tim Mathews procured a number of young plants and seeds of the Ceylon cinnamon from the Royal Botanic Garden. He planted these on his lands, and by the end of 1807 he had an estate with approximately 1500 thriving trees. This success inspired Mathews to expand cultivation but, uncertain of the market, he sought help from Governor Beckwith to secure preferences in Britain. Beckwith took up the matter with Lord Castlereagh, Secretary for War in 1807, "feeling such encouragement was necessary in light of the declining condition of the sugar industry."[77]

At this critical juncture, the severe shortages of food, lumber, and other plantation articles forced the planters to look outside the sugar industry for survival. They took more seriously the dire need to raise cattle and to extend the cultivation of provisions generally. The planters of St. Vincent and Tobago established agricultural societies, with the governor as president. The St. Vincent society experimented, almost immediately upon its formation, with the production of bread from yams and breadfruit. Its members also produced flour from the arrowroot. This proved immediately satisfactory and was of immense significance. The society continued and improved the practice of curing pork. It encouraged the colonists to manufacture staves from hardwoods.[78]

Frustrated by their failure to achieve a meaningful rationalization of the sugar industry and to revive the profitability of the plantation system, many planters took the short way out. Some abandoned their estates; others sold portions of estate lands in order to raise money to make up the shortfall in rum production. The money was used to assist with the annual expenses, including the commissions of their attorneys and managers, to purchase slaves and other supplies, and to pay taxes and other debts.[79] The number of these insolvency-induced sales had become alarming in 1792. The trend continued through the 1790s, and in 1804 one report contended that numerous British merchants were foreclosing on West Indian plantations. By 1807 a report of the Jamaica House of Assembly estimated that "the sugar estates lately thrown up, brought to sale and now in the Court of Chancery, amount to about one-fourth of the whole number in the colony."[80]

Even well-known planters were not immune to economic hardship.[81] There were not always purchasers for these estates. In some cases, prices were decidedly too high. Few planters had ready cash, and little or no credit was available. Owners therefore sold at vastly reduced prices. Some staggered the payments, with half the cost put up when the sale was negotiated and the remainder to be paid off in two or more years.[82] The austerity measures recommended by several absentees were attempts to curb unwarranted increases in such areas as supplies ordered out from Britain and salaries paid to white employees on the estates.

The sugar industry had reached fresh crossroads in its development. The cries of the plantation owners in the 1790s were preceded by similar cries in the 1690s. In both periods there were various reasons for colonial complaints. However, certain threads can be found linking the claims of decline a century apart. The predecessors, even ancestors, of these eighteenth- century planters also pegged their losses on wartime conditions. They charged that the convoy system was inadequate and could not protect their trade, just as the Royal Navy was accused of being unable to protect West Indian commerce from privateers during the American and French Revolutionary Wars. British bureaucracy imposed greater control on the islands' trade with the entrenchment of mercantilism, in the same way that the Colonial Office was limiting United States–West Indian commerce. In this period Parliament adopted legislation, including the income tax, that seriously affected the ability of the sugar planters to rejuvenate and expand their economy.[83]

Throughout the eighteenth century, the West Indian planters and merchants expanded the production of sugar and secondary staples and in so doing became the chief object of British taxation. Taxes were blamed for destroying the indigo and cocoa industries, thus making the islands a monocultural sugar economy. Even though profits became "exceedingly *low*" towards the end of this period,[84] there was vibrancy among the planters right up to the American War. But the islands emerged from the conflict with a severely damaged economy. The plantation system was greatly weakened by the severing of this umbilical cord that nurtured West Indian prosperity. Its lifeline, its central keel, having been damaged, the sugar producers looked on anxiously as British policy on United States–West Indian commercial relations was unveiled. One Dominica attorney in 1782 explained that all the "demands ag't the Estate must be satisfy'd as ruin will ensue we have by fair winds kept the Creditors from extremities but I fear these next Courts, nor will your whole crop suffice without Assistance, cou'd you & Mr. Fordyce determine on what to do, it would be infinitely for your Interest. If you neglect doing it, I again repeat nothing can save the Estate, & as to selling it I don't suppose without reck'ning the negroes (ten of whom I am sorry to tell you are run away . . .) You w'd get 500£ sterling tho' the works alone are worth 1500£."[85]

This aptly describes the state of many estates at that time, not only in Dominica but in Barbados, where creditors sold the slaves and cattle by auction for a fraction of their costs. They ripped up coppers and tore down timbers from mills and other structures, destroying £5,000 to £6,000 of the real value of an estate in order to recoup £200 or £300 or whatever they could.[86] These reports illuminate the deteriorated condition of many estates. The odd one made marginal profits, but only if certain payments were not considered, such as the purchase of new slaves or provision for meeting the costs of natural and other disasters. One owner observed: "The Bills you drew on me, together with the articles sent out exceeded the produce of the estate by £500. I expect it will be the same again this year which certainly does not induce me to purchase negroes—nor to expand the estate—more than I can help—until it is more productive."[87]

Higher local costs for supplies pushed up these charges. Planters who had repeatedly advocated the establishment of penns to satisfy the needs of the stock were incensed by quite substantial sums for these estate animals. In response to expenditures of "£340 for steers & £250 for Mules besides a still for Mesopotamia," Barham told his managers: "Charges like this must weigh down any produce." High annual charges remained a sore point throughout the period 1790–1807. Even when estates made reasonably good crops, the expenses and taxes swallowed up any returns, and except for the penns no profits were left for the planters. Of this, Barham wrote: "You will perhaps have already calculated that with a crop of 300 hhds if I take the profits of the pen out, little or no ballance would be left to me."[88]

How profitable were the sugar estates at the end of the eighteenth century? Correspondence between planters and their managers document the issue of profitability and decline. To many, there was a significant decline in the gross returns from sugar in the course of the century. One estimate contended that "an estate which 105 years ago did with a capital of less than £10,000 in slaves produced an average income of above £5,000 per annum does now with a capital of about 3 times that number not produce £3000."[89] Other assessments give greater details of the losses that some planters bore in the period. Nisbet carefully described his own and those of Lady Stapleton's estate.[90]

Observers always considered measuring the income and profitability of

West Indian plantations a very tricky exercise. Conditions in the region varied, and production from one year to the next was uncertain because of pest attacks and blasts, droughts and floods and hurricanes, and accidents such as fires to the buildings and cane fields.[91] In general terms, however, commentators were able to gauge the performance of the economy. It was commonly accepted that the sugar industry was reasonably healthy until about the beginning of the American War. Consistent with views examined earlier is Barham's 1823 judgment that the returns from sugar production were "larger about seventy or eighty years ago than they have ever been since; from that date they fluctuated variously till about the year 1789, when they again became very considerable; but about the beginning of this century they received a severe shock by . . . withholding a portion of the drawback on exportation."[92]

After the revolution in St. Domingue "the British planters for a short time had the markets of the world,"[93] and prices were very high. The future of the sugar industry in the West Indies looked bright until the British Parliament destabilized it by the measures to reduce the price of sugar for domestic consumers. This not only stimulated imports of sugar into America but also invigorated the Cuban and Brazilian sugar industries, which undersold the British planters at home. Increased taxation also helped to weaken the West Indian plantation system. Writing in 1803, one manager estimated that "the neat [sic] proceeds of sugar for the last five years, has been very little, if at all more than £16 per hhd, upon an average, which is just equal to the present duty of 24/per cwt. & our expenses are so very great, that our rum is not only swallowed up by them, but also a great part of our sugar."[94]

The net revenue from sugar production worsened towards the end of the eighteenth century.[95] Before the American War, planters received on average 64 to 70 percent of their gross incomes from the sale of their sugar. This declined to about 48 percent in 1781. One estimate noted that it took 52 hogsheads of sugar to discharge the duty on 100 hogsheads at 12 hundredweight each; that is, it cost planters 10s 6d in the pound for duty.[96] This worsened towards the end of the period. Annual charges upon estates then stood at 11s 4½d in the pound on gross annual revenue from sugar and rum production, or nearly 57 percent of earnings. The ray of hope that came with the destruction of the French sugar industry soon dimmed, and net returns dropped to barely 40 percent by the end of the slave trade in 1807. In July 1808, Barham communicated to his managers his "determination to make alterations" in the operation of his estates. He wrote: "In truth one cannot afford to keep an estate at a regular loss which now for three successive years is the case (for this year will not compensate for the loss of the last)."[97]

The accounts of individual estates submitted on the eve of the abolition of the slave trade paint a most depressing picture. Conditions were worsening rapidly. Plans to purchase slaves were scrapped in spite of attorneys' urgings to add fresh blood to the understrength slave population before the trade was terminated.[98] Both of Joseph Foster Barham's accounts for 1806, given in table 9.2, show that he was losing money. Many did not include several items of expenditure. For example, Irish supplies were omitted from the Mesopotamia calculations. Planter concerns about the state of the sugar industry had materialised by the end of the first decade of the nineteenth century. Barham called for a lower quantity and higher quality of sugar in order to regain profits. This created a further dichotomy between the interests of the planters and merchants, with the latter preferring greater quantity so that, irrespective of the

Table 9.2. Barham's estate accounts, 1806

Island plantation

Debit		Credit	
Bills	£1,335 10s	135 hhds sugar at £14	£1,890
Invoice	£1,000	96 puncheons rum at £10	£960
Insurance	£100	Total crop	£2,850
Total debits	£2,435 10s	Insurance	-£285
		Total credits	£2,565
		Total debits	£2,435 10s
		Balance	£129 10s

Mesopotamia estate

Debit		Credit	
Bills	£2,498 2s	193 hhd sugar at £15.10	£2,991 10s
Invoice	£1,700	90 puncheons rum at £15	£1,350
Insurance	£170	Total crop	£4,341 10s
Total debits	£4,368 2s	Insurance	-£434
		Total credits	£3,907 10s
		Total debits	£4,368 2s
		Balance	-£461 8s

Source: Barham to Wedderburn Grant and Blyth, 8 January 1807, Bdl., Barham Papers 428, fol. 121.

Note: The balance represented the amount from which he was to deduct the loss of slaves. The insurance in the credit column must be deducted from the total credit.

state of the colonial economy, they were "sure of their profit & if on one hand they are kept out of their money on the other they get the estates for a third or fourth."[99]

Recent scholarship, led by Seymour Drescher, has contended that the West Indian plantations were highly profitable at the end of the eighteenth century and down to the attainment of peace in 1815. This interpretation, undoubtedly made on inadequate information, has led many historians to believe that the trade was "highly beneficial in the period after the American War."[100] It was certainly of benefit to a few very wealthy planters who made profits, but for most plantations there were only losses. There were no advantages to the community as a whole, because the plantation system could not "replace the capital employed in it, with a profit adequate to the risk of loss in deterioration to which it is exposed."[101] Some modern historians have drawn on Bryan Edwards, in particular, and a few managers for the view that the abolition of the slave trade ruined the economy of the West Indies. David Eltis, for example, argues that Britain reduced its own economic growth through the abolition of the slave trade, which he argues was unprofitable. This was certainly not the case.

Several factors at the end of the eighteenth century point to an economy in distress. Land prices were low; there was very little money in the colonies; many plantations upon which significant amounts of capital had been expended were simply abandoned; the capital in slaves wasted away because of high mortality rates from overwork, malnutrition, and disease; cotton became the major crop on several of the islands for part of the period; coffee plantations and penns were replacing sugar estates as the more profitable economic activities in Jamaica; numerous planters became insolvent during the period. One contemporary essayist, assessing the claims of apologists for slavery, pointed out that, while the facts about the unprofitability of the sugar industry were misunderstood, the attitude of the planters could be employed in evaluating the state of the plantations. He wrote: "Many of them are now *not* the enemies of the abolition of the slave trade. Some of them it is hoped are friends to annihilation of this infamous traffic from a conviction of enormity, but by far the greater number it is probable not from motives purely selfish. They are satisfied that the trade being already too much expended has ceased to be profitable."[102]

The sugar industry was certainly not destroyed by the abolition of the slave trade. The decline of the West Indian plantation system had long been in train. There were numerous structural weaknesses, which were well on the way to achieving this without the abolition of the slave trade. The contribution of the

West Indian sugar industry to the development and then expansion of the Atlantic economy had been made from the first half of the seventeenth century right up to the outbreak of the American War of Independence in 1776. By this time, the islands' economy had reached the point where expansion would have been difficult. There was little uncultivated land to increase the units of production, and the technological changes that would have enhanced the manufacturing sector came late in the eighteenth century and required large sums of unavailable money, as well as a restructuring of the agricultural sector, as occurred in Cuba later in the nineteenth century.

There was simply not enough land or capital to make these adjustments at the end of the eighteenth century. Capital could be attracted to the West Indies only by increasing the rate of interest. Jamaica experienced a 30 percent increase at the beginning of the nineteenth century. But this did not improve the situation for the sugar industry or halt the flight of the remaining capital to Britain. In spite of mortgage rates of 8 percent in the colonies, financiers preferred to transfer their mortgages to Britain where they received only 4 percent.[103] Resident planters who had the resources were packing up and investing in England. The best-recorded example was John Pinney. Walter Nisbet also concluded that the islands were limited areas for further investment. Absenteeism increased as a result of the economic conditions and the scare from the St. Domingue Revolution of 1791. Mrs. Susannah Goulburn was advised by William Gore to invest the savings of her son's share from the Jamaica estate "in some substantial property" in England, as "West Indian property is but precarious at all times, & the example of St. Domingo will make it still more so."[104]

Simon Taylor, after assessing the state of the sugar industry, advised his brother on several occasions to use the profits of their Jamaican estates to establish a business in England and reduce dependency on West Indian property whose profitability could not "last forever." For nearly twenty years Taylor threatened repeatedly to leave the West Indies, expressing a preference for the United States, although he was no "Republican." He did not want to continue under British rule because "Ill usage will exhaust the Patience of Man and God knows the Colonies have experienced nothing else for these thirty five years." He never carried out these threats because he was a "die-hard" Jamaican planter. Summing up conditions in 1799, he wrote: "The Duty Freight and Insurance on my Goods is more than I receive for them. Every article of clothing Provisions are 100 per or more than they used to be. Lumber or Timber Staves Boards Hoops are £200, Negroes £100. While I used to labour and gett something to lay by for myself and Relations and also to assist the State I was satisfied but I am determined not to exist for that alone and if this becomes general and it assuredly be the case they would loose the West India Income altogether."[105]

On the other hand, Barham, whose views could be considered representative of the absentee planters, believed the changes taking place in the economy of Britain, as against the static nature of that of the West Indies, brought about a change in the compact between the colonists and the residents of Britain. These alterations, which were so important to the advancement of free trade and the capitalist mode of production in Britain, worked against slavery and the general interest of the colonial planter class. To operate the sugar industry in a capitalist system without any significant structural changes only impoverished the planters. This maintained a plantation system that, most owners recognized, had "for a long time past ... been considered as very unprofitable."[106]

The West Indian economy was indeed in decline at the end of the eighteenth century. Therefore, the sugar estates were no longer attractive as investment centres, and financiers, including absentee planters, refused to send out capital to the "old colonies" even for the improvement of the logistics of sugar production. For their part, resident planters were committed to returning to Britain to invest their incomes there because the economies of the islands were declining markedly.[107]

❧ 10 ❧

War, Trade, and Planter Survival, 1793–1810

For the planters, the eighteenth century was the best of times and the worst of times—in rapid succession. Richard Pares designates "the years between the Peace of Paris (1763) and the outbreak of the American Revolution" as "above all, the silver age of sugar." The long-drawn-out international conflict, "even the vast acquisition of sugar-growing territory" in the Treaty of Paris and the development of new islands, had little or no negative effect on the older colonies up to 1770. The price of sugar in the home market remained approximately 50 percent higher than the level in the 1730s. "From this point everything went to the bad. . . . Great Britain had the worst of it in the War of the American Revolution. Far more serious was the break in the intercourse with the sources of food supply in North America, which was continued long after the peace treaty."[1]

Not only did the war years have a devastating impact on the development of the colonies, the continued imposition of British mercantilist policies and the restrictions on the admission of United States produce lessened the profitability of the West Indian plantations and certainly speeded their decline.[2] While the economic consequences of the American Revolution and Britain's United States policy could be measured statistically, it has always been difficult to assess the psychological impact of these factors on the planters. One can divine from their letters and those of their attorneys that a sort of helplessness had crept into the psyche of the planter class. The driving spirit that had pitted the planters against all possible odds—slave revolts, natural disasters, indebtedness, and the disappearance of fortunes into bankruptcy—had never forced them into submission until the loss of the American colonies and the imposition of British trade restrictions. One manager observed: "Since the American War, the Gentlemen of Jamaica sadly neglected their Estates, their conduct towards them . . . has been ruinous in the extreme."[3]

The planters had certainly had devastating experiences. The war had caused shortages, high prices, and declining incomes. Many were longing for peace, as one wrote to his correspondent in England: "We continue in very great distress for want of provisions & necessaries. Peace is our dayly wish which if it don't happen soon, the most independant man here must be ruined."[4] Many had indeed reached this state by the end of the war. They lost their capital in slaves as the result of diseases caused in part by malnutrition and overwork. Natural disasters also took their toll as severe dry weather was followed by devastating hurricanes throughout the Caribbean in the 1780s. Of the destruction in Barbados one year, Henry Duke, Solicitor General and member of the Assembly, wrote that "most of the Plantations have been laid in Ruins."[5]

Even though times were hard and losses great, West Indian planters were accustomed to war and hardship. At each return of peace, they would take measures to rationalize their plantation operations and regain their profitability. On previous occasions, prosperity had continued or returned immediately. After 1783, because of Britain's insensitive and restrictive commercial policies towards the United States, and her undermining of the slave system, prosperity was very slow to return.[6] The possible outcome of Britain's restrictive policy was not lost on either the absentee planters or their attorneys on the islands.

The adoption of the order-in-council of 2 July 1783 engraved indelibly the psychological scar that seven years of deprivation from the the American War of Independence had caused. Writing from the islands, both managers and resident planters forecast from experience that the restrictions would most likely inflate the prices of foodstuffs and send the costs of sugar production exorbitantly high. Add to this the increased duty on West Indian products, wrote planter-manager Walter Nisbet, and the result "must so much reduce the nett value of our Estates, as to render it unprofitable for us to carry on their culture; for our expences are certain, and enormous; & . . . our profits very much the reverse." There emerged the general belief that Britain had no interest in preserving the West Indian colony's monopoly of its market for tropical products. British policy itself had spawned such thinking. Parliamentary restrictions were viewed as certain to ruin the islands' economy. Nisbet wrote: "For if we are to be reduced to the necessity of carrying on the cultivation of our Estates, at an expence beyond our profits, it very obviously follows, that every Plantation must be ruined, and the cultivation of sugar cease."[7]

Complaints against British policy evoked little or no concern. This was one of the rare times when the West Indian interest did not get its way. The opposition to its pro–United States trade policy was led by Lord Sheffield and supported by British shipping interests, the North American loyalists, and even the West India Committee, which favoured the American trade without United States shipping. Members of the resident West India planter-managerial class recognized the changed attitude of the British administration and its interest groups. As sources of revenue, the islands remained important to the British Treasury, as Nisbet also noted: "This country seems to care little about us, or our remonstrances, as long as a certain revenue is raised. Tis true, it may last for a short time; but like the Dog in the Fable, they are likely to lose the whole, by grasping at too much."[8]

This bleak outlook on the economic picture in the sugar colonies was corroborated by the London West Indian merchants. Richard Neave wrote to Catherine Stapleton: "In answer to what you mention about the consequence of the American prohibition will be to the West Indian concerns I cannot do it better than sending you a letter I received from a very sensible Man & of great consideration in Antigua by which you will find it a very serious affair to all concerned in the islands."[9]

These were still early days, and worse British restrictions, culminating in the abolition of the slave trade, were yet to come. But by the late 1780s West Indian estates were in severe financial straits. In this decade of war and trade restrictions that cut off a significant portion of the plantations' supplies, the government had also destabilized the American market for secondary West Indian products such as coffee and rum. Rum sales to the United States were fundamental to the entire working of the plantation system. Rum was the commodity that had enabled the estates to replace their labour force annually. It also met the costs of the contingencies, including taxes. Rum now had to be sent to England, "for we cannot sell rum here for cash. We can only get rid of it by way of barter for any American articles such as lumber, corn, flour etc," wrote one manager.[10] British commercial policy caused the Americans not only to refuse to take British West Indian rum, which accumulated unsold in the colonies, but to discriminate against the British planters, forcing them to give better terms in the exchange of West Indian products for American supplies.

These changes had greatly increased the contingent expenses of West Indian estates, exclusive of the purchase of new Africans and livestock. In the earlier part of the century, the first year or two after a war would have seen normal operating costs, increased supplies to the plantations, and restored profits. In the case of the American Revolution, normal peacetime operations never truly returned before the plantations had to face the economic rigours caused by the French Revolution. It is certainly a misreading of conditions in the islands to claim that prosperity had returned almost immediately after the American War. Reports from managers continued to highlight the serious financial state of the plantations, their reduced production and their ever increasing costs. One wrote: "I have had, indeed, to lament that for many years after the commence- ment of the American War & the capture of this Island, the accounts run very high, but that was owing to the high price of many necessary for the estate, and the losses it sustained."[11]

The financial cost of the capture of St. Kitts continued to be felt long after the resumption of peace and was the result of British policy, which in the long run would destroy the entire credit system in the British West Indies. Rum was previously the major commodity capital in the West Indian economy and al- lowed for effective United States–Caribbean commercial dealings. Once the trade was restricted, no bilateral trade agreements could be effected. The United States had the upper hand. With rum now being manufactured throughout the Caribbean, the United States could get what it needed elsewhere, and the British planters, instead of continuing to use rum as capital, had to expand their in- debtedness in Britain by drawing on the merchants there.

The sugar crop, which was normally used to pay the capital expenditure in England, now had to be sold locally to meet the contingencies of the estate and such local costs as taxes and purchasing new Africans. In any case, the price "clear of all charges" was better than in England.[12]

Planters and managers who, only a short while before, seemed so assured in their business were now relegated to living in hope of a return to ante–Ameri- can War conditions. Nisbet wrote: "I hope ere long we shall see better times, when my letters will afford you more comfort than they can do at present, and to these times we must look forward struggling through the present as well as we can."[13] Declining profits and repeated calamities led some to invoke the blessings of a higher power to relieve the stresses in the economy. Thus Richard Pennant wrote, "But I hope it would please God . . . that we may see good times again."[14]

These once prosperous islands, where not only planters and managers but also officeholders had dreamt of making fortunes, were slipping fast and steadily. Plantation production figures give only a part of the picture. Local customhouse revenues offer a more comprehensive view of the health of the economy. From this standpoint, Walter Nisbet's report is very enlightening. He observed that, as collector of the customs in St. Kitts, he was well placed to comment on the island's economy. He stated: "These places, at home, in point of profit, are very much exaggerated. All similar offices have very much de-creased since the prohibition of our former intercourse with America, and I had no conception that the collection of Basseterre was so reduced. I have now had the best information of the amount of it, for the last four years, and it has not cleared twelve hundred sterling per annum."[15]

These conditions went unchanged throughout the 1780s, and the 1790s be-gan much the same. However, revolution in France, a slave revolt and civil war in St. Domingue, and war between France and Britain kindled hope. Pennant's invocation for better times and Lady Stapleton's correspondent's prayer for their changed circumstances seemed to have been answered with the destruc-tion of the French sugar industry. But, was this enough to guarantee planter survival? Initially the upheaval promised brighter times, but this was not to last, and the British government's measures to limit any profits from higher prices destabilized the market and smashed the dreams of the sugar interests.

These restrictions, coming at a time when the debate on ending the slave trade was also taking place in Parliament, reopened in the islands the old dis-cussion about the relationship between Britain and the sugar colonies. The colonists argued that the compact between the colonies and Britain was in-tended to be a symbiotic arrangement, but instead it worked to their detriment, with all the advantages going to Britain. One argument went:

Not only the colonist is obliged to deposit, in a state particularly subject to loss by drainage and to expense by carriage, the chief of his produce for sale in Great Britain, but he is restricted to Great Britain for his principal purchases, and to British ships for his sole conveyances, even in time of war, when he might avail himself both of the cheapness and convenience of neutral bottoms. He is allowed indeed to purchase building timber, packages, livestock and certain articles of provision, from the neighbour-ing continent of North America; but though, from the circumstances of the islands, his wants of these articles are progressively multiplying, he must obtain them under such disadvantages, that, when the obstacles attending the sale of his melasses and rum are considered, it is 100 percent, beyond their price before the American War, and 50 percent beyond the prices at which rival colonies may obtain them. It happens unfortunately, also, that the same causes, which produce a shortness of crops, commonly occasion an increase of expence, from an accompanying dearth of provisions.[16]

In the Leeward and Windward Islands, daily meetings were held, circulars and advertisements were published and distributed throughout the region, highlighting the problems of the planters. These meetings resulted in the second call for united West Indian action against Britain. The appeals to the Jamaicans for a meeting of the most important and influential proprietors from all the sugar colonies to be held at a central place, advantageous to the group, to consider British policy that was inimical to the islands went unheeded. United action foundered in the depths of the Caribbean Sea. The planters' call was rejected. It was certainly the ideal time for a joint position, given "the Concurrence as it were (eadem flates) of so many things as the Resolution for abolishing the Slave Trade; and the several Resolutions for prohibiting the exportation of sugar, in order to lower the price of it; and the encouragement given the East India Company to import clayed sugar from India; with admission of foreign sugar to be imported into Nassau in New Providence, and exported from thence to England."[17]

British West Indian sugar planters retained their belief that their contribution to the expansion of the Atlantic economy in general, and to British economic development in particular, was significant. Unfortunately, by the end of the eighteenth century the islands and their trade were seen as having conflicting roles in British economic development. Looking at their trade, the vast quantity of their production was shipped to Britain, consuming in return large quantities of British manufactures. Late in the century, estimates showed that the West Indian trade utilized annually some 238,450 tons of shipping employing over 20,000 seamen. The exports were valued at £5,264,107, of which 94 percent went to Britain. The total production, however, was estimated at £7,243,266. This was earned from an investment of £50 million in 1788, rising above £70 million in the last decade of the century for a return of more than 10 percent.[18] About half of the investments came from British residents.[19] The duty on sugar for home consumption had risen tremendously, from something over £1 million sterling in 1791 to a high of roughly £4,178,000 in 1808. It is likely that the duties and excise taxes collected on other West Indian products would have raised the aggregate duty above £5 million.

Historians cite this growth as evidence of development in the economy.[20] The rise in the tax and excise revenue resulted from a stupendous rise in the duty charges on sugar, from 12s 4d per hundredweight in 1790 to 27s in 1808. This represented an increase of 119 percent during the war years. In this period the sugar consumed rose from 1,536,232 hundredweight in 1790 to 2,842,818 hundredweight in 1808, for an increase of 85 percent. The combined result was that the revenue from duties on sugar almost quadrupled between 1790 and 1808, increasing by approximately 289 percent. But it is quite clear that the growth in revenue from sugar duties, while linked to a rise in consumption, was primarily the result of greater taxes.[21]

Based on the available statistics, there arises the interpretation that the West Indian colonies were of pivotal importance to Britain. Contemporary writers considered "the loss of the sovereignty of those islands as equivalent to the destruction of that trade, ... the annihilation of this branch of the revenue" and to reduced investments in the trade of the region. Modern scholars have made only a slight alteration. They see the abolition of the slave trade as having negative consequences for the British economy. Assessing the contemporary viewpoint, it is possible to illustrate the impracticability of the contention by an assessment of the American situation. The possible separation of the mainland colonies was considered to be synonymous with the ruin of the British economy. In fact, this did not happen. The independence of the American colonies did not destroy the British trade or English investments in the United States. Few had "anticipated that the Mother Country, thereby freed from the necessity of defending or rather watching the colonies, would still continue to monopolize its infinitely more extensive trade. But the issue of that context has taught the politician to distinguish between the advantages resulting from the *sovereignty* of Colonial possessions, and those resulting from the intercourse of trade between them considered as independent States."[22]

British politicians had certainly acquired the most profound "lessons of Colonial policy" from the outcome of the separation of the mainland colonies. Likewise, it had done more "to enlighten [their] minds in political jurisprudence than any other event" during the eighteenth century. As far as the West Indies were concerned, while the contribution of the duties and taxes to the Treasury was recognized, the view was held that the only internal tax that provided revenue to the Treasury was the 4½ percent duty collected in Barbados and the Leeward Islands. Of the £200,000 collected, only about £40,000 went to the British Exchequer. The remainder went to pay administrative costs. Furthermore, as an internal tax it had done grave damage to those societies and economies. For example, "Barbados has in the course of the last century been reduced from 150,000 to 78,000 and in shipping from 60,000 tons to 27,000 tons." It was therefore indeed impracticable "of ever deriving any considerable revenue from internal taxation in the Colonies." Even if the islands ceased to be tied politically to Britain, writers noted they would continue to be inextricably linked to England for the following reasons: "Powerful as she is by sea, the trade of the Indies could sail the ocean safely under no other flag. Possessed of capital more than any other nation, from none could the planter receive equal accommodation, and to none other could they carry their produce whatever were its quantity, to a secure market. The manufacture of Britain, alone can supply the Colonists with *all* the implements of their husbandry, *all* the furniture of their houses; and the dress at once for the master, and the slave; while its fisheries, and its fields produce for them the great staple articles of their food. The character of the British merchant for integrity, her superior knowledge of markets are sufficient to command the confidence of the Colonists, who residing at a distance must naturally feel the importance of these qualities."[23]

The debate on the value of the West Indies to the British economy had taken a new turn by the end of the eighteenth century. The most influential and significant contention held initially by the West Indian interest was that the colonies were important nurseries for British seamen and that their commerce was fundamental to the growth of a strong navy. But now these claims were denied. It was held that the islands' commerce did not employ the number of seamen for which it was credited, and that the British coal, fishing, and coasting trades were the nurseries of British seamen, the foundation of its merchant marine and the bastion of its Royal Navy. What did the West Indian trade contribute in this area? It was credited with being "the nursery and the bulwark of the trade to the Coast of Africa, which, alone, destroys more of our seamen than fall by the hands of our enemies. Beneficial to the Country in other respects, the West Indian trade may be but assuredly to the naval power of Great Britain it is not."[24]

It was in this type of debate that the West Indian planters found themselves during the 1780s and early 1790s just before St. Domingue economy was rent asunder by civil war and rebellion. The destruction of the French cane sugar industry relieved the decay that had set in throughout the British West Indies where "the labour of the Planter" was "rendered unprofitable and many facilities reduced from affluence to want." One petition emphasised that, because of the rapid decline of the commerce of the West Indies, Antigua exhibited "a melancholy picture of poverty and decay—streets once crowded with industrial Inhabitants now trodden and solitary; shops and warehouses formerly filled with Manufactures of Great Britain and Ireland, now empty and shut up, Dwelling houses untenanted. Harbours without shipping, Mechanics without work, and men of every profession in want of employment."[25]

West Indian plantations had existed on a break-even profit level. They were able to do so because estates produced, in addition to sugar, a number of secondary items that allowed the white population to maintain its hold on society and also because planters allowed their enslaved workers to engage in private income-producing activities that provided all categories of food for the plantations even if not for themselves. Hence, although most estates netted less than the legal 6 percent interest on their capital, they survived. Late in the century, some estates in Barbados varied the acreage of their cultivation between canes and cotton as a survival strategy. It was indicative of the decline of the Barbados economy that cotton was replacing sugar as the principal crop. Sugar production levels had declined below 18 hundredweight per acre. The decline of the industry from the outbreak of the American War caused many planters to lose their investments for some "8 or 10 yrs together."[26] This falloff of the Barbados economy is clearly demonstrated in the decline of the slave population and the decrease in the number of windmills. The number of new Africans imported did not compensate for the annual average losses of about 1.25 percent. On the other hand, there was only minor fluctuation in the number of cattle mills. Table 10.1 illustrates the marked decrease in some categories.

Many colonial officials shared the experiences of the planter class. Governor George Ricketts of Barbados in order to reduce the cost of his government adopted a "rigid economy." Reports contend that during his administration he refrained from drawing bills on the Treasury "except for his fixed salary, and his contingent allowance ... for payment of a Secretary."[27] Yet the expenditure of governments throughout the West Indies kept increasing because of rising defence costs. Hence planters were forced to pay higher local taxes.

Faced with ever increasing costs and declining profitability, all absentee planters ordered their attorneys to restore the viability of the estates. This was not always taken kindly by the management, which felt that the austerity measures were not usually in its best interest. In one instance Barham, attempting to make redress for his criticisms of the high contingencies, apologised to Wedderburn and Graham, assuring them that he had not lost confidence in

Table 10.1. Slaves, windmills, cattle mills, and Africans imported, Barbados, 1780–89

Year	Slave population	Windmills	Cattle mills	Africans imported
1780	68,270	396	7	0
1781	63,248	345	4	1,138
1782	—	—	—	303
1783	62,258	335	3	0
1784	61,808	322	3	0
1785	62,775	319	7	149
1786	62,115	325	7	482
1787	62,712	323	5	713
1788	63,557	318	6	1,502
1789	61,703	314	7	371

Source: "An Account of the Number of Slaves, Windmills, Cattle-mills and the Number of Slaves Imported, 1780–1789," PRO, CO 28/62, fol. 262.

their austere management. Because of "the late falling off of my estates," he wrote, "the present low prices (not I fear likely to improve) make the clear profit a subject of rather melancholy contemplation."[28]

As the costs of operating the estates mounted, both managers and attorneys avoided expenditures that were likely to be viewed as unnecessary. One area subjected to almost immediate cutback was the maintenance of buildings. In the case of the "hothouses" where ailing workers were sent to recuperate, this only added to the costs. Worse, there was a general belief that the dilapidated conditions of some of these structures increased mortality rates among the occupants. With buildings continuing to deteriorate and United States supplies for repairs unavailable, many attorneys advised selling to reduce expenses.[29]

Planters were now ever careful that all expenditures were legitimately made on authorised work and not on the managers' pet projects. For example, after the death of her husband, Susannah Goulburn, as trustee for Henry Jr., wanted assurances that he had previously endorsed the projects that James Craggs, her manager, was besieging her to undertake. She told him: "the purchase of the Morocco land will certainly be allowed if it is proved that Mr. Goulburn wished to make the purchase before his death, & that the contiguity of the land & the necessity of it authorised such a purchase—that Mr. Craggs will likewise be permitted to purchase negroes & stock for the estate on making an affidavit that there is not at present a sufficient number to cultivate the estate—that he also will be allowed to rebuild & repair the different buildings which may require it on making an affidavit that such building & repairs are necessary and attested by witnesses competent to judge & resident on the Island."[30]

Such a policy became even more necessary with the impending abolition of the slave trade. It is quite evident that many planters were for the first time scrutinizing the invoices of supplies ordered for their estates. Previously they had simply paid the bills, unconcerned as long as they did not have to make any additional payments. Now they were finding fault with every expenditure. For example, in the late 1700s, coal became a major item on the supply lists. It was a surprise to owners that their estates were using as much as fifty to a hundred tons of coal annually, even after managers had initiated significant reductions, in one case 50 percent. Some estate owners showed ignorance of the law regarding items that estates were to provide for defence. The repeated importation of large quantities of gunpowder met with criticisms that were resented by managers, creating ill feeling.[31]

In several cases, they also appear uninformed about the logistics of sugar production and slavery. Many absentees had inherited their estates and never visited them, so they did not understand such concepts as "Negro houses" when viewed in the context of housing for the labouring class in Britain. When the lists of supplies showed repeated charges for material to repair and rebuild "Negro houses," many absentees objected that they were unnecessary. One instance brought this curt response: "I have read with infinite concern, what you have said on the subject of the 'building & repairing of negro houses,' I conclude that you are of opinion, that such are built in the country, somewhat in the same manner & at the same expence as farm houses are built in England. But in reality all estates negro houses are made of [cheap] material, & in such a manner as repeatedly to require repairs & in the process of time to be put up a new."[32]

The economic situation of the plantations demanded a stamping out of wastage, which was certainly a feature of the system, but not at the expense of the enslaved population, already receiving the minimum. Luxury items such as wines were better targets. These reductions were necessary because the cost of producing sugar was spiralling while the price of that commodity was falling steadily around the turn of the century.

One computation undertaken by John Wedderburn, based on the returns of the six largest and most profitable estates in Jamaica, showed that the cost of producing a hundredweight of sugar had risen to £1 0s 10d after deducting the value of the rum made. The cost of producing a hundredweight of sugar on the other islands was estimated at 19s 6d. A committee of the Jamaica House of Assembly accepted the quotation from Wedderburn and Company but pointed out that the cost of production was higher for the smaller planters, who formed the backbone of the Jamaica sugar industry. The committee noted that while the price of sugar had depreciated continuously since 1799, the duties had been "injudiciously increased" and "at least operated, not only to deprive the planter, generally speaking, of any interest whatsoever on his capital, but to oblige him, if he continues the cultivation of the sugar cane to do it at a considerable actual loss."[33]

The cost of raising a hundredweight of sugar had increased steadily after 1751. Between then and 1787, this figure rose by roughly 75 percent while the London price, exclusive of duty, declined by 6.5 percent. In the latter year, the duty on sugar increased 155 percent over the 1751 cost. Table 10.2 gives the cost of producing sugar, its price, and duty charges on one hundredweight. It must be stressed that several charges such as the price of new Africans, the 4½ percent duty, the interest on the capital, damages by natural disaster, and depreciation on capital items are not included in the prime cost.

While the British government, after the destruction of the sugar estates in St. Domingue and the initial steep rise in prices, effectively lowered the price and thus the returns to the West Indian planters, the latter now had to pay more for their supplies from the United Kingdom. The case of Simon Taylor reflects the plight of the planter class. Taylor, although a wealthy man, was squeezed as the cost of his supplies including charges, insurance, and freight from Britain almost doubled between 1792 and 1798, as table 10.3 shows.

Meanwhile the return on sugar sold in Britain became progressively lower.

Table 10.2. Sugar costs, duty, and price, 1751–1807

Year	Island	Prime cost	Duty	Gross price
1751	Jamaica	11s 7d	4s 10d	39s 10d
1774	Jamaica	15s 10d	6s 4d	35s 6d
1787	All islands	20s 3d	12s 4d	45s
1807	Jamaica	20s 10d	27s	32s 9d
	Others	19s 6d	27s	35s 4d

Sources: Journals of the House of Assembly of Jamaica, 10:44; Dickson, *Mitigation*, 387, 388; Report of the House of Assembly, 13 November 1807, PRO, CO 137/122.

Note: Figures are quoted per hundredweight, in sterling.

Table 10.3. Gross cost of supplies, 1792–98

Year	Total cost £ sterling	Percentage increase
1792	4,343	
1793	4,050	-6.7
1794	6,293	44.9
1795	6,608	52.2
1796	7,688	77.0
1797	6,355	46.3
1798	8,444	94.4

Source: *Journals of the Assembly of Jamaica*, vol. 9.

Table 10.4. Account of sugar sales in England, 1792–98

Year	Hogsheads	Weight	Gross sales	Duties	Freight	Charges	Insurance	Net return	% return
1792	1034	15,022	51,632	11,272	3,009	2,093	1,095	34,163	66.2
1793	1133	12,655	42,604	10,480	4,199	1,903	3,175	22,847	53.6
1794	1136	14,228	37,491	10,678	5,979	1,715	3,341	15,778	42.1
1795	1107	13,264	51,588	9,950	5,970	2,104	4,995	28,569	55.4
1796	232	3,274	12,645	2,550	1,493	535	1,640	6,427	50.8
1797	758	10,259	42,360	8,979	4,613	1,843	5,069	21,856	51.6
1798	707	9,840	42,272	9,512	4,428	2,049	4,664	21,619	51.1

Source: "An Account of Sales of Sugar Shipped by the Honourable Simon Taylor . . . commencing with crop 1792 and ending with crop 1798," *Journals of the Assembly of Jamaica*, 10:429–35.
Note: Weights are in hundredweights, money in pounds sterling.

The planter who had netted 66 percent of sales in 1792 was finding that his returns had fallen below 50 percent in 1794, then settled around 51 percent until 1798. This was the experience of Simon Taylor, whose account books for 1792–98 are summarised in table 10.4.

Taylor's case is quite reflective of the general trend. Though the West Indies planters' share of gross sales had stood at about 70 percent before the American Revolution, it dropped significantly during the French wars, especially after 1791, falling from 71 percent in that year to 51 percent in 1799 and to 40.4 in 1807. An assessment of the statistical information indicates that planters' incomes were indeed declining when sugar prices were highest. One reaches, then, the incontrovertible observation that higher prices did not guarantee increased gains to the planters.[34]

Management, colonial administrators, and owners had to endeavour to limit the decline of the West Indian plantations by reducing the expenses of government in order to achieve a measure of profitability. In reality, however, any significant turnaround required a change of policy towards the supply markets of the colonies, and effective strategies for raising sugar prices on the London market. These did not seem possible, and the islands' economies were poised to continue sliding for a long time. The plantation interests were not the only ones worried. The concerns of the colonial officials were demonstrated in a letter written by Governor Maitland of Grenada:

> At this present Time it is notorious—how extremely he is suffering in a Twofold view—1. All he buys is greatly increased in Price—2. All he sells has fallen equally, and the difference rises to an Evil that ruin many, unless some Channels should offer by which the Price of their Produce may rise to a level with the price of the supplies they must buy. The chief article of West Indian Produce is sugar—and this article . . . may therefore be allowed to regulate—the Planter ought to receive £20. sterl. clear Money upon each hogshead of good Muscovado sugar—to satisfy him. If the times will yield more; he will become rich—If the Market will not yield that Rate, he will quickly become in Debt and have to struggle with Distress. At this time, the best muscovado will not/by the last Prices/give £15 sterl. a Hhd—and the Cause is—that sugar cannot be sold—Another article of main importance is Rum. The Sale of this is now made mostly with the Americans. . . . It *was* a rule with Planters, that the Rum should pay all Expences of Cultivation—but this will not do now.[35]

Maitland's words are a fair summary of the problems of the planter class. Others also reported the extent of the crisis in their own colonies and the planters' reaction. As we have seen, this led to significant migration of planters and their families from the older colonies to the new British colonies and some foreign islands. While government was unable to prevent this migration, some governors attempted "to discourage the emigration of persons in considerable trust" to the foreign colonies.[36] This massive flow was blamed on British policy, which continued to spur the decline of the West Indian economy.[37]

The space left by the departing British planters and their families was quickly filled by a large influx of residents from the French islands fleeing the atrocities of war. Their arrival occasioned grave strain, both social and financial. Many of those arriving were free coloureds and free blacks, which created an imbalance in the free population and threatened the domination of the white planter class. In Jamaica, some officials issued proclamations restricting the entrance of these persons—a restriction later extended to white persons whose presence placed a great strain on supplies.[38] The flood of immigrants to the Leeward Islands, put at about 2,000, threatened distress to the separate islands' governments. Lord Lavington, governor-general of the Leeward Islands, estimated that his administration had spent £28,000 in money and rations for the subsistence of new residents. This seriously affected the credit of those islands.[39]

With significant new demand on already short supplies, prices went even higher and made conditions worse. Governor Woodley of the Leeward Islands defied British policy and opened the ports to American ships and goods. In Jamaica too, the flood of immigrants from St. Domingue overstretched the food supplies. The island Privy Council recommended the importation of all kinds of provisions in neutral vessels for five months upon the same terms, charges, and conditions as British vessels. As the war in St. Domingue gave rise to increased trade between Jamaica and the foreign islands, many foreign merchants moved to Kingston to carry on the trade, thus threatening the islands' security. While British officials were aware of the need to impose restrictions on these new residents inhabiting mainly the coastal areas, they were reluctant to do anything that would interfere with the valuable commercial intercourse that had emerged.[40]

This trade was particularly important for British reexports; it had only minimal effect on the domestic market. The outbreak of rebellion and revolution in St. Domingue and then war between Britain and France merely deepened the already stressed situation in the West Indies. Relief loomed with the high prices of sugar in Britain, but the government supported by public opinion ended this interlude. In reality, sugar prices had not increased "more in proportion than that of meat, butter, cheese and a variety of other articles of the first necessity. The freight of all the heavy articles from England to the Islands has been very considerably augmented and the North American produce is twice as high as it used to be," observed one disenchanted individual.[41] The rise in prices of West Indian commodities was just a response to the worldwide inflation caused by the French war in which privateering activities along the trade routes in the Caribbean sent insurance rates skyrocketing.

Privateering in addition to British policy also affected the supply of North American food. Corn became scarce and prices jumped markedly. The quantity of local supplies was inadequate to fill the vacuum. Provisions for the enslaved population again became a worry. Supplies from Canada, Ireland, and Britain were far too scant and unreliable to meet West Indian demands.[42]

Several survival strategies were adopted. First, the colonists, especially the merchant class, sought and took every opportunity to continue trading with the United States. The contribution of the merchant class to the survival of the West Indian plantation system is clearly highlighted in a joint petition of the Council and Assembly of Antigua in which the two houses emphasised that it was "by means of a liberal credit from the Merchant class and by that means only that the slaves can be maintained, and the cultivation of the earth carried on, till circumstances more favourable produce crops more abundant; but while the Merchant is compel'd to struggle with the difficulties of a confined trade, he is unable to furnish adequate assistance to the Planter and both are in danger of being permanently crushed under calamities."[43]

One of the principal contributions of the continental trade to the development of the sugar industry was that it continued, much longer than British merchants, to allow transactions for lumber, provisions, and other supplies to be undertaken with sugar and rum as payment. While West Indian commodities were still being used as cash, attorneys could honour the requests "not to draw Bills on their absentee owners."[44] The commodity cash system favoured the British West Indies, and its loss was very much against the interests of the West Indian planters. Without the use of commodity cash and ready access to credit, the hands of the planters were tied. Some were advised to lease their estates; Clement Tudway was urged "to grant a lease of the Estate to Mr. Crawford, as you have neither the Works or Negroes to carry it on as a Sugar Plantation; indeed Crawford's Works might be bought at a reasonable rate, but where would you get slaves? You have not a sufficient number for the two estates now in your possession."[45] Heeding his attorney, Tudway leased the estate to Crawford for £450 sterling per annum.

Before the American War and for a while at the end of the century, rum sales with a small amount of sugar provided for the payment of the contingencies, including the purchase of new Africans. However, with the redirection of trade to Britain, Canada, and Ireland where rum was little needed, planters had to find more money and bills of exchange to pay their expenses in England and the local contingencies. The practice of covering bills with West Indian products was, like the sources of credit, coming to a quick end in Britain.[46]

In such a delicately balanced situation, any rumblings of war sent waves of panic through the sugar colonies. A recovery after the American War was just about to gain momentum when yet another war broke out in the West Indies. The downside was that most islands were defenceless.[47] The upside was the prospect of increased prices and profits for the sugar industry. This time, however, war brought consequences that would immediately distress the sugar economy. The merchants, on whose shoulders the future of the plantations rested, were forced to raise the prices of their flour and other provisions by a good half. And supplies remained precariously low for most of the period.

There were calls throughout the colonies for opening up the ports to United States shipping and provisions. Attorneys also made individual appeals to their absentees for larger quantities of provisions from Britain.[48] While these requests resulted in some shipments, the amounts were much less than the demands, and delays were regular and prolonged. In general, the French Revolutionary Wars caused further dislocation to the West Indian economy.[49] Planters protested, but they were forced to endure excessive hardships. Most of these complaints were centred on the fears of prolonged shortages of provisions, which would affect the enslaved population seriously and increase the threat of revolt. The example of St. Domingue was kept alive among West Indian planters, who were sympathetic to their French counterparts.[50]

Leaving little to chance, several planters defied British regulations and established their private trading arrangements with North American merchants or with agents in the United States to whom they shipped their produce. While the supply of American foodstuffs was assured under these arrangements, they did not guarantee cheaper food. In some instances, prices were as much as 30 percent higher than for similar articles purchased in some major towns. These merchants also charged high freight rates without any guarantee of adequate supplies to the planters.[51]

There were limited direct efforts to supply some plantations, but there continued to be times when American corn was very scarce and expensive. The situation became chronic, and grew worse as natural disasters hit the islands.[52] Drought was the most common. One manager wrote: "I do not know what we shall do to feed your People next year for there will be none fore sale in the Parish."[53] Simon Taylor said: "the drougth we had in Dec. Jan'y & Feb'y we are in a very alarming and Critical Situation, and Famine staring us in the Face. Upon an Exact acct. taken, there are only about 2000 Blls of Flour and 300 Trcs of Rice, Hardly any Corn or Biscuit or other Provisions to be had, for the support and existence of 20,000 Souls."[54]

The shortage of foodstuffs was not the only important problem that West

Indian planters faced throughout the period of the French Revolutionary and Napoleonic Wars. Lumber of all categories was very scarce. This was crucial since the planters were unable to construct casks for shipping their sugar and rum to London. Planters feared that it was "useless to send out ships . . . from England to bring home produce from this Island for there will be none to send for want of packages to put it into by this means the Canes must rott on the ground."[55] To ease the problem, absentee planters were advised to send out plantation supplies of flour, beans, and oatmeal "in good puncheons without sap in the staves." These were then reused to ship rum to England.[56] In some cases, managers experimented with alternative material. Local staves were produced on plantations where wood was available, but on the whole West Indian timber was unsuitable for containers for sugar and rum. One manager experimented with bamboo and lancewoods for hoops.[57]

Even when casks were available, there was a dreadful shortage of ships to take the goods either to the United States or to Britain. Added to this, the convoy system had been virtually nonexistent owing to a lack of both naval vessels and arms. There were constant requests to open the ports to send ships to America for supplies according to the law. Simon Taylor observed that it was "mockery to apply to the commander to send a convoy with ships to gett these articles from the only place they are to be had . . . for he has no ships to send as convoy. To arm vessels we cannot for we have no Guns or arms to putt on board them."[58]

Privateers in conjunction with French warships infested the Caribbean Sea, causing panic among the inhabitants. They blamed the Royal Navy for not relieving their fears of being captured. One manager wrote: "I think we are in a fair way of being literally starved in the Islands, for we have just received advice that two French frigates are on the coast of America which have taken several of our vessels going there for supplies of Provisions, and some of them can neither get in nor out of the American Ports. . . . The only means left of deriving supplies will be through the foreign Islands, & they will thereby be rendered very precarious and excessively dear—That an ill-judged Policy it is to debar us from the American Trade, which never can hurt the Navigation of the Mother Country, & is so essentially necessary to us."[59]

Even before the outbreak of the French Wars and the renewed struggle for supplies for the plantations, there were numerous efforts by the planters and merchants to safeguard their interests. Thus they established a circuitous trade through the French islands. In response, Parliament prohibited American supplies reaching the British colonies by this way. The planters sought to circumvent the measure by applying to their local commanders-in-chief "to suspend the operation of the Act" for limited times.[60] These applications were not always successful, and in order to resuscitate the estates to a measure of prosperity, some planters and managers adopted other practices. Local merchants who had devised ways of receiving regular supplies from the United States were given contracts to furnish the estates, as one planter-manager wrote: "I have curtailed all the expensive articles of Provisions from England & entered into a contract with a merchant here, on the same terms for you, that I have contracted for myself."[61]

Despite all these circuitous ways of supplying the estates, the most effective and direct method was to get the governors to open up shipping for a time in order to relieve severe shortages and so avoid death and disaster among the slave population. From the very inception of the prohibition of United States–West Indian trade, planters availed themselves of every opportunity to secure American goods by applying to the Assembly and Council to request the governors to open the ports of the islands to prevent famine. According to the regulation, the governors had to take the advice of their councils. On most occasions, the councillors supported the requests because the evidence was so overwhelming or because their interests were also served by the application. The practice was general throughout the British West Indies, as a letter to Lord Sydney indicates: "On account of the Scarcity of those Articles in the said Islands, arising from the intermediate Demand which had happened there, in consequence of Permissions granted by the Governors of His Majesty's other Islands, the authority conveyed to me by your Lordship's Letter of the 25th will I conceive afford a Seasonable Relief to Grenada and I shall not fail to avail myself, under that authority of the Powers given by the 3ᵈ clause of the said Act with the approbation of the Council."[62]

Requests for opening West Indian ports to American trade were made repeatedly after 1783. The responses of the commanders-in-chief varied from island to island. In colonies where the residents easily influenced the governors, assent was readily given; in others, the requests led to long-drawn-out battles with local planters. In Barbados, Governor Parry set a trend. Requests were speedily endorsed, as he noted that "a combination of circumstances rendered it absolutely necessary for me to open the ports . . . to vessels of all nations, for a limited time. As soon as that necessity ceases they shall again be shut."[63] Adam Williamson, lieutenant governor of Jamaica, in spite of his personal awareness of the degree of scarcity, was reluctant to take action to relieve the situation until he was assured of "the most urgent necessity."[64]

As a military man, Williamson stuck doggedly to regulations. His failure to allow American shipping to enter Jamaican ports was transmitted to the island agent, who wrote to the Colonial Secretary asking him to intervene and to order Williamson to accede to the planters' requests. Fuller's intervention had the desired result. The Colonial Office clearly enunciated the position that it was prepared to allow governors the freedom to adopt measures to forestall famine even though these were contrary to British commercial policy. However, Dundas warned, opening the ports was illegal and should not be continued beyond the period of absolute necessity. Williamson, although he felt that he was treated with the greatest civility on his opening of the Jamaica ports to United States trade, criticised the Colonial Office's opposition to opening the ports. He believed that the secretaries could not "be judges of the necessity & if I had not opened the ports for . . . provisions and lumber, the island would have been very much distressed & the revenue home fall short. I hope some arrangement may take place between us & the Americans. They are absolutely necessary to the welfare of all our Islands. . . . it would ruin America to be at War with us, but we should also suffer exceedingly."[65]

Conditions were indeed very poor, and there were repeated periods of significant scarcity of food and clothing among all classes in the West Indies.[66] There thus emerged hope among the West Indian interest that changes might be implemented in United States–West Indies commercial relations as a result of the negotiations with Chief Justice John Jay. For many years after the American Revolution and the imposition of British mercantilist policy, it had been impossible to maintain the effective operation of the plantation as a business enterprise. The logistics of sugar production necessitated the annual supply of millions of feet of staves, hoops, heading, and shingles, thousands of barrels of pork and beef and flour, hundreds of thousands of bushels of corn for the enslaved population. Supplies of these and other items were very inadequate, and the planter class was always in fear either of the starvation of its people or of its inability to produce and ship sugar and rum.

Severe losses in sugar production had the potential to establish a domino effect in the British and West Indian economies. The customs collected diminishing duties; British shipping suffered severe losses, having to return home in ballast. English merchants in the West Indian trade received reduced annual remittances, leading to further indebtedness of the plantations and further depressed trade conditions. But the ones who had the most to lose were the planters who went bankrupt. The very fact that commercial relations between the sugar islands and the United States had to rely on the intervention of the governors after repeated appeals and solicitations for help created the wrong atmosphere for business.

There was too much uncertainty, and the planters were placed at too great a disadvantage vis-à-vis the United States merchants. Most of the opinions on the value and necessity of bilateral trade between the West Indies and the United States did not cite the carrying trade as a major element. Nor was it crucial to the continued development of British naval power. Above everything else, some observers believed that if the British government were "seriously to investigate the Business, they will find it not an object any longer to sacrifice the planter's Interest for the sake of it."[67]

Even the West India Committee of Merchants and Planters, which had gone along with British exclusionist policy in the formulation of the order-in-council of July 1783, now implored the British government to maintain the trade between America and the West Indies in British ships in order to provide the several necessities for the plantations so evident in wartime. Thus, from time to time, down to the end of this study, the West India Committee supported appeals from the colonial planters for relief from catastrophic economic disasters because of the shortage of food and lumber. For much of the time and throughout most of the islands, the governors were prevailed upon to open the ports to United States goods and vessels. In most cases, the proclamation for this purpose stipulated the categories of goods to be imported. On nearly all occasions, lumber, flour, and corn were allowed, while salted meats and fish, unless brought in British ships, were debarred.[68]

The evidence is overwhelming that the British government's efforts to restrict and control United States trade to the West Indies had only limited success. Although not in the same quantity, the commerce continued through the regular opening of the ports, through the foreign islands, and through other illegal methods of trade. The islands remained, however, dependent on the United States for lumber and provisions. The continuance of the trade and its immense value to the plantations are amply told in the records. Managers were adept at carrying on the trade when, in their opinion, scarcity threatened famine among the enslaved people, as one wrote to Barham: "I have sent four puncheons Rum to New York to purchase corn meal, rice etc. thinking of doing the same for Mesopotamia."[69]

One of the most significant consequences of the French Wars and the continued restrictions placed on United States trade was the rapid increase in the price of most articles imported into the islands. The restrictions remained a sore point with the colonists because their forced dependence on Ireland for meats and other dairy products increased costs: "I find by the correspondence between the Island agent and the ministers for the colonies, he lays great strictures on the intercourse between us and the Americas. There is no probable cheaper [way] of importation of salted meats into the Islands again, as he considers Ireland to be very competent to furnish us with that article & at a cheap rate; that is not the case; for two years back the colonies have been very badly supplied at high rates, and inferior qualities, especially herrings."[70]

From the outset of the fighting in the West Indies, the costs of all supplies soared to new heights. Herring rose from 45s per barrel in 1790 to above 65s in 1793; shad was only a couple of shillings less. Flour had been relatively so cheap that planters preferred to sell their locally grown plantains at 5s–6s 3d per hundred to raise cash to buy American flour for the slaves, as Barritt told his absentee owner: "I have judged it proper to purchase 50 barls of best 2nd flour quite fresh out of the vessels @ 37/6 per Barrel with which I mean to feed the negroes that are in want, twice a week to enable me to sell more plantains." Within two years, Barritt reported an increase of over 220 percent to approximately £6 per barrel.[71] Prices for supplies for the enslaved people remained very high. Corn increased from 7s 6d per bushel after the American War to 10s–10s 7½d per bushel by 1793. Attorneys could not purchase at these prices and they therefore reverted to sending requests home for well-dried flour, beans, or oatmeal if they were cheaper.[72]

British naval activity and impressments of United States citizens threatened further the trade relationship between the latter and the West Indies. The American government retaliated with an embargo, which seriously affected the small supplies reaching the islands. Corn prices increased phenomenally. Even after the embargo was removed and larger quantities of provisions were sent to the islands, lumber remained scarce and prices were high, ranging from £18 to £20 per thousand feet.[73] As the crisis in food supplies deepened, the attorneys turned to importing peas from Britain. However, very little corn could be sent, and the price soared to the extraordinary height of 24s 9d per bushel late in 1797.[74] Conditions continued along these lines for at least the first quarter of 1798.[75]

While all provisions and lumber were fetching record prices, rum fell quite markedly because there was no market either in England or in the United States. The combination affected seriously the contingencies of the estates. To meet the problem, planters called for the British merchants to institute the use of rum as cash to pay for supplies. But advanced British capitalism had long gone past the days when commodities were used as currency or barter was employed in exchange transactions.[76]

Even the traditional and historic system of drawing bills of exchange on absentees' accounts guaranteed solely by sugar shipments to England was now frowned upon and cast aside by both absentees and their merchant factors. The former were convinced that they were throwing good money after bad and that the sugar estates should be self-financing. The latter were not confident that the sugar market could maintain high prices and did not want to be caught extending to the plantations credit they could not reclaim. The situation puzzled resident West Indian planters and attorneys. One manager explained: "With respect to the Bill drawn on Messrs. Thompson & Litt I consider were the only persons to draw upon. Indeed I had no directions who to apply to but from former Bills which have been drawn on them. In the year 1797 Mr. Craggs drew on that House for £395 9s 10. In 1798 for £1061 11s. In 1801 £945. In 1802 I drew for £1120 & 451 & 909. And in 1803 £1029 & 126 and £157 10, which were all, paid. I cannot see their reason why they refused accepting the Bill."[77]

The new financial arrangements did not suit the West Indian plantations. They had no control over the British sugar market and could not determine the prices for their products. Now when sugar prices were no longer at the £30 to £35 level per hogshead that made production profitable, estate owners were calling for rigid economy in order "that sugar could have been imported without loss" into England. Areas where this could be achieved were singled out: "The purchase of furniture in Jamaica which is necessary might have been sent out at much less expence—The new Survey of estate which is merely a copy what . . . I could have sent you together with some other points however inconsiderable yet might have served to save me at least from loss."[78]

The restrictions on drawing bills and the limitations on United States trade affected supplies to the enslaved workers most. Often they were forced to consume "green food which brings on the fluxes that are much to be dreaded," wrote one attorney.[79] Many blacks died from these attacks and from diseases arising from malnutrition. On some estates, managers considered it too much a risk to purchase new Africans.[80]

The severe shortages during the French Wars, which were reminiscent of conditions during the American War, led planters once again to cultivate provisions locally. On some estates they planted corn and yams, but the worms that were ravaging the cane fields destroyed these crops.[81] In any case, it was difficult to operate a sugar plantation and at the same time maintain self-sufficiency. Food production called for the employment of large gangs of labourers who were also needed for cultivating the cane fields. One crop normally suffered, and this was the corn.

The corn crops, like the young canes, were also nearly always subjected to exceedingly long periods of severe dry weather which burnt them up.[82] Another problem was that such food crops as yams were usually planted on the best lands, injuring the soil for cane cultivation. Yet as long as the war and the restrictions on American trade kept provisions scarce and costly, these efforts had to be pursued along with the normal activities on the estates.[83] Maize, yams, and other provisions were also grown for the overseers and their assistants. The slaves were also allowed to plant crops on as much land as they wished for their own subsistence. Generally, however, they had only Sundays for this purpose and could not make much of the offer.[84]

It was certainly not possible to plant corn and cane with the same labour force. The number of field hands was small and declining steadily, and estates could not afford to replace them. Consequently, in spite of the restrictions on United States trade, the islands remained dependent on supplies from the main towns frequented by North American merchants. When the trade was allowed to operate freely, the islands had been well supplied with cheap and plentiful provisions, and sugar production could progress without impediment.[85] Now, because of the numerous restrictions on both the trade and agriculture, the planters looked for a more durable food crop. Some felt that the plantain was satisfactory, but the trees were affected by long dry spells. After years of the planters' search for a replacement for American supplies, Captain William Bligh imported the breadfruit tree into the West Indies in 1794. As a sign of its appreciation and its high expectations for the breadfruit, the Assembly of Jamaica voted him a thousand guineas.[86]

Throughout most of the eighteenth century, the Royal Navy had been able largely to control shipping in the Caribbean. The British government had established a convoy system that protected both the outward and homeward trade as the ships made their way among the foreign islands to their destinations in the British ports. As in the America War, during the French Wars privateering was a major setback to trade with Britain and greatly inhibited the interisland and United States trade. Early in 1793 there were complaints of the lack of protection from attacks on Jamaica and its trade. Simon Taylor wrote: "Our supplies from British America and the United States is cutt off by 2 French Frigates and some

Privateers who range along the whole coast of America without British Men of Warr there, by which means almost all the Vessells with Provisions, lumber etc. are take there."[87]

With the Caribbean infested with privateers and Britain unable to provide adequate protection, merchant vessels had to acquire their own guns.[88] The privateers were active right into the nineteenth century. The failure of the British convoy system to protect the West Indian trade can be gleaned from a report that reached Antigua around 8 June 1805 conveying news of the capture by a combined French and Spanish convoy of the Leeward Islands merchant fleet under convoy of the schooner *Netley*. This incident occurred at a time when the islands were least able to withstand such a blow to their commerce. Every ship carrying "the whole Pittance of the present miserable crop, the only means by which the new Taxes could be defray'd, or Public or Private Credit in any Degree restored; the only means by which the Bills ... drawn this Year by the Island were to be answered, and the only means by which stores and Provisions were to be purchas'd for the ensuing crop ... was taken," wrote Lord Lavington dejectedly.[89] The numerous captures of all types of merchant vessels regularly disrupted the supply lines to the islands and threatened their enslaved population.[90]

Wars always gave rise to increased insurance costs, and planters had no control over these. The activities of the privateers in the Caribbean and Atlantic, and the risks of merchant vessels being captured even when under convoy, sent the premiums on all goods to or from the West Indies rising after 1793 to 10 guineas percent (that is, 10 guineas per hundred pounds of insured value). Three years later, the price of insurance on Jamaican sugar doubled to 20 guineas percent, with a rebate of £10 percent if convoyed. The cost of insurance varied with the state of the war and the fate of Britain. Conditions of the policies also differed frequently. In 1797 premiums remained at 20 guineas percent, but only £8 percent was returned for convoy, plus a further £2 percent for sailing before a certain date.[91]

By the turn of the century and with the possibility of peace, insurance rates on sugar from Jamaica declined to 15 guineas percent, returning £5 percent for convoy. Yet the brokers still made profits in excess of 10 guineas percent. Any real fall in premiums came only with peace. In 1801 premiums fell to 12 guineas percent to return £4 percent for convoy, £1 for sailing on a particular date, and a further £1 percent for going to the outports. In the following year, there was a further decline to £8 if the ships sailed to London, with premiums as low as £4 and £3 percent for ships sailing to Liverpool.[92] When war resumed in 1803, insurance premiums on the homeward cargo increased immediately to 12 guineas percent to return £5 percent for convoy with a further £1 percent for sailing before a specified date.[93]

Premiums were set at fixed rates on sugar and rum. On sugar, the charges were £20 per hogshead and £15 per tierce for most of the 1790s. With the return of war in 1803, the rates on sugar increased to £30 per hogshead and £22 per tierce. There was also a marked difference on the charges for insurance on goods shipped to the West Indies from England. In 1801 premiums were quoted at 8 guineas percent. A decade later, in 1811, insurance premium on coal exported to the islands amounted to 6 guineas percent to return £3 percent for convoy.[94] While the insurance business was profitable, very often the underwriters were subjected to severe losses, especially when privateers were active in the shipping lanes and the protection of the Royal Navy was at a low ebb, as occurred regularly during the French Wars.

The rising cost of insurance was a severe burden to the planters whose gross earnings were declining, as table 10.5 shows. As in the American War, insurance became a major expenditure.

From the outbreak of the American Revolution, a combination of wartime conditions, British policy, and natural disasters shattered the West Indian sugar economy. This was mainly felt in the area of finance. Because of cash flow problems and the ruinous condition of many public buildings including several churches in Barbados, the House of Assembly passed an act to raise £50,000 by two public lotteries, with ten thousand pounds earmarked for rebuilding the Parish Church of St. Michael. The Council refused its support because the measure contravened the governor's ninth Royal Instruction, which required

Table 10.5. Insurance costs as percentage of gross earnings, 1792–98

Year	Gross earnings	Insurance cost	Percentage
1792	51,632	1,095	2.12
1793	42,604	3,175	7.45
1794	37,491	3,341	8.91
1795	51,588	4,995	9.69
1796	12,645	1,640	12.97
1797	42,360	5,069	11.97
1798	42,272	4,664	11.03

Source: "An Account of Sales of Sugar Shipped by the Honourable Simon Taylor . . . commencing with crop 1792 and ending with crop 1798," Journals of the Assembly of Jamaica, 10:429–35.

Crown permission for such legislation, and because no money was allocated to four other churches—Christ Church, St. George's, St. Thomas and St. Lucy's—that were in similar condition. In March 1784 the act was sent to the Privy Council, which approved the legislation, allowing the governor to give his assent.[95]

Lotteries certainly could not resolve the cash flow problems occurring throughout the West Indies. The trade between St. Domingue and Jamaica, valued around £150,000 annually, was one route through which Jamaica lost its cash. Previously, the French merchants took British manufactured goods, but with the rebellion raging, they demanded cash. British restrictions on the West Indian trade with the United States influenced the American merchants to refuse to accept rum for their supplies of lumber and provisions. In the majority of cases, West Indian traders had to make cash payments.[96] This soon drained the islands of their money supply.

The British Treasury sent out £60,000 sterling in specie to Jamaica to relieve the cash flow problem and to act as security against any further scarcity of money. The Assembly promised to reimburse the home government.[97] But the money was only a drop in the bucket. Most of it immediately found its way back to England and very little remained on the island for any length of time. During periods of normal trading, large sums of money flowed into the British colonies from the free port trade with the Spanish colonies and also from their illegal trade in new Africans and manufactured goods with the foreign islands. However, captives who were formerly purchased at Jamaica were now bought in Hispaniola where prices were very much lower. Added to this, the Spanish *guardacostas* were extraordinarily vigilant in their efforts to prevent the trade in "Spanish dollars" with Jamaica.[98]

The Anglo-Spanish War reduced the flow of specie into Jamaica, in particular. This was worsened by the large outflow of cash in the trade with Santo Domingo and St. Domingue.[99] From as early as 1794, Jamaica merchants had established meaningful trade links with St. Domingue, whose trade was divided up by the merchants of several European colonial powers and the United States. The latter controlled the northern and western ports; the Danes from St. Thomas and the Jamaicans established control over the south side, while other West Indian merchants played minor roles.[100] The trade was welcomed by Jamaican officials as being of a "prodigious quantity" and sure to "add considerably to the Revenue" of Britain.[101] It continued throughout the period and probably beyond. The figures available for the period February to August 1801 put the imports into Jamaica at 2,443,095 pounds of coffee, 789,877 of cotton, 209,478 of sugar, and 93,070 of cocoa, with a total value of some £165,541 sterling.[102]

The sizeable loss of specie in the trade was seriously affecting Britain's war effort in the West Indies. The earlier shortage of specie also had grave domestic consequences. It restricted the Assembly's payment and subsistence of the army, and it restricted its ability to meet the normal contingent expenses of government, as it could collect few taxes from an impoverished planter class. Summing up the impact of the specie crisis on the island, the Committee of Correspondence wrote: "Its fatal effects on the Commercial operations of this colony are already felt in the highest degree—there is no market whatever for the manufactures of Great Britain, with which the stores in the different trading ports are filled, nor for the produce of this Island, which lie on the wharves without demand. Bills of Exchange, which formerly bore a premium of 10 percent, are now at a discount of 5 percent."[103]

In an effort to resolve the shortage of specie and fund the Jamaica government, a local bond issue of £80,000 currency was offered to the public, but there was no response, primarily because of the very shortage of specie that prompted it. Another attempt to solve the crisis, this time by drawing bills of exchange on the British Treasury by depositing certificates to the sum of £80,000 bearing 10 percent interest annually, met with the same fate: there was "little or no effect owing to the want of specie."[104] The British government itself was faced with cash flow problems. It therefore directed the lieutenant governor of Jamaica, the Earl of Balcarres, to resume the free port trade with the Spanish merchants.[105] The severe shortage of specie throughout the West Indies worsened towards the end of the eighteenth century and deepened as the war continued into the nineteenth century. It led Lord Seaforth, governor of Barbados, to make drastic and unconventional recommendations. He saw "no remedy for this within colonial reach, nothing I am convinced can remedy the evil, but either checking the exuberance of the Neutral Flags that swarm like bees all around us, and monopolize everything, or to allow those Neutrals to carry off a part of our produce for cash, the latter remedy in my humble opinion would be a dire remedy and as loud as the disease as it would lead to increased depositions that are but too prevalent already, yet I see no other resource, and if the evil increases as it has done within these last two years the scarcity will be very serious."[106]

In the Leeward Islands, the specie crisis had reached epic proportions. The authorities applied to the Secretary of State for help from Jamaica, since they believed that there was an improvement in that island resulting from the resumption of the free port trade. But this was a case of the poor begging from the poor. The merchant class rejected the appeal as being "entirely impossible" because Jamaica's supply of silver money was "scarcely equal" to the demands of the North American trade.[107]

This refusal motivated Lord Lavington to write one of the most penetrating and painful reports on the state of any colonial government in the West Indies. For several years Lavington had stuck doggedly to British trade policy in the face of petitions and appeals from the merchants and planters to open the Leeward Islands ports to United States ships and supplies. Only about three months earlier he had turned down another such request. Unable to withstand any longer the degradation of his government partly because of the loss of the trade, and more so because he believed that British policy was unsound, at the end of July 1805 he wrote on the condition of the Leeward Islands because "events of such absolute Importance and of such imperious and immediate necessity" threatened further disaster. The cash flow crisis was not confined solely to the public credit, it was of a more diverse nature, and the governments and their people faced bankruptcy. He emphasised: "There has been no year of Abundance since . . . 1799; and then the sudden fatal unprecedented Fall of the Price of the Produce render'd it difficult . . . for many Proprietors to pay the ordinary Expences of their Estates. Half of the canes intended for the Crop of 1806 have perish'd; the other Half will follow their Example, unless retriev'd by most speedy and Seasonable weather and the whole fall of the country wears an adjust and most melancholy appearance."[108]

Added to the shortness of the crops, the steep decline in prices, and the near bankruptcy of both the planters and the local treasuries, the continuation of war accompanied by the threat of capture had forced the plantations to employ their entire resources in the service of the government in order to preserve British rule. The repeated summoning of the militia had led to the total suspension of agriculture and sugar manufacture. The several colonies had to meet the costs of subsistence of their militias and other contingent expenses associated with direct warfare in the region. These exercises had virtually drained every treasury and had plunged the Leeward Islands into debt in excess of £20,000.[109] Jamaica faced a similar problem, with its public debt from Balcarres's Maroon War alone exceeding £231,000 currency.[110] Yet in spite of debt, crop losses, reduced prices, and restriction of the United States trade, the colonial governments were repeatedly called upon to expend large sums of money on the defence of the islands.

Lord Lavington, recognizing the impossibility of the Leeward Islands solving their financial woes internally, supported a call from the Council and Assembly of Antigua to the British government for assistance. He used the precedent of the government of Mathew Burt in 1779 when the Leeward Islands were also near bankruptcy to appeal for Treasury permission to draw bills of exchange to the sum of £10,000 in order to save his government from the "Brink of Ruin." Most of the money would help to repair the islands' credit. As in 1779, the Leeward Islands governments were rescued from the edge of the precipice of financial collapse.[111]

In the face of economic disasters, the West Indian planters always sought ways to wait out the difficult times. One such measure, which Barbados and the Leeward Islands imposed upon themselves and which proved a millstone around their necks, was the 4½ percent duty adopted in the 1660s when their economy was flourishing. This tax on the exports of participating islands was intended to help defray the administrative costs of government. Jamaica rejected it, preferring to impose a system of quitrents on land. When the Ceded Islands were faced with similar demands for the adoption of the 4½ percent duty, they refused. This led to the lawsuit Campbell vs. Hall, in which Lord Mansfield handed down his historic ruling that the Crown could not tax the colonies that had their own legislatures. This inspired the American rebels to adopt the slogan "No taxation without representation." The 4½ percent duty continued to be extracted from the imports of Barbados and the Leeward Islands throughout the eighteenth century with virtually no complaints until the Barbados legislature sought to repeal the measure during the American War when its economy was severely depressed. Until the American rebellion, conditions were good and planters could pay their way. The 4½ percent duty became burdensome after the war, and the planter assemblies tried to repeal the legislation. It became a bone of contention until it was repealed in the 1850s.

The bulk of the revenue from the tax went to pay "charges of collection and other allowances connected with colonial affairs" but not all related to the interests of the islands concerned. However, as decline gripped the islands' economies, appeals were repeatedly made for the abolition of the duty. Complaints included claims that the tax was equal to a 10 percent charge upon their capital. One report stated that it was mainly responsible for distressing the economy of "every Island where it" existed and it was blamed for Barbados's marked decline.[112]

As the economy of the Leeward Islands declined even further, the General

Council and Assembly in 1798 passed legislation entitled "An Act to Restrict the Collection of the Four and a half percent Duty granted to His Majesty on the Exportation of the Produce of the Leeward Charibbee Islands." Robert Thomson, commander-in-chief, local planter, and manager, refused his assent, although he favoured the passage of the act, because the 20th Royal Instruction on adopting such legislation restricted him. In supporting the bill, however, he recommended a general tax on all West Indian produce as being less burdensome and less likely to damage the economy of any one group of colonies.[113]

There was absolutely no way the burden of the 4½ percent duty would have been shared by all the West Indian colonies. It was also the wrong time from a financial standpoint to expect the British Government to surrender the proceeds of the tax; it too was strapped and wanted every penny it could lay its hands on, however limited the net deposit to the Treasury. Consequently, the Board of Trade disallowed the act.[114]

Coming so soon after the American War of Independence, the French Wars deepened the economic problems of the planter class, which was still clinging to the philosophy of the compact between the sugar colonies and the mother country. But British policymakers had come to understand two important features of economic growth. First, to control the economy of an area, there was no need for colonies. This was clearly demonstrated in Britain's relationship with the United States and Brazil. While the policy of mercantilism was still to be enforced on colonial trade, the British market and British merchants were to operate on free trade principles. Second, Britain had become a European power after the American War. Her economic interest lay more in exploiting European and other world markets through laissez-faire capitalism and less in bilateral trade.

The struggles of the planters to survive clearly indicate that, without favourable legislation from Britain, very few individuals could make profits in the West Indian plantation system. By the 1790s it was also clear that sugar plantations based on slavery could not be a long-term profitable capitalist activity. From this research, it is quite evident that the sugar plantation had reached a desperate level of distress, which was then increasing with alarming rapidity.[115] The struggle for survival began with the American Revolution and continued through the French Wars. And just when the planters began to see a light at the end of the tunnel, the British Parliament again subjected them to a host of restrictions that aborted their hopes and plans.[116]

❧ 11 ❧

Profitability and Decline

Issues and Concepts—An Epilogue

History is an analysis of events and issues that have occurred over time. It certainly cannot simply be a detailed regurgitation of the events of particular periods in the past. Probably the most satisfying achievement is when, having amassed a wealth of information and data, the researcher is enabled to answer the many questions that arise, or to substantiate a thesis on some aspect of human activity—social, economic, political. *The Sugar Industry and the Abolition of the British Slave Trade, 1775–1810* has sought to illustrate the state of the British sugar industry during a critical period in its development, a period in which the West Indian economy declined.

In so doing, the work has illustrated and analysed the concepts of decline through the detailed assessment of several themes and statistical data. It is now left to summarise the findings of the study and to reach a decision on whether or not the economy of the British West Indies had declined to the point where it could be safely said that slavery had become unprofitable.

It is certainly clear that the economy of the sugar islands was operating smoothly in the years prior to the outbreak of the American War. Although the islands had grown dependent on the American colonies because of the nature of West Indian production, its labour system, and the diverse market needs, this artificial economy moved along without any significant fear that the logistics of its very existence would soon be called into question.

The American War shattered this complacency and threatened the existence of the sugar colonies. The islands struggled through difficult years when the slave trade virtually came to a standstill. The Prohibitory Act restricted commercial relations between the mainland continental colonies and the sugar islands. The system of slavery was threatened by the shortage of supplies of food and lumber; by high mortality rates caused by excessive labour, malnutrition, and disease; by repeated natural disasters which took a heavy toll on the already weakened and depleted slave population. Alternative sources of supply brought only limited relief. Increased planting of provisions and cutting of lumber only shifted the focus of West Indian agriculture without achieving its goals. These changes led to the expansion of and reliance on hired labour, increasing the costs to the estates and forming another factor in the long list of evidence for decline. Prime lands, previously devoted to cane, were planted during the war and even afterwards in yams and provisions. This cutback on sugar production weakened the profitability of the estates and impoverished the soil. The ultimate result was increased indebtedness of the planters. This worsened with each passing decade and shortly before the abolition of the slave trade many West Indian plantations were weighed down by heavy debts.

The restrictions on United States trade virtually closed the most important market for West Indian secondary products and forced the islands to rely on Britain, Ireland, and Canada. These countries consumed only a minimal part of West Indian rum. After the 1780s this product could hardly be sold locally. Most of it had in the end to be bartered with the Americans, on their terms, or sent to England to be sold by factors to enable attorneys to draw bills of exchange to pay the contingencies of estates—something that had never occurred in the earlier period. Peace in 1783 did not initiate the significant changes required to forestall the decline the war had initiated. The British market was overstocked and could not respond to peacetime conditions, and foreign buyers stayed away because money was short and sugar from St. Domingue was cheaper. Poor-quality sugar, a feature of West Indian production, could not be sold at a profit. The estates were further distressed by the wholesale attack on the canes by disease and pests. With the quality of sugar thus low, West Indian securities could not meet the annual interest, much less help in reducing planter debt.[1]

Cane lands that earlier in the eighteenth century had been revered as the best in the world and brought a premium from investors were now viewed as "incumbrances" which could not be operated "to any advantage" given the increased taxes, high duties, and restricted West Indian trade. The introduction of the new income tax in 1798 further reduced returns to estate owners, even when crops were "pretty good." West Indian lands were being sold to pay contingency charges, and the small profits or annuities paid to the children of estate owners were not reinvested in the islands but were used to buy properties in England.[2] Absentees gave their managers power of attorney to sell portions of their land. The money was put in current accounts to bolster the scant proceeds of rum production and pay the contingencies of the estates.

A matter of grave concern was the decline of the slave population. One contemporary commentator wrote that the number of enslaved workers in Barbados declined by 1¼ percent annually within a forty-year period after the middle of the eighteenth century. Since the American War, figures for Barbados showed that the rate of decline in the five years 1778–80 averaged approximately 2¼ percent per annum.[3] The diminution of the enslaved population on the other islands was about the same. In Jamaica, Long's estimate placed the decline of this group at a fortieth part, or 2½ percent annually. Antigua's enslaved population fell off by an estimated 1½ to 2 percent per year, which was almost on par with Barbados and may be representative of the diminution of the enslaved population on the Leeward Islands. The highest rate of decline, amounting to 3 percent, occurred in Dominica and could probably be taken as representing the rate at which the enslaved people declined in the Windward Islands.[4]

It was quite evident that a steady supply of new blood was needed to maintain an adequate labour force. With the returns showing that in nearly all the colonies there was no natural increase, many commentators shared the view that the ground on which the planter stood was "now fast sinking under his feet,"[5] and that slavery was the most costly labour system in the world. An economic activity that consumed its labour force at the rate the sugar industry was doing was in the long term unprofitable, and the advancement of capital modes of production could not be founded on such investment. The ruin of the planter class was the inevitable result.[6]

Several estimates were made at the end of the eighteenth century showing the high cost of slave labour and illustrating the improbability of retrieving investments in this activity. The cost of maintaining an enslaved person was placed at £8 (Edward Long—always conservative—reduced it to £5). The cost rose to £9–10 when insurance of 5 percent and deaths from seasoning are included in the evaluation. After paying interest on the capital invested in enslaved labour, land, and animal stock employed in the sugar industry, the lowest estimate of the cost of slave labour exceeded the production of the slaves employed on sugar plantations at the end of the eighteenth century. "In short, a working slave and the property he occupies," wrote one analyst "cannot be less than £200 sterling."[7] Taking into account all the calculations, the total annual charge on an enslaved person's labour amounted to £17, apart from the current expenses. This was significantly in excess of what the planters thought that their slaves should produce annually. Hired slave labour increased the overall costs of the estates. The cost of hiring field hands was approximately £12 per annum, with employers paying insurance and maintenance.[8]

On most plantations the decline in the enslaved population was not arrested by the purchase of new Africans because prices were too high. Only the old established West Indian planters remained committed to buying them. While those living on and managing their estates invested, however unprofitably, what little money they could find on improving their human stock, absentee planters chose to neglect this investment. They preferred to spend the money "on themselves at a distance from their plantations in Europe." The West Indian economy was so precariously based that "every lot of new slaves helped to precipitate the planter sooner into ruin." By the 1780s and 1790s, the advantages the British had in the slave trade and slavery were passing to the Americans, French, and Spaniards. The debt situation in the colonies deepened to such an extent that "the creditors could get no fool to take" properties off their hands, so West Indian estates continued to be owned nominally by debt-ridden planters.[9]

To meet these crises, as we have seen, planters adopted changes in the management of their estates. First they concentrated on limiting expenses.[10] One absentee, after costing the goods sent out to the West Indies in 1787, observed that they exceeded the revenue from the estates by £500 over and above the value of the rum. He took solace in the expectation of better times.[11] To revive the profitability of their estates, many absentee planters restricted the purchase of new Africans, since the capital for such investment could not now be procured from West Indian securities. There was certainly no desire whatsoever among absentees in Britain to send out money to invest in an economy where profits were not guaranteed, when that capital or half of it could earn much greater profits from exchequer bills in England.[12]

The "greatest economy & management" remained the most effective way for owners to achieve reduced cost.[13] One significant area of change was planter amelioration of the living conditions of the slaves. In the view of one manager, the slave population on his estate was "wearing out for want of a regular supply of new negroes as none has been purchased for some years."[14] This was a general complaint as owners insisted on every effort to achieve natural increase by a change in the stocking of the plantations and care of the enslaved population.

A preference now emerged for purchasing females with the express aim of breeding them. Women were no longer required to perform strenuous jobs. They were removed from activities such as lifting trash baskets; from feeding mills or removing the trash and in some cases they were put into separate gangs from the men and were not allowed to do heavy digging with the hoe. The merciless beating of women, even when they were pregnant, was prohibited in all reported cases, and the guilty overseers were dismissed.

In a few instances, absentees insisted on a system of rewards for all the people directly connected with the birth of children on the plantations, including the overseers, managers, and especially the midwives whose responsibility it was to deliver the babies—though, interestingly, no rewards were ever made available to the "fathers" of these children. The attitude of planters and managers reveals an insensitivity to black womanhood. No manager or planter seems to have respected the right of women, as individuals and human beings, to refuse to become pregnant, though Barham did recognize this as an issue among black women. Try as they might, no overseer, no planter could have inspired young black women on estates to produce and rear children to whom they had no claim.

Under amelioration, some estates prepared all meals for the young children, who were fed under the watchful eyes of the overseers. Superannuated slaves were selected for this job. In Barbados, reports indicate that housing was improved on a limited number of estates and there were healthy children playing in the yards. In some cases, slave huts were removed from unhealthy surroundings and the slaves resettled in more suitable areas on the estates. Even the diet was improved in terms of quantity, though there is no evidence of significant changes in the quality.

To achieve their goals, planters began hiring labour for the most laborious tasks on estates, in spite of their sensitivity to the increased costs. Amelioration was indeed a costly exercise. Its implementation called for a drastic reduction of labour from at least the enslaved women, which meant increasing jobbing, raising the contingencies, and lessening profits.[15]

While the 1790s and the early 1800s up to the end of the slave trade are important in establishing a connection between decline and abolition, the last years of the 1780s are very informative on the attitude of Parliament and the Colonial Office towards the slave trade and slavery. The Colonial Secretary sent out between 1787 and 1788 the most searching inquiries, eliciting information on all aspects of slavery from the individual governments and interested persons. This information, and evidence given before a Parliamentary Committee in 1790, clearly hardened the feeling of some members against slavery. It is thenceforth quite noticeable that influential members of the government, while not prepared in the first instance to adopt legislation to abolish the slave trade, were convinced that "a total abolition of that traffic would not be a detriment to European settlement in the West India Islands, as the propagation of the African (if well treated) might answer every purpose."[16]

Reducing slavery meant reducing North American influence on the islands. Throughout the first three-quarters of the eighteenth century, there developed in the eyes of British policymakers too great a dependence by the British West Indies on the commerce of the American Colonies for the proper operation of the slave system. This dependence led to a fear that the sugar islands would follow them in revolution. Consequently, British policymakers were adamant that no dependence be developed on the United States: "it highly becomes us to adopt such measures as may lessen if not destroy a dependence which must be prejudicial to this Country whether we reduce America to Subjection again or not." It was certainly against the interests of Britain to allow West Indian commercial relations with the United States to return to their former status because it would be "establishing and perhaps increasing that dependance and connection which is our Policy to break as much as possible."[17] Thus the Colonial Office insisted on forcing the islands to rely on Canadian supplies, though all the evidence indicated that Canada could not supply the sugar islands sufficiently with lumber and foodstuffs, except for fish.[18]

With all these problems, West Indian property kept declining after the American War of Independence. Some hope appeared with the destruction of St. Domingue's sugar industry in 1791, but at the same time that the planters saw this possibility of change, they had to contend with the negative fallout of the Parliamentary investigation into the slave trade and slavery and the fears caused by the upheavals in St. Domingue. The British government clearly demonstrated its readiness to legislate the reduction of West Indian commodity prices. It was not concerned about the interests of the sugar producers. British consumers came first, and the market was to operate in their favour. West Indian monopoly was handcuffed.

Although it was good domestic politics for the British Government to reduce the drawback and bounty, for the West Indian planters it was bad business. To them, the government was insensitive, and was prepared to use them as scapegoats for the high price of sugar. The planters made no gains, since sugar went up no more than food supplies and lumber, and freight rates on imports from London and Ireland doubled.[19] It was one thing for the government to limit West Indian participation in the United States market; it was certainly another to limit the price of West Indian sugar in the home market.

Thus the 1790s, which began fairly well for the sugar planters, deepened the decline of the economy. The French Wars exacerbated the dearth of North American lumber and provisions, and the decade opened up a more important debate over the possible abolition of the slave trade.

Once more the planters attempted to find a way out. They adopted a new type of cane which, when planted on the same acreage as the traditional Creole cane, produced about 30 percent more sugar. It was also better able to withstand attacks by the borer and blasts. However, the Otaheite cane had the opposite effect to that desired. The quality of its sugar was inferior, bringing poor prices in Britain. And the increased production led to overstocking of the British market, which in turn was blamed for the abolition of the slave trade.

In their search for ways to survive, planters adopted whatever technology emerged. Both the steam engine and the plough were brought into operation to reduce labour while increasing production. Although the plough was used in Jamaica just after the middle of the eighteenth century, it was not generally adopted as a labour-saving device until shortly before the abolition of the slave trade. The steam engine, where planters and managers introduced it, was successful in production—and, like the Otaheite cane, led to overproduction and low sugar prices.

The plantation papers document the decline of the British West Indian economy in the period before the abolition of the slave trade. The sugar industry was reliant on the smooth functioning of numerous activities in order to achieve profits. This study has highlighted and analysed several themes that had an impact on it. It remains now to determine whether or not the economy of the West Indies was in irreversible decline. Almost one hundred years earlier, in 1695, there were complaints about the decline of the Barbados economy. One commentator wrote: "It must therefore be owned that we ought to exert ourselves to the utmost for their preservation, and to the restoring them to their former flourishing State; for otherwise, if they continue thus, bleeding in their trade, it will issue in Death with speedy redress, by producing an utter Cessation in Trade."[20]

Conditions seemed not to have changed. Decline was still a major complaint of the island governments and planters, and it took on greater force towards the end of the eighteenth century. In 1787 Penrhyn cited the large sum he had lost that year, saying he expected the trend to continue. Another observer summed up the state of the sugar industry by pointing out that for more than five years, the net proceeds to the planters amounted to a sum equal to the duty. Hence, planters were investing solely to pay British duty charges.[21] But if this was true for sugar production, the penns were not expected to lose money. It certainly came as a surprise to Joseph Foster Barham when he discovered that he had lost more than £500 in the penn operation, for the profits of penns were about the only gains that the planters made at the end of the eighteenth century.[22]

More often than not, the profits of the estates were either trifling or nonexistent. In 1802 Barham stressed that he had been losing money for four consecutive years, and it was "highly imprudent" to invest any further money since it was "likely to make no return." One year later, Barham made the further observation that it was great "impropriety" to extend business ventures in the West Indies. His solution was to reduce the "losses" resulting from the low price of sugar.[23] Declining sugar prices and lower incomes plagued the planters in another way. They had "little credit in England." Merchants were refusing to take West Indian rum and sugar for consignments from England, as was previously the case.[24] Credit was the lifeline of the West Indian economy. Its unavailability was a death knell.

It was abundantly clear that the West Indian economy had fallen off. Assessing the situation, one factor pointed out that estates 105 years after their establishment were losing returns on their capital investment.[25] As early as 1787, one writer on slavery contended that in thirty-six years the cost of producing a hundredweight of sugar had increased by 75 percent, while the price of slaves had risen by 140 percent. On the other hand, the price of sugar, exclusive of duty, fell by 6.5 percent.[26] Writing in 1823, Barham observed that returns from West Indian properties were substantial up to the third quarter of the eighteenth century. They then fluctuated until about 1789. Following the revolution in St. Domingue they increased significantly, but the adoption of a policy reducing the drawback and bounty charged European consumers with a British duty and thus destroyed the competitiveness of British sugar.[27]

British policy, in attempting to eradicate the dependence of the islands on the United States and in curtailing the drawback and bounty, stimulated American reexports of West Indian, Brazilian, and Cuban sugar. These sugars undersold British West Indian and forced the planters to rely solely on the British market. Calculations show that fresh captive Africans amounted to £50–200 sterling each. Then there was an annual maintenance charge of feeding and clothing the workers. Enslaved labour was short-lived and could be replaced only at ever increasing cost. Consequently, free labour now had the competitive edge and provided greater benefits to the capitalists.[28] Calculations show that the returns on sugar were less than the cost of producing and marketing it. In Jamaica, one estimate had the planters losing as much as £5 5s on every hogshead of sugar. In Barbados, the planters made nothing on their investments, while in Dominica there was an estimated 1 percent profit. The consensus was that the importation of new Africans to maintain the sugar industry was an unprofitable business and served only to add to existing debts. Several plans were emerging to counter the use of enslaved people. One called for the introduction of Chinese labour, which would be "free, industrious," and would introduce to West Indian estates "ingenuity and voluntary exertion."

It is evident from the study that the economy of the British West Indies was in decline after 1783. The planters who remained solvent had very little room in which to manoeuvre. New investments in the West Indian plantation system were indeed risky ventures. The system itself was in need of detailed restructuring. Self-sufficiency and the plantation system were incongruous within the limitations of the economy of the British Caribbean islands, where good sugar land was at a premium and where a peasant class had not yet developed sufficiently. The markets for foodstuffs were present, but the shortage of good arable land was restrictive. The growth of the British Caribbean plantation system was best ensured by its total commitment to external markets. This guaranteed the enslaved workers' dependence on the plantation owner, who could impose greater control on his labour force if it was foreign fed than if it grew its own food.[29] As the cost of producing sugar remained very high and prices fell, leading to markedly reduced profits, the economic situation looked bleak at best. Table 11.1 shows the production costs and the returns on a hundredweight of sugar landed in Britain between 1781 and 1805 just before the abolition of the slave trade.

As this study has demonstrated in detail, the American War and then British policy greatly distressed the planters. There were periods of near famine on many of the islands; thousands of enslaved workers died as a result of malnutrition. By the end of the 1780s the value of many West Indian plantations had declined significantly.

The establishment of the plantation system had several weaknesses, which

Table 11.1. Sugar production costs and proceeds, 1781–1805

	1781	1785	1795	1805
British supplies	8s	7s	20s 10d	20s 10d
Island expences (planting/transport)[a]	14s	14s	19s 6d	19s 6d
Duty	11s 8d	12s 3d	15s	27s
Freight	8s	5s 6d	7s 6d	9s 1d
Insurance[b]	10s	9s 8d	2s	2s
Port charges	8d	10d	1s 2d	10d
Commission[c]	1s 3d	1s 10d	2s 4d	2s 10d
Wastage[a]	3d	3d	3d	3d
Total cost[d]	45s 10d	44s 4d	47s 9d	61s 6d
Price of sugar, highest	72s	42s	75s	75s
Price of sugar, lowest	55s	26s	42s	32s
Gross proceeds, highest	+26s 2d	-2s 4d	+27s 3d	+13s 6d
Gross proceeds, lowest	+9s 2d	-18s 4d	-5s 9d	-29s 6d

Sources: "Charges on 1 cwt. Sugar," [1781], BL, Add. MSS 12,412, n.fol.; Deerr, *The History of Sugar*; W. Young, *Common- Place Book,* 47.

Note: Figures, in sterling, are for one hundredweight of sugar.

a. Approximately.

b. A hogshead of sugar was valued at £25 in 1781, and insurance was as high as 25 percent. In 1795 and 1805 a rate of 5 percent was charged.

c. Commission was 2½ percent in 1781 and 1785, and 3 percent in 1795 and 1805.

d. The cost of British supplies is not counted in the "total cost"—nor is the cost of slaves or interest on capital.

had to be overcome in the period after 1776 if the planters were to survive the effects of the American War, postwar British policy, and the French Wars. They never succeeded in doing this; the economy did not adjust to the new commercial system, and its decline was set in motion. From the commencement of the American Revolution, the foreign islands became important centres of trade for their British counterparts. This situation continued during the 1780s right down to the French and Napoleonic Wars. It is therefore not surprising that these wars, which ended all major fighting in the Caribbean theatre, had the appearance of being for commercial control of the region.

Several answers emerge from this monograph. The most obvious is: Were the West Indian islands in a serious state of decline? The work leaves absolutely no doubt that the West Indian economy was on the downturn after 1776. All the statistical information and graphic illustrations show quite clearly that the economy did not rebound after the American War, as was normally the case after eighteenth-century wars in the Caribbean. Added to this situation, the agitation for the investigation of the slave trade and slavery began in Parliament at the end of the 1780s, and hearings by a Parliamentary Committee revealed hideous atrocities. The St. Domingue slave revolt and the attempts in Parliament to legislate the end of the slave trade spelled disaster for the plantation system. A large "docile" and unskilled labour force was indeed the major single component of sugar production. These circumstances combined to curtail major capital investments in the British Caribbean sugar business at the end of the eighteenth century.

Diversification of the British West Indian sugar economy was not a serious alternative. Seventeenth-century West Indian agriculture had demonstrated that, while the islands could produce cotton and tobacco and coffee, sugar brought them wealth and fame. Diversification would mean a return to the problems of the preplantation West Indian economy. Furthermore, over 90 percent of capital investment in the West Indies was in sugar-related businesses. This money could not have been reinvested successfully in other crops. Richard Pares in assessing this call for diversification has written that it was extremely difficult to convert a sugar plantation, which was a "factory in a field," into another form of agriculture. Besides, those islands that contained the necessary land resources were already producing large quantities of tropical staples in addition to sugar. Most of the new colonies, and Jamaica and Barbados, produced significant quantities of cotton. Coffee and cocoa were grown on the Ceded Islands and in Jamaica. The latter developed into a major coffee exporter at the close of the eighteenth century. Other minor staples were also exported from the islands. All in all, the planters attempted to make the best use of the available resources in spite of the changing nature of the Atlantic economy.

Increased shipments of sugar to Britain caused a marked decline in prices in the 1790s and the 1800s. Sugar prices stood as low as £16–23 per hogshead in 1806, about 75 percent less than the planters received between 1793 and 1795. The study has shown clearly that both production and profit levels of sugar estates worsened at the end of the eighteenth century. A committee of the House of Commons, appointed about 1803 to investigate the condition of the British West Indies, placed the blame on the burdensome charges, inconveniences, risks, and heavy expenses of the sugar planters.

During the height of the American trade, West Indian estates made an estimated annual profit of as much as 12 percent. Profits declined to 6 percent in 1801 to 1804. They fell further to 3 percent in 1805 and to virtually nothing in 1807. Sir William Young, governor of Tobago and himself a planter, best expressed the fate of the British Caribbean planters: "I must consider the decline from the immediate and progressive distress of the planter, continuing to work for returns inadequate to his labour. He will struggle for a while to procure the means of subsistence, and of satisfaction to his creditors and consignees. He will be supported for a time by the latter, through liberality or from interest—shooting forth another arrow to follow and recover the arrow lost, till the quiver is exhausted, or the archer prudently desists from further attempt."[30]

Young's words perfectly sum up the fate of the West Indian planters and their struggles to retain their estates at the level of a previous time of fame and glory. They were looking backwards while British capitalism was marching boldly forwards. Undoubtedly, slavery and the slave trade had contributed to British economic growth and industrialisation. Now they were incapable of evolving to meet the dynamism of finance capitalism. It is evident that very little, if any, reinvestment occurred on the islands throughout the glory days of sugar. British policy forced the colonies to continue in an agricultural mode.

There were unmistakable signs of a faltering system. Planter flight or absenteeism was at a high level, especially at the end of the eighteenth century. Many islands had deficiency laws forcing absentees to have adequate white supervisory personnel in relation to the number of enslaved persons. Failing this, they were fined. But these laws did not arrest white depopulation. Investments were being made in other locations, not always outside sugar, and in other commodities. When the planters struggled to reduce sugar imports into England as a way of raising prices, they found that such days were long gone. West Indian influence ended with the debate over British acquisition of Guadeloupe or Canada. The sugar planters won that round, but they lost the rest. As the work clearly illustrates, Britain adopted a policy of legislating for the islands.

The movement for the abolition of the slave trade rose on the back and contentions of Adam Smith's *Wealth of Nations*. The period of the growth of economies through trade and commerce aimed at a monopolistic market ended with the fall of the First British Empire. The Second, concerned chiefly with the innovation of technology and the mass production of goods, called for entrepreneurial energies in home-based industries funded and guaranteed by a rising set of financial institutions. The islands had become "nuisances" and "millstones." Money invested in bonds and industry in England was bearing higher profits than capital investments in the West Indian sugar industry, leading to greater "national prosperity—a greater public revenue, more shipping, more seamen, more wealth." Everything with which the islands were associated in the early eighteenth century was now credited to England.[31] The sugar colonies were too small to rationalize their industry to take advantage of the new economic wave. They were now irrelevant to the new economic life that Williams refers to as "mature capitalism."[32]

Although sugar was still important and was produced in larger quantities, the British islands had begun losing their place to such giants as Cuba, Brazil, and even the United States. Beet sugar was also discovered; it would eventually replace cane sugar in the British market. The fortune of the sugar islands had come full circle during the long eighteenth century. It began with the islands as the stalwarts of the British economy and ended with them clinging tenaciously to British coattails, afraid to "let go" lest they sink to the depths of the Caribbean Sea and the Atlantic Ocean which had become the graveyards for hundreds of thousands, probably millions, of Africans on their hapless journey to the islands to produce sugar. This sweetener laid the foundations of a bitter experience for African people turned into "slaves." In the end, however, African labourers, the source of West Indian contribution to British, European, and American wealth, had lived to see the impoverishment of the planters who had exploited them. These once great islands whose beauty had captivated Christopher Columbus had become, in the eyes of British policymakers and political commentators, "millstones" around the neck of Britain. The archer's quiver was now empty.

Abbreviations

Adm.	Admiralty Papers (in PRO)
BL	British Library, London
Bodl.	Bodleian Library, Oxford
BRL	Bristol Reference Library
BRO	Bristol Record Office
BT	Board of Trade Papers (in PRO)
CH	Custom House Accounts (in PRO)
CO	Colonial Office Papers (in PRO)
HMSO	His Majesty's Stationery Office
ICS	Institute of Commonwealth Studies, University of London
IUP	Irish University Press
JAA	Journal of the Assembly of Antigua (in CO)
JAB	Journal of the Assembly of Barbados (in CO)
JAJ	Journal of the Assembly of Jamaica (in CO)
JRO	Jamaica Record Office
L.Bk.	Letter Book
LMA	London Metropolitan Archives
NAS	National Archives of Scotland
NLS	National Library of Scotland
NLW	National Library of Wales
PRO	Public Record Office, Kew, London
RHL	Rhodes House Library, Oxford
SomRO	Somerset Record Office
SurRO	Surrey Record Office
T	Treasury Papers (in PRO)
UBL	University of Bristol Library
UWB	University of Wales, Bangor

Notes

Introduction: Methodology and Historical Assessment of the Literature

1. Carrington, "Economic and Political Development"; Carrington, *British West Indies.*

2. Williams, *Capitalism and Slavery,* 120.

3. Pringle, *Fall,* 13.

4. Makinson, *Barbados*; Sheridan, "Crisis of Slave Subsistence"; Solow, "Capitalism and Slavery"; Darity, "Williams Abolition Thesis."

5. D. B. Davis, "Reflections," 806 ff.; *Problem of Slavery,* 62.

6. Pringle, *Fall,* intro., 16.

7. Davis, *Problem of Slavery,* 61.

8. Eltis, *Economic Growth.*

9. Minchinton, "Williams and Drescher," 91.

10. Ward, "Profitability."

11. Richardson, "Slave Trade," 742.

Chapter 1. Sugar Production and British Caribbean Dependence on External Markets, 1769–1776

1. Unless otherwise noted, in this section (up to note 10), figures on imports to Britain from her Caribbean island colonies are drawn from the Public Record Office, Custom House papers, class 3; volumes are numbered by year, so records for 1774 are found in PRO, CH 3/74.

2. Long, *History of Jamaica,* BL, Add. MSS 12,404, fol. 37d.

3. Mocha coffee, produced in the East Indies, was a favourite drink in England.

4. JAJ, 21 December 1774, PRO, CO 140/46, p. 563; see also 1 November 1775, p. 575.

5. JAB, 16 March 1777, PRO, CO 31/39, fol. 138.

6. Pinckard, *Notes,* 214.

7. Long, *History of Jamaica,* BL, Add. MSS 12,404, fol. 448d.

8. Ibid., fol. 348.

9. Sir Ralph Payne to the Earl of Dartmouth, 17 December 1773, 10 October 1774, PRO, CO 152/54, fols. 14, 103–4.

10. *Parliamentary Papers* (HMSO), vol. 84: *Accounts and Papers,* vol. 26, no. 6.

11. Long, *History of Jamaica,* BL, Add. MSS 12,404, fol. 401.

12. Long, "Notes for the History of Jamaica," BL, Add. MSS 12,411, fol. 28.

13. "An Account of the Number of Ships, with Their Tonnage, Which Cleared Outwards from Great Britain to the British West India Islands, in Each Year, from 1765, Together with the Total Value of Exports from Great Britain to the West Indies . . . to the nearest £," n.d., *Parliamentary Papers* (HMSO), vol. 84: *Accounts and Papers,* vol. 26, pt. 4, nos. 687.

14. Sheffield, *Observations,* 20.

15. Long, *History of Jamaica,* BL, Add. MSS 12,404, fol. 402d.

16. Ibid., fol. 433.

17. Lord Macartney to Lord George Germain, 30 June 1776, PRO, CO 101/20, fol. 29.

18. Ibid.; A. Henderson to Governor Leyborne, 27 November, PRO, CO 71/4, fol. 96; Address of the Assembly of Dominica to the King, 24 April 1776, PRO, CO 71/6, fol. 53.

19. Long, *History of Jamaica,* BL, Add. MSS 12,404, fols. 402, 464. American beef was bought by the West India merchants at 18–20s per barrel, about 30s cheaper than Irish beef.

20. "Answer to Queries," 1774, PRO, CO 137/70, fol. 89; "Answer to Queries," 26 June 1774, PRO, CO 152/54, fol. 63.

21. Long, *History of Jamaica,* BL, Add. MSS 12,404, fols. 433–433d.

22. *Cornwall Chronicle and Jamaica General Advertiser,* 12 April 1777 (supp.), vol. 1, no. 124:1 (in BRL).

23. Lieutenant-Governor Stuart to Dartmouth, 24 September 1773, PRO, CO 71/4, fol. 71.

24. Dartmouth to Stuart, 6 April 1774, fol. 118.

25. "Remarks on the Trade of the Different Government on the Continent of North America," n.d., BL, Add. MSS 38,342, fols. 211–211d.

26. Ibid., fols. 211d–212.

27. Ibid., fols. 212–212d; Pares, *Yankees and Creole,* 27.

28. "Remarks on the Trade," fols. 213–213d.

29. "Account of the Total Quantities of Imports from North America to the British West Indies," n.d., BL, Add. MSS 12,431, fol. 170; Long, *History of Jamaica,* BL, Add. MSS 12,404, fols. 463d, 433.

30. Ibid., fol. 422; Minutes of the Committee of the Privy Council, Appointed for All Matters Relating to Trade and Foreign Plantations (hereafter cited as "Minutes of the Committee for Trade"), 16 April 1784, PRO, BT 5/1, fols. 158–59.

31. Sheffield, *Observations,* app. 5.

32. Long, *History of Jamaica,* BL, Add. MSS 12,404, fols. 390, 402. Jamaica provided a larger part of her own food than the other islands, but the provisions taken lasted only a few weeks.

33. "Imports from North America," BL, Add. MSS 12,431, fol. 170.

34. Edwards, *History,* 2:409; Ragatz, *Fall,* 38.

35. "Memorial and Petition of the Assembly and Council of Jamaica to the King," 11 December 1784, PRO, BT 6/83, pt. 1, fol. 20; Long, "Collections for the History of Jamaica," BL, Add. MSS 12,413, fol. 15.

36. Minutes of the Committee for Trade, 3 April 1784, PRO, BT 5/1, fol. 137.

37. Sheffield, *Observations,* app. 4.

38. Long, *History of Jamaica,* BL, Add. MSS 12,404, fols. 420–421d.

39. Sheffield, *Observations,* app. 4.

40. Minutes of the Committee for Trade, 16 March 1784, PRO, BT 5/1, fol. 25; "Answers to Queries," 1774, PRO, CO 137/70, fol. 90.

41. Long, *History of Jamaica,* BL, Add. MSS 12,404, fols. 458, 464d.

42. Ibid., fol. 450; Long, "Collections," BL, Add. MSS 12,413, fol. 18.

43. Long, "Notes," BL, Add. MSS 12,411, fol. 29d.

44. Ibid., fol. 46d.

45. Pares, *Yankees and Creoles,* 40–41.

46. "Account of the Quantity of Rum Exported from the Late British Colonies between 5 January 1770 and 5 January 1774," n.d., BL, Add. MSS 38,342, fol. 52.

47. Long, *History of Jamaica,* BL, Add. MSS 12,404, fol. 447.

48. Long, "Collections," BL, Add. MSS 12,413, fol. 66.

Chapter 2. The American War and the British Caribbean Economy

1. The Earl of Dartmouth to Sir Ralph Payne, October 1774, CO 152/54, fol. 101d; Payne to Dartmouth, 3 July 1774, ibid., fol. 84.

2. Barritt, "Navy and the Clyde," 34.

3. Glover, *Substance of the Evidence,* 24–25; Ragatz, *Fall,* 133; Sheridan, "Crisis of Slave Subsistence," 615–16.

4. Payne to Dartmouth, 12 January 1775, PRO, CO 152/55, fol. 7.

5. Edward Hay to Dartmouth, 6 April 1775, PRO, CO 28/56, fol. 101.

6. John Pinney to John Hayne, 10 April 1775, UBL, Pinney L.Bk. 5, p. 305.

7. Pinney to Simon Pretor, 1 June 1775, UBL, Pinney L.Bk. 3, p. 13; Pinney to Mills and Swanston, 9 December 1775, UBL, Pinney L.Bk. 4, p. 21.

8. JAJ, 1 November 1775, PRO, CO 140/46, p. 575; Sir Basil Keith to Dartmouth, 18 January 1776, PRO, CO 137/71, fol. 43.

9. JAJ, 1–3 November 1775, PRO, CO 140/46, pp. 575, 579–80; JAJ, 22 December 1775, PRO, CO 140/46, p. 631; JAJ, 18 August 1779, PRO, CO 140/59, p. 146; see Deerr, *The History of Sugar,* vol. 1.

10. Minutes of the West India Merchants, 7 March 1775, vol. 1, fol. 73; 4 June 1776, 1:87; 18 February 1777, 1:104, microfilm copies at the Institute of Commonwealth Studies, London; originals are in the West India Library in Trinidad. Hereafter cited as "Minutes of the West India Merchants."

11. D. Hall, *West India Committee,* 2. Although Bligh's mission ended in disaster, he carried mountain rice from Timor to England. The rice was sent to Jamaica to be grown in the mountainous regions to encourage settlement; see Jefferson, *Papers,* 17:564.

12. Sheridan, "Crisis of Slave Subsistence," 619.

13. Hay to Dartmouth, 6 April 1775, PRO, CO 28/56, fol. 1; 29 August 1775, PRO, CO 29/21.

14. Ragatz, *Fall,* 151.

15. Hay to Dartmouth, 6 April 1775, PRO, CO 28/56, fol. 1; Hay to Germain, 12 February 1776, PRO, CO 28/56, fol. 27; see PRO, CO 29/1.

16. JAB, 13 February 1776, PRO, CO 31/39; see Makinson, *Barbados,* 91.

17. JAA, 3 February 1776, PRO, CO 9/33. The supplies in the warehouses were 102 tierces of rice, 13,840 barrels of grain, 1,740 barrels of flour, 340 barrels and tierces of bread (300 tierces), 295 barrels of beef and pork, 1,250 bushels of beans, 200 bushels of peas, 513 firkins of butter, and 200 bushels of oatmeal. By the completion of the report, large quantities of all articles were sold.

18. Captain Benjamin Payne to Major-General Howe, 15 February 1776, PRO, CO 5/93, pt. 1, fols. 127–127d; see also Ragatz, *Fall,* 151.

19. JAB, 13 February 1776, PRO, CO 31/39; minutes of the Council of Barbados, 31 January 1776, PRO, CO 31/38; Hay to Germain, 13 February 1776, PRO, CO 28/56, fols. 27–27d; *West India Merchant,* no. 16; Ragatz, *Fall,* 151; Address of the Assembly to the King, 15 February 1776, PRO, CO 28/56, fols. 33–33d, 35–35d. The address was signed by thirteen of twenty-two members.

20. Hay to Germain, 13 April 1776, PRO, CO 28/56, fol. 70.

21. Makinson, *Barbados,* 91–92, 99.

22. Payne to Howe, 15 February 1776, PRO, CO 5/93, pt. 1, fols. 126–127d.

23. Dickson, *Mitigation of Slavery,* 308–10, quoted in Sheridan, "Crisis of Slave Subsistence," 620.

24. Bennett, *Bondsmen and Bishops;* "Planter in Barbados to Gentleman in Kingston," *Cornwall Chronicle and Jamaica General Advertiser,* 10 May 1777 (supp.),

vol. 1, no. 128:4 (in BRL); Rear-Admiral Barrington to Phillip Stephens, 13 July 1778, PRO, Adm. 1/310, p. 299.

25. Hay to Germain, 4 June 1778, PRO, CO 28/57, fols. 41–42.

26. Hay to James Young, 24 March 1776, PRO, CO 28/56, fol. 51; minutes of the Council of Barbados, 6 April 1776, PRO, CO 31/38; Hay to Germain, 10 May 1776, PRO, CO 28/56, fol. 59.

27. *West India Merchant,* no. 16:123–24.

28. Young to Stephens, 7 April 1776, PRO, Adm. 1/309, fol. 458d; Jameson, "St. Eustatius," 683; Matthew Burt to Germain, 7 June 1777, PRO, CO 152/56, fol. 108d.

29. "Extract of a letter from Antigua, May 17," in the *Antigua Mercury,* 20 September 1777, PRO, CO 152/56, fol. 22; Assembly of Antigua to Burt in Council, 14 August 1777, PRO, CO 152/56, fols. 203–203d. The Council passed a resolution supporting the Assembly; see Council and Assembly of St. Kitts to Burt, 25 August 1777, PRO, CO 152/56, fol. 201.

30. Council and Assembly of Montserrat to Burt, 4 September 1777, PRO, CO 152/56, fol. 205.

31. *Connecticut Gazette,* 6 February 1776, in Clarke, *Naval Documents,* 4: 1319.

32. Burt to Germain, 1 December 1777, PRO, CO 152/57, fol. 151; Petition of the Council and Assembly of Nevis to the King, n.d., PRO, CO 152/59, fol. 75; Pinney to William Croker, June 1778, UBL, Pinney L.Bk. 4, p. 220.

33. Clement Tudway, M.P. for Wells, owned five hundred slaves on two plantations in Antigua; see Sheridan, "Crisis of Slave Subsistence," 623–24. His papers are at the Somerset Record Office. Quote found in Sheridan, *Subsistence,* 623–24.

34. Quoted in Pinney to Sarah Maynard, 3 May 1777, UBL, Pinney L.Bk. 2, p. 111.

35. Ibid.; Pinney to Pretor, 12 June 1777, p. 114; see also Pares, *A West-India Fortune,* 93–94.

36. JAA, 6 February 1776, PRO, CO 9/33.

37. Burt to Germain, 17 September 1777, PRO, CO 152/56, fols. 193–193d; March 1778, fols. 247–247d; 14 December 1777, CO 152/57, fol. 165.

38. Burt to Germain, 17, 30 June 1778, PRO, CO 152/57, fols. 192–192d; 14 June 1779, CO 152/59, fol. 208; 19 December 1778, CO 152/60, fols. 59d–60; Ragatz, *Fall,* 157–58.

39. Assembly to Keith in JAJ, 22 December 1775, PRO, CO 140/46, fol. 630.

40. Dalhousie and Stephens to Sir Hugh Smyth, 23 July 1776, BRO, Ac/Wo 16(27), pp. 89–101.

41. Keith to Germain, 20 December 1776, PRO, CO 137/72, fol. 34d.

42. Pasley, *Private Sea Journals,* 256.

43. Macartney to Germain, 3 September 1776, PRO, CO 101/20, fol. 203; 28 July

1777 ("List of Topsail Vessels from Grenada"), fol. 243; 21 April 1778, CO 101/21, fol. 189; 23 May 1779, CO 101/23, fol. 159; 30 June 1778, CO 101/20, fol. 30; 10 October 1778, CO 101/22, fol. 139; 3 April 1779, CO 101/23, fol. 116d.

44. Shirley to Dartmouth, 4 February 1776, PRO, CO 71/6, fols. 31–31d.

45. Young to Stephens, 7 April 1776, PRO, Adm. 1/309, fol. 458d.

46. Syrett, *Shipping and the American War,* 165–71.

47. Pares, *A West-India Fortune,* 91–92; Southey, *Chronological History,* 2:425.

48. William Smelling to Sir Joseph Foster Barham, 10 July 1777, Bodl., Barham Papers 357/1.

49. "Answers to Heads of Inquiry," 22 January 1785, PRO, CO 71/9, fol. 61.

50. "A State of the Prices of Provisions and the Value of Sugar and Rum in the Years 1774, 1775 and 1776," 8 September 1776, PRO, CO 28/60, fol. 209; "Heads of Inquiry with Answers," 7 September, PRO, CO 152/64, fol. 115; "Answers" of Edmund Lincoln to Sydney, 8 January 1785, PRO, CO 260/7, no. 14; Craton and Walvin, *A Jamaican Plantation,* 119.

51. Houston and Co. to Houston and Paterson, 19 June 1776, NLS, MSS 8793, p. 45; to Charles Irvine, 28 August 1777, p. 259; to Jonas Akers, 31 December, p. 227; to Thomas Froth, p. 328.

52. Houston and Co. to Josias Jackson, ibid., p. 230; to Gill and Nisbet, 30 July 1778, NLS, MSS 8794, p. 40; to Turner and Paul, 23 November 1778, fol. 78; "Jamaica Advices," 27 July 1778, BL, Add. MSS 12,412, fol. 19d.

53. Houston and Co. to Houston and Paterson, 19 June 1776, NLS, MSS 8794, p. 45; to Irvine, 28 August 1777, MSS 8793, p. 259; "The Price of Sugar," 6 July 1778, BL, Add. MSS 12,404, fol. 445.

54. William Cunninghame to Robert Dunmore, 9 July 1776, NRA, GD 247/59/Q; Houston and Co. to Gill and Nisbet, 30 July 1778, NLS, MSS 8794, p. 40.

55. Cunninghame to Dunmore, 9, 21, 27 July 1778, NRA, GD 247/59/Q; Charles Cowes to Dunmore and Co., 9 July 1778; Robert Colquhoun to Dunmore, 6 August 1779; see also Cunninghame to Dunmore, 3 August 1778.

56. Cunninghame to Dunmore, 13 August 1778, ibid.; Ragatz, *Fall,* 167.

57. "Rise of Sugar," 6 July 1778, BL, Add. MSS 12,404, fol. 445; also see H. Allen, "British Commercial Policy."

58. "Sales of Sugar," 6 April 1782, NLS, MSS 188:75, fol. 63.

59. D. E. Hall, "Incalculability," 343; "Comparative Prices and Charges Attending the Jamaican Planter at and since the Commencement of the War" n.d., BL, Add. MSS 12,413, fol. 45; Van Keelen to Barham, 9 September 1782, Bodl., Barham Papers 357/1; Graham to Germain, 27 July 1779, PRO, CO 101/23, fol. 203.

60. William Cunninghame to Robert Dunmore, 9 July 1778, NAS, MS AD.

247/59/2; Houston & Co. to Gill and Nisbet, 30 July 1778, NLS MSS 8,794, p. 40.

61. Prices were taken from Houston and Co. letter books, NLS, MSS 8793, 8794.

62. "Jamaican Advices," November 1778, BL, Add. MSS 12,412, fol. 3.

63. Cunninghame to Dunmore, 9 July 1778, NRA, GD 247/59/Q.

64. Minutes of the West India Merchants, vol. 1, fols. 76, 83, 115, 147, 174; vol. 2, fols. 30, 58, 92, 112.

65. Ibid.; "An Account of the Quantity of British Sugar Imported into England between 1772 and 1791," BL, Add. MS 12,432, fol. 18.

66. "An Account of the Quantity of Rum and Sugar Imported into North America from the West Indian Islands, 1768–1783," 1 February 1786, PRO, BT 6/84, fol. 297.

67. Ragatz, *Statistics,* 22; Schumpeter, *English Overseas Trade,* 60–62.

68. See Ragatz, *Fall,* 169, 50d–51, 55; Minutes of the West India Merchants, 29 May, 21 June 1781, vol. 2, fols. 62–63; Instruction from the Earl of Shelburne, 7 June 1782, in JAJ, 12 February 1783, PRO, CO 140/59, p. 549.

69. See "Charges on 1 cwt Sugar," [1781], BL, Add. MSS 12,413, fol. 44; see also Add. MSS 12,412, fol. 24 (Long calculated that the foreign producers were making about 240 percent per cwt. more on sugar shipped to England in neutral vessels); JAJ, 12 January 1783, PRO, CO 140/59, p. 545.

70. JAJ, 27 February 1783, PRO, CO 140/59, p. 567.

71. "History of the Policy Hitherto Pursued by England with Respect to the Trade of Sugar," n.d., BL, Add. MSS 38,759, fols. 32, 52; *Parliamentary Papers* (HMSO), 19 Geo. III chap. 25; see 22 Geo. III chap. 5.

72. Houston and Co. to Walter Nisbet, 17 April 1781, NLS, MSS 8794, p. 521.

73. Charles Ruddach to Charles Steuart, 30 October 1780, Charles Stewart Papers, NLS, MSS 5032, fols. 57d–58; extract from supp. to the *Kingston Gazette,* 14 October 1780, PRO, CO 137/79, fols. 41–42d; Dalling to Germain, 20 October 1780, PRO, CO 137/79, fol. 13d.

74. "An Account of the Damage Done by the Hurricane in Barbados," 10 October 1780, *Parliamentary Papers* (HMSO), vol. 84, pt. 2, no. 15; Rodney to Stephens, 12 November 1780, PRO, Adm. 1/311, fols. 423–423d.

75. Dalhousie and Stephens to Smyth, 14 January 1778 and 20 May 1779, BRO, Ac/Wo 16(27), pp. 89–101, 102–12.

76. Van Keelen to Barham, 7 April 1781, Bodl., Barham Papers 357/1; Sheridan, "Crisis of Slave Subsistence," 627; Southey, *Chronological History,* 2:479; "Statement of Circumstances Relating to the Slave Trade, 1789," *Parliamentary Papers* (HMSO), vol. 82, no. 626, p. 4; "An Account of the Number of Slaves Returned into the Treasurer's Office of Barbados from 1780 to 1787 Inclusive," PRO, CO 28/61, fol. 204.

77. Macartney to Germain, 25 October 1778, PRO, CO 101/22, fol. 157.

78. JAB, 25 July 1780, PRO, CO 31/41; Cunninghame to the Board of Trade, 28 November 1781, PRO, CO 28/35, fol. 93; see "The Answer of Major-General James Cunninghame to the Petition of the House of Assembly of Barbados to the King," PRO, CO 28/35; Hay to Germain, 2 June 1778, PRO, CO 28/57, fols. 41–42.

79. Cunninghame to Welbore Ellis, 23 April 1782, PRO, CO 28/59, fol. 320.

80. Journal of the Assembly of St. Kitts, 1 December 1779, PRO, CO 241/11; JAJ, 19 August 1779, PRO, CO 140/59, p. 147; 20 August 1779, pp. 148–49.

81. Minutes of the Assembly of Montserrat, 25 September 1777, PRO, CO 177/12.

82. "Extract of Minutes of the Council of Antigua," 9 June 1779, PRO, CO 177/12, fol. 208; JAA, 20 September 1780, PRO, CO 9/41.

83. Germain to Burt, 4 October 1780, PRO, CO 152/60, fol. 102; Ragatz, *Fall*, 158; Macartney to Germain, 25 October 1778, PRO, CO 101/22, fols. 156–57; "Jamaica Advices," 21 June 1778, BL, Add. MSS 12,412, fol. 6.

84. Charles Stirling to Sir William Stirling, 23 April 1778, Abercairny MSS, NRA, GD 24/1/461.

85. Macartney to Germain, 25 October 1778, PRO, CO 101/22, fol. 157.

86. Germain to Dalling, 15 May 1779, PRO, CO 137/74, fol. 158; 7 December 1780, CO 137/78, fol. 344d.

Chapter 3. British Policy, Canadian Preference, and the West Indian Economy, 1783–1810

1. Minutes of the Committee for Trade, 11 March 1784, PRO, BT 5/1, fols. 20, 33–33d, 56.

2. John Adams to Robert Livingston, 23 June 1783, *Works*, 8:74–75.

3. "A Jamaican Planter to the Editor," *Cornwall Chronicle and Jamaica General Advertiser*, 1 March 1783 (supp.), vol. 1, no. 427:2 (in BRL).

4. John Van Keelen to Sir Joseph Foster Barham, 18 August 1783, Bodl., Barham Papers 357/1.

5. Robert Livingston to John Adams, 29 August 1782, *Revolutionary Diplomatic Correspondence*, ed. Wharton, 5:678; to Benjamin Franklin, 5 September 1782, 696–99, 5:597–598; to John Jay, 12 September 1782, 5:721.

6. James Madison to Thomas Jefferson, 13 May 1783. Madison, *Writings*, 1:462–64.

7. Minutes of the West India Merchants, 25 February 1783, vol. 2, fols. 111–111d; see also "Extracts from the Minutes of a General Meeting of the West India Merchants," 25 February 1783, PRO, CO 137/83, fol. 182.

8. Bell, "British Commercial Policy," 434–36.

9. Pares, "Merchants and Planters," 23.

10. Thomas Shirley to Lord Sydney, January 1785, PRO, CO 162/64, no. 95; see also Makinson, *Barbados,* 123.

11. Langford Lovell to Kender Mason (extract), 26 November 1783, PRO, BT 6/84, p. 75.

12. Minutes of the Committee for Trade, 11 March 1784, PRO, BT 5/1, fols. 10–12.

13. "Extract of a Letter from a Planter in St. Vincent," 25 February 1787, PRO, BT 6/77, fol. 208; see Pares, *War and Trade;* "Prices of the Following Are Compared with Average before and since the War," 11 November 1784, PRO, CO 137/85, fol. 115; "Answer to Queries," 1786, PRO, CO 152/64; Governor Shirley to Lord Sydney, 31 July 1784, PRO, CO 152/63.

14. Archibald Campbell to Lord North, 26 November 1784, PRO, CO 137/84, fols. 6d–7.

15. Address of Assembly of Jamaica to Governor Campbell, 20 November 1783, PRO, CO 137/84, fols. 20–20d; Campbell to Assembly, 20 November 1783, fols. 21–21d; Wise, "British Commercial Policy," 67–68; Campbell to Governor Haldimand, 16 October 1783, BL, Add. MSS 21,809, fols. 307–307d.

16. John Orde to Sydney, 19 March 1778, PRO, CO 71/8, fol. 150.

17. Edward Long to Mrs. George Ricketts, 23 March 1783, BL, Add. MSS 30,001, fol. 66d.

18. Craton and Walvin, *A Jamaican Plantation,* 114.

19. David Parry to Lord North, 11 November 1783, PRO, CO 28/60, fol. 68d; Wise, "British Commercial Policy," 66; Bell, "British Commercial Policy," 438.

20. Ehrman, *The Younger Pitt,* 1–2:332–33.

21. Orde to Sydney, 13 August 1784, PRO, CO 71/8, fol. 234; Wise, "British Commercial Policy," 76–77.

22. Shirley to Sydney, 30 July 1783, PRO, CO 152/63, no. 81.

23. Parry to the Committee for Trade, 7 September 1784, PRO, BT 6/84, fols. 273d–274d; PRO, CO 28/60, fols. 183–184d; Representation of Stephen Fuller to His Majesty's Ministers, 8 March 1785, PRO, BT 6/83, pt. 1, fol. 23d.

24. Parry to Sydney, 16 June 1785, PRO, CO 28/42, fols. 88d–90.

25. Evan Nepean, "Trade between North America and the British West Indies," [1787], BL, Add. MSS 38,348, fol. 20d.

26. Parry to the Committee for Trade, 7 September 1784, PRO, BT 6/84, fol. 275; see Fuller to His Majesty's Ministers, 8 March 1785, PRO BT 6/83, pt. 1, fols. 24–24d.

27. Edward Lincoln to Sydney, 1 December 1785, PRO, BT 6/85, pp. 185–86.

28. Shirley to Sydney, January 1785, PRO, CO 152/64, no. 95; Cuthbert Collingwood to Shirley, 16 December 1784, PRO, CO 152/64; copy of the cargo manifest of the brigantine *Belvidere,* CO 152/64.

29. Horatio Nelson to Sydney, 20 March 1785, PRO, CO 152/64.

30. The chief articles and quantities taken were 27,260 barrels of flour, some 2,000 barrels of bread, 3,413,000 feet of lumber, 5,437,000 staves and shingles, 262,000 hoops, 258 horses, and 59,171 bushels of grain.

31. "Remarks Relative to the Laws of Navigation," 5 January 1789, BL, Add. MSS 38,224, fols. 80d–81.

32. "A Comparative State of the Trade between the West Indies and North America from 1 October 1785 to 1 October 1787," PRO, CO 318/1, fol. 135; for the illegal trade between the French at Cape Francois and the Jamaicans, see "Extracts of Letters from Elisha Tyler of Kingston to Caleb Mumford of Cape Francois," n.d., BL, Add. MSS 38,376, fols. 99–100d.

33. "An Account of Ships and Their Cargoes Entered Inwards in the British Islands, from the United States, British North America and the Foreign West Indies," n.d., PRO, CO 318/1, fols. 142–48; for Dominica, see PRO, CO 318/2, fol. 264; see also Wise, "British Commercial Policy," 74–75, 79.

34. Sheridan, "Crisis of Slave Subsistence," 636. Breadfruit has become acceptable to many West Indians only recently; see Brathwaite, *Creole Society in Jamaica,* 86.

35. "An Account of the Number of Slaves Returned into the Treasury Office of Barbados from 1780 to 1787 Inclusive," PRO, CO 28/61, fol. 204. Figures for the remaining years were: 1781, 63,248; 1782, no figures; 1783, 62,258; 1784, 61,808; 1785, 62,775; 1786, 62,115.

36. "Extracts of Two letters from Jamaica to a Gentleman Now in London," 21 September 1786, PRO, BT 6/76, fol. 1; see Stephens Raester and Co. to Sir John Hugh Smyth, 8 December 1783, BRO, Ac/Wo 16(27), pp. 113–22; see Brathwaite, *Creole Society in Jamaica,* 85–86. He estimated that 15,000–24,000 slaves died as a result of the many problems in Jamaica.

37. Extract of letter from Jamaica, 28 December 1786, PRO, BT 6/76, fols. 1–1d.

38. Edwards, *History,* 2:53–54.

39. Ibid.; see Macpherson, *Annals of Commerce,* 4:228. He has an error in the calculation of the 1791 figures.

40. For further information on West Indian prosperity, see Edwards, *History,* 448. Exacerbating the decline in exports of sugar and other staples, the cost of production of every item was rising with the cost of slave subsistence, wrote Goveia in *Slave Society,* 142–43. For example, in the Leeward Islands, the price of Indian corn, a staple diet of slaves, increased from 5s to 9s per bushel. In St. Kitts flour cost nearly 50 percent more after the war than before, and in Antigua the rise was even higher. The available statistics for West Indian economic study cannot be taken at face value. They change from source to source, and historians must recognize that

instead of stressing quantities, the trend of rise or decline is probably more important. For the quantity of West Indian sugar imported into England between 1772 and 1791, see "An Account of the Quantity of British Sugar Imported into England between 1772 and 1791," BL, Add. MSS 12,432, fol. 18.

41. Parry to North, 11 November 1783, PRO, CO 28/60, fol. 69.

42. Charles Avril to Charles Spooner, 4 March 1784, PRO, BT 6/83, pt. 1, fol. 179.

43. "Extract of a Letter from One of the Most Considerable Planters in St. Vincent to His Merchants in London," 25 February 1787, PRO, BT 6/77, fol. 207.

44. Ehrman, *The Younger Pitt,* 1–2:359.

45. Robert Thomson to Spooner, n.d., PRO, BT 6/83, pt. 1, fol. 179; Mr. Covy to Spooner, 28 February 1784; John Julius to Spooner, n.d., fol. 179d; Avril to Spooner, 4 March 1784, fols. 179d–180.

46. Van Keelen to Barham, 24 July 1786, 24 July 1787, Bodl., Barham Papers 357/1; see Nepean, "Trade between North America and the British West Indies," BL, Add. MSS 38,348, fols. 20d–21.

47. "Report from the Committee to Enquire into the Present State of the Intercourse between the British West India Islands, and His Majesty's Colonies in North America," 8 January 1788, PRO, BT 6/76, fol. 30.

48. Ehrman, *The Younger Pitt,* 1–2:338.

49. 27 Geo. III chap. 7; see also 28 Geo. III chap. 6.

50. Ehrman, *The Younger Pitt,* 1–2:337.

51. "A Proclamation," 29 November 1804, PRO, CO 152/86.

52. George Metcalfe to Lord Castlereagh, 27 November 1807, PRO, CO 71/42.

53. *Barbados Mercury,* n.d., PRO, CO 28/74.

54. Protheroes and Claxton, Bristol, to A. Cumming, St. Vincent, 20 April 1807, PRO, CO 260/22.

55. Metcalfe to Castlereagh, 27 November 1807, PRO, CO 71/42.

56. Protheroes and Claxton to Cumming, 20 April 1807, PRO, CO 260/22; see Fawkener to Edward Cooke, 5 May 1807, PRO, CO 260/23.

57. "Canadian Bounty," 28 August 1807, PRO, CO 28/76.

58. Eyre Coote to William Windham, 10 November 1806, PRO, CO 137/117; "An Act for Granting Certain Bounties on Salted and Pickled Fish Imported into the Island from Newfoundland or Any of the British Colonies, Provinces or Settlement in North America in British Vessels," 14 November 1806, PRO, CO 137/117.

59. Coote to Windham, 30 May 1806, PRO, CO 137/116.

60. Assembly to the Council, 27 July 1806, PRO, CO 152/88.

61. Metcalfe to Castlereagh, 27 November 1807, PRO, CO 71/42.

62. Speaker and Gentlemen of the Assembly to the Governor, 2 July 1807, PRO, CO 260/22.

63. "Resolutions of the House of Assembly," n.d., PRO, CO 137/119.

64. President of the Council to Members of the Assembly, 29 July 1806, PRO, CO 152/88.

65. Assembly to President and Council, 20 June 1806, PRO, CO 152/88; see Assembly to the Council (St. Christopher), 29 July 1806, ibid.; resolution of the Assembly of Nevis, 9 September 1806, ibid.; Coote to Windham, 30 May 1806, PRO, CO 137/116.

66. Speaker and Members of the Assembly to the Governor, 25 October 1806, PRO, CO 101/44.

Chapter 4. The Sugar Market after 1775

1. "The Case of the British Sugar Colonies," n.d., BL, Add. MSS 12,431, fol. 171.

2. "The State of the West India Islands Laid before Parliament," March 1775, BL, Add. MSS 12,431, fol. 20.

3. Hibbert Purrier and Co. to Nathaniel Phillips, 6 July 1781, NLW, Slebech Papers 8588.

4. Ragatz, *Fall.*

5. Hibbert Purrier to Phillips, 1 January 1783, NLW, Slebech Papers 8591.

6. 23 Geo. III chap. 14; Ragatz, *Fall,* 172; Hibbert Purrier to Phillips, 5 March 1783, NLW, Slebech Papers 8621.

7. James Nisbet to Mrs. Catherine Stapleton, 12 November 1783, UWB, Stapleton-Cotton MSS 18.

8. Thomson to Stapleton, 9 June 1785, NLW, Bodrhyddan MSS, box 2.

9. Petition of the Assembly of Jamaica, 23 December 1786, PRO, CO 137/86.

10. Edward Fuhr to Phillips, 6 September 1786, NLW, Slebech Papers 9102.

11. Hibbert, Fuhr and Hibbert to Phillips, 1 July, 30 September 1788, NLW, Slebech Papers 11555, 11565.

12. Ibid., 1788, 11556.

13. Copy of a letter to George Scott, 15 October 1788, Cooper-Franks MSS, LMA, Acc. 775/930.

14. Evidence of Thomas Irving, Inspector-General, to the Select Committee on the Slave Trade, in Minutes Reported to the House of Commons.

15. "Reasons, general and particular, on the subject of certain innovations projected in the long-established Laws of Great Britain respecting Sugars; drawn up in consequence of communications made by the Chancellor of the Exchequer to a Deputation of West India Planters and Merchants, and presented to Mr. Pitt and Mr. Dundas on 1 March," 28 February 1792, NLW, Slebech Papers 11540.

16. John Nesbitt to Jacob Franks, 27 January 1792, Cooper-Franks MSS, LMA, Acc. 775/945, fols. 1–2.

17. Barham to Wedderburn and Graham, 15 September 1791, Bodl., Barham Papers 428, fol. 12.

18. George Turner to M. D. Hodgson, 26 October 1791, JRO, Tweedie Estate Records 4/45/66, fol. 23.

19. J. Lindsay, "The Pennants and Jamaica," 61.

20. Turner to Hodgson, 16 April 1792, JRO, Tweedie Estate Records 4/45/66, fol. 70.

21. Ragatz, *Fall*, 205–9.

22. *Journal of the Assembly of Jamaica* 12 (1813): 543.

23. Ragatz, *Fall*, 207.

24. *Journal of the Assembly of Jamaica* 12 (1813): 546.

25. Edward Mathew to Lord Hawkesbury, n.d., BL, Add. MSS 38,228; Ragatz, *Fall*, 209.

26. "East India Trade," 23 November 1792, BL, Add. MSS 38,228.

27. "Reasons," 28 February 1792, NLW, Slebech Papers 11540.

28. "The Memorial of the Agents for the Several British West India Colonies," 30 March 1792, SomRO, DD/DN 508/67–75.

29. "At a General Meeting of the West India Planters and Merchants Held at the London Tavern," Melville MSS, RHL, W.Ind. s.8.

30. "Reasons," 28 February 1792, NLW, Slebech Papers 11540.

31. Thomas Plummer to Barham, 1792, Bodl., Barham Papers 361/2.

32. "Resolution of the House of Assembly of Jamaica," 8 November 1791, PRO, CO 137/91.

33. Letter to Lord Hawkesbury, September 1792, BL, Add. MSS 38,228, fol. 62.

34. Dickinson and Dickinson to Salmon, 1 December 1792, 25 January 1793, SomRO, DD/DN 468.

35. Plummer to Barham, 30 July 1794, Bodl., Barham Papers 361/2.

36. Rose Fuller to Stephen Fuller, 9 August 1794, SomRO, DD/DN 508/103–46.

37. Walter Nisbet to Rev. William D. Shipley, 5 August 1794, NLW, Bodrhyddan MSS, box 2.

38. Thomson to Shipley, 21 July, 31 October 1794, ibid.

39. Major-General Adam Williamson to Henry Dundas, 11 June 1794, PRO, CO 137/93; Minvan Home to Dundas, 28 June 1794, PRO, CO 101/33; Thomson to Shipley, 1 May 1794, NLW, Bodrhyddan MSS, box 2.

40. Plummer to Barham, 24 September, 24 December 1795, 5 October 1796, Bodl., Barham Papers 361/2.

41. Plummer to Barham, [?] February, 30 August, 25 September 1797, ibid.

42. Plummer to Barham, 12 August 1797, 17 January, 25 August 1798; John Davis to Lord Penrhyn, 12 November 1798, UWB, Penrhyn MS 1292.

43. Williams, *Capitalism and Slavery,* 152; Drescher, Econocide, 16, 24, chap. 2.

44. J. Lindsay, "The Pennants and Jamaica," 59.

45. Plummer to Barham, 9, 13 August 1799, Bodl., Barham Papers 361/2.

46. Val and M. O'Connor to Clement Tudway, 4 September 1799, SomRO, DD/ TD 12/1.

47. Charles Brooks to Sir William Young, 3 August 1808, Young Papers, RHL, W.Ind. t.1, vol. 1, fol. 112.

48. Plummer to Barham, 3 October 1799, Bodl., Barham Papers 361/2.

49. Ibid.

50. Robert Johnson to Tudway, 8 October 1799, SomRO, DD/TD 12/1.

51. Plummer to Barham, 22 October, 2 November 1799, 4 January 1800, Bodl., Barham Papers 361/2.

52. Plummer to Barham, 23 November 1801.

53. Moses Benson and Son to William Chisholme, 24 April 1800, NLS, MSS 5465.

54. Plummer to Barham, 11 February 1802, Bodl., Barham Papers 362/1.

55. Davidson and Graham to Lord Penrhyn, 14 February 1803, UWB, Penrhyn MS 1362.

56. John Davies to Penrhyn, 10 March 1803, UWB, Penrhyn MS 1313.

57. Plummer to Barham, 26 August 1803, Bodl., Barham Papers 362/1.

58. Davidson and Graham to Penrhyn, 12 October 1805, UWB, Penrhyn MS 1346; 12 November 1805, MS 1351.

59. H. O'Connor to E. Moore, 7 September 1804, SomRO, DD/TD 12; Davidson and Graham to Penrhyn, 27 December 1804, UWB, Penrhyn MS 1359.

60. "A Comparative View of the Produce and the Supplies of the British West Indies," Liverpool Papers, BL, Add. MS 38,346, fols. 85–86.

61. Hibbert Purrier to Phillips, 6 July 1781, NLW, Slebech Papers 8588.

62. Franks to Scott, 15 October 1788, Cooper-Franks MSS, LMA, Acc. 775/930.

63. Thomson to Stapleton, 9 June 1785, NLW, Bodrhyddan MSS, box 2.

64. Turner to Hodgson, 26 October 1791, JRO, Tweedie Estate Records 4/45/66; Plummer to Barham, 30 July 1794, Bodl., Barham Papers 361/2; Fuller to Fuller, 9 August 1794, SomRO, DD/DN 508/103–46.

65. Thomson to Shipley, 12 November 1795, 12 January 1799, NLW, Bodrhyddan MSS, box 2.

66. Robert Greaves to Tudway, 24 February 1800, SomRO, DD/TD 12/1.

67. Plummer to Barham, 20 August 1803, Bodl., Barham Papers 362/1; also see Plummer's letter of 20 December 1803; Rowland Williams Fearon to Penrhyn, 10 October 1805, UWB, Penrhyn MS 1396.

68. Thomas Samson to Henry Goulburn, 10 June 1807, SurRO, Goulburn Papers 319/53.

69. Richard and Thomas Neave to Dear Sir (Rev. Shipley), 6 January 1799, NLW, Bodrhyddan MSS, box 2.

70. Gilbert Franklyn to Lord Hawkesbury, 15 September 1792, BL, Add. MSS 38,228, fol. 63.

71. Penrhyn to Samuel Jefferies, 26 February 1807, UWB, Penrhyn MS 1461.

72. Davidson to Penrhyn, 24 July 1803, MS 1322.

73. John Maxset to Tudway, 21 January 1805, SomRO, DD/TD 12.

74. Davidson and Graham to Penrhyn, 22 July 1803, UWB, Penrhyn MS 1322.

75. Fearon to Penrhyn, 10 July 1806, 2 April 1807, MSS 1429, 1468.

76. Barham to Plummer, December 1808.

77. Barham to Grant and Blyth, 11 December 1808, Bodl., Barham Papers 428.

Chapter 5. Debt, Decline, and the Sugar Industry, 1775–1810

1. See Sheridan, *Sugar and Slavery.*

2. Pares, *A West-India Fortune,* 250.

3. Sheridan, *Sugar and Slavery,* 466.

4. See Carrington, *British West Indies.*

5. Sheridan, *Sugar and Slavery,* 262–63.

6. Pares, "Merchants and Planters," 50.

7. Carrington, *British West Indies,* 21–22.

8. Long, *The History of Jamaica,* 1:451–61.

9. Richard Brissett, John Sharp, William Barnett, 10 February 1775, JRO, Tweedie Estate Records 4/45/11, fol. 119.

10. Rooke Clarke to Brothers, 10 May 1774, JRO, Tweedie Estate Records 4/45/6.

11. Clarke to Mary Clarke, 10 May 1774, ibid.

12. "A List of Debts Due from the Estate of Rooke Clarke," 1 January 1789, 4/45/65.

13. Mary Clarke to Ann Clarke, 13 May 1791, 4/45/17.

14. Clarke to Clarke, 10 December 1781, 4/45/7; see Pares, *A West-India Fortune,* 244.

15. Houston and Co. to Alexander Wilson, 7 February, NLS, MSS 8793, fol. 166.

16. Sheridan, *Sugar and Slavery,* 266–67.

17. Rowland Williams Fearon to Lord Penrhyn, 16 March 1805, UWB, Penrhyn MS 1366.

18. John Kelly to Jacob Franks, 16 October 1810, Cooper-Franks MSS, LMA, Acc. 775/928/4.

19. Rooke Clarke to Brothers, 10 May 1774, JRO, Tweedie Estate Records 4/45/6.

20. Mary Clarke to Ann Clarke, n.d., 4/45/16; see also 31 March 1789.

21. Rooke Clarke to Mary Clarke, 10 December 1781, 4/45/7.

22. Carrington, "British West Indies Economic Decline and Abolition," 54.

23. Pares, "Merchants and Planters," 38.

24. Sheridan, *Sugar and Slavery,* 278.

25. John Shickle to John Pennant, 21 December 1772, UWB, Penrhyn MS 1207; 6 March 1775, MS 1219; 2 October 1775, MS 1225; 30 September 1776, MS 1224.

26. Pares, "Merchants and Planters," 40.

27. Taylor, "Planter Attitudes," 113, 114; see J. Lindsay, "The Pennants and Jamaica."

28. Pares, *A West-India Fortune,* 244; Edwards, *History*; J. Lindsay, "The Pennants and Jamaica," 66; *Journals of the Assembly of Jamaica,* 9:145.

29. Houston and Co. to Turner and Paul (St. Vincent), 27 May 1778, NLS, MSS 8794, fol. 3.

30. Carrington, *British West Indies,* 125; Thomas Shirley to Lord Sydney, 7 May 1785, PRO, CO 152/64; A. Nugent to Earl of Camden, 18 November 1804, PRO, CO 137/113; see chaps. 8–10.

31. Richard Pennant to Alexander Falconer, 25 March 1783, UWB, Penrhyn MS 1255.

32. Pennant to Shickle, 12 February 1781, MS 1236; to Falconer, 1782, MS 1248.

33. James Nisbet to Stapleton, 28 August 1784, UWB, Stapleton-Cotton MSS 18.

34. Walter Nisbet to Madam (Stapleton), 15 January 1784.

35. Letter to Mr. Hering, 28 August 1787, UWB, Penrhyn MS 1264; see Penrhyn to Fearon, 8 January 1805, MS 1379; 2 April 1805, MS 1371.

36. Fearon to Penrhyn, 25 April 1806, MS 1419.

37. "Charges in Peace, Exclusive of Duty," [1781], BL, Add. MSS 18,273, fol. 44.

38. Pennant to Hering, 14 October 1787, UWB, Penrhyn MS 1265.

39. J. Robley and Co. to Sir William Young, n.d., Young Papers, RHL, W.Ind. t.1., vol. 1, fol. 88.

40. [Nisbet] to Stapleton, 18 March 1789, UWB, Stapleton-Cotton MSS 23(vi); Nisbet to Madam, 23 May 1788, ibid.

41. Thomson to Stapleton, 21 April 1789, ibid.

42. Transactions between Sir William Young and Messrs J. Robley & Co., n.d., MSS W.Ind. t.1, vol. 1.

43. Houston and Co. to Walter Nisbet, 2 May 1777, NLS, MSS 8793, fol. 238; see 28 May 1778, fol. 18; 20 July 1778, fol. 41.

44. Rooke Clarke to Mary Clarke, 10 December 1781, JRO, Tweedie Estate Records 4/45/7.

45. Nisbet to Madam, 12 April 1791, UWB, Stapleton-Cotton MSS.

46. Kelly to Franks, 25 October 1809, Cooper-Franks MSS, LMA, Acc. 775/928/1.

47. J. Lindsay, "The Pennants and Jamaica," 79.

48. "Old Road Estate, Antigua," n.d., Young Papers, RHL, W.Ind. t.1, vol. 1, fol. 17.

49. Shickle to Pennant, 30 September 1776, UWB, Penrhyn MS 1224.

50. Pennant to Shickle, 28 December 1781, MS 1247; 24 March 1782, MS 1250.

51. Pennant to Hering, 28 January 1787, MS 1259.

52. Barham to Wedderburn and Graham, n.d., Bodl., Barham Papers 428, fols. 8–9.

53. Turner to Hodgson, 16 April 1792, JRO, Tweedie Estate Records 4/45/66, fols. 75–76.

54. Penrhyn to Falconer, 10 December 1782, MS 1253.

55. Turner to Hodgson, 16 April 1792, JRO, Tweedie Estate Records 4/45/66, fols. 75–76.

56. Fearon to Penrhyn, 26 January 1805, UWB, Penrhyn MS 1361.

57. Penrhyn to Fearon, 20 December 1804, MS 1357; see also letters dated 25 October 1805, MS 1364; 16 March 1806, MS 1366.

58. See Pares, *A West-India Fortune,* 120.

59. Penrhyn to Hering, 28 April 1787, UWB, Penrhyn MS 1261.

60. Penrhyn to Hering, 26 July 1878, MS 1263; to Fearon, 30 October 1804, MS 1349.

61. Pares, *A West-India Fortune,* 126, 250, 263; Pares, "Merchants and Planters," 41; J. Lindsay, "The Pennants and Jamaica," 40, 59.

62. Richard and Thomas Neave to Stapleton, 1 June 1792, UWB, Stapleton-Cotton MSS 9(ii); Richard Neave to Stapleton, [1787/1788].

63. Drescher, *Econocide*; Ward, *British West Indian Slavery.*

64. Neave to Stapleton, 1 August 1796, UWB, Stapleton-Cotton MSS 9(ii).

65. Pares, *A West-India Fortune,* 120.

66. Davidson and Graham to Penrhyn, 22 July 1803, UWB, Penrhyn MS 1322.

67. Ibid.

68. Pares, *A West-India Fortune,* 258.

69. Henry Davidson to Penrhyn, 13 November 1806, UWB, Penrhyn MS 1442.

70. Mary Marchant to Lady Liston, 10 February 1806, NLS, MSS 5610, fol. 14; Fearon to Penrhyn, 10 July 1806, UWB, Penrhyn MS 1429.

71. Pares, "Merchants and Planters," 41.

Chapter 6. New Management Techniques and Planter Reforms

1. Long, *History of Jamaica,* BL, Add. MSS 12,404, fol. 345.

2. Sheridan, *Doctors and Slaves,* 145; Roughley, *A Jamaican Planter's Guide,* 3–9.

3. Roughley, *A Jamaican Planter's Guide,* 3–9.

4. Ibid., 10–11; Sheridan, *Doctors and Slaves,* 145–46.

5. Luffman, *Antigua,* 43–45, 49.

6. Roughley, *A Jamaican Planter's Guide,* 39, 9.

7. Walter Nisbet to Catherine Stapleton, 10 July 1783, UWB, Stapleton-Cotton MSS 18.

8. Nisbet to Madam, 18 June 1786, NLW, Bodrhyddan MSS, box 2.

9. Robert Logan to Nathaniel Phillips, 23 May 1784, NLW, Slebech Papers 8878; Thomas Barritt to Phillips, 23 May 1784 bundle 9634.

10. Barham to Jefferies, 26 June 1801, Bodl., Barham Papers 428.

11. Barham to Plummer, 21 July 1798, Bodl., Barham Papers 357.

12. Barham to White and Webb, 1 July 1804, Bodl., Barham Papers 428.

13. Simon Taylor to Jack (Sir John Taylor), n.d. and 24 November 1783, ICS, Simon Taylor Letter Books, vol. 1A.

14. *Short Sketch,* 11; Luffman, *Antigua,* 99–100.

15. Roughley, *A Jamaican Planter's Guide,* 79; for a detailed look at the issue of labour and mortality, see Higman, *Slave Populations.*

16. Barham to Rowe, April 1789, Bodl., Barham Papers 428.

17. Ward, *British West Indian Slavery,* 209–15.

18. Barham to Wedderburn, Grant and Blyth, n.d., ibid.; see Pinckard, *Notes,* 198.

19. Barham to Jefferies, 23 June 1801, Bodl., Barham Papers 428; to Webb and White, 1 July 1804.

20. Barham to Grant and Blyth, 10 December 1808.

21. Barham to Grant and Blyth, 3 July 1809.

22. J. Lindsay, "The Pennants and Jamaica," 77.

23. Barritt to Phillips, 8 October 1784, NLW, Slebech Papers 8437.

24. "Negroes Imported from Africa into Jamaica, 16 December 1787," BL, Add. MSS 12,431, fol. 222.

25. "An Act to Repeal Several Acts, and Clauses of Acts Respecting Slaves, and for the Better Order and Government of Slaves, and Other Purposes," 2 December 1787, PRO, CO 137/87; "Code of Laws for the Government of Slaves in Jamaica," 23 January 1789, PRO, CO 137/88; J. Lindsay, "The Pennants and Jamaica," 87.

26. Thomson to Shipley, 16 December 1798, 22 June 1799, NLW, Bodrhyddan MSS, box 2.

27. Pinckard, *Notes,* 198; see Dickson, *Letters on Slavery.*

28. "Notes," n.d., NLW, Slebech Papers 8874.

29. James Laing to N. W. Senior, 6 September 1786, NLW, Nassau-Senior Papers E81.

30. Dickson, *Mitigation of Slavery.*

31. *Short Sketch,* 11.

32. Luffman, *Antigua,* 93–97.

33. Dickson, *Letters on Slavery,* 13.

34. Pinckard, *Notes,* 301.

35. J. Lindsay, "The Pennants and Jamaica," 60–62.

36. Main Swete Waldron to Tudway, 3 May 1788, SomRO, DD/TD 11/6. The issue was whether beans or corn was more wholesome for Negroes.

37. Frederick Goulburn to Henry Goulburn, 22 February 1818, SurRO, Goulburn Papers 319/51/3Q.

38. J. Lindsay, "The Pennants and Jamaica," 79.

39. Ibid., 82.

40. John Mair to Senior, [1782], NLW, Nassau-Senior Papers E51.

41. Barham to Grant and Blyth, 10 December 1808, Bodl., Barham Papers 428.

42. Letter from Catherine Stapleton, 24 October 1794, NLW, Bodrhyddan MSS, box 2.

43. Barham to Wedderburn and Graham, 4 December 1794, Bodl., Barham Papers 428.

44. Pinckard, *Notes,* 179, 299–300; Kelly to Franks, Cooper-Franks MSS, LMA, Acc. 775/928/4.

45. Luffman, *Antigua,* 130–34.

46. Pinckard, *Notes,* 343.

47. Ibid., p. 140.

48. Penrhyn to Fearon, 3 December 1804, UWB, Penrhyn MS 1354; Simon Taylor to John Taylor, 6 August 1798, ICS, Simon Taylor Letter Books, vol. 1B.

49. Fearon to Penrhyn, 20 January 1805, UWB, Penrhyn MS 1361.

50. Pinckard, *Notes,* 457.

51. Luffman, *Antigua,* 112–13.

52. Plummer to Barham, 23 September 1799, Bodl., Barham Papers 357; Barham to White and Webb, 1 July 1804, Bodl., Barham Papers 428.

53. J. Lindsay, "The Pennants and Jamaica," 78.

54. Barham to Dear Sir, n.d., Bodl., Barham Papers 428, fol. 22.

55. Hibbert and Taylor to Sir Hugh Smyth, 10 August 1797, BRO, Ac/Wo 16(27) 171(a).

56. Fearon to Penrhyn, 16 March 1805, UWB, Penrhyn MS 1366.

57. Penrhyn to Fearon, 25 October 1805, MS 1364.

58. J. Lindsay, "The Pennants and Jamaica," 63–64.

59. Pares, "Merchants and Planters," 39.

60. Penrhyn to Falconer, 10 December 1782, UWB, Penrhyn MS 1253.

61. Penrhyn to Hering, 18 February 1788, MS 1267; Turner to Hodgson, 16 April 1792, JRO, Tweedie Estate Records 4/45/66, fols. 75–76.

62. Barham to Wedderburn and Graham, 23 June 1792, Bodl., Barham Papers 428, fols. 16–17; Henry Goulburn to Samson, 29 June 1804, SurRO, Goulburn Papers 319/54; Fearon to Penrhyn, 26 January 1805, UWB, Penrhyn MS 1361.

63. Simon Taylor to Sir John Taylor, 3 December 1798, ICS, Simon Taylor Letter Books, vol. 1B.

64. Thomson to Nisbet, 23 April 1789, UWB, Stapleton-Cotton MSS 23(vi).

65. Penrhyn to Mr. Fraser, 30 October 1804, UWB, Penrhyn MS 1349; Barham to Grant and Blyth, 10 December 1808, Bodl., Barham Papers 428.

66. Ibid.

67. Evidence of John Giles, in Lambert, *Sessional Papers*, vol. 82, pp. 77 ff.; Luffman, *Antigua*, 93–97.

68. Pinckard, *Notes*, 300.

69. Frederick Goulburn to Henry Goulburn, 22 February 1818, SurRO, Goulburn Papers 319/51/3Q.

70. Evidence of Mr. Towne, in Lambert, *Sessional Papers*, 82:43.

71. Luffman, *Antigua*, 54.

72. "Queries and Answers from His Excellency," 18 August 1788, PRO, CO 28/61.

73. Evidence of Dr. Harrison and of John Giles, in Lambert, *Sessional Papers*, 82:52; see Pinckard, *Notes*, 198 ff.

74. Barham to Grant and Blyth, 4 June 1811, Bodl., Barham Papers 428.

75. Barham to Wedderburn and Graham, 23 June 1792, Bodl., Barham Papers 428, fols. 16–17; Penrhyn to Falconer, 10 December 1792, UWB, Penrhyn MS 1253; Turner to Hodgson, 16 April 1792, JRO, Tweedie Estate Records 4/45/66, fols. 75–76.

76. David Ewart to Penrhyn, 6 August 1807, UWB, Penrhyn MS 1477.

77. Barham to Webb, 7 June 1810, Bodl., Barham Papers 428.

78. Penrhyn to Fearon, 25 May 1807, UWB, Penrhyn MS 1478.

79. Samson to Goulburn, 19 January 1806, SurRO, Goulburn Papers 319/51/3Q.

80. Evidence of Mr. Coor, in Lambert, *Sessional Papers*, 82:89; for a comparison, see Samson to Goulburn, 19 January 1806, SurRO, Goulburn Papers 319/51/3Q.

81. "Notes," n.d., NLW, Slebech Papers 8874; Penrhyn to Fraser, 30 October 1804, UWB, Penrhyn MS 1349.

82. Barham to Wedderburn and Graham, 23 June 1792, Bodl., Barham Papers 428; see Turner to Hodgson, 16 April 1792, JRO, Tweedie Estate Records 4/45/66, fols. 75–76; see Barham to Webb, 7 June 1810, Bodl., Barham Papers 428.

83. Ewart to Penrhyn, 6 August 1807, UWB, Penrhyn MS 1477.

84. Thomson to Nisbet, 23 April 1789, UWB, Stapleton- Cotton MSS 23(vi).

85. Pinckard, *Notes*, 199–200.

86. Penrhyn to Fearon, 23 August 1805, UWB, Penrhyn MS 1388; Barham to Webb and White, 1 July 1804, Bodl., Barham Papers 428.

87. See Fearon to Penrhyn, 9 June 1804, UWB, Penrhyn MS 1327; also Dickinson to Salmon, 1 December 1792, SomRO, DD/DN 468.

88. Thomson to Mrs. Shipley, 26 October 1798, NLW, Bodrhyddan MSS, box 1; Jefferies and William Rodgers to Barham, 22 September 1802, Bodl., Barham Papers 357; see Barham to Jefferies and Rodgers, 8 July 1802, Bodl., Barham Papers 428; George Ottley to Tudway, 1 February 1809, SomRO, DD/TD 11/7.

89. Richard Pennant to John Shickle, 12 February 1781, UWB, Penrhyn MS 1236; Fearon to Penrhyn, 27 July 1805, MS 1383; J. Lindsay, "The Pennants and Jamaica."

90. Galloway, *The Sugar Cane Industry*, 95.

91. Fearon to Penrhyn, 9 June 1805, UWB, Penrhyn MS 1327; Penrhyn to Fearon, 28 August 1804, MS 1337; see J. Lindsay, "The Pennants and Jamaica," 79.

92. Fearon to Penrhyn, 26 January 1805, MS 1361; Galloway, *The Sugar Cane Industry*, 95.

93. J. Lindsay, "The Pennants and Jamaica," 79.

94. Fearon to Penrhyn, 8 June 1805, UWB, Penrhyn MS 1378.

95. Barham to Grant and Blyth, 10 December 1808, Bodl., Barham Papers 428.

96. Stephens and Co. to Smyth, 20 September 1782, BRO, 16(27) 112(b).

97. Richard and Thomas Neave to Stapleton, 4 May 1795, NLW, Bodrhyddan MSS, box 2.

98. Barham to Jefferies, 25 June 1801, Bodl., Barham Papers 428; "A Paper," n.d., SurRO, Goulburn Papers 319/52.

99. Penrhyn to Hering, 14 October 1787, UWB, Penrhyn MS 1265.

100. Barham to Jefferies, May 1802, Bodl., Barham Papers 428.

101. Barham to Wedderburn and Co., 5 September 1806, Bodl., Barham Papers 428.

102. Plummer to Barham, n.d., Bodl., Barham Papers 375.

103. Barham to Wedderburn and Co., 15 September 1806, Bodl., Barham Papers 428; July 1808, fol. 125.

104. Barham to Wedderburn and Graham, 28 August 1794, Bodl., Barham Papers 428.

105. Penrhyn to Falconer, 19 May 1782, UWB, Penrhyn MS 1256.

106. J. Lindsay, "The Pennants and Jamaica," 66.

107. Jefferies to Penrhyn, 20 April 1807, UWB, Penrhyn MS 1463.

Chapter 7. Hired Slave Labour

1. Higman, *Slave Populations*, 226–45.

2. See James Craggs to Henry Goulburn, 1 September 1793, SurRO, Goulburn Papers 319/53.

3. Higman, *Slave Populations*, 226.

4. Dickson, *Mitigation of Slavery*, 11.

5. See Higman, *Slave Populations*, and Johnson, *Bahamas*, for their views on the issue.

6. "Answer to Queries," December 1788, PRO, CO 152/67.

7. "Answers to Queries," 1 July 1788, PRO, CO 260/8; "Queries from His Excellency Governor Parry in Barbados—Answers by a Planter," 18 August 1788, PRO, CO 28/61, fols. 216d–217. It has been suggested that cane holes were smaller than the size used in this book. The Barbados measurements given here are applicable to discussion on Jamaica.

8. Samson to Goulburn, 4 October 1804, SurRO, Goulburn Papers 319/51.

9. Hibbert, Stephens and Raester to John Hugh Smyth, 28 March 1785, BRO, Ac/Wo 123/16(27).

10. Simon Taylor to Jack (Sir John Taylor), 13 April 1784, ICS, Simon Taylor Letter Books, vol. 1A; see also Samson to Goulburn, 7 December 1812, SurRO, Goulburn Papers 319/51.

11. "Answers to Queries," December 1788, PRO, CO 152/67.

12. "Answers to Queries," 4 October 1788, PRO, CO 71/4; December 1788, PRO, CO 152/67.

13. Lambert, *Sessional Papers*, 82:96.

14. "Settlers in the Parish of St. James Next in Degree to Sugar Planters," September 1774, BL, Add. MSS 12,435, fol. 3d.

15. Dickson, *Mitigation of Slavery*, 22.

16. Barham to Graham and Plummer, n.d., Bodl., Barham Papers 428.

17. For a discussion of early attempts to ameliorate slave conditions, see Ward, *British West Indian Slavery*, chap. 6.

18. Barham to Gentlemen, 1 June 1796, Bodl., Barham Papers 428.

19. J. Lindsay, "The Pennants and Jamaica," pt. 1; Penrhyn to Hering, 28 April 1787, UWB, Penrhyn MS 1261.

20. Ward, *British West Indian Slavery*, 209–15.

21. Samuel Eliot to Tudway, 1 January 1801, SomRO, DD/TD, 11/617; see Sheridan, *Doctors and Slaves*.

22. Samson to Goulburn, 22 June 1812, SurRO, Goulburn Papers 319/51.

23. Bernard and William Dickinson to Thomas S. Salmon, 1 December 1792, SomRO, DD/DN 468.

24. Letter to George Scott, 15 October 1788, Cooper-Franks MSS, LMA, Acc. 775/943/1.

25. Carrington, "Economic and Political Development."

26. List of Negroes belonging to Spring Plantation, 1 January 1784, BRO, Ac/Wo 16(27) 120(e); also 166(d); "Inventory of Slaves on Grand Bras Estates," De-

cember 1805, Cooper-Franks MSS, LMA, Acc. 775/953/13; Ottley to Tudway, 1 February, SomRO, DD/TD, 11/7.

27. Thomson to Catherine Shipley, 25 October 1798, NLW, Bodrhyddan MSS, box 1.

28. Stephens and Co. to John Hugh Smyth, 20 September 1782, BRO, Ac/Wo 16(27) 112(b); 28 March 1785, Ac/Wo 16(27) 123(b).

29. James Seton to Lord Sydney, 29 December 1789, PRO, CO 260/8.

30. Dundas to Williamson, 8 March 1792, PRO, CO 137/90.

31. Samson to Goulburn, 7 December 1812, SurRO, Goulburn Papers 319/51.

32. Evidence of Captain Cook, 5 March 1791, and William Fitzmaurice, 12 March 1791, in Lambert, *Sessional Papers,* vol. 82.

33. Pinckard, *Notes,* 111–17.

34. See Johnson, *Bahamas,* 1–13.

35. Luffman, *Antigua,* 99–100. A "dog" was a unit of money used in Antigua. For the practice, see evidence of Thomas Clapperon, 10 March 1791, in Lambert, *Sessional Papers,* 82:211.

36. *Papers,* ibid.; evidence of Fitzmaurice, ibid., 82:220; Higman, *Slave Populations,* 245; Johnson, *Bahamas,* 6.

37. Higman, *Slave Populations,* 244–45; Johnson, *Bahamas,* 1 ff.

38. Thomas Barritt to Nathaniel Phillips, 4 August 1792, NLW, Slebech Papers 8402.

39. Extract from *St. Vincent Gazette,* Saturday, 4 October 1806, PRO, CO 260/20.

40. John Kelly to Jacob Franks, 28 October 1809, Cooper-Franks MSS, LMA, Acc. 775/928/1.

41. Higman, *Slave Populations;* he discusses hard labour and high mortality rates on West Indian plantations.

42. "Settlers," BL, Add. MSS 12,435, fols. 3–3d.

43. Dalhousie and Stephens to Smyth, 14 January 1778, BRO, Ac/Wo 16(27), pp. 84–106.

44. Falconer to William Gore, 3 September 1802, SurRO, Goulburn Papers 319/52/3B1; Craggs to Mrs. Goulburn, 23 October 1798, 319/53.

45. Barritt to Phillips, 11 April 1793, NLW, Slebech Papers 8414; Craggs to Mrs. Goulburn, 12 October 1789, SurRO, Goulburn Papers 319/53; Craggs to Goulburn, 13 February 1801, 319/51; Plummer to Barham, 19 February 1800, Bodl., Barham Papers 357; John Wedderburn to Barham, 14 December 1789.

46. Stephens and Co. to Smyth, 20 September 1782, BRO, Ac/Wo 16(27) 112(b).

47. Falconer to Gore, 3 September 1802, SurRO, Goulburn Papers 319/52/3B1.

48. Craggs to Mrs. Goulburn, 23 October 1798, SurRO, Goulburn Papers 319/53.

49. Racher Webb to Barham, 30 September 1801, Bodl., Barham Papers 357/3.

50. Wedderburn to Barham, 24 October 1795, Bodl., Barham Papers 357.

51. Thomson to William Shipley, 22 July 1800, NLW, Bodrhyddan MSS, box 2.

52. "Answers to Head of Enquiry," 13 May 1788, PRO, CO 28/61, fol. 164; Craggs to Mrs. Goulburn, 12 October 1798, SurRO, Goulburn Papers 319/53.

53. J. Lindsay, "The Pennants and Jamaica," 57; Webb to Barham, 30 September 1801, Bodl., Barham Papers 357/3.

54. Craggs to Mrs. Goulburn, 6 August 1801, SurRO, Goulburn Papers 319/51.

55. Craggs to Mrs. Goulburn, 13 February 1801.

56. Craggs to Mrs. Goulburn, 12 October 1798, 319/53; letter to George Scott, 15 October 1788, Cooper-Franks MSS, LMA, Acc. 775/943/1; Barham to Rowe, 31 March 1794, Bodl., Barham Papers 428.

57. Mair to A. W. Senior, 1782, NLW, Nassau-Senior Papers E51(a).

58. "Answers to Queries," 13 May 1788, PRO, CO 28/61, fols. 157d–158.

59. "The State of Dominica," n.d., PRO, CO 318/2, fol. 18; Ragatz, Statistics, 5.

60. "Answers to Queries: Queries from Parry—Answered by a Planter," 18 August 1788, PRO, CO 28/61, fols. 216d–217.

61. Evidence of Captain Giles, 21 February 1791, in Lambert, Sessional Papers, vol. 82.

62. William Peete and James Clarke to George Sobin, 21 May 1785, BRO, Ac/Wo 16(27) 126(c).

63. "Answers to Queries," December 1788, PRO, CO 152/67.

64. "Answers to Queries," 4 October 1788, PRO, CO 71/14. In Grenada, Lord George Macartney paid £292 10s to hire thirty-one Negroes for the period 1 May to 4 July 1779; this amounted to 90s per day, or a scant 3s a day for each Negro (Government of Grenada to Rowley Lascelles, RHL, W.Ind. s.9, fol. 94).

65. "Answers to Queries," 1 July 1788, PRO, CO 260/8.

66. Muir to Senior, 15 May 1782, NLW, Nassau-Senior Papers E53; Samson to Goulburn, 7 December 1812, SurRO, Goulburn Papers 319/51.

67. "Answers to Queries," 4 October 1788, PRO,CO 71/14; evidence of Thomas Clapperon, 8 March 1791, in Lambert, Sessional Papers, 82:211.

68. Journal of the Assembly of Jamaica 9 (1792).

69. Robert Hibbert and Co. to Smyth, 6 March 1785, BRO, Ac/Wo 16(27) 161.

70. Wedderburn to Barham, 14 December 1789, Bodl., Barham Papers 357.

71. Graham to Barham, 5 October 1794, Bodl., Barham Papers 357/2; Rowe to Barham, 4 July 1789.

72. Craggs to Madam (Mrs. Goulburn), 20 November 1798, SurRO, Goulburn Papers 319/53.

73. Barritt to Phillips, 7 August 1793, NLW, Slebech Papers 8420; 4 April 1792, bundle 8390.

74. Butler, "Mortality and Labour," 57.

75. Craggs to Mrs. Goulburn, 28 February 1797, SurRO, Goulburn Papers 319/54.

76. Plummer to Barham, 8 September 1800, Bodl., Barham Papers 357.

77. Duckenfield Hall Plantation Account with Turney and Jameson, [1789], Cooper-Franks MSS, LMA, Acc. 775/943/6; Duckenfield Hall Plantation Account with George Scott, 31 December 1790, Acc. 775/943/5; Duckenfield Hall Plantation Account Current with George Scott, 31 December 1791, Acc. 775/943/5; Duckenfield Hall Estate Account with MacBean and Bagnold, 31 December 1793, Acc. 775/947/6; Jacob Franks and John Nesbitt in Account Current with Sandford Peacocke, 31 December 1794, Acc. 775/948/2.

78. Account with J. C. Hughes, 18 July 1805, Cooper-Franks MSS, LMA, Acc. 775/953/10; Account Current with John Peter Hankey, 20 February 1806, Acc. 775/953/11; Duckenfield Hall Plantation Account Current, 30 June 1807, Acc. 775/953/20.

79. Ottley to Tudway, 1 February 1809, SomRO, DD/TD, 11/7.

80. Bernard and William Dickinson to Salmon, 1 December 1792, SomRO, DD/DN 468.

81. Estate of Nathaniel Phillips Esqr. in the Parish of St. Thomas, East Jamaica, n.d., NLW, Slebech Papers 8864.

82. Barham to Rowe, 31 March 1794, Bodl., Barham Papers 428.

83. Barham to Rowe, 5 December 1792.

84. Barham to Wedderburn Grant and Blyth, n.d.

85. Goulburn to Samson, 25 October 1814, SurRO, Goulburn Papers 319/51.

86. Barham to Jefferies, 7 July 1803, Bodl., Barham Papers 428.

87. Barham to Wedderburn and Co., 5 September 1806.

88. Penrhyn to Hering, 29 July 1777, UWB, Penrhyn MS 1263.

89. Penrhyn to Fearon, 30 October 1804, MS 1349.

90. Fearon to Penrhyn, 27 July 1805, MS 1383.

91. Muir to Senior, 15 May 1782, NLW, Nassau-Senior Papers E53.

92. Gore to Mrs. Goulburn, 28 October 1800, SurRO, Goulburn Papers 319/52.

93. Dickson, *Mitigation of Slavery*, 11.

94. Plummer to Barham, 31 January 1798, Bodl., Barham Papers 357.

95. Aufhauser, "Slavery and Technological Change," 36–50.

96. Frederick Goulburn to Henry Goulburn, 22 February 1818, SurRO, Goulburn Papers 319/51/3Q.

97. Dickson, *Mitigation of Slavery*, 11.

Chapter 8. British Caribbean Slavery and Abolition

1. Dickson, *Mitigation of Slavery*, 15.

2. Barham, *Considerations*, 29–30.

3. Klingberg, *Anti-slavery Movement*, 57.

4. "Letter to Proprietor on the Suspension of the Trade," n.d., Bodl., Barham Papers 377.

5. Letter from William Wilberforce, 23 November 1787, BL, Add. MSS 38,227, fols. 122–122d.

6. While there are statistics for all the islands, those for Jamaica are the most complete and illustrate the point quite well.

7. Sir John Gay Alleyne to H. T. Senior, 24 June 1785, NLW, Nassau-Senior Papers E64.

8. Parry to Dundas, 13 June 1793, PRO, CO 28/63, fols. 95d–96.

9. Rowe to Barham, 4 July 1789, Bodl., Barham Papers 387.

10. Wedderburn to Barham, 17 February 1791, ibid.

11. Jefferies and Rodgers to Barham, 3 August 1803, ibid.

12. Plummer to Barham, 10 June 1799, ibid.

13. Dickson, *Mitigation of Slavery*, 33–34.

14. Henry Goulburn to Samson, 3 August 1813, SurRO, Goulburn Papers 319/51.

15. Van Keelen to Barham, 4 June 1785, Bodl., Barham Papers 357; Graham to Barham, 6 September 1780, 5 September 1794; Wedderburn to Barham, 4 November 1794.

16. Thomson to Rev. Shipley, 16 March 1791, NLW, Bodrhyddan MSS, box 2.

17. White to William Dickinson, 17 November 1802, SomRO, DD/DN 474.

18. "Negroes Drafted from Watchwell to Pepper Penn," 1 January 1803, SomRO, DD/DN 473.

19. See James Laing to N. W. Senior, 5 September 1786, NLW, Nassau-Senior Papers E81; Henry W. Plummer to Barham, 10 June 1799, Bodl., Barham Papers 357/2; Dickson, *Mitigation*, pp. 33–34; Hibbert Hall and Fuhr to Smyth, 15 May 1790, BRO, Ac/Wo 16(27) 142(a).

20. Walrond to Tudway, 9 July 1784, SomRO, DD/TD 11/6; John Gray to Tudway, 15 October 1792, ibid.; Graham to Barham, 18 December 1792, Bodl., Barham Papers 357.

21. Thomson to Stapleton, 17 December 1787, UWB, Stapleton-Cotton MSS 23(vi).

22. Walrond to Tudway, 26 January 1790, SomRO, DD/TD 11/6; see Barritt to Phillips, 16 December 1789, NLW, Slebech Papers 8349; see also 29 June 1791, bundle 8376.

23. Barritt to Phillips, 9 September 1789, NLW, Slebech Papers 8345; see Barritt letter, 10 December 1797, bundle 8439.

24. Barritt to Phillips, 15 December 1793, NLW, Slebech Papers 8426; Graham to Barham, 29 January 1793, Bodl., Barham Papers 357/2.

25. Craggs to Goulburn, 8 August 1793, SurRO, Goulburn Papers 319/53.

26. Thomson to Shipley, 17 December 1793, NLW, Bodrhyddan MSS, box 2.

27. Graham to Barham, 15 October 1793, Bodl., Barham Papers 357 (in this letter he reported losing six slaves; he had fears of more dying); 2 November 1793.

28. Jefferies to Barham, 5 August 1802, Bodl., Barham Papers 357/3; Rodgers to Barham, 14 November 1803; J. Lindsay, "The Pennants and Jamaica," 79; Samson to Goulburn, 17 May 1810, SurRO, Goulburn Papers 319/52.

29. Sheridan, Doctor and Slaves, 279 ff.

30. Barham to Jefferies and Rodgers, 8 July 1802, Bodl., Barham Papers 428.

31. Thomson to Shipley, 16 March 1791, NLW, Bodrhyddan MSS, box 2; Barritt to Phillips, 6 September 1791, NLW, Slebech Papers 8382; Graham to Barham, 18 December 1792, Bodl., Barham Papers 357; Dickinson to Salmon, 28 February 1794, SomRO, DD/DN 468; letter to White, 4 August 1794.

32. J. Lindsay, "The Pennants and Jamaica," 83; see also UWB, Penrhyn MS 1484.

33. Penrhyn to Falconer, 17 April 1793, UWB, Penrhyn MS. 1256.

34. Evidence of Henry Coor, 18 February 1791, in Lambert, Sessional Papers, 82:89.

35. Evidence of John Giles, 82:77.

36. Ibid.

37. Samson to Goulburn, 28 April 1813, SurRO, Goulburn Papers 319/51.

38. Dickson, Mitigation of Slavery, 75.

39. Barham to Grant and Blyth, 3 July 1809, Bodl., Barham Papers 428; see J. Lindsay, "The Pennants and Jamaica," 74.

40. Claim for Fresh Evidence, 13–14.

41. Barham to Grant and Blyth, 4 June 1811, Bodl., Barham Papers 428.

42. Barham, "Increased Population," [1832], Bodl., Barham Papers 381/2, fols. 4–7.

43. Ibid.

44. Jefferies and Rodgers to Barham, 22 September 1802 (see also 3 August 1803), Bodl., Barham Papers 357.

45. J. Lindsay, "The Pennants and Jamaica," 75–76.

46. Ibid.

47. "Answers to Queries," 31 May 1788, PRO, CO 101/28.

48. "Of Particulars . . . in the Communication: Increased Population," n.d., Bodl., Barham Papers 381/2, fol. 3.

49. Pennant to Hering, 14 October 1787, UWB, Penrhyn MS 1265.

50. Eliot to Tudway, 4 December 1786, SomRO, DD/TD 11/6.

51. Dickson, *Mitigation of Slavery,* 101.

52. Ibid., 63, 101.

53. Barham to Grant and Blyth, 4 June 1811, Bodl., Barham Papers 428.

54. Dickson, *Mitigation of Slavery,* 205 n.

55. Lord Sydney to Governor Mathews, 6 November 1788, PRO, CO 101/28.

56. "Report of the Committee of the Assembly on the Subject of the Slave Trade and Treatment of Negroes," 19 October 1788, PRO, CO 137/87.

57. Extract of letter from Spanish Town to Stephen Fuller, 25 April 1788, PRO, CO 137/87.

58. Fuhr to Phillips, 6 February 1788, NLW, Slebech Papers 9105.

59. Hibbert, Fuhr and Hibbert to Phillips, 30 May 1788. ibid., 11554.

60. Nisbet to Madam, 23 May 1788, UWB Stapleton-Cotton MSS 23(vi).

61. Richard and Thomas Neave to Stapleton, 22 July 1788, UWB, Stapleton-Cotton MSS 9.

62. Hibbert, Fuhr and Hibbert to Phillips, 1 July 1788, NLW, Slebech Papers 11555; see copy of letter to Thomas Hibbert, 26 July 1788, bundle 9097; Hibbert Fuhr and Hibbert, 6 January 1789, bundle 11565.

63. Lord Grenville to Major-General Williamson, 21 April 1791, PRO, CO 137/89.

64. Barham to Rowe, 23 June 1791, Bodl., Barham Papers 428.

65. "Sketch of Report on the Slave Trade," n.d., Bodl., Barham Papers 377.

66. Richard and Thomas Neave to Stapleton, 6 March 1788, UWB, Stapleton-Cotton MSS. 9 (ii).

67. Turner to Hodgson, 16 April 1792, JRO, Tweedie Estate Records 4/45/66.

68. Report, 19 October 1788, PRO, CO 137/87.

69. David Evans to A. Dundas, 3 April 1792, Melville MSS, RHL, W.Ind. s.8, vol. 11.

70. Barham to Wedderburn and Graham, 3 June 1793, Bodl., Barham Papers 428.

71. Dickinsons to Salmon, 1 December 1792, SomRO, DD/DN 468.

72. Fuller to Sydney, 25 June 1788, PRO, CO 137/1788.

73. Parry to Grenville, 23 May 1791, PRO, CO 28/63; to Nepean, 13 June 1792, fols. 95d–96; to Dundas, 11 June 1793, fol. 93d.

74. Parry to Dundas, 26 December 1791, PRO, CO 28/63.

75. Thomson to Shipley, 20 July 1792, NLW, Bodrhyddan MSS, box 2.

76. Williamson to Dundas, 18 September 1791, PRO, CO 137/89.

77. Earl of Effingham to Dundas, 17 September 1791, PRO, CO 137/89.

78. Williamson to Dundas, 23 January 1793, PRO, CO 137/91, fol. 100.

79. Barritt to Phillips (P.S.), 8 December 1791, NLW, Slebech Papers 8386.

80. Statement made by Michael Keane, Attorney-General, 3 June 1792, PRO, CO 260/11.

81. Ibid.

82. Williamson to Dundas, 6 November 1791, PRO, CO 137/87.

83. Osborn to Phillips, 8 February 1792, NLW, Slebech Papers 9228.

84. Hibbert and Taylor to Smyth, 17 February 1787, BRO, AC/WO 16(27) 168(b).

85. Governor Ricketts to the Duke of Portland, 20 March 1795, PRO, CO 28/65.

86. Thomson to Shipley, 20 July 1792, NLW, Bodrhyddan MSS, box 2; see Barritt to Phillip, 8 February 1792, NLW, Slebech Papers 8388; also see Plummer to Barham, 24 May 1797, Bodl., Barham Papers 357.

87. Wedderburn to Barham, 22 January 1796, Bodl., Barham Papers 357/2.

88. Parry to Dundas, 26 December 1791, PRO, CO 28/63, fol. 76.

89. Barham, *Considerations*.

90. "Computation of the Annual Gain of a Jamaica Planter," n.d., BL, Add. MSS 12,413, fols. 70d–71.

91. Dickson, *Mitigation of Slavery*, 199.

92. A. Young, *Annals of Agriculture*, 4: 6, 96.

93. Dickson, *Mitigation of Slavery*, 15.

94. "Letter on the Suspension of the Trade," n.d., Bodl., Barham Papers 377.

95. Pringle, *Fall*, 13.

96. Dickson, *Mitigation of Slavery*, 43.

97. Pringle, *Fall*, 13.

98. Draft letter to Major-General Nugent, 1 August 1804, PRO, CO 137/112, fols. 82, 83, 84d.

99. George Nugent to E. Cooke, 30 August 1804, ibid.; see Jefferies to Penrhyn, 7 March 1807, UWB, Penrhyn MS 1463.

100. Jefferies to Penrhyn, 20 April 1807, MS 1463; Penrhyn to Jefferies, 26 February 1807, MS 1461.

101. Fearon to Penrhyn, 2 April 1807, MS 1468.

Chapter 9. The Sugar Industry and Eighteenth-Century Revolutions

1. Sheridan, *Sugar and Slavery*, 263.

2. J. Lindsay, "The Pennants and Jamaica," 39–40.

3. "Essay for Ascertaining the Value of the British Colonies," n.d., RHL, W.Ind. r.2.

4. Notes to the letter from the Committee of Correspondence of Jamaica to Stephen Fuller, 23 May 1792, PRO, CO 137/89.

5. Thomson to Shipley, 20 July 1792, NLW, Bodrhyddan MSS, box 2.

6. Nisbet to Madam, 23 May 1788, 24 January 1785, UWB, Stapleton-Cotton MSS 23(vi).

7. Thomson to Shipley, 21 July 1794, NLW, Bodrhyddan MSS, box 2.

8. Nisbet to Madam, 18 June 1786, ibid.

9. Eliot to Tudway, 15 June 1787, SomRO, DD/TD 11/6; see Eliot's letter of 3 November 1787; Thomson to Stapleton, 8 May 1788, NLW, Bodrhyddan MSS, box 2; Nisbet to Madam, 23 May 1788, UWB, Stapleton-Cotton MSS 23(vi).

10. Ibid.; Eliot to Tudway, 23 June 1789, SomRO, DD/TD 11/6; letter to Stapleton, 18 March 1789, UWB, Stapleton-Cotton MSS 23(vi).

11. Nisbet to Stapleton, 22 January 1790, UWB, Stapleton-Cotton MSS 18.

12. Eliot to Tudway, 24 July 1792, SomRO, DD/TD 11/6; Thomson to Shipley, 29 May 1793, NLW, Bodrhyddan MSS, box 2; Nisbet to Shipley, 23 September 1794; Thomson to Shipley, 25 July 1795, NLW, Bodrhyddan MSS, box 2.

13. Barritt to Phillips, 7 July 1789, NLW, Slebech Papers 8342; see his letter of 13 March 1790, bundle 8353.

14. Dickson, *Mitigation of Slavery,* 29.

15. Nisbet to Madam, 12 April 1791, UWB, Stapleton-Cotton MSS.

16. Ibid.; Wedderburn to Barham, 15 March 1791, Bodl., Barham Papers 357/2; Craggs to Goulburn, 8 August 1793, SurRO, Goulburn Papers 319/53; Craggs to Mrs. Mumbee Goulburn, 22 December 1796; see also letters of 15 February 1797 and 20 February 1800.

17. Ibid.; Thomson to Shipley, 25 July 1796, NLW, Bodrhyddan MSS, box 2.

18. Bishop to Duke of Portland, 15 October 1800, Seaforth Papers, NRA, GD 46/17/11.

19. Craggs to Mrs. Goulburn, 12 July 1797, SurRO, Goulburn Papers 319/53.

20. Hibbert Stephens Raester to Smyth, 16 November 1786, BRO, AC/Wo 16(27) 127(a). There were five hurricanes in the Caribbean region between 1780 and 1786. See also letter of 21 March 1800.

21. Penrhyn to Hering, 26 July 1787, UWB, Penrhyn MS 1263.

22. Barham to Charles Rowe, 5 December 1792, Bodl., Barham Papers 428.

23. President Bishop to Portland, 16 February 1800, PRO, CO 28/66, fol. 10d.

24. Thomson to Shipley, 21 July 1794, NLW, Bodrhyddan MSS, box 2.

25. Barham to Dear Sir, 6 July 1799, Bodl., Barham Papers 428.

26. Craggs to Goulburn, 1 September 1793, SurRO, Goulburn Papers 319/53; Craggs to Mrs. Goulburn, 18 March 1800.

27. Thomson to Shipley, 17 December 1793, NLW, Bodrhyddan MSS, box 2.

28. Nisbet to Shipley, 5 August 1794, NLW, Bodrhyddan MSS, box 2.

29. "Answers to Queries," n.d., PRO, CO 71/14; Thomson to Shipley, 17 December 1793, NLW, Bodrhyddan MSS, box 2.

30. Barham to Jefferies and Rodgers, May 1802, Bodl., Barham Papers 428.

31. Barham to Wedderburn and Co., 5 September 1806.

32. Galloway, *The Sugar Cane Industry*, 97.

33. Barritt to Phillips, 26 January 1791, NLW, Slebech Papers 8367.

34. Penrhyn to Fearon, 2 April 1805, UWB, Penrhyn MS 1371; see 24 April 1805, MS 1374.

35. Pares, *A West-India Fortune*, 111.

36. Fearon to Penrhyn, 16 March 1805, UWB, Penrhyn MS 1366.

37. See Galloway, *The Sugar Cane Industry*, 96.

38. Ibid.

39. Graham to Barham, 16 August 1797, Bodl., Barham Papers 357.

40. Thomson to Shipley, 16 February 1798, NLW, Bodrhyddan MSS, box 2; Plummer to Barham, 4 March 1800, Bodl., Barham Papers 357/3.

41. Plummer to Barham, 19 February, 8 September 1800, Bodl., Barham Papers 357; see his letter of 4 March 1800, 357/3.

42. Rodgers to Barham, 5 July 1802.

43. Pares, *A West-India Fortune*, 110.

44. Jefferies to Barham, 12 January 1804, Bodl., Barham Papers 357/3.

45. Barham to Jefferies and Rodgers, 7 July 1803, Bodl., Barham Papers 428, fol. 78.

46. Pares, *A West-India Fortune*, 110.

47. Penrhyn to Fearon, 24 April 1805, UWB, Penrhyn MS 1374.

48. Samson to Goulburn, 16 May, 1 May 1807, SurRO, Goulburn Papers 319/53.

49. Barham to Jefferies and Rodgers, 7 July 1803, Bodl., Barham Papers 428.

50. Barham to Plummer and Webb, 8 July 1802; to Plummer, 7 July 1803.

51. Barham to Wedderburn Grant and Blyth, 8 January 1807.

52. Kelly to Franks, 28 October, Cooper-Franks MSS, LMA, Acc. 775/928/1.

53. Barham to Wedderburn and Co., 5 September 1806, Bodl., Barham Papers 428.

54. Thomson to Stapleton, 21 April 1789, UWB, Stapleton-Cotton MSS 23(vi); Thomson to Shipley, 20 July 1792, NLW, Bodrhyddan MSS, box 2.

55. Nisbet to the Dean of St. Asaph, 13 April 1793.

56. Craggs to Goulburn, 11 June 1798, SurRO, Goulburn Papers 319/53; Samson to Goulburn, 4 July 1806, 319/51/3Q1.

57. Thomson to Shipley, 29 May 1798, NLW, Bodrhyddan MSS, box 2; see also Thomson to Stapleton, 16 July 1787, UWB, Stapleton-Cotton MSS 23(vi).

58. Nisbet to the Dean of St. Asaph, 13 April 1793, NLW, Bodrhyddan MSS, box 2.

59. Barritt to Phillips, 14 May 1794, NLW, Slebech Papers 8429.

60. Gray to Tudway, 28 July 1790, SomRO, DD/TD 11/6.

61. Barham to Webb, 1 July 1809, Bodl., Barham Papers 428, fol. 133.

62. Franklyn to My Lord (Hawkesbury), 16 September 1792, BL, Add. MSS 38,228, fol. 62.

63. Barham to Wedderburn Grant and Blyth, 8 January 1807, Bodl., Barham Papers 428.

64. Pennant to Falconer, 1782, UWB, Penrhyn MS 1248.

65. Dickinsons to Salmon, 2 September 1792, SomRO, DD/DN 468.

66. Barham to Wedderburn and Co., 5 September 1806, Bodl., Barham Papers 428.

67. Susannah Goulburn to Samson, 1802, SurRO, Goulburn Papers 319/52.

68. Penrhyn to Falconer, 25 March 1783, UWB, Penrhyn MS 1255.

69. Hibbert, Stephens, and Raester to Smyth, 28 March 1785, BRO, Ac/Wo 16(27) 123(b).

70. Letter to Dear Sir, 6 July 1799, Bodl., Barham Papers 428; Dickinson to Salmon, 1 December 1792, SomRO, DD/DN 468.

71. "Essay," RHL, W.Ind. r.2, fol. 74.

72. Muir to Senior, 20 July 1786, NLW, Nassau-Senior Papers E78.

73. Howard Johnson, *The Bahamas*, 26; Penrhyn to Falconer, 10 December 1782, UWB, Penrhyn MS 1253.

74. Nisbet to Madam, 23 May 1788, UWB, Stapleton-Cotton MSS 23(vi).

75. Parry to Nepean, 22 December 1787, PRO, CO 28/61, fols. 106–106d.

76. Mary Clarke to Ann Clarke, 13 May 1791, JRO, Tweedie Estate Records 4/45/17.

77. Mathews to Beckwith, 5 October 1807, PRO, CO 260/22; Beckwith to Castlereagh, 27 October 1807.

78. Beckwith to Castlereagh, 19 October 1807.

79. Penrhyn to Hering, 21 July 1787, UWB, Penrhyn MS 1263; to Hering, 28 August 1787, MS 1284; to Fearon, 8 January 1805, MS 1329.

80. Pringle, *Fall*, 13.

81. Barritt to Phillips, 18 January 1794, NLW, Slebech Papers 8426.

82. Fearon to Penrhyn, 25 April 1806, UWB Penrhyn MS 1419; Penrhyn to Fearon, 2 April 1805, MS 1371.

83. For a discussion of the earlier period, see *A Brief Account of the Present Declining State of the West Indies*," in West India Merchant.

84. Plummer to Barham, n.d., Bodl., Barham Papers 375.

85. Muir to Senior, 2 December 1782, NLW, Nassau-Senior Papers E54.

86. Dickson, *Mitigation of Slavery*, 43.

87. Pennant to Hering, 14 October 1787, UWB, Penrhyn MS 1265; see Plummer to Barham, 13 December 1800, Bodl., Barham Papers 362/1.

88. Barham to White and Webb, 1 July 1804, Bodl., Barham Papers 428; to Rodgers and Jefferies, 8 July 1802.

89. Plummer to Barham, n.d., Bodl., Barham Papers 375.

90. Nisbet to Madam, 12 April 1791, UWB, Stapleton-Cotton MSS.

91. "Answer to Queries," December 1788, PRO, CO 152/67.

92. Barham, *Considerations*, 51.

93. Plummer to Barham, n.d., Bodl., Barham Papers 375.

94. Eliot to Tudway, 31 July 1803, SomRO, DD/TD 11/7.

95. Ramsay, *Objections*, 17–18.

96. "Charges in Peace, Exclusive of Duties," [1781], BL, Add. MSS 18,273, fol. 44.

97. Barham to Gentlemen, July 1808, Bodl., Barham Papers 428, fols. 124–25.

98. Barham to Wedderburn Grant and Blyth, 8 January 1807, Bodl., Barham Papers 428, fol. 121.

99. Barham to Grant and Blyth, 3 July 1809, Bodl., Barham Papers 428, fol. 124.

100. Drescher, *Econocide*, 24, chap. 2.

101. "Essay," RHL, W.Ind. r.2, fol. 38.

102. Ibid.

103. Pares, *A West-India Fortune*, 259.

104. Nisbet to Madam, 12 April 1791, UWB, Stapleton-Cotton MSS; Gore to Mrs. Goulburn, 20 October 1803, SurRO, Goulburn Papers 319/52.

105. Simon Taylor to Sir John Taylor, 30 October 1782, ICS, Simon Taylor Letter Books, vol. 1A; see letters dated 30 March, 11 May, and 1 July 1783; Simon Taylor to Robert Taylor, 29 April 1799, vol. 1C.

106. Plummer to Barham, 7 January 1796, Bodl., Barham Papers 361/2.

107. Dickson, *Mitigation of Slavery*, 388.

Chapter 10. War, Trade, and Planter Survival, 1793–1810

1. Pares, "Merchants and Planters," 40–41.

2. J. Lindsay, "The Pennants and Jamaica."

3. Falconer to Gore, 3 September 1802, SurRO, Goulburn Papers 319/52/3B1.

4. Muir to Senior, 25 July 1780, NLW, Nassau-Senior Papers E46.

5. Henry Duke to Senior, 28 November 1780, NLW, Nassau-Senior Papers E49.

6. Taylor, "Planter Attitudes," 118, 119.

7. Nisbet to Madam, 15 January 1784, UWB, Stapleton-Cotton MSS 18.

8. Ibid.

9. Richard Neave to Stapleton, 3 April 1784, UWB, Stapleton-Cotton MSS 9(1).

10. Nisbet to Stapleton, 18 March 1789, UWB, Stapleton-Cotton MSS 23(vi).

11. Thomson to Stapleton, 21 April 1789, UWB, Stapleton-Cotton MSS 23(vi).

12. Hibbert, Stephens and Raester to Smyth, 28 March 1785, BRO, Ac/Wo 16(27) 123(b).

13. Nisbet to Stapleton, 18 March 1789, UWB, Stapleton- Cotton MSS 23(vi).

14. Pennant to Hering, 14 October 1787, UWB, Penrhyn MS 1265.

15. Nisbet to Madam, 12 April 1791, UWB, Stapleton-Cotton MSS.

16. "Reasons," 28 February 1792, NLW, Slebech Papers 11540.

17. Keane, 3 June 1792, PRO, CO 260/11.

18. Duffy, *Soldiers, Sugars, and Seapower,* chap. 15.

19. "Essay for Ascertaining the Value of the British Colonies," RHL, W.Ind. r.2.

20. Drescher, *Econocide*; Duffy, *Soldiers, Sugar, and Seapower.*

21. "Sugar Quantities Retained for Home Consumption," Dalhousie Papers, NAS, GD 45/7/5.

22. "Essay," RHL, W.Ind. r.2.

23. Ibid.

24. Ibid.

25. "Humble Petition of the Council and Assembly of Antigua," 28 June 1792, PRO, CO 152/72.

26. "Answers to Additional Heads of Enquiry No. 1," 13 May 1788, PRO, CO 28/61, fol. 170d.

27. M. Lewis to the Duke of Portland, 14 December 1798, PRO, CO 28/65, fol. 254.

28. Barham to Wedderburn and Graham, 28 August 1794, Bodl., Barham Papers 428, fol. 29.

29. Jefferies and Rodgers to Barham, 20 September 1802, Bodl., Barham Papers 357.

30. Appended to James Craggs, 16 October 1800, SurRO, Goulburn Papers 319/53.

31. Kelly to Franks, 28 October 1809, Cooper-Franks MSS, LMA, Acc. 775/928/1.

32. Kelly to Franks, 16 December 1810, Acc. 775/928/4.

33. Report of House of Assembly, 13 November 1807, PRO, CO 137/122.

34. See Carrington, "American Revolution, British Policy," 28–29.

35. Maitland to Windham, 9 February 1807, PRO, CO 101/45.

36. Shirley to Sydney, 4 September 1787, PRO, CO 152/65, no. 178.

37. Keane, 3 June 1792, PRO, CO 260/11.

38. Woodley to Dundas, 13 March 1793, PRO, CO 152/73, no. 41.

39. Lavington to Camden, 30 July 1805, PRO, CO 152/87.

40. Woodley to Dundas, 7 January 1793, PRO, CO 152/73, no. 133; "In Privy Council," 7 August 1793, PRO, CO 137/91, fol. 252d; Williamson to Dundas, 9 February 1794, PRO, CO 137/92, fol. 315; Balcarres to Portland, 14 August 1796, PRO, CO 137/98.

41. Gilbert Franklyn to Lord Hawkesbury, 15 September 1792, BL, Add. MSS 38,228, fol. 63.

42. Graham to Barham, 27 June 1792, Bodl., Barham Papers 357/2; Eliot to Tudway, 16 July 1793, SomRO, DD/TD 11/6.

43. "Humble Petition of the Council and Assembly of Antigua," 28 June 1792, PRO, CO 152/72.

44. Penrhyn to Falconer, 4 March 1783, UWB, Penrhyn MS 1255.

45. Walrond to Tudway, 29 April 1784, SomRO, DD/TD 11/6.

46. Walrond to Tudway, 14 March 1786.

47. Eliot to Tudway, 3 November 1787, ibid.

48. Thomson to Shipley, 6 April 1793, NLW, Bodrhyddan MSS, box 2.

49. Davis to Penrhyn, n.d., UWB, Penrhyn MS 1283.

50. Taylor, "Planter Attitudes," 121.

51. Davis to Penrhyn, n.d., UWB, Penrhyn MS 1253; Rodgers to Barham, 4 July 1801, Bodl., Barham Papers 357; John White to William Dickinson, 30 March 1803, SomRO, DD/DN 474; Fearon to Penrhyn, 1 September 1805, UWB, Penrhyn MS 1392.

52. Taylor, "Planter Attitudes," 123.

53. Craggs to Goulburn, 2 December 1793, SurRO, Goulburn Papers 319/53.

54. Simon Taylor to Fuller, 20 June 1793, SomRO, DD/DN 508/29–40.

55. Ibid.

56. Craggs to Goulburn, 13 December 1793, SurRO, Goulburn Papers 319/53.

57. Barritt to Phillips, 11 February 1794, NLW, Slebech Papers 8426.

58. Taylor to Fuller, 20 June 1793, SomRO, DD/DN 508/29–40.

59. Thomson to Shipley, 29 May 1793, NLW, Bodrhyddan MSS, box 2.

60. Thomson to Stapleton, 16 July 1787, UWB, Stapleton-Cotton MSS 23(vi).

61. Nisbet to Stapleton, 22 January 1790, UWB, Stapleton-Cotton MSS 18.

62. Lucas to Sydney, 19 July 1787, PRO, CO 101/27. Lucas refers to An Act to Continue the Laws for Regulating the Trade between the subjects of His Majesty's Dominions and the United States of America.

63. Parry to Dundas, 3 August 1793, PRO, CO 28/64, fol. 117.

64. Williamson to Dundas, 29 June 1793, PRO, CO 137/91, fol. 224.

65. Fuller to Dundas, 8 September 1793, PRO, CO 137/91, fols. 407–8; Dundas to Williamson, 8 November 1793, PRO, CO 137/91, fols. 298–298d; Williamson to Fuller, 11 June 1794, SomRO, DD/DN 508/103–46.

66. Charles Stirling, 1 March 1794, Abercairny MSS, NRA, GD 24/1/459.

67. Thomson to Shipley, 17 January 1794, NLW, Bodrhyddan MSS, box 2.

68. Fearon to Penrhyn, 1 September 1805, UWB, Penrhyn MS 1378.

69. Jefferies to Barham, 29 April 1802, Bodl., Barham Papers 357/3.

70. Fearon to Penrhyn, 17 November 1805, UWB, Penrhyn MS 1402.

71. Barritt to Phillips, 8 December 1791, NLW, Slebech Papers 8386; 4 July 1793, bundle 8421.

72. Craggs to Goulburn, 13 December 1793, SurRO, Goulburn Papers 319/53.

73. Eliot to Tudway, 3 May 1794, SomRO, DD/TD 11/6; Barritt to Phillips, 8 October 1794, NLW, Slebech Papers 8437.

74. Eliot to Tudway, 2 March, 15 November 1797, SomRO, DD/TD 11/71; see Ewart to Penrhyn, 4 July 1807, UWB, Penrhyn MS 1475.

75. Nisbet to the Dean of St. Asaph, 18 March 1798, NLW, Bodrhyddan MSS, box 2.

76. Thomson to Shipley, 22 June 1799, NLW, Bodrhyddan MSS, box 2.

77. Samson to Mrs. Goulburn, 13 April 1804, SurRO, Goulburn Papers 319/54; Samson to Goulburn, 3 August 1804, 319/51.

78. Barham to Wedderburn Grant and Blyth, 8 January 1807, Bodl., Barham Papers 428.

79. Ewart to Penrhyn, 4 July 1807, UWB, Penrhyn MS 1475.

80. Samson to Goulburn, 7 October 1803, SurRO, Goulburn Papers 319/53.

81. Eliot to Tudway, 15 November 1797, SomRO, DD/TD 11/7; see 5 November 1801, ibid.

82. Craggs to Thomas Lee, 17 August 1797, SurRO, Goulburn Papers 319/54; to Mrs. Goulburn, 20 September 1797, ibid.

83. Thomson to Shipley, 22 July 1800, NLW, Bodrhyddan MSS, box 2.

84. Pringle, *Fall,* 16.

85. See Pares, *A West-India Fortune,* 126; Samson to Mrs. Goulburn, 27 May 1805, SurRO, Goulburn Papers 319/53.

86. Barham to Fuller, 19 February 1794, SomRO, DD/DN 510/14–55; see "Extract from the Minute of a General Meeting of the West India Planters and Merchants," ibid.; William Bligh to West India Planters and Merchants, SomRO, DD/DN 511.

87. Taylor to Fuller, 20 June 1793, SomRO, DD/DN 508/29–40.

88. Plummer to Barham, n.d., Bodl., Barham Papers 362/1.

89. Lavington to Camden, 30 July 1805, PRO, CO 152/87.

90. Nisbet to the Dean of St. Asaph, 18 March 1798, NLW, Bodrhyddan MSS, box 2; Eliot to Tudway, 15 November 1797, SomRO, DD/TD 11/7.

91. Plummer to Barham, 5 September 1796, 4 July 1797, Bodl., Barham Papers 361/2.

92. See "Insurance," [1801], Cooper-Franks MSS, LMA, Acc. 775/946.

93. Davidson and Graham to Penrhyn, 20 July 1803, UWB, Penrhyn MS 1322; "Insurance," [1803], Cooper-Franks MSS, LMA, Acc. 775/946.

94. "Insurance," 14 November 1811, Cooper-Franks MSS, LMA, Acc. 775/946.

95. Parry to North, 16 December 1783, PRO, CO 28/60, fols. 71–72; draft letter to Parry, March 1784; Parry to Lord Sydney, 15 August 1784, fol. 149.

96. Atkinson to Nugent, 15 May 1803, PRO, CO 137/90.

97. Dundas to Williamson, 8 December 1792, PRO, CO 137/90.

98. Merchants of Kingston to Williamson, 4 September 1792, PRO, CO 137/90.

99. Earl of Balcarres to Portland, 9 July 1797, PRO, CO 137/98, fol. 258d.

100. Nugent to the Earl of Camden, 15 December 1804, PRO, CO 137/114.

101. Williamson to Dundas, 9 February 1794, PRO, CO 137/92, fol. 315.

102. "An Account of the Trade between St. Domingue and Jamaica," 31 August 1801, CO 137/107.

103. Committee of Correspondence to Sewell, Agent, 15 May 1797, PRO, CO 137/97.

104. Ibid.

105. Draft letter to the Earl of Balcarres, 1 December 1797, PRO, CO 137/98.

106. Seaforth to Castlereagh, 20 December 1805, PRO, CO 28/73, fols. 186–186d.

107. Draft letter to Major-General Nugent, 2 February 1803, PRO, CO 137/110; Atkinson to Nugent, 15 May 1803.

108. Lavington to Camden, 30 July 1805, PRO, CO 152/87.

109. Ibid.

110. Nugent to Camden, 18 November 1804, PRO, CO 137/113.

111. Address of the Council and Assembly to Lavington, 19 June 1805, PRO, CO 152/87; Lavington to Camden, 19 June, 30 July 1805; draft letter to Lord Lavington, 2 October 1805.

112. "Essay," RHL, W.Ind. r.2.

113. Thomson to Portland, 4 May 1798, PRO, CO 152/78, fol. 321.

114. Thomson to John King, 20 June 1799, PRO, CO 152/79.

115. Pringle, *Fall,* 13.

116. Gilbert Franklyn to My Lord [Hawkesbury], 15 September 1792, BL, Add. MSS 30,228, fol. 63.

Chapter 11. Profitability and Decline: Issues and Concepts–An Epilogue

1. See letter to Stapleton, 18 March 1789, UWB, Stapleton-Cotton MSS 23(vi); Nisbet to Stapleton, 10 July 1783, MSS 18; Neave to Stapleton, [1787/88], MSS 7(ii).

2. Davidson and Graham to Lord Penrhyn, 15 December 1804, UWB, Penrhyn

Papers; Barham to Dear Sir, 6 July 1799, Bodl., Barham Papers 428; Gore to Mrs. Goulburn, 24 October 1803, SurRO, Goulburn Papers 319/52.

3. Dickson, *Mitigation of Slavery*, 33–34.

4. "Diminution of Slave Population," n.d., BL, Add. MSS 18,273, fol. 92d.

5. Dickson, *Mitigation of Slavery*, 388.

6. Pringle, *Fall*, 11, 13; A. Young, *Annals of Agriculture*, 92–93.

7. Ramsay, *Objections*, 17–19.

8. Ibid., 26.

9. Ibid., 20.

10. Nisbet to Stapleton, 28 March 1794, 18, UWB Stapleton-Cotton MSS. 18; Barham to Wedderburn and Graham, 20 November 1790, Bodl., Barham Papers 428.

11. Pennant to Hering, 14 October 1787, UWB, Penrhyn MS 1265.

12. Barham to Wedderburn and Graham, 20 November 1790, Bodl., Barham Papers 428.

13. Barham to Jefferies, 8 July 1802.

14. Craggs to Madam, 12 October 1798, SurRO, Goulburn Papers 319/53.

15. Barham to Wedderburn and Graham, 1 June 1796, Bodl., Barham Papers 428; see also 23 June 1792; Pringle, *Fall*, 11.

16. Lord Dorset to Lord Hawkesbury, 21 May 1789, BL, Add. MSS 38,224, fol. 140.

17. "Thoughts on the Importance of Our Colonies in the West Indies," n.d., BL, Add. MSS 38,387, fols. 8–9.

18. The Committee of the Privy Council for Trade, July 1804, PRO, BT 6/88, fols. 3–5.

19. Gilbert Franklyn to Lord Hawkesbury, 15 September 1792, BL, Add. MSS 30,228, fol. 63.

20. *A Brief Account of the Present Declining State of the West Indies*, in West India Merchant.

21. Eliot to Tudway, 30 July 1803, SomRO, DD/TD 11/7; Penrhyn to Hering, 14 October 1787, UWB, Penrhyn MS. 1265.

22. Barham to Jefferies, 25 June 1801, Bodl., Barham Papers 428; to Rodgers and Jefferies, 8 July 1802.

23. See letters of May 1802, 7 July 1803, 5 September 1806.

24. "Thoughts on the Importance of our Colonies in the West Indies," n.d., BL, Add. MSS 38,387, fol. 7.

25. Plummer to Barham, n.d., Bodl., Barham Papers 375.

26. Dickson, *Mitigation of Slavery*, 388.

27. Barham, *Considerations*, 51.

28. James Ramsay to the Lord Bishop of London, 1 March 1778, Lambeth Palace Library, Fulham Papers, vol. 15.

29. This is supported by the later action of the planters of Guyana who destroyed the fruit trees and provision grounds to force the ex-slaves to be dependent on them after emancipation.

30. W. Young, *Common-Place Book,* 48.

31. A. Young, *Annals of Agriculture,* 96.

32. G. Wright, "Capitalism and Slavery," 867–69.

Bibliography

Primary Sources

Note: The repositories of manuscripts consulted include: in London, the British Library, Institute of Commonwealth Studies, Lambeth Palace Library, Public Record Office (with papers of the Admiralty, Board of Trade, Colonial Office, Custom House, High Court of Admiralty, Privy Council, and Treasury), and University of London; in Oxford, the Bodleian and Rhodes House Libraries; in Bristol, the Bristol Reference Library, Bristol Record Office, and University of Bristol Library; Somerset Record Office; Surrey Record Office; in Scotland, the National Archives and National Library; in Wales, the National Library and University of Wales, Bangor, Library; the Jamaica Record Office; the Elsa Goveia West India Reference Library, UMI; Mona and West India Library, St. Augustine. They are presented alphabetically.

BODLEIAN LIBRARY, OXFORD

The Barham Family Papers in the Clarendon MSS include these consulted items (Bodl. MSS Clarendon dep. C):

357–60. Letters and papers pertaining to the Barhams' Jamaica estates, 1747–1835; in 357, bundle 1, in the period of the American Revolution, letters from overseers in Jamaica about estate conditions, slaves, effect of the war on Jamaica, trade, shipping, and sugar and rum prices.

361. Letters on trade.

362. Information on problems of the sugar market.

375. Information on decline; issue of profitability of the estates.

381. Estimation of slave value and performance of slave labour.

428. Letters between Sir Joseph Foster Barham and estate managers.

BRISTOL RECORD OFFICE (BRISTOL ARCHIVES)

Woolnough Papers in the Ashton Court Collection Ac/Wo, 16(27). In the Spring Plantation Papers, letters of interest for the period.

BRISTOL REFERENCE LIBRARY (BRISTOL CITY LIBRARIES)

Cornwall Chronicle and Jamaica General Advertiser. 5 vols. 1776–94.

C. T. Jefferies Collection of Manuscripts. 16 vols. Vols. 8–13 used; in vol. 13, material on the

African slave trade of Bristol, also letters from the West Indies to Isaac Hobhouse and Partners regarding their estates and the slave trade.

BRITISH LIBRARY, LONDON

The manuscripts of the British Library (originally consulted at the British Museum reading room and now found at St. Pancras) include two collections of particular interest. The papers of Edward Long, planter, historian, and colonial official, invaluable for any study of West Indian history, comprise Add. MSS 12,402–40. The Liverpool Papers, the official papers of Charles Jenkinson, first earl of Liverpool, in Add. MSS, contain West Indies trade statistics, shipping returns, and information on British policy. The British Library papers consulted are Add. MSS 38,218–387.

Add. MSS 12,402–4. Long's manuscript copies of his *History of Jamaica* with corrections and additions.

Add. MSS 12,411–14. Notes on Jamaican history; trade statistics.

Add. MSS 12,415–21. James Knight's unpublished *History of Jamaica to 1746.*

Add. MSS 12,430. "Code de Noir 1788."

Add. MSS 12,431. Papers relating to Jamaican affairs.

Add. MSS 12,432. List of ships captured by American privateers during the American Revolution.

Add. MSS 12,435. Papers on the statistics of Jamaica, 1739–70.

Add. MSS 18,270, 18,273, 18,961. Information on slavery, population figures (diminution), slave imports in British West Indies and St. Domingue, sugar prices, subsistence for troops.

Add. MSS 21,254–56. Minutes and resolutions of the Committee for the Abolition of the Slave Trade.

Add. MSS 21,809. Haldimand Papers. Letters on the condition of Jamaica after the prohibition of American shipping in 1783; calls for immediate supply from Canada.

Add. MSS 22,677. Letters of James Knight and others relating to Jamaica, 1725–89; material on neutral shipping with special reference to the West Indies during the Anglo-French War.

Add. MSS 30,001. Letters of the Rickets and Jervis family on Jamaican matters, mostly property issues, 1757–99.

Add. MSS 30,870–71. Letters of West Indian planters to John Wilkes.

Add. MSS 33,316. Diary of James Pinnock, a Jamaican planter.

Add. MSS 38,218–19. Letters from Jamaica and other papers on the West Indies.

Add. MSS 38,224. "Remarks Relative to the Laws of Navigation and of the Revenue of the Customs in Jamaica."

Add. MSS 38,227. Wilberforce Papers: letters on slavery

Add. MSS 38,228. Information on East Indian–West Indian trade.

Add. MSS 38,309, 38,342–43. West Indian trade statistics.

Add. MSS 38,345–51. Material on American–West Indian trade, the French West Indies, trade among the British sugar islands.

Add. MSS 38,352. Trade information on St. Domingue; British West Indian trade statistics.

Add. MSS 38,376. Shipping statistics, 1784–93; papers on Grenada and on smuggling in the West Indies.

Add. MSS 38,387. Paper on the importance of the sugar colonies to Britain with suggestions for their extension and improvement.

Add. MSS 38,717. Letters from Lord George Germain to Lord Macartney, 1776–79.

Add. MSS 38,718. Letters from Lord Macartney to Lord George Germain, 1776–79 (duplicates of correspondence in CO 101/20–23).

Add. MSS 38,759. Contains a letter on British sugar policy.

Add. MSS 59,239. Dropmore Papers. Information on Tobago.

Egerton MSS 2,135. Letters and papers relating to the American War of Independence, and to the surrender of Grenada to the French in 1779.

Kings MSS 214. Governor Archibald Campbell's *Memoir of Jamaica*.

Stowe MSS 922. Historical, Statistical and Descriptive Account of the Island of Tobago.

JAMAICA RECORD OFFICE (JAMAICA ARCHIVES, SPANISH TOWN)

Tweedie Estate Records. Files 4/45/6, 7, 11, 16, 17, 65, 66.

INSTITUTE OF COMMONWEALTH STUDIES, UNIVERSITY OF LONDON

Simon Taylor Letter Books. Collection dealing with Jamaica estates, condition of island, trade with United States, some political matters.

LAMBETH PALACE LIBRARY, LONDON

Fulham Papers. Vols. 15–20: material on the Society for the Propagation of Christian Knowledge, religious education of slaves on its estate in Barbados.

LONDON METROPOLITAN ARCHIVES (FORMERLY GREATER LONDON RECORD OFFICE)

Cooper-Franks MSS. Acc. 775/928, 930, 935, 942–46, 953: papers on the Duckenfield Plantation in Jamaica, production, slave population, sugar prices, and other trade matters; some information on Dominica.

NATIONAL ARCHIVES OF SCOTLAND, EDINBURGH

Abercairny MSS. GD 24/1/461: letters, accounts, papers of planter Charles Stirling relating to plantations in Jamaica, 1765–97.

Cunningham of Lainshaw MSS. GD 247/59/Q: letters from William Cunninghame, a partner of, and Henry Clarke, an agent for, Robert Dunmore and Company, 1777–78, concerning shipping, freight rate, sugar prices, the state of the market, insurance premiums.

Dalhousie Papers. GD 45/7/5, 45/7/75, 45/3/629: statistics on the slave trade, prices of sugar, net revenue and duties; table in 45/7/5 of sugar consumption in England between 1700 and 1790. GD 45/3/629: discussion of the value to Britain's economy of her West Indian and North American colonies.

Logan Home of Edrom Muniments MSS. GD 1/384, bundles 5 and 7: accounts by Captain

Home, commander of one of His Majesty's warships, of the war in America and the West Indies.

Seaforth Papers. GD 46/17/11: Barbados–United States trade; subsistence for the enslaved population.

NATIONAL LIBRARY OF SCOTLAND, EDINBURGH

William and James Chisholme Papers in the Nisbet Collections. MSS 5464–66 and 5475–80: accounts of provisions and other supplies sent to Jamaica and of sugar sent from Jamaica, insurance documents, sugar sales and prices, lists of slaves, and correspondence with estate overseers, mainly after 1784. MS 5484: statistical information on Jamaica.

Ellice Papers. MS 15137: estate material, loss of investment, debts, information on Balfour estates in Tobago.

Houston Papers. MSS 8793–94: letters from Houston and Company to business correspondents mainly in Grenada, St. Vincent, Tobago, St. Kitts, and Nevis regarding trade, freight rates, insurance charges, and shipping between Glasgow and the West Indies. MSS 8795: letters to associates in Greenock, London, Bristol, and other places concerning West Indian products, shipping, insurance and related matters. Houston and Company's 1775–79 sale book detailing sales in Glasgow of West Indian sugar, rum, cotton, logwood, and tobacco.

Liston Papers. MS 5610: information on estate conditions in Antigua, efforts to solve debt problems.

Melville Papers. MS 1075: information on the slave trade in Jamaica and restricted slave imports. MS 1711: Barbados population and production figures.

Robertson-Macdonald Papers. MSS 3942: letters from R. Lindsay of St. Catherine, in Jamaica, about Jamaican affairs in 1776. MS 3982: information on Jamaica estate.

Charles Steuart Papers. MSS 5028–40. MSS 5028–34: letters to Charles Steuart, Surveyor-General of Customs in North America, mostly from his nephews Thomas Ruddach, a merchant and planter in Tobago, and Charles Ruddach, a plantation overseer in Jamaica, about commercial conditions in the islands.

NATIONAL LIBRARY OF WALES, ABERYSTWYTH

Bodrhyddan Collection. Boxes 1–2: letters (part of the Stapleton-Cotton Papers at the University of Wales, Bangor) concerning estate matters and conditions on Nevis and St. Kitts.

Nassau-Senior Papers. E31–81: problems of investing in the West Indies, conditions of estates and slaves, mainly in Dominica; some letters on Barbados.

Slebech Papers. Bundles 8639–8721: Nathaniel Phillips's Jamaica estate papers, a wide array of material on the sale of sugar and on slavery and estate-management issues.

PUBLIC RECORD OFFICE, LONDON

Admiralty Papers

Series 1. Letters from commanders-in-chief of the West Indian fleets to the Secretary of the Admiralty:

Adm. 1/309. Dispatches of Admirals Man, Parry, and Young, 1769–77.

Adm. 1/310. Dispatches of Admirals Young and Barrington and Commodore Hotham, 1776–81.

Adm. 1/311. Dispatches of Admiral Rodney, 1779–80.

Board of Trade Papers

BT 5/1. Minutes of the Committee of the Privy Council, Appointed for All Matters Relating to Trade and Foreign Plantations (cited as the Committee for Trade).

BT 6/20. Letter permitting West Indian governors to import American food; correspondence on the unprofitability of slavery; West Indian slave trade papers.

BT 6/70. Commercial papers: ser. 2, 1784–91, American trade.

BT 6/75. Miscellaneous papers on the West Indies, 1786–89.

BT 6/76. Papers on Jamaica, West Indies, 1786–91.

BT 6/77. Papers on the West Indies, 1787–91; price of American goods.

BT 6/78. Act regulating slaves on hire and stipulating treatment.

BT 6/80. Correspondence: American commercial intercourse, 1783–84.

BT 6/81. Papers on American intercourse, 1783–86: minutes of the Committee of the Privy Council on American Trade.

BT 6/83, pts. 1 and 2. American–West Indian commercial intercourse: minutes and statistics; prices of American goods.

BT 6/84. Correspondence on American–West Indian trade; imports into Quebec.

BT 6/85. Concerned with correspondence and other papers on U.S.–West Indian trade relations.

BT 6/88. Regulation of American–West Indian trade; prices of American goods.

BT 6/96. Material on shipping and proposed new Navigation Act.

BT 6/185. Sir Charles Whitworth's *State of the Trade of Great Britain*, published in 1776; this manuscript copy contains tables from 1697 to 1801.

BT 6/186. Jamaica shipping returns.

Colonial Office Papers

The largest single collection of documents for any study of West Indian history, the Colonial Office papers contain correspondence between the governors and the Secretaries of State for the Colonies, and from the governors to the Board of Trade. Those used in this work are:

America

Series 5. Vols. 93–94: correspondence with the Secretary of State, military dispatches concerning the American war.

Antigua

Series 9. Vols. 33, 41: Journals of the Assembly of Antigua for the period 1775–1810.

Barbados

Series 28. Vols. 34–35: correspondence with the Board of Trade, 1772–82. Vols. 42–77: correspondence with the Secretary of State for the Colonies, 1773–1808.

Series 29. Governors' commissions, instructions, and "out" letters from the Board of Trade to the governors (correspondence is usually a duplicate of series 28). Vol. 21: material on the period 1767–78.

Series 31. Invaluable material, for any study of the period, on relations between the governors and the Barbados Assembly; copies of many speeches made in the Assembly on important political and constitutional issues. Vols. 38, 42: minutes of the Council of Barbados. Vols. 39, 41, 43: journals of the Assembly.

Dominica

Series 71. Vols. 1–2: correspondence with the Board of Trade, 1730–1801. Vols. 3–42: correspondence with the Secretary of State, 1770–1807; information on slave imports and trade.
Series 72. Vols. 3–5: sessional papers.

Grenada

Series 101. Vols. 1–7: correspondence with the Board of Trade. Vols. 18–46: correspondence with the Secretary of State for the Colonies, 1774–1807, with many statistics on trade, prices, and production.

Jamaica

Series 137. Vols. 38–40: Board of Trade correspondence. Vols. 68–122: correspondence with the Secretary of State, 1772–1807; extensive information on trade.
Series 140. Vols. 46, 59: journals of the Assembly of Jamaica.

Leeward Islands

Series 152. Vols. 31–34: correspondence with the Board of Trade. Vols. 49–91: correspondence with the Secretary of State, 1768–1808, dealing with trade, condition of the islands, and general correspondence with the Board of Trade.

Montserrat

Series 177. Sessional papers of the legislative bodies; vol. 12 contains Minutes of the Assembly.

St. Kitts

Series 239. Vol. 1: correspondence with the Secretary of State, 1702–1812.
Series 241. Minutes of the Assembly and Council, vols. 11, 12, 14, and 17.

St. Vincent

Series 260. Vols. 4–23: correspondence with the Secretary of State, 1776–1807, on all aspects of slavery, slave trade, American–West Indian trade, prices of goods.

West Indies

Series 318. Vols. 1–2: correspondence with the Board of Trade, 1624–1808; notes, statistical tables regarding trade between the United States, British North America, Britain, and the West Indies. Vol. 7: West Indies miscellany.
Series 325. Miscellany. Vol. 6, "The State of Trade with America": mainly after 1783.

Custom House Accounts

Class 3, vols. 64–82. Ledgers of imports from the British West Indies into London and the outports in England.

Privy Council Papers

Series 1, 19A/24: "Report of the Lords of the Committee for Trade, upon Two Acts passed by the Congress of the United States of America in July 1789."

Treasury Papers

Series 1. Papers, accounts, reports, petitions, and other material pertaining to trade, land grants, illicit commerce, and other British West Indies issues; the pieces consulted in this study are 338, 515, 516, 526, 528, 530, 531, 534, 535, 539, 540, 542, 551, 623.

T 38/269 (ser. 38, vol. 269). Account of English–British West Indian trade, 1773–83.

RHODES HOUSE LIBRARY, OXFORD

W.Ind. r.2. Essay on the value of the British colonies in the West Indies to the mother country.

W.Ind. r.5–6. William Senhouse's *Diary, 1750–1800,* 2 vols., compiled by Sir H. F. Senhouse. Material on William Senhouse's work as Surveyor-General of the Customs in the West Indies, his family, character sketches of Governor Hay, social life in Barbados.

W.Ind. s.8. Melville MSS. Information on the slave trade and the humanitarians' attack, also on American–West Indian trade.

W.Ind. s.9. Information on the cost of hiring slaves.

W.Ind. s.24. Material on Nevis, Leeward Islands, and Alexander Hamilton.

W.Ind. s.37. Arthur E. V. Barton Papers.

W.Ind. t.1. Young Papers. Vols. 1–3: material on Sir William Young's estates in Antigua, St. Vincent, and Tobago, and the loss of some of these due to indebtedness.

SOMERSET RECORD OFFICE, TAUNTON

Dickinson MSS. DD/DN 468, 471–511: information on Jamaica estates of Appleton, Barton Isle, and Pepper Penn; general estate conditions in the West Indies; production and price figures.

Tudway Papers. DD/TD 11–12: information on estate production and market conditions in Antigua, Jamaica, and Britain.

SURREY RECORD OFFICE, KINGSTON-UPON-THAMES

Goulburn Papers. Acc. 319. Boxes 51–54 contain letters about conditions, trade, the African population, production, and profitability or losses of estate.

UNIVERSITY OF BRISTOL LIBRARY

Pinney Papers, Letter Books 3–5. Letters mainly about trade and conditions in the Leeward Islands during the American War of Independence.

UNIVERSITY OF LONDON LIBRARY

Newton MSS. Information on plantation in Barbados, accounts and correspondence.

UNIVERSITY OF WALES, BANGOR

Penrhyn MSS. MSS 1207–1442: letters to and from Richard Pennant, Lord Penrhyn, from Jamaica on all aspects of estate matters.

Stapleton-Cotton Papers. MSS 6–23(vi): estate matters on Nevis and St. Kitts.

Secondary Sources

Adams Family Correspondence. Edited by L. H. Butterfield. 6 vols. Cambridge: Harvard University Press, 1963–93.

Adams, John. *The Works of John Adams: Second President of United States.* Edited by Charles F. Adams. 10 vols. Boston: Little, Brown, 1850–56.

Allen, Helen M. "British Commercial Policy in the West Indies 1783–1793." Ph.D. diss., University of London, 1938.

Allen, James. *Considerations on the Present State of the Intercourse between His Majesty's Sugar Colonies and the Dominions of the United States of America.* London, 1784.

Allen, Joseph. *Life of Nelson.* London, 1852.

Andrews, Charles McLean. *Guide to the Materials for American History, to 1783, in the Public Record Office of Great Britain . . .* 2 vols. Washington, D.C.: Carnegie Institution of Washington, 1912–14.

Andrews, Charles M., and Frances G. Davenport. *Guide to the Manuscript Materials for the History of the United States to 1783, in the British Museum, in Minor London Archives, and in the Libraries of Oxford and Cambridge.* Washington, D.C.: Carnegie Institution of Washington, 1908; reprint, New York: Kraus Reprint Corp., 1965.

Anstey, Roger. *The Atlantic Slave Trade and British Abolition, 1760–1810.* London: Macmillan, 1975.

Armytage, Frances. *The Free Port System in the British West Indies: A Study of Commercial Policy, 1766–1822.* London: Longmans, Green, 1953.

Ashton, T. S. *An Economic History of England: The Eighteenth Century.* London: Methuen, 1955.

Atwood, Thomas. *The History of the Island of Dominica: Containing a Description of its Situation, Extent, Climate, Mountains, Rivers, Natural Productions . . .* London: J. Johnson, 1791.

Aufhauser, Fitzzroy R. "Slavery and Technological Change." *Economic History Review* 34 (1974): 36–50.

Augier, F. R. *The Making of the West Indies.* London: Longmans, 1960.

Barham, Joseph Foster. *Considerations of the Abolition of Negro Slavery, and the Means of Practically Effecting It.* London: J. Ridgway, 1823.

Barritt, M. K. "The Navy and the Clyde in the American War, 1777–1783." *Mariner's Mirror* 55 (1969): 33–42.

Basye, Arthur Herbert. *The Lords Commissioners of Trade and Plantations, Commonly Known as the Board of Trade, 1748–1782.* New Haven: Yale University Press, 1925.

Beer, George Louis. *British Colonial Policy, 1754–1765.* New York: Macmillan, 1907.

————. *The Commercial Policy of England toward the American Colonies.* New York: Columbia College, 1893.

Bell, Herbert C. "British Commercial Policy in the West Indies, 1783–1793." *English Historical Review* 21 (1916).

————. "The West India Trade before the American Revolution." *American Historical Review* 22 (June 1917).

Bell, Herbert C., and David W. Parker. *Guide to British West Indian Archive Materials, in London and in the Islands, for the History of the United States.* Washington, D.C.: Carnegie Institution of Washington, 1926.

Bemis, Samuel Flagg. *The Diplomacy of the American Revolution.* New York: D. Appleton–Century Company, 1935.

————. *Jay's Treaty: A Study in Commerce and Diplomacy.* 2d ed. New Haven: Yale University Press, 1962.

Bennett, J. Harry. *Bondsmen and Bishops: Slavery and Apprenticeship on the Codrington Plantations of Barbados, 1710–1838.* Berkeley and Los Angeles: University of California Press, 1958.

Bingham, William. *A Letter from an American Now Resident in London, to a Member of Parliament, on the Subject of the Restraining Proclamation, and Containing Strictures on Lord Sheffield's Pamphlet on the Commerce of the American States.* London: J. Stockdale, 1784.

Bonsal, Stephen. *When the French Were Here: A Narrative of the Sojourn of the French Forces in America, and Their Contribution to the Yorktown Campaign, Drawn from Unpublished Reports and Letters of Participants in the National Archives of France and the Ms. Division of the Library of Congress.* Garden City, N.Y.: Doubleday, Doran, 1945.

Boyd, Julian P. "Jefferson's Expression of the American Mind." *Virginia Quarterly Review* 50, no. 4 (1974).

Brathwaite, Kamau. *The Development of Creole Society in Jamaica, 1770–1820.* Oxford: Clarendon Press, 1971.

Brown, Margaret L. "William Bingham: Agent of the Continental Congress in Martinique." *Pennsylvania Magazine of History and Biography* 61 (1937).

Buckley, K. "The Role of Staple Industries in Canada's Economic Development." *Journal of Economic History* 18 (December 1958).

Burns, Alan Cuthbert. *History of the British West Indies.* London: Allen and Unwin, 1954.

Butler, Mary. "Mortality and Labour on the Codrington Estates, Barbados." *Journal of Caribbean History* 19, no. 1 (1984).

Carrington, Selwyn H. H. "The American Revolution and the British West Indies Economy." *Journal of Interdisciplinary History* 17, no. 4 (1987).

————. "The American Revolution, British Policy and the West Indian Economy, 1775–1808." *Review Interamericana* 12, nos. 1–2 (1992): 72–108.

————. *The British West Indies during the American Revolution.* Leiden: Foris, 1988.

————. "British West Indian Economic Decline and Abolition, 1775–1807: Revisiting Econocide." *Canadian Journal of Latin American and Caribbean Studies* 14, no. 2 (1989): 33–59.

————. "'Econocide'—Myth or Reality? The Question of West Indian Decline, 1783–1806." *Boletín de Estudios Latinoamericanos del Caribe* 36 (June 1984): 49–65.

————. "Economic and Political Developments in the British West Indies during the Period of the American Revolution." Ph.D. diss., University of London, 1975.

————. "Management of Sugar Estates in the British West Indies at the End of the Eighteenth Century." *Journal of Caribbean History* 33 (1999).

————. "The State of the Debate on the Role of Capitalism in Ending the Slave System." *Journal of Caribbean History* 22, nos. 1–2 (1990).

Cateau, Heather. "Management and the British West Indian Sugar Industry, 1750–1810." Ph.D. diss., University of the West Indies, St. Augustine, 1995.

Cateau, Heather, and S.H.H. Carrington, eds. *Capitalism and Slavery Fifty Years Later: Eric Eustace Williams—A Reassessment of the Man and His Work*. New York: Peter Lang, 2000.

The Claim for Fresh Evidence on the Subject of the Slave Trade Considered. London: Phillips and Fardon, 1807.

Clark, Dora Mae. *British Opinion and the American Revolution*. New Haven: Yale University Press, 1930.

Clark, George N. *Guide to English Statistics, 1696–1782*. London: Royal Historical Society, 1938.

Clarke, Mary Patterson. *Parliamentary Privilege in the American Colonies*. New Haven: Yale University Press, 1943.

Clarke, William Bell, ed. *Naval Documents of the American Revolution*. 10 vols. Washington, D.C.: Government Printing Office, 1964–69.

Cole, W. A. "Trends in Eighteenth-Century Smuggling." *Economic History Review*, 2d ser., 10, no. 3 (April 1958): 395–410.

Coupland, Reginald. *The American Revolution and the British Empire*. London: Longmans, Green, 1930.

Craton, Michael, and James Walvin. *A Jamaican Plantation: The History of Worthy Park, 1670–1970*. London: W. H. Allen, 1970.

Crowhurst, R. P. "British Oceanic Convoys in the Seven Years War, 1756–1763." Ph.D. diss., University of London, 1970.

Cundall, Frank. *Historic Jamaica*. London: Institute of Jamaica/West India Committee, 1915.

Curtin, Philip D. *The Atlantic Slave Trade: A Census*. Madison: University of Wisconsin Press, 1969.

Darity, William, Jr. "Eric Williams and Slavery: A West Indian Viewpoint?" *Callaloo* 20, no. 4 (1997).

————. "The Williams Abolition Thesis Before Williams." *Slavery and Abolition* 9, no. 1 (1988).

Davis, David Brion. *The Problem of Slavery in the Age of Revolution, 1770–1823*. Ithaca: Cornell University Press, 1975.

————. "Reflections on Abolitionism and Ideological Hegemony." *American Historical Review* 92, no. 4 (1987): 797–812.

Davis, Ralph. *The Rise of the English Shipping Industry in the Seventeenth and Eighteenth Centuries.* London: Macmillan, 1962.

Deane, Phyllis, and W. A. Cole. *British Economic Growth, 1688–1959: Trends and Structure.* London: Cambridge University Press, 1967.

Deerr, Noël. *The History of Sugar.* 2 vols. London: Chapman and Hall, 1949–50.

Devine, T. M. "A Glasgow Merchant during the American War of Independence: Alexander Speirs of Elderslie 1775 to 1781." *William and Mary Quarterly,* 3d ser., 33 (1976).

————. "Transport Problems of Glasgow West India Merchants during the American War of Independence, 1775–1783." *Transport History* 5, no. 3 (1971).

Dickerson, Oliver Morton. *American Colonial Government 1696–1765: A Study of the British Board of Trade in Its Relation to the American Colonies, Political, Industrial, Administrative.* Cleveland: Arthur H. Clark, 1912.

————. *The Navigation Acts and the American Revolution.* Philadelphia: University of Pennsylvania Press, 1951.

Dickson, William. *Letters on Slavery.* Westport, Conn.: Negro Universities Press, 1970.

————. "Letters and Papers of the Hon. Joshua Steele." Pt. 1 of *Mitigation of Slavery.* N.p., 1814.

————. "Letters to Thomas Clarkson by William Dickson." Pt. 2 of *Mitigation of Slavery.* N.p., 1814.

Donoughue, Bernard. *British Politics and the American Revolution: The Path to War, 1773–75.* New York: St. Martin's Press, 1965.

Dookhan, Isaac. "War and Trade in the West Indies, 1783–1815: A Preliminary Survey." *Journal of the Colleges of the Virgin Islands* (1975).

Drescher, Seymour. *Econocide: British Slavery in the Era of Abolition.* Pittsburgh: University of Pittsburgh Press, 1977.

Duffy, Michael. *Soldiers, Sugar, and Seapower: The British Expeditions to the West Indies and the War against Revolutionary France.* Oxford: Clarendon Press, 1987.

Egnal, Marc. "The Changing Structure of Philadelphia's Trade with the British West Indies, 1750–1775." *Pennsylvania Magazine of History and Biography* 99 (April 1975).

Ehrman, John. *The Younger Pitt.* 3 vols. London: Constable, 1969–96.

Edler, Friedrich. *The Dutch Republic and the American Revolution.* Baltimore: Johns Hopkins Press, 1911.

Edwards, Bryan. *The History, Civil and Commercial, of the British Colonies in the West Indies.* 2 vols. 1784; London: Stockdale, 1994.

————. *The History, Civil and Commercial, of the British West Indies.* 5th ed. 5 vols. London: G. and W. B. Whittaker, 1819.

————. *Thoughts on the Late Proceedings of Government Respecting the Trade of the West India Islands with the United States of North America.* London: T. Cadell, 1784.

Eltis, David. *Economic Growth and the Ending of the Transatlantic Slave Trade.* New York: Oxford University Press, 1987.

Farnie, D. A. "The Commercial Empire of the Atlantic, 1607–1783." *Economic History Review,* 2d ser., 15, no. 2 (1962).

Fay, Bernard. *The Revolutionary Spirit in France and America: A Study of Moral and Intel-*

lectual Relations between France and the United States at the End of the Eighteen Century. Translated by Ramon Guthrie. New York: Harcourt, Brace, 1927.

Galloway, J. H. *The Sugar Cane Industry: An Historical Geography from Its Origins to 1914.* Cambridge: Cambridge University Press, 1989.

Giesecke, Albert Anthony. *American Commercial Legislation Before 1789.* Philadelphia: University of Pennsylvania, 1910.

Gipson, Lawrence Henry. *The British Empire in the Eighteenth Century.* Oxford: Clarendon Press, 1952.

———. *The Coming of the Revolution, 1763–1775.* New York: Harper, 1954.

Glover, Richard. *The Substance of the Evidence on the Petition Presented by the West-India Planters and Merchants to the Hon. House of Commons . . .* London: T. Cadell, 1775.

Goveia, Elsa V. *Slave Society in the British Leeward Islands at the End of the Eighteenth Century.* New Haven: Yale University Press, 1965.

Great Britain. *Papers Presented to Parliament. Accounts and Papers.* London: HMSO, 1787–91.

———. *Parliamentary Papers Relating to the Slave Trade (1801–1815).* Vols. 4–6. Shannon: Irish University Press, 1968–.

Hall, Douglas. *A Brief History of the West India Committee.* St. Lawrence, Barbados: Caribbean Universities Press, 1971.

Hall, Douglas G. "Incalculability as a Factor of Sugar Production in the Eighteenth Century." *Social and Economic Studies* 10, no. 3 (1961).

Hannay, David. *Rodney.* London: Macmillan, 1891.

Hewitt, M. J. "The West Indies in the American Revolution." D.Phil. diss., University of Oxford, 1936.

Higman, B. W. *Slave Population and Economy in Jamaica, 1807–1834.* Cambridge: Cambridge University Press, 1976.

———. *Slave Populations of the British Caribbean, 1807–1834.* Baltimore: Johns Hopkins University Press, 1984.

Hughes, Sarah S. "Slaves for Hire: The Allocation of Black Labour in Elizabeth City County, Virginia, 1782 to 1810." *William and Mary Quarterly,* 3d ser., 35, no. 3 (1978): 200–286.

Inikori, Joseph E. *Slavery and the Rise of Capitalism.* Mona, Jamaica: University of the West Indies, 1993.

Inikori, Joseph E., and Stanley L. Engerman, eds. *The Atlantic Slave Trade: Effects on Economies, Societies, and Peoples in Africa, the Americas, and Europe.* Durham: Duke University Press, 1992.

James, W. M. *The British Navy in Adversity: A Study of the War of American Independence.* London: Longmans, Green, 1926.

Jameson, Franklin J. "St. Eustatius in the American Revolution." *American Historical Review* 8 (1903).

Jefferson, Thomas. *Papers.* Edited by Julian P. Boyd. 28 vols. Princeton: Princeton University Press, 1950–2000.

Johnson, Howard. *The Bahamas in Slavery and Freedom.* Kingston, Jamaica: Ian Randle and James Carry, 1991.

Journals of the Assembly of Jamaica. 14 vols. Kingston, Jamaica: Alexander Aikman, 1811–29.

Kammen, Michael G. *A Rope of Sand: The Colonial Agents, British Politics, and the American Revolution.* Ithaca: Cornell University Press, 1968.

Kerr, Wilfred Brenton. *Bermuda and the American Revolution: 1760–1783.* Princeton: Princeton University Press, 1936.

Klingberg, Frank J. *The Anti-slavery Movement in England: A Study in English Humanitarianism.* New Haven: Yale University Press, 1926.

Lambert, Sheila, ed. *House of Commons Sessional Papers of the Eighteenth Century.* 147 vols. Wilmington, Del.: Scholarly Resources, 1975.

Levi, Leone. *The History of British Commerce and of the Economic Progress of the British Nation, 1763–1878.* 2d ed. London: J. Murray, 1880.

Lindsay, Jean. "The Pennants and Jamaica, 1665–1808." Part 1, "The Growth and Organization of the Pennant Estates." *Caernarfonshire Historical Society Transactions* 43 (1982): 37–82; part 2, "The Economic and Social Development of the Pennant Estates in Jamaica," ibid. 44 (1983): 59–96.

Lindsay, W. S. *History of Merchant Shipping and Ancient Commerce.* 4 vols. London: S. Low, Marston, Low, and Searle, 1874–76.

Long, Edward. *The History of Jamaica.* 3 vols. London: T. Lowndes, 1774. *See also* BT, Add. MSS 12,402–4.

Luffman, John. *A Brief Account of the Island of Antigua.* 2d ed. London: J. Luffman, 1790.

MacIntyre, Donald G.F.W. *Admiral Rodney.* New York: Norton, 1962.

Mackesy, Piers. *The War for America, 1775–1783.* Cambridge: Harvard University Press, 1964.

Macpherson, David. *Annals of Commerce, Manufactures, Fisheries, and Navigation . . .* 4 vols. London: Nichols and Son, 1805.

Madison, James. *The Writings of James Madison.* Edited by Gaillard Hunt. 9 vols. New York: Putnam's, 1900–1910.

Makinson, David H. *Barbados: A Study of North-American–West-Indian Relations, 1739–1789.* London: Mouton, 1964.

Manning, Helen Taft. *British Colonial Government after the American Revolution, 1782–1820.* New Haven: Yale University Press, 1933.

Manross, William Wilson. *The Fulham Papers in the Lambeth Palace Library.* Oxford: Clarendon Press, 1965.

Martin, Asa E. "American Privateers and the West India Trade, 1776–1777." *American Historical Review* 39 (1933–34).

Metcalf, George. *Royal Government and Political Conflict in Jamaica, 1729–1783.* London: Longmans, 1965.

Minchinton, Walter. "Williams and Drescher: Abolition and Emancipation." *Slavery and Abolition* 4, no. 2 (1983).

O'Shaughnessy, Andrew Jackson. *An Empire Divided: The American Revolution and the British Caribbean.* Philadelphia: University of Pennsylvania Press, 2000.

Pares, Richard. "Merchants and Planters." *Economic History Review,* supp. no. 4 (1960).

———. *War and Trade in the West Indies, 1739–1763.* Oxford: Clarendon Press, 1936.

————. *A West-India Fortune.* London: Longmans, Green, 1950.

————. *Yankees and Creoles: The Trade Between North America and the West Indies Before the American Revolution.* Cambridge: Harvard University Press, 1956.

Parry, J. H. "Eliphalet Fitch: A Yankee Trader in Jamaica during the War of Independence." *History*, n.s., 40 (February 1955).

————. *Trade and Dominion: The European Oversea Empires in the Eighteenth Century.* London: Weidenfeld and Nicolson, 1971.

Pasley, Sir William. *Private Sea Journals, 1778–1782.* Edited by Rodney M. S. Pasley. London: J. M. Dent, 1931.

Paullin, Charles O. *The Navy of the American Revolution: Its Administration, Its Policy, and Its Achievements.* Cleveland: Burrows Brothers, 1906.

Penson, Lillian Margery. *The Colonial Agents of the British West Indies.* London: University of London Press, 1924.

————. "The London West India Interest in the Eighteenth Century." *English Historical Review* 36 (1921).

Phillips, Deane. "Horse Raising in Colonial New England." *Cornell University Agricultural Station Memoir*, no. 54 (May 1922).

Phillips, J. D. "Salem Revolutionary Privateers Condemned at Jamaica." *Essex Institute Historical Collections* 76 (1940).

Pinckard, George. *Notes on the West Indies.* 2d ed. 2 vols. London: Baldwin, Cradock, and Joy, 1816.

Pitman, Frank Wesley. *The Development of the British West Indies, 1700–1763.* New Haven: Yale University Press, 1917.

Porter, Dale H. *The Abolition of the Slave Trade in England, 1784–1807.* Hamden, Conn.: Archon Books, 1970.

Poyer, John. *A History of Barbados from the First Discovery in the Year 1605 till the Accession of Lord Seaforth, 1801.* London: J. Mawman, 1808.

Pringle, Hall. *The Fall of the Sugar Planters of Jamaica.* London: Trübner, 1869.

Ragatz, Lowell J. *The Fall of the Planter Class in the British Caribbean, 1763–1833: A Study in Social and Economic History.* New York: Century, 1928.

————. *The Old Plantation System in the British West Indies.* London: Bryan Edwards Press, 1953.

————. *Statistics for the Study of British Caribbean Economic History, 1763–1833.* London: Bryan Edwards Press, 1927.

Ramsay, James. *Objections to the Abolition of the Slave Trade, with Answers.* 2d ed. London: J. Phillips, 1788.

Richardson, David. "The Slave Trade, Sugar, and British Economic Growth, 1748–1775." *Journal of Interdisciplinary History* 17, no. 2 (1987).

Ritcheson, Charles R. *Aftermath of Revolution: British Policy Toward the United States, 1783–1795.* Dallas: Southern Methodist University Press, 1969.

Robertson, M. L. "Scottish Commerce and the American War of Independence." *Economic History Review*, 2d ser., 9, no. 2 (1956).

Rodney, George Brydges. *Letters from Sir George Brydges now Lord Rodney, to His Majesty's*

Ministers, &c., &c., Relative to the Capture of St. Eustatius... London: A. Grant, 1789.

Roughley, Thomas. *The Jamaican Planter's Guide.* London: Longman, Hurst, Rees, Orme, and Brown, 1823.

Schomburgk, Robert H. *The History of Barbados.* London: Longmans, 1848.

Schumpeter, E. B. *English Overseas Trade Statistics, 1697–1800.* Oxford: Clarendon Press, 1960.

Setser, Vernon G. *The Commercial Reciprocity Policy of the United States, 1774–1829.* Philadelphia: University of Pennsylvania Press, 1937.

Sheffield, John Holroyd, Lord. *Observations on the Commerce of the American States with Europe and the West Indies...* London: J. Debrett, 1783.

Sheridan, Richard B. "The British Credit Crisis of 1772 and the American Colonies." *Journal of Economic History* 15, no. 2 (1960).

———. "The Crisis of Slave Subsistence." *William and Mary Quarterly,* 3d ser. 33, no. 4 (October 1976): 615–41.

———. *The Development of the Plantations to 1750: An Era of West Indian Prosperity, 1750–1775.* St. Lawrence, Barbados: Caribbean Universities Press, 1970.

———. *Doctors and Slaves: A Medical and Demographic History of Slavery in the British West Indies, 1680–1834.* Cambridge: Cambridge University Press, 1985.

———. "The Rise of a Colonial Gentry: A Case Study of Antigua, 1730–1775." *Economic History Review,* 2d ser., 13, no. 3 (1961): 342–57.

———. *Sugar and Slavery: An Economic History of the British West Indies, 1623–1775.* Baltimore: John Hopkins University Press, 1973.

———. "The Wealth of Jamaica in the Eighteenth Century." *Economic History Review,* 2d ser., 18, no. 2 (1965).

———. "The Wealth of Jamaica in the Eighteenth Century: A Rejoinder." *Economic History Review,* 2d ser., 21 (1968).

A Short Sketch of the Evidence for the Abolition of the Slave Trade: Delivered before a Committee of the House of Commons... London, 1792.

Siebert, Wilbur H. *The Legacy of the American Revolution to the British West Indies and Bahamas: A Chapter out of the History of the American Loyalists.* Columbus: Ohio State University, 1913.

Solow, Barbara. "Capitalism and Slavery in the Exceedingly Long Run." *Journal of Interdisciplinary History* 17, no. 4 (1987): 711–37.

Solow, Barbara L., and Stanley L. Engerman, eds. *British Capitalism and Caribbean Slavery: The Legacy of Eric Williams.* New York: Cambridge University Press, 1987.

Southey, Thomas. *Chronological History of the West Indies.* 3 vols. London: Longman, Rees, Orme, Brown, and Green, 1827.

A Speech, which was Spoken in the House of Assembly of St. Christopher, upon a Motion made on Tuesday the 6th of November, 1781, for Presenting an Address to His Majesty, Relative to the Proceedings of Admiral Rodney and General Vaughn at St. Eustatius... London: J. Debrett, 1782.

Stephenson, O. W. "The Supply of Gunpowder in 1776." *American Historical Review* 30 (1924–25).

Syrett, David. *Shipping and the American War 1778–83: A Study of British Transport Organization.* London: University of London, Athlone Press, 1970.

Taussig, Charles William. *Rum, Romance and Rebellion.* London: Jarrols, 1928.

Taylor, Clare. "Planter Attitudes to the American and French Revolutions." *Clychgrawn Llyfrgell Genedlaethol Cymru* 21, no. 2 (1979(: 113–30.

Thomas, Robert P. "The Sugar Colonies of the Old Empire: Profit or Loss for Great Britain?" *Economic History Review,* 2d ser., 21 (1968).

Valentine, Alan Chester. *Lord George Germain.* Oxford: Clarendon Press, 1962.

Walne, Peter, ed. *A Guide to Manuscript Sources for the History of Latin America and the Caribbean in the British Isles.* London: Oxford University Press, 1973.

Ward, J. R. *British West Indian Slavery, 1750–1834: The Process of Amelioration.* Oxford: Clarendon Press, 1988.

———. "The Profitability of Sugar Planting in the British West Indies, 1650–1834." *Economic History Review,* 2d ser., 31, no. 2 (1978): 197–213.

Waters, Ivor. *The Unfortunate Valentine Morris.* Chepstow, Wales: Chepstow Society, 1964.

The West India Merchant: Being a Series of Papers Originally Printed in the London Evening Post. London: J. Almon, 1778.

Wharton, Francis, ed. *The Revolutionary Diplomatic Correspondence of the United States.* 6 vols. Washington, D.C.: Government Printing Office, 1889.

Whitson, Agnes M. "The Outlook of the Continental American Colonies on the British West Indies, 1760–1775." *Political Science Quarterly* 45 (1930).

Williams, Eric. *Capitalism and Slavery.* Chapel Hill: University of North Carolina Press, 1944.

———. "The Economic Aspect of the Abolition of the West Indian Slave Trade and Slavery." D.Phil. diss., University of Oxford, 1938.

———. *From Columbus to Castro: The History of the Caribbean, 1492–1969.* London: Andre Deutsch, 1970.

Wise, John P. "British Commercial Policy, 1783–1794: The Aftermath of American Independence." Ph.D. diss., University of London, 1972.

Wright, Charles, and C. Ernest Fayle. *A History of Lloyd's from the Founding of Lloyd's Coffee House to the Present Day.* London: Macmillan, 1928.

Wright, Gavin. "Capitalism and Slavery on the Islands: A Lesson from the Mainland." *Journal of Interdisciplinary History* 17, no. 4 (1987): 867–69.

Young, Arthur. *Annals of Agriculture.* Published 1784–92. Bound copy in the British Library.

Young, Sir William. *The West-India Common-Place Book.* London: R. Phillips, 1807.

Index

Note: page references in italics indicate a table.

Selwyn H. H. Carrington, associate professor of history at Howard University, Washington, D.C., is a specialist in eighteenth-century Caribbean economic history and has published numerous works related to the topic. He is the author of *The British West Indies during the American Revolution* and coeditor with Heather Cateau of *Capitalism and Slavery Fifty Years Later.*